# Resistance and Theological Ethics

# Resistance and Theological Ethics

Edited by Ronald H. Stone and
Robert L. Stivers

ROWMAN & LITTLEFIELD PUBLISHERS, INC.
*Lanham · Boulder · New York · Toronto · Oxford*

ROWMAN & LITTLEFIELD PUBLISHERS, INC.

Published in the United States of America
by Rowman & Littlefield Publishers, Inc.
A wholly owned subsidiary of the Rowman & Littlefield Publishing Group, Inc.
4501 Forbes Boulevard, Suite 200, Lanham, Maryland 20706
www.rowmanlittlefield.com

PO Box 317
Oxford
OX2 9RU, UK

British Library Cataloguing in Publication Information Available

**Library of Congress Cataloging-in-Publication Data**

Resistance and theological ethics / edited by Ronald H. Stone and Robert L. Stivers.
    p. cm.
    Includes bibliographical references and index.
    ISBN 0-7425-4159-2 (hardcover : alk. paper) — ISBN 0-7425-4160-6
(pbk. : alk. paper)
    1. Christian sociology—Presbyterian Church—Congresses. 2. Christian ethics—
Presbyterian authors—Congresses.  I. Stone, Ronald H. II. Stivers, Robert L., 1940–

BX9199.S62R47 2004
241'.045—dc22                                                                         2004005593

Printed in the United States of America

♾ᵀᴹ The paper used in this publication meets the minimum requirements of
American National Standard for Information Sciences—Permanence of Paper
for Printed Library Materials, ANSI/NISO Z39.48-1992.

# Contents

*1*

# Introduction: Contemporary Resistance Ethics

## Ronald H. Stone

The twenty-first century opens with a mixture of order and chaos. Globalization from its American-European center advances while its economic giants Enron and the World Trade Center falter and fail or are blown away. A partially democratic laissez-faire economic order seems to be struggling to be born, but the significant worlds of China, Indonesia, and Islam thwart the new order. Africa declines. Latin America stagnates. The promises of 1776 for the wealth of nations and freedom seem beyond the grasp of most who reach for them.

In the summer of 1999, a group of ethicists, the Theological Educators for Presbyterian Social Witness, met in Geneva, Switzerland, and Sommiéres, France, historic centers of Presbyterian formation and resistance. There it was easy to recall how in the sixteenth century forces of renewal were unleashed through resistance to an imperial church and society. Our group of seminary and university professors discussed and ultimately concurred with the need for theologies and policies of resistance, applicable to both church and society.

They visited the prison for Huguenot women in Aigues-Mortes, France. They marveled at the courage of Durand, who scratched with her fingernail the cry "Résistez" in the rock of her tower cell. As they adopted this project of resistance to their vocations as ethicists, they knew they were walking in very big shoes.

Thousands of Christians have resisted to the death, from the original disciples through to Martin Luther King Jr. and Dietrich Bonhoeffer in our lifetimes. We do not anticipate martyrdom nor even imprisonment. Our resistance is the more modest vocational resistance of attempting, with our writing and actions, to normalize resistance against the negativities of our time. As scholars, we reflect on the work of others, but we try to find our own actions of resistance.

Also, we have chosen to limit our recommended forms of resistance to those of nonviolent resistance. We mean to enter into the coercive realms of economics and politics, but we are not here reflecting on the sometimes necessary options of violent resistance. This is not a book on revolution; it is a study on nonviolent resistance, including the coercive force of demonstrations, negotiations, boycotts, and politics. Jesus was reported as saying "Do not resist the evil one"; our interpretation is: "Do not engage evil power violently." We think Jesus encouraged confrontations with oppressors and that he initiated the church movement in which we live today. Part of our vocation as church scholars is to ensure that the church continues to confront oppression and bear witness to the biblical prophets who preceded Jesus and in whose tradition his own prophetic ministry is founded.

The church is, of course, part of the social problem as well as an aspect of the struggle for solutions. Since Constantine (ca. 312 A.D.) the church has integrated itself into the social life of the world. Church members participate in the management of globalization and in armies as well as among the poor of the world. Church scholars must advise rulers about responsible rule as well as assist the poor in overcoming their poverty. Hopefully, church scholars will live neither as the outrageously privileged nor as the outraged poor. They can do their work best when they have neither too much nor too little. Hopefully, by associations with both the suffering of the poor and knowledge of the ways of the rulers, they can locate points of decision-making where critical ethics can inform social action.

The authors of this volume go into specific reflections on particular means of resistance to social forces. All of the authors recognized a specific call to resistance against powers grounded in particular forms of sin. The project named four human sins all grounded in human nature and reinforced by social reality. The logic of the book is that specific structural forces can be understood to be outgrowths of these sins and that Christian morality requires particular strategies of resistance. The four forms of sin highlighted are religious pride, greed, violence, and domination.

Where we were, we are not now. In the second half of the twentieth century, Protestant theology could correlate its theological answers with cultural trends toward greater freedom, empowering science, advances in psychology, existentialism, and process philosophy.[1] At that earlier time, it was essential that we resist both Nazism and communism, yet we could correlate our thought with the freeing aspects of existentialism and secularism. Early trends of the twenty-first century are ominous for Christianity. The church is called to resist many trends as well as to correlate its thought with others. Our destiny as church and as Christians will depend on the wisdom of our choices to resist or correlate.

The work of the church is to develop Christians who are governed by love of neighbor and God and who seek justice in society as in the church. Love is expressed in life by forgiveness, service, understanding, and care; justice is approximated in fairness, community, human rights, increasing freedom, and equality. This love and justice seeking is supported by Christian community responding to the revelation of God's love in Jesus Christ. While the focus of the church is positive toward the development of love and justice, certain aspects of life must be surrendered and others resisted for that love and justice to flourish.

Protestantism, at its best, grounds both its religious and its social critique in the faith of the prophets and the faith and life of Jesus Christ as well as in the formal creeds, structure, and doctrines of organized religion. From Moses through the revelation of John, complacent religion, which is at ease with imperial greed, domination, and violence, is critiqued and opposed in a multiplicity of actions and insights. It is our responsibility to apply those biblical insights and actions to our lives, our time, and the emerging world of the future. The scriptural references for each of the trends to be resisted are from the gospel writers' interpretation of Jesus. They are not to be understood as proof texts, but as gospel-attested expressions of deep religious protest against perennial sins posing dangers to our spiritual well-being.

## RELIGIOUS PRIDE

The expulsion of Eve and Adam from the garden represents the transition of dreaming, animal-like essentiality into the world of human existence. Still, Adam and Eve were only fallen humanity, punished for the basic and "original sin" of religious hubris. Deep evil arose in the next generation. Cain slew Abel over a religious dispute: when Abel's offering to God was perceived as more acceptable, Cain, in religious fury, killed his brother.

In the emerging twenty-first century, peoples on a crowded planet rise up to destroy each other in the name of parochial religious identities. Through the middle latitudes, from North Africa through the Middle East to Indonesia, Islam is involved in a religious struggle of modernist versus fundamentalist, Muslim versus Christian, Jew versus Muslim, Hindu versus Muslim, and Muslim versus Buddhist. In Europe, we see Protestant versus Catholic, Catholic versus Orthodox, and Orthodox versus Muslim. China, the most populous country of the world, still represses most religious

expression or insists on regulating it in the name of its old-fashioned Mao-
ism. In the few places of the earth still not subject to Western technology,
aggressive Christian missionaries seek out unbaptized peoples to bring
them within the Western-Christian orbit. Unfortunately, the collateral aspects of Western Christianity will destroy the culture and Western diseases
will probably end the lives of the newly evangelized.

The term "fundamentalism" has emerged through common usage as a
term to describe this violence-prone, aggressive assertion in the name of religion. People of deep faith do not need defensive claims for a particular religion. Our search for peace requires global ethics and religious appreciation of
the ways others worship. In Isaiah there is no turning of swords into plow-
shares until there is a common vision and religious peace. Even Moses' exodus, basic to our faith understanding, is the seeking of worship freedom from
the pharaonic-imposed cult of state religion. Through education, developed
free spirituality, and acts of ecumenical imagination, fundamentalism must be
resisted and overcome first in ourselves and then in our neighbors.

Religious absolutism is expressed in forms other than fanatical loyalty
to a particular interpretation of a text. Roman Catholicism's opposition to
democracy and modernism was not grounded in scripture but in tradition.
Nor is its medieval repudiation of the marriage of priests and the exclusion
of women from ordination scripturally based. Absolutism to creed and practice beyond their time is grounded in a gender-specific priesthood, mores,
and traditions. Loyalty to God's love must be central in Christian existence,
but the pretense that a Polish or an Italian priest speaks for Christ in the ac-
cents of a Roman curia is silly. The famed pluralism of Hinduism can succumb to religious fanaticism and murder when grounded in politics and the
practice of caste.

Even Presbyterians can use sentences of scripture or phrases from creeds
to shame their brothers and sisters and obscure the witness of the church.
Many Presbyterians appear most fundamentalistic when trying to discuss or
reason about sexuality. But, as they are not fundamentalists on other matters,
their motivations must be grounded elsewhere than in textual absolutism.
Our task is to give our loyalty absolutely to God, while resisting absolutism
on religious grounds in ourselves and others.

The danger always is that religious leadership will fall prey to religious
pride. Jesus particularly denounced the scribes and Pharisees for this: "But
woe to you, scribes and Pharisees, hypocrites! For you lock people out of the
kingdom of heaven. . . . Woe to you, scribes and Pharisees, hypocrites! For you
tithe mint, dill, and cumin, and have neglected the weightier matters of the
law: justice and mercy" (Matt. 23:13, 23).

## GREED

Similarly, we must resist greed in ourselves and in our neighbors. There truly are human needs that our bodies and psyches incline us to fulfill. Our freedom, including our imagination and our anxiety, inclines us to reach beyond our real needs for more. In this reaching, we eclipse the needs of the less strong. The salaries, perks, and stock options of America's chief executive officers, star entertainers, and best athletes are gross and have no rational place in a society seeking fairness. Our patterns of inheritance, organization, and taxation encourage some of us to have more money and give us power to take more. This vicious spiral encourages individuals, organizations, corporations, and governments to dominate others for their own gain.

Thousands of years of accumulation and refinement of these patterns have produced our system as the United States, Europeans, and Japanese dominate the world in neo-liberal capitalist terms. The system, given population expansion, produces both more people with more affluence than ever before and more people living miserable lives of poverty and malnutrition than before. America drowns in consumerism and the consequent pollution of the environment while the world's poor suffer from corruption, inflation, underemployment, stagnation, and pollution from unregulated capitalism or declining socialism. While an expanding middle class can be seen in Latin America, India, and elsewhere, the power accumulated at the top continues to enforce a growing population of poor and malnourished human beings.

The Presbyterian Church's goals of fairness in the economy of the United States and sustainable human development as an international reality cannot be achieved without revolution from below and regulation from above. The suppression of welfare and unions may encourage the stock market. But greed and the over-accumulation of capital resources require countermovements for the health of society. The equalitarian and libertarian principles of justice require resistance to organized greed for the good of society.

We in the United States are in danger of acquiring the world's wealth through our cleverness, power, and technology. Such acquisition destroys our souls and sows seeds of destruction. Were we not warned by the prophets and by Jesus: "Do not store up for yourselves treasures on earth, where moth and rust consume and where thieves break in and steal; but store up for yourselves treasures in heaven" (Matt. 6:19–20)?

## VIOLENCE

The third trend to resist is the violence of humanity. Obviously, since Cain slew Abel, it has been part of our existence to be violent. But the twentieth century saw horrible new expressions of the culture of violence. We perfected mass destruction and a culture of death. American culture, with its power of sophisticated organization of mass retailing, is the most guilty of this as the twenty-first century begins. We encourage children, neurotic or normal, to play games of violent death, to learn music of death, to read literature of death, and, as an end-of-the-millennium celebration, to project human wars into the stars. Our movie theaters become temples of the gods of death, which are projected in huge images on screens while we stuff ourselves full of non-nutritious calories to compensate as the horror fills our minds. Beyond this, we fill our kids with drugs and arm them for self-destruction. This sick culture sustains and defends the arms industry that arms children here while arming the armies and paramilitaries of the rest of the world. We first arm countries and then have to crush them, isolate them, embargo them, and bomb them. This culture is related to our reliance on nuclearism, regarded by the Defense Department as our "ultimate assurance." The absurdity of tens of thousands of nuclear weapons ready to launch has recently called forth a campaign to abolish nuclear weapons.

Since 1946 the Presbyterian Church has called for the end of the development of nuclear weapons and the reduction and elimination of all weapons of mass destruction. Religion in the most general terms consists of a diagnosis of the human situation and human suffering; then, it suggests healing or salvation from human estrangement, alienation, and suffering; and finally, it offers a vision of hope and eternal meaning. The burden of nuclear weapons contributes to the human condition: fear, suspicion, a tendency to violence, and economic dislocation. The religious response is to show that the weapons are unnecessary and that, through diplomacy, understanding, creative politics, and mutual security, they can be eliminated. The belief is that meaning is not found in weapons, but in faith, hope, and love. The divine wills peace and gives us all we need to secure peace.

As we increase security, weaponry will decrease. We must move the United States toward increasing world security through policies that really improve the standards of living for the poor of the world, including in Russia, China, India, and Pakistan, and that cease to punish them for being poor.

Our best tools for moving our society toward increasing security and decreasing weapons are worship, education, organizing for peace, using peace politics, and using our funds creatively to divest from war. Then we must move toward investing in peace organizations, peace politics, and sustainable development. We must use our ordinary means of change with extraordinary energy, skill, and religious passion.

One does not need to believe that Jesus was addressing state policy or that he taught a full-blown theory of nonviolence to recognize his rejection of violence and his insight that violence begets violence. His followers were not to trust it or increase it. When Jesus was facing his own execution, he still urged his disciples to reject violent defense: "Put your sword back into its place; for all who take the sword will perish by the sword" (Matt. 26:52).

## DOMINATION

Jean-Jacques Rousseau was mistaken about many things. But his insight that our institutions tend to enslave us is basically correct. Minor differences in strength, gender, racial characteristics, birthplace, and family have evolved in human history into vicious powers that threaten the meaning of humanity in the twenty-first century. As the church affirms God, it also affirms humanity in the image of God and opposes all that defaces the image.

Our spiritual nature leaves us vulnerable in our psyches to insecurities, including our own finitude and death. If we do not accept faith in God's grace, we are inclined to fight insecurity by dominating others. This is the classic meaning of sin. In history, the victors enshrine their victories in powers; then, they and their kind use the powers to oppress others. The classic powers of domination have been patriarchy, racism, nationalism, oppression of the stranger or alien, classism, and exploitation of nature. These basic social powers have been embodied in our institutions of religion, politics, economics, law, and custom to the extent that they are almost undislodgable.

Some functional hierarchy is inevitable. But the inevitable functional hierarchy has become a repressive, nonfunctional lordship. The church must resist patriarchy until full mutuality in all of the life of the church is achieved. Intermediate steps until the whole church shares commonalty might include women popes, matriarchs, and bishops. Racism must be smashed and its subtle manifestations of privilege for the former white masters unmasked and undone. Nationalism, a liberating holdover from the nineteenth century, became demonic in the twentieth century and threatens the twenty-first century in its armed fury and genocidal tendencies. In our insecurity, we oppose the stranger and we fear the alien. This hatred must be overcome by love. A concrete result would be to humanize our immigration and naturalization processes. Classism in privileged education, inherited wealth, family connections, and elite privileges divides our societies, misuses power, and corrupts democracy. It evokes resistance from a church obedient to love and seeking justice.

The fundamental form of domination for humanity has been its exploitation of nature. Rather than preserving and living with nature as a friend on whom we depend, we have misused it and destroyed it. As we depend upon nature's generosity, our war against nature has been terribly short-sighted. Jesus' harsh words against dominating authority apply by reasonable extension to all of the above forms of domination, though he was particularly hard on religious legitimation of domination. Jesus had to resist the tendency among his own disciples to want the privileges of hierarchy, but Matthew saw him condemning the religious hierarchy of his own religious system: "But you are not to be called rabbi, for you have one teacher, and you are all students. And call no one father on earth, for you have one Father—the one in heaven. . . . The greatest among you will be your servant. All who exalt themselves will be humbled, and all who humble themselves will be exalted" (Matt. 23:8–12).

These six forms of human domination—patriarchy, racism, nationalism, oppression of the stranger or alien, classism, and exploitation of nature—have inspired revolutions against the evil systems that protected them. Each one is the subject of many studies and the sacrifice of many lives against the corrupting powers. The different forms of power are demonic in their own spreading, corrupting influence. The means against each of the six forms of domination will, in part, be unique. In their unity they are subject to the church's resistance in loyalty to Jesus as it articulates creative, imaginative acts of courage against these sins.

## RESISTANCE

Resistance to certain trends of the new century is here considered within loyalty to a protesting, resisting Protestant understanding of reality. Of course, much is to be affirmed, but much also must be resisted in the coming years. The acceptance by Protestant denominations of the need for resistance to much of American life can produce a joyous Christian confidence in Christian life that is noticeably different from lives of religious pride, greed, violence, and domination.

Of course, the clear articulation of the theology of resistance, as well as specifics to be resisted and the particular means of resistance to be undertaken, is an ongoing task. May many people of faith join in this task in the name of Jesus the Christ and the bringing of God's realm to reality.

So, organizations of resistance against religious pride, greed, violence, and domination need to be strengthened and rebuilt. One small organization committed to resistance is the Theological Educators for Presbyterian Social Witness. For fourteen years, they have met to strengthen the social witness of one church and, through it, modern ecumenical social witness. They are the contributors to this volume, from a professional economist to a minister, though most are professors of Christian ethics. All but two of the chapters are by active participants in the group.

The study begins with the reshaping of our world by economic forces. Globalization has been attracting resistors who oppose it for a variety of reasons. Ethicist Robert L. Stivers seeks out reasons for protesting the emerging order. While grounding resistance in realism, he seeks out the significant actors that could balance the power of the transnational corporations promoting globalization. Noting the sin in which we live, he articulates ethical norms and begins the discussion of means of resistance.

Economist Gordon K. Douglass, hesitating between reform and resistance to globalization, analyzes its various forms. The concerns of the church rest between the human development model and the people-centered protest against globalization while realizing the energy derived from the Washington consensus model of globalization. Douglass argues for a broad-based set of reforms to humanize the globalization trends. The enactment of the reform calls for resistance to domination and greed.

Seminary President Heidi Hadsell draws upon her years of teaching Christian social ethics and her Brazil experience to focus on environmental movements and resistance. She chooses to frame her essay as a biblical meditation and to emphasize land, human relationships, and the task of faithful resistance. As the environmental movement is furnishing many of the more profound examples of resistance, the conjoining of these themes with explicitly biblical reflections establishes the possibility of uniting the ecological movement with faith commitments.

Laura Stivers, a university religious ethics professor, addresses the normative and practical failures of the structural adjustment policies of globalization in Central America. The negative consequences of these policies have particularly increased the burden of suffering on the women and poor of Central America. Inequality, domination, and suffering have increased. Her essay carefully works through several ethical criteria that are violated by the structural adjustment policies and notes the size of resistance movements to these policies.

Dana W. Wilbanks, an ethicist well known for his writings on both immigration and resistance to militarism, focuses on nationalism in an age of globalization. Resistance to the national state system is probably, in his estimation, too utopian. Resistance to rather than support of nationalism is called for when it is connected to racism and exclusivism or to narrow pursuits of national interest. The role of nationalism in the twentieth century was particularly evil, and the role of the nation-state must be relativized by critique and resistance in the twenty-first century.

F. E. Bonkovsky, a former Presbyterian seminary professor, now teaches and researches medical ethics in universities in Austria and Germany. His essay surveys emerging issues in bioethics to provide insight for the arguments to resist certain tendencies in emerging medical and biological science.

Ronald H. Stone writes on militarism as expressed in emerging U.S. imperial tendencies and suggests ethical, theological, and organizational resources for resistance to the trend toward U.S. military dominance.

Paul Hertig offers an exegesis of the Gospel of Luke with a resistance hermeneutic, confirming that to follow Jesus calls one to acts of resistance. This seminary New Testament professor finds Luke placing Caesar in a relativized position, with Jesus challenging oppressive religious authorities and adopting servanthood as social resistance. Jesus' subversion of authorities of domination in religion and society is directly relevant, Hertig claims, for his followers in contemporary churches.

Brian K. Blount, professor of New Testament, finds in John's poetic, apocalyptic language of Revelation the call to choose nonviolent, transformative resistance. He finds a correlation between Martin Luther King Jr.'s urging to active, nonviolent, transformative marching and John's call in Revelation to resistance against oppression. Such response may result in death, but its purpose is, as in King's case, the transformation of society. Blount's heightened awareness of the witness of King helps him to find in Revelation the summons to active witness. He sees the gospel working to subvert the tyrannical forces of dominion, whether the racism of white America or the tyranny of the Roman Empire.

John C. Raines chaired a major religion department at Temple University and now is invested in establishing a religion department in heavily Muslim Indonesia. Here he presents his theoretical work on resistance drawn out of his own radical involvement in the civil rights struggle and the anti–Vietnam War movement. He finds the roots of resistance to domination in human nature. From our very birth, when we hurt, we cry. He finds that resistance is always there in our human nature, ready to protest, and the protests have "anticipatory memories" of the Kingdom of God. Raines's long friendship with the editors includes his arrest and trial with Stone for occupying the South African embassy in New York City in demanding that Nelson Mandela not be executed. Twenty-five years later, we saw Mandela released to lead South Africa into its new freedoms. Raines's chapter echoes the need for resistance to be both persistent and patient.

Frances S. Adeney's participation in demonstrations against war-making policies of her government drove her to reflect on fundamental issues of loyalty to God and to the state. She found in Augustine a helpful model of dual loyalty to God and state that helped her understand how her protests of state action were loyal to God and also loyal to the best of the state. Understood theologically, resistance is a normal part of adequate citizenship that is also loyal to God. She could not directly apply Augustine's theology in the Roman situation to our contemporary situation. Moreover, many conceptual moves separate contemporary theology from Augustine's theology. But she argues that, following Augustine, resistance to state policy can be seen as loyalty both to the state and to God.

Ethicist Scott C. Williamson moves the discussion into the complexities of resistance with the case of Frederick Douglass, who moved from a pacifist stance to the necessary acceptance of violence for protection in some cases. Douglass also found it necessary to break with some of his white abolitionist allies who could not overcome their paternalism. Tempted by German philosophers toward atheism, he retained his faith and increased the role of human agency beyond what William Lloyd Garrison was willing to affirm.

Young Lee Hertig, a professor of missions, internationalizes the discussion by presenting two Christian women martyrs from Korea. The women rose up and led in the Korean movement for independence from Japanese occupation. She recognizes the importance of their lives and martyrdom for the awakening of the Korean church today against the oppression of Korean culture, faith, self-understanding, and identity by international and domestic forces. She, more than many of our authors, spells out some of the implications of her research for reforming theological education.

Mark Douglas, a seminary professor of ethics who emphasizes the theological roots of Christian ethics, uses the tension between the Jubilee 2000 campaign and the International Monetary Fund to show how distinctively reformed theological insights can contribute nuance and subtlety to the debate. Christian resistance must first be resistance grounded in the calling of faithfulness to God. Resistance ought not to be an end in itself; it is rather a means of being loyal to God in our complex world. Douglas finds at least four essential theological concepts necessary to shape the resistance discussion for Christian consideration.

Pastor Robert A. Chesnut provides a sermon that reflects his thoughtful criticism of contemporary fundamentalism. The selection of a few presumed biblical teachings as a moral creed or litmus test of faith is an example of Edward LeRoy Long Jr.'s category of "malpraxis." Here Chesnut carries it into the very specific dangers rooted in Protestant fundamentalism in the context of western Pennsylvania. Fundamentalism in the passion for a rigid formula of someone's orthodoxy is in danger of missing the large picture of God's love, grace, and mercy.

Ronald E. Peters, a professor of urban ministry, examines black resistance to the white-dominated church. His participation and leadership in the "New Wine Project" was among the more significant challenges presented to the Presbyterian Church's failure to overcome the domination of racism. Peters's educational leadership only a few blocks from the exciting ministry of Robert Chesnut at East Liberty Presbyterian Church is witness to the Presbyterian feistiness in one contemporary city.

Lora M. Gross, a visiting professor at Pacific Lutheran University who visited the sites of Huguenot resistance with the Theological Educators group, wrote on the doctrine of the Spirit, examining its expression in the bold resistance of Lillian Hellman. A broad understanding of the Holy Spirit's work in the world allows Christians to understand spiritual resources at work in non-Christians who join in movements of resistance to evil.

The volume provides two examples of twentieth-century theologians' resistance to Nazism. Matthew Lon Weaver, pastor and doctor of philosophy candidate, reflects on the meaning of two seminal works of Dietrich Bonhoeffer and Paul Tillich. Particularly in his engagement with Bonhoeffer's developing into a radical resister, he analyzes the correlation of his Christological development with his radicalization. Paul Tillich's movement to resistance was more of a social-political development in its origins. Both show the impingements of history on theology that lead Christians into resistance out of loyalty to God and country.

As an emeritus professor of Christian ethics, Edward LeRoy Long Jr. coins and defines the term "malpraxis of religion." While most chapters in the book utilize religious resources for resistance in society, it is also necessary to resist the deleterious practice of religion. He finds the association of religion with exclusion, violence, and moralistic condemnation particularly problematic. Concluding the book, he argues that religion at its best preserves a prophetic role that is critical of religious malpraxis as well as social evil.

The editors express their thanks to Mrs. Sheryl Gilliland, faculty secretary at Pittsburgh Theological Seminary, for her typing and assistance in the project. The fellowship of the Theological Educators for Presbyterian Social Witness, who sponsored the project of this study, maintains a mutually helpful partnership with the Advisory Committee on Social Witness of the Presbyterian Church (U.S.A.). The Rev. Peter Sulyok, the coordinator of the ACSWP, was helpful to the project, as was Professor Lois Livzey of McCormick Theological Seminary, the chair of the TEPSW.

## NOTE

1. Ronald Stone, "21st Century Trends: Resist or Correlate," *Church and Society* 90, no. 2 (November/December 1999): 26–33. The following paragraphs and the discussion of religious pride, greed, violence, and domination are from this founding essay of the project.

*I*

# RESISTANCE TO SOCIAL FORCES

## 2

# Resistance and
# Economic Globalization

## *Robert L. Stivers*

*S*ince the meeting of the World Trade Organization (WTO) in Seattle in November 1999, demonstrators have frequently taken to the streets to resist economic globalization. At first glance the demonstrators seem, in the words of *New York Times* columnist and globalization supporter Thomas Friedman, "senseless." Who could object to globalization? Its advocates promise to deliver universal economic prosperity as the next step after the "defeat" of communism in the evolution of the free market system.

The demonstrators tell a different story, refusing to accept inevitability at least on the terms of those who currently lead globalization. They decry the many abuses of globalization: the loss of cultural diversity, the spirit-numbing materialism, the environmental destruction, the secrecy of deliberations, the exploitation of labor, the bypassing of those on the margins of society, the increasing maldistribution of income and wealth, the corruption of governments, and the imbalance of political power.

Economic globalization is the term used to describe the dominant trends in the worldwide expansion of market capitalism. The trendsetters are the large transnational corporations (TNCs) that increasingly dominate world trade. In support are the governments of most developed countries, whose function is to maintain the stability of the overall system and openness to market penetration by TNCs. Also in support are groups of workers, especially those in the hi-tech and export industries.

By any historical measure, this expanding system has been enormously productive and has improved material well-being. In terms of injustice, there have been far worse systems. To call attention to certain abuses is not to gainsay the successes of this system, for example, expanded freedoms for many individuals, and the desirability of retaining these successes. Nor is it to will some generalized overthrow and the substitution of some non-existent alternative economic organization. It also does not mean naivete about changing the system. What it means is resistance to the abuses with the goal of mitigating them. Although TNCs dominate, there are important new forces already working to counter their power. The task for Christians interested in justice and environmental preservation is to resist the worst manifestations of globalization through the use of nonviolent forms of power, to preserve and build on the successes, and to discern the difference between abuse and success.

## HOMESTEAD, PENNSYLVANIA, JULY 1892

A social-critical analysis of economic globalization requires an understanding of economic trends over the past century. The United States is an appropriate focus because it is the leader in economic globalization, the foremost military power, and home to many of the most powerful TNCs. Homestead, Pennsylvania, in 1892 is an appropriate place and time to start such a critical analysis because the strike of millworkers in Andrew Carnegie's Homestead works near Pittsburgh represents one of the first efforts by labor to rein in the power of economic interests.

Andrew Carnegie and his chief lieutenant Henry Clay Frick had built Carnegie Steel into the largest, most efficient, lowest-cost big producer of steel in the United States. Both held to the prerogatives of capital and private property and espoused a form of social Darwinism. In the face of increasing labor unrest and demands for higher wages, Frick, who was in charge of day-to-day operations, held the line. When Frick's private army of Pinkerton agents rushed to the mill to expel the workers who were occupying it, violence erupted. The National Guard was finally called in to set things in order for Frick and Carnegie.

Frick, Carnegie, and their supporters not only knew how to use police power but, for their day, were accomplished ideologists. Appeals to the prerogatives of capital and private property were effectively presented and reached willing ears. Equally convincing were their paternalistic claims to represent the best interests of their workers and to be the benevolent leaders of an expanding capitalism that promised general prosperity. Their claims seemed validated by increasing production and efficiency. By combining police, ideological, and economic power Carnegie, Frick, and other early industrialists achieved nearly total power.

Carnegie and Frick trumped the steelworkers in 1892, but countervailing forces were already beginning to emerge. In Christian circles the so-called social gospel emerged as a distinctly American contribution to thought and action. The easy laissez-faire arrangement between industrialists and government officials gradually gave way. The federal government began to flex its muscles under Theodore Roosevelt. Congress enacted antitrust laws and established the Forest Service under conservationist Gifford Pinchot. Power shifted back to industry in the 1920s, but the Great Depression, Franklin Delano Roosevelt, and an increasingly powerful labor movement brought on an era of government regulation, unions, and a rough balance of power that lasted beyond mid-century into the 1970s. By the early 1980s, capital had again reasserted itself, and the era of globalization and TNCs began in earnest.

The reasons for this shift of power back to capital are complex. TNCs developed new strategies that achieved greater centralized control with the appearance of decentralization. One strategy was for TNCs to form strategic alliances with each other.[1] Another was to centralize the essential operations of capital investment, design, and marketing and to cultivate a core group of well-paid, hard-to-replace workers to perform these functions. All other operations were decentralized or, to use the current terminology, outsourced to dependent, competitive bidders who were responsible, among other things, for environmental protection and employee wages and benefits. This strategy has been called "lean" production and highly praised in terms of efficiency. TNCs also developed computerized management systems to control far-flung operations and, in conjunction with financial institutions, to move capital easily and swiftly.

To increase autonomy, TNCs have lobbied all levels of government with considerable success to reduce taxes, to deregulate, to cut public spending in general, and to lower or not to enforce environmental standards. This effort to engage government has gone far beyond lobbying and other forms of political influence to active government bashing. The "evils" of big government have been droned into and sold to an electorate on the move from traditional blue- to white-collar jobs, from inner city to suburb, and from north to south. The business wing of the Republican Party carried this charge with the help of conservative Democrats. That this critique of big government sold while equally strong critiques of bigness in industry went unheeded is a testament to the power of ideology and the degree to which the economic realm has come to dominate the larger social realm.

Ironically, at the same time economic interests were successfully bashing government, they were also enlisting its support to help penetrate new markets. Hidden and not-so-hidden subsidies and the promotion of business interests by foreign embassies were two traditional strategies. The really novel innovations, however, were to persuade the federal government to take responsibility for overall market stability and to encourage the establishment of supranational organizations such as the WTO, the International Monetary Fund (IMF), the World Bank, and the North American Free Trade Agreement (NAFTA), to smooth the way for successful penetration of markets worldwide. Structural adjustment loans, privatization, reduced government expenditures and regulation, and the liberalization of trade were the instruments of these organizations, and they went a long way to improve the climate for TNC investment.

As these supranational organizations and the TNCs waxed in power, other international organizations with potential to be a counterbalancing force, such as the United Nations, remained weak and subject to the anarchy of the nation-state system. This turn of events was no mere coincidence.

As for governments in poor countries, they have been no match for the power of TNCs.[2] If they resist TNC penetration, investment and foreign aid dry up. But seldom do they resist, because control by narrow oligarchies favorable to business interests is the norm. If all else fails, the armies of TNC-based countries are always available to restore "order."

The increasing mobility of capital and the relative immobility of labor and land have made unions and local communities easy marks. Rapid technological innovations that increased capital-intense methods of production and decreased labor-intense methods have added to this effect. Threat of job loss has been a potent weapon against labor. The traditional conservatism of labor in the United States has not helped. Local communities capitulated in much the same fashion, taking seriously TNC threats to move operations elsewhere and competing with each other over who could offer the greatest benefits.

Finally, nature has always been without voice, vote, new techniques, or military power. The only threat it could muster was the potential of economic decline because of degraded ecosystems and the extinction of species. Good public relations and the clean-up of the most serious toxic wastes made this seem improbable.

The result of these trends is that once again, as in the age of Carnegie and Frick, the power of large business concerns is largely unchallenged. Many cheer this state of affairs and for good reason. Economic gains have been impressive for a large number of people. The gross domestic products (GDPs) of most countries are up. Trade has increased dramatically, as has private investment. More goods and services are available at lower prices. Production is more efficient. Employment levels are high. Workers are flocking from rural areas to take new jobs. So why the protest? Why would anyone want to resist?

## WHY RESIST?

It is easy to write off resistance as the antics of anti-authoritarian youth, the self-interest of workers trying to protect noncompetitive jobs, or the obstructionist tactics of "extreme" environmentalists. But the matter runs deeper. The situation is not as rosy as we are told, the protesters not as crazy or self-interested as charged.

To start with, there are specific and persistent injustices.[3] While the winners win big, the losers lose big as economic gains bypass large segments of populations in most countries. Even among the so-called winners, all is not well. The gap between rich and poor and between the really well off and those in the middle has widened in terms of the distribution of income and wealth. Equity is suffering as those well connected to TNC-led globalization arrogate the first and best fruits to themselves, as witnessed by the salaries and benefits of TNC executives.

It is the poor who bear the brunt of suffering. Peasants who flock from impoverished rural areas to the new plants constructed to handle outsourcing often encounter low wages, harsh working and living conditions, exploitation, and environmental hazards. Little matter that their incomes are higher than before and some have the potential to advance. Their lives are still impoverished, and they have little if any control over their lives. As for the workers in developed countries they in effect replace, the result is usually new jobs with lower wages and fewer benefits.

Finally, TNCs manipulate local communities to gain even greater advantage. As we have seen, threats to move create docility among workers and community leaders. Corporations play communities off against each other to gain increased concessions. Tax avoidance through creative accounting among branches in different countries goes unchecked. Corruption is widespread, especially in countries governed by narrow oligarchies.

Turning to the environment, while TNCs have done a fairly good job of cleaning up the worst abuses in developed countries (for example, the chemical industry in its production processes, the dumping of toxic substances from point sources, and cleaner air in developed countries) global warming, the destruction of ecosystems, the extermination of species, animal cruelty, nonpoint sources of pollution, and visual ugliness continue to cause or threaten environmental degradation. As with equity considerations, indeed as with anything that cannot be counted in monetary terms, these costs are not factored into market transactions. To achieve a clean environment and more equity, real people need to intervene in the supposedly impersonal marketplace. But, of course, such interventions violate the ideology of "free" markets and are stoutly resisted.

A still deeper complaint is directed at the role of TNCs in setting social direction and policy in countries throughout the world. The charge is not one of conspiracy so much as a sense that outsiders with special interests are setting agendas. Actually, no conspiracy is needed. The combination of profit motive, the will to power, disproportionate amounts of power, and a pervasive ideology and the means to sell it are enough. The result is what theologian John Cobb calls "economism," the determination of social arrangements on the basis of economic criteria, especially those that benefit the most powerful economic interests. The issue is, who should set the agenda? Should it be impersonal economic forces controlled by not-so-impersonal TNCs, or local communities?

Related to this complaint is the growing dominance of economic criteria and business practices in all fields of endeavor. Education is a good example. Education is more and more judged on numerical and economic criteria, less and less on qualitative considerations. Teachers are expected to produce "good" scores. Money dominates sports. Perceived human economic well-being takes precedence over aesthetic or environmental criteria. However overstated these complaints often are, there remains a sense that communities no longer control the common life, and those who do are most concerned with their own economic well-being.

Related also is the loss of cultural diversity that globalization fosters in its drive to reduce things to the common denominator of economics. Not all traditions deserve preservation, for example, traditions that discriminate on the basis of race, gender, class, and sexual orientation. But others do, especially those that foster authentic spirituality, local knowledge, and the richness of different cultures. The loss of these traditions does not appear on financial records but is real nonetheless. It is the same as the loss of biodiversity, as in the replacement of an ancient forest by a monoculture of biologically similar trees that are planted in rows and cut in fifty years. So a magnificent cultural diversity gives way to modern economic culture. Humans become consumers, land becomes real estate and resource, and traditional peoples are reduced to selling mass-produced trinkets to cruise-ship customers.

So how are we to assess globalization? Should we give priority to the material gains that have accrued to many people, judging on balance that, among the evils in human history, TNC-led globalization is by no means the most pernicious? Or in the name of justice, environmental protection, and the preservation of local initiative and diverse cultures, are we called to resistance? And if resistance, who should lead? Before deciding, we must consider ethical foundations.

## ETHICAL FOUNDATIONS FOR RESISTANCE

At the root of the injustice, environmental degradation, and threats to culture resulting from TNC-led globalization are disproportions of power. Political and economic power is unbalanced, powerful technologies destroy ecosystems, and popular Western culture overwhelms ancient traditions. A disproportion of power seldom promotes the well-being of the weak, and the corruption of unbalanced power has a long history.

To deepen foundations, it is helpful to return to the insights of American theologian Reinhold Niebuhr (1892–1970), who was so influential in building a rational and religious basis for countering the power of early industrialists. Niebuhr's political philosophy is often called Christian realism because of its appeal to Christian ethical principles and its insistence that sin be factored into political calculations.

Niebuhr had ample reason to stress the Christian *understanding of sin*.[4] Tuned historically, he saw the abuses of early capitalism that culminated in the Great Depression. He sounded a loud trumpet against the rise of Fascism and Stalinism. To his historical observations he applied traditional Christian understandings—passing from the Apostle Paul through Augustine and the reformers to the present—that stress the thoroughness and universality of sin.[5] Resistance to the will to power of large industrial organizations and authoritarian nation-states was the order for his day.

The appeal to resistance was not just negative. Niebuhr was a Christian who appreciated the *image of God* in humans and understood the *spiritual power* released by the resurrection of Jesus. He was also well acquainted with the Western philosophical traditions on the concept of *justice*. There are, he always insisted, resources that should be tapped to move society to higher levels of morality.

For Niebuhr, justice was the working out of love in social situations.[6] As a concept, justice has an ideal component (equality and freedom as regulative principles) and a real component (the activity of balancing power). The ideals of freedom and equality are important because, like a magnet, they attract individuals—and, to a lesser degree, groups—to higher levels of moral endeavor. They also serve as a plumbline (Amos 7:7–17) by which to judge social justice and the claims of those who determine what is fair.

Starting with the equal worth of each human being, the regulative principle of equality says that departures from equality—for example, from the equal distribution of income and wealth—are ethical only when some exceptional good is to be achieved, and then only in proportion to the degree of good to be achieved. In like manner, persons are to remain free from restraint unless they commit some act that violates a law justly established and administered.

Needless to say, the application of these principles is notoriously difficult. What qualifies as an exceptional good? Who judges degree, and how do the judges compare the relative merits of different goods? How can such subtle discriminations be made in large groups? The list goes on. Even so, the Christian realist insists these discriminations are important. Political institutions can be devised and administered that answer these questions in a way that permits a rough kind of justice. The discriminations also serve as rationale for improving levels of justice and provide a framework for determining when resistance is appropriate. There is no reason to give up on idealistic principles just because they are difficult to implement and perfection is not possible.

These complications when added to the reality of sin do, however, force those who make ethical judgments to add other considerations to the ideal. In reality, what goes in any society as equitable or fair is the result of power balances between contending individuals and groups. In the present market economy and its political companion democracy, for example, power accrues to those who have better access to markets and are active participants in them. The distribution of income and wealth and the power to command resources, set social agendas, and exploit the environment are largely in the hands of the owners and managers of capital. In the last third of the twentieth century, the balance of power shifted back to large corporations, and the public must rely on the good will of corporate leaders for justice and environmental health.

The powers of TNCs are not absolute, however. Other centers of power exist, and there are forms of power that TNCs do not control. The task for Christian realists is to use available forms of power to achieve higher levels of justice and environmental preservation. The use of power for good ends is not evil, but a moral requirement.

In keeping with Niebuhr's analysis and Christian realism, four other ethical foundations are worthy of note. The first is the *biblical concern for the poor*. This concern is found in both Hebrew and Christian scriptures. In Exodus, it is the liberation of oppressed slaves in Egypt. For the prophets, this concern is a matter of God's righteousness. In Luke, it is a special identity with the poor and the promise of good news. For Paul, it is sharing. Few other Christian norms are as solidly based as this one. This concern for the poor pushes those who seek justice to make the relief of poverty the first goal; it translates into resistance when economic and political systems fail to meet basic needs and disproportions of wealth and power are present.

The second of these foundations is the Christian understanding of *community*. The essence of Christian community is *koinonia*, which is the spirit of fellowship and unity in Jesus Christ. *Koinonia* is the glue of the church and makes possible closer-knit communities. The ideals are established in the opening chapters of the book of Acts and include sharing through work and gifts, fellowship, and unity in Christ, ideals that Paul confirms in Romans 12 and in his call to the Greek churches to share with the poor Jerusalem community. To translate these ideals into a normative statement about the wider community is problematic. As the size of groups increases, the sense of cohesion decreases. Few nation-states have ever even approximated such community. Nevertheless, the norm of community sets direction. From the Christian perspective, churches and nation-states should be working toward sharing, fellowship, and unity. The participation of people in decisions that affect their lives becomes a paramount norm. The effects of economic programs on community solidarity must be carefully evaluated.

The third of these foundations arises from the *tension between the way things are and the way things ought to be.* This tension appears in the first pages of the Bible. People are made in the image of God but, starting with Adam and Eve, fall into sin. In Exodus, God establishes a covenant with the Hebrews, and Moses descends from the mountain to witness the worship of a golden calf. It reappears again and again in the history of Israel as the Israelites wrestle with the obligations of the covenant, comparing their own situation to the responsibilities God has set forth.

In Jesus' message, the tension appears in his teaching that the community of God is at hand. Later Christians reformulated this to say the community of God had been inaugurated in the life, death, and resurrection of Jesus Christ, but that its fulfillment awaited his return. "Here, but yet to come," repeats this tension. The tension also turns up in other teachings of Jesus. In Matthew 10:16, for example, Jesus advises his disciples to be sheep among the wolves and to have the wisdom of the serpent and the innocence of the dove.

This tension is found preeminently in the cross and resurrection. The cross is reality at its worst. The cross points to the depth of human sin. It points as well to the limitations of individuals and groups and to the need for structures and order to keep sin in bounds. Yet the cross is not the last word. It is followed by the victorious new word of the resurrection. The resurrection points to God at work in the present situation, overcoming sin and death. It points as well to the possibility of "new creations" in the lives of individuals and groups and to the creative potential of love and justice. It teaches that while the present is the age of sin and death, God's love breaks in, there is hope, and efforts to achieve greater justice and environmental health are not in vain.

Finally the tension is highlighted by Paul's sense that Christians live between the ages. They live in the old age of injustice, but are called to live a way of life according to the new age. Insofar as they live in the old age, they give limited support to systems that perform economic tasks and preserve order, however imperfect. Building and maintaining functioning economic and political systems is no easy task to be taken lightly by romantic appeals to resistance. Nevertheless, Christians are called to live according to the new age. More equitable economic and political systems are the true direction. Tolerance for disproportions of power is limited. Mere order is not enough. Resistance at some point becomes an option.

The fourth foundation is *care for creation*. That Judaism and Christianity have contributed to the environmental crisis through popular interpretations of certain biblical texts such as Genesis 1:26–28, major emphases such as human sin, and lack of attention to nature is generally accepted today. While this criticism is valid, it often overlooks themes and texts that encourage a more caring relation to nature. It also ignores the tremendous changes in our relation to the natural environment since the Industrial Revolution. What was wise counsel in a previous period ("be fruitful and multiply") is no longer helpful.

An impressive body of theological and ethical work has emerged in the past twenty-five years to challenge popular interpretations and to bring out the long-neglected nature side of Judaism and Christianity. This is not the place to explore this work, but it is important to recognize that care for creation is now well established as a norm. The popular notion of dominion as domination or license to exploit nature is under heavy criticism from traditional sources, such as the notion of stewardship or the repeated declaration of Genesis 1, "and God saw that it was good," as well as from new explorations of incarnational and sacramental theology, nature spirituality, and the meaning of Jesus as caregiver extended to nature. The new stress is on care for creation, as in the way God cares for humans and nature. This norm challenges the heavy emphasis on economic criteria in social decisions and the assault of powerful technologies on the environment.

Given these foundations and the existing situation, the case for resistance is reasonable, even compelling. The task is to establish a new power balance between capital, labor, diverse communities, the poor, and the earth's ecosystems and species. It remains to speak about how this balance might be achieved and who should lead such an endeavor.

## THE "HOW" OF RESISTANCE

Following Niebuhr, the "how" of resistance should be based on appeals to ideal foundations and on building alliances with sufficient strength to balance the power of TNCs. Basic to the *ideal approach* are the ethical norms developed in the preceding section. These norms provide the guidelines for making ethical discriminations and motivating behavior. To prevent discussions, however, from deteriorating into narrow conflicts over norms or equally narrow calculations of economic good, relative risk, and competing ideologies, visions of alternative futures are needed. The process of globalization leading to a vague future cornucopia is not a very satisfactory vision. At its best it offers the possibility of rising income and wealth. At its worst it is narrowly materialistic and indifferent to the needs of the poor, the degradation of the environment, and the preservation of traditional cultures. It reduces justice to the freedom of entrepreneurs to make exchanges. The resistance being advocated here needs imaginative visions to stimulate the human spirit and guide action. Without exhausting the possibilities, two such visions are worth mentioning.

The first is Martha Nussbaum's capabilities theory, which offers a comprehensive ethic to assess and guide development policy.[7] Nussbaum rejects freedom of exchange as an adequate conception of justice and proposes to take the concept of development beyond the provision of basic material needs. For Nussbaum, the goal of development is a flourishing life. Following Aristotle, her first question is to ask what it means for human life to flourish. In answering this question she offers two general lists of human capabilities that give life a human shape and should direct social policy.

The first of these lists defines the "human form of life" and the basic capabilities required to function as a human: (1) mortality; (2) the human body, including the needs for food and drink, for shelter, and for sexual desire; (3) the capacity for pleasure and pain; (4) cognitive capability, including perceiving, imagining, and thinking; (5) early infant development; (6) practical reason; (7) affiliation with other human beings; (8) relatedness to other species and nature; (9) humor and play; (10) separateness; (11) space to move around in.[8]

The second list is called "basic human functional capabilities" and defines what "good" human functioning is: (1) being able to live to the end of a human life of normal length; (2) being able to have good health; (3) being able to avoid unnecessary and nonbeneficial pain; (4) being able to use the senses; (5) being able to have attachments to things and persons outsides ourselves; (6) being able to form a conception of the good and to engage in critical reflection about the planning of one's life; (7) being able to live for others, to recognize and show concern for other human beings, and to engage in various forms of social interaction; (8) being able to live with concern for and in relation to animals, plants, and the world of nature; (9) being able to laugh, play, and enjoy recreational activities; (10) being able to live one's own life and nobody else's in one's own surroundings and context.[9]

These lists are specific, yet general: specific to indicate that some things are essential or universal to human flourishing, general to allow for local and pluralistic specification of detail. Nussbaum goes on to insist that it is the function of the state and the good of development to provide the institutions and services that ensure everyone is capable of functioning at a human level. The details of functioning and flourishing are left to individuals in communities to work out.

In stating the basic capabilities that are the responsibility of the state and economic institutions to establish as possibilities for all, Nussbaum sets very different goals for development than are found in TNC-led globalization. Her list redefines equality and freedom and redirects the work of TNCs to the provision of material goods sufficient for the exercise of basic capabilities while caring for the environment. It respects pluralism and a large degree of local determination. It saves the concept of development from a too materialistic definition that serves TNC interests.

The second example of a vision for stimulating the human spirit and guiding action is the Earth Charter patterned in part on the Universal Declaration of Human Rights.[10] Championed by different international secular and religious groups, the purpose of the Earth Charter is to build a sustainable global community. The charter sets forth sixteen major principles, each with subprinciples under four headings: (1) respect and care for the community of life; (2) ecological integrity; (3) social and economic justice; and (4) democracy, nonviolence, and peace. Currently a commission is leading efforts to secure adoption by the United Nations.

At first glance, the Earth Charter elicits skepticism. The principles are numerous and lofty, adoption by the United Nations is by no means certain, and implementation is beyond any existing organization. Yet such vision is needed to give spirit to resistance, to offer an alternative for resistors to rally around, and to set clear goals for development.

Basic to the *realistic approach* is the task of balancing power as a mode of resistance in order to move from the existing state to one of greater justice, environmental preservation, and respect for cultural diversity. To accomplish these objectives, individuals and groups must first be empowered. For Christians this empowerment comes from the Holy Spirit. A loving relationship to God is therefore essential. This task will not be accomplished, however, by lone individuals in relation to God, although charismatic leaders may help. The focus will be on groups working cooperatively and using a variety of tactics and available media to engage in political give-and-take. What groups will undertake this task, and what tactics should they use?

Starting with tactics, a commitment to nonviolence is fundamental, even allowing for rare occasions when a large measure of justice, preservation, and

respect is attainable with a small measure of violence. Faith calls Christian resistors to this commitment; pragmatic calculation confirms it. In a world of 6
billion-plus people, degraded ecosystems, and vanishing diversity, violent tactics will only exacerbate suffering and destruction.

Nonviolent resistance tactics have a long history. Among the most often
used are *political demonstrations*, whose efficacy often lies more in calling attention to a problem than attaining tangible results. Given media hunger for
anything out of the ordinary, this can be a powerful tool, as witnessed by recent demonstrations held in conjunction with meetings of key international
economic organizations. Demonstrations are important in calling attention to
the abuses of globalization, since the process moves forward in small, decentralized decisions largely without critical attention.

Over the long haul, when the enthusiasm of direct action wanes, the
nitty-gritty of *political organization* is a necessity. This, of course, means attention to human institutions with all inherent dangers of bureaucracy. Here
the use of new electronic technologies comes into play. The *electronic revolution* that has so aided the mobility of capital and corporate control of far-flung
operations has also provided the means for resistors to come together and to
transmit news of corporate abuses. TNCs are increasingly finding it difficult
to hide environmental abuses and the exploitation of labor. Observers are ever
present and quickly report such abuses, often to the embarrassment of corporate leadership. TNCs are vulnerable to such exposure. Bad publicity can have
an effect on the financial bottom line, and it takes only a minority of resistors
to mount a fairly effective boycott or threaten disinvestment.

As for groups, first come the organizations that have traditionally and in
varying degrees countered corporate power. During the period of the mid-
twentieth century when power was roughly in balance, *government* was a fairly
effective counterforce to corporate power. This is no longer the case, for reasons previously considered. In the short term, local, state, national, and even
international institutions will not be very effective forces for resistance, except
perhaps in environmental protection. With exceptions, they are captive to the
interests of globalization. They remain a potential future source of resistance,
however, and therefore should be engaged by resistors, if for no other reason
than to weaken support for the status quo. The range of options to engage political process is quite large and beyond the scope of this chapter. Whatever
the tactic, the three primary concerns of social justice, environmental protection, and respect for diversity should govern avenues of engagement.

*International political organizations*, however weak they are now, will increasingly become important if resistance is to be effective. The international
arena, in spite of efforts to order it both formally with new institutions and
informally with the economic power of TNCs, continues to be characterized

by anarchy. On the one hand, this anarchy threatens the entire process of globalization, especially where local interests continue to take priority over global ones. Resistors will not want to side with unjust local interests, but with a measure of discrimination they may find common cause among the numerous local abuses created by globalization. Sweatshops, cut-and-run forestry, and careless mining practices are just a few examples.

On the other hand, global organizations themselves have potential for supporting programs of resistance. Social criticism has had some effect on organizations such as the WTO, the IMF, and the World Bank and should be intensified. The United Nations, however weak, is not fully captive to TNC power. Nation-states vary in their captivity; some, like Cuba, still offer an economic if not a democratic alternative. Efforts to come to international agreements on protecting the environment—for example, in the case of global warming—deserve support and political engagement.

*Labor organizations* show signs of new life. Their primary motivation must still be the protection of jobs and the interests of workers, but some unions are moving on larger social agendas and reaching out to other resistance-movement groups. Unions were in the vanguard in Seattle at WTO demonstrations, even providing buses for college students to participate.

Still another form of resistance is the deconstructing work of *intellectuals and academics*. The classic example is Karl Marx, of course, whose deconstruction of early capitalism, including its ideological foundations, spurred earlier efforts to balance corporate power. The phenomenal growth of academic institutions in the post–World War II period has greatly enlarged the potential number of critics. Anti-intellectualism is still strong in the United States, however, and universities are a major cog in the machinery of globalization. They turn out engineers and business majors in large numbers and are supported heavily by corporate research dollars. Partnerships with TNCs are increasingly common at large research universities. But they also educate social critics on a large scale, many of whom are not captive to business interests. Indeed, universities are one of the few remaining bastions of critical thinking. Resistance movements need sound ideological grounding, and academics have a role in providing it. There is even a bit of irony here as the critics educate the new leaders of globalization.

These traditional groups will be important in any resistance movement. More is needed, however, since the power balance has deteriorated even as these traditional groups have been in place. Where might this more come from?

First, a new group of groups has emerged to observe abuses, to report them, and to act in concert to counterbalance TNC power. The term *nongovernmental organizations* (NGOs) has been applied to the burgeoning number of activist organizations put together in the last two or three decades. These organizations are often small, private, grassroots, nonprofit, voluntary, and single issue, but can join forces with amazing speed to bring pressure to bear, as they did in protest of the Multilateral Agreement on Investments, the WTO, and the World Bank.[11] Rough estimates place the number of NGOs working on the environment alone at more than 100,000.[12] The movement is international, South Korea being one example where they have been effective politically. In most countries, however, they stick to education, health, and social services.

NGOs are certainly a force to be reckoned with, so much so that corporate interests are setting up front groups that use the same tactics.[13] Gifts to NGOs from corporate interests also threaten to stifle effectiveness. It remains to be seen if NGOs become the critical new force to balance TNC power.

Second, *the churches* have both a direct and indirect role as NGOs. The churches manage substantial endowment and pension portfolios of stocks and bonds, and most have set policy, established an institutional presence, and managed portfolios with an eye to ethical investment. Activities range from jawboning with corporate executives and submitting shareholder resolutions to disinvestment and support of boycotts. In addition, as a direct role, the vast majority of mainline churches have offices that formulate social policy. On the basis of established policy, church leaders are permitted and even encouraged to lead the church in much the same way as a leader of an NGO. Indirectly, the church educates its members on ethics, and while this influence is often weak and disorganized, it does make some difference and offers further potential.

Churches also enter into coalitions with other churches and even NGOs. Two such organizations are the Interfaith Center for Corporate Responsibility (ICCR) and CERES. The latter has developed a set of principles for corporate environmental responsibility and seeks to enlist corporations in voluntary compliance. Associations of churches and para-church organizations are still other examples.

The witness of the churches on corporate social responsibility is ambiguous. Many conservative churches champion TNC leadership. In the mainline churches there is hardly a consensus on how the churches should address TNCs. But again, the influence of NGOs is not dependent on majorities and unambiguous witness, but rather on hard work, organization, and a just cause.

Third, *investigative journalists* expose corporate abuses. Many journalists work for large news organizations that are susceptible to advertising pressures. In spite of these influences, investigative journalists are a remarkably independent lot, and news organizations often pride themselves on their independence. Most NGOs send periodic updates to constituents in the form of magazines and newsletters that also provide alternative sources of information.

Finally, *managers of major corporations* are increasingly aware that social justice and environmental concern make for second and third bottom lines that are connected to the financial bottom line. John Elkington details the transformation of corporate executives who no longer find the tactics of Carnegie and Frick palatable.[14] This transformation is not so much a change of heart, although there is some of that, as it is an awareness that concern for people and care of the earth are also financial concerns. It is difficult to say how deep this transformation runs, but whatever the depth is, it means that acts of resistance will find an audience among some corporate leaders.

So there are signs of hope. To repeat, the task is not the achievement of perfection, but higher levels of justice, environmental protection, and respect for diversity. That task is achievable, but it will require those who are willing to challenge power to act. Otherwise self-interest will go unchecked, and the current situation will deteriorate further.

## NOTES

1. Gordon Douglass, "The Globalization of Economic Life," a study paper prepared at the request of the Advisory Committee on Social Witness Policy of the Presbyterian Church (U.S.A.), 2002, pp. 3ff. Available from Presbyterian Distribution Center, 100 Witherspoon Street, Louisville, KY 40202.

2. Ibid., pp. 7–9.

3. International Labor Rights Fund, "The Employment Effects of Free Trade and Globalization," a study paper prepared at the request of the Advisory Committee on Social Witness Policy of the Presbyterian Church (U.S.A.), 2002. Available from Presbyterian Distribution Center, 100 Witherspoon Street, Louisville, KY 40202.

4. Reinhold Niebuhr, *The Nature and Destiny of Man*, vol. 1 (New York: Charles Scribner's Sons, 1941), chs. 6–10.

5. Reinhold Niebuhr, *Christian Realism and Political Problems* (New York: Charles Scribner's Sons, 1953), ch. 9.

6. Reinhold Niebuhr, *Love and Justice*, ed. D. B. Robertson (Louisville: Westminster/John Knox Press, 1957), part 1.

7. I am indebted for this brief analysis to Laura A. Stivers, "A Development Ethic of Capabilities and Liberation: Structural Adjustment and the Rural Poor of Central America," unpublished doctoral dissertation presented to the faculty of the Graduate Theological Union, April 2000, ch. 5.

8. Martha Nussbaum and Jonathan Glover, *Women, Culture, and Development: A Study of Human Capabilities* (Oxford: Clarendon Press, 1995), pp. 76–80.

9. Ibid., pp. 83–85.

10. The Earth Charter Commission, *The Earth Charter*, http://www.earthcharter.org, 2000.

11. Curtis Runyan, "Action on the Front Lines," in *World Watch* 12, no. 6 (November/December 1999): 12.

12. Ibid., p. 13.

13. Ibid., p. 21.

14. John Elkington, *Cannibals with Forks: The Triple Bottom Line of 21st Century Business* (Stony Creek, Conn.: New Society Publishers, 1998).

*3*

# Globalization:
# Reform or Resist?

*Gordon K. Douglass*

*M*ary Jo stood contentedly in her front yard, as firmly planted in Middle America as any of the cornstalks out back. "I wouldn't invest in Asia," she said, shaking her head decisively. A fifty-nine-year-old secretary with big, sparkling eyes, a plaid shirt, and no pretensions, she added, "Investing in Asia frightens me."

Yet Mary Jo, who has never traveled outside the United States, is in fact invested in Asia and all over the world, although she does not know it. After retiring in April from her job as a secretary with the state government, she has relied on a pension fund that has large investments abroad, giving her indirect ownership of stocks in Indonesia and Russia and Brazil. And the cash she tucked away in an A. G. Edwards money market account was funneled to big banks, which helped build elegant hotels and office towers from Argentina to Vietnam.

Meanwhile, sitting on the ground beside her hut, Bangon chopped up wild plants for lunch and pondered a wrenching question: what does her four-year-old daughter need more, food or a mother? A gentle woman whose soft face is framed by thick black hair, she explained that the family cannot afford both. As a result of the Asian financial crisis, her husband has lost his job as a construction worker, and so the family earns only a trickle of cash through odd jobs in this tiny village in northeast Thailand. That money can be used to buy rice and milk for the little girl, Saiyamon, who has become anemic and malnourished. Or Bangon can try to save the tattered small-denomination bills to pay for a stomach operation that she needs to save her own life.[1]

In its broadest sense, globalization refers to the rapid growth of linkages and interconnections between nations and social communities that make up the present world system. While this world system involves many aspects of society, its economic dimension—the erasing of economic borders to allow the free flow of goods and money—is the subject of this chapter. As economic globalization occurs, decisions and activities taking place in one part of the world have more and more consequences for people and communities elsewhere in the world. A question before the church is whether these consequences, on balance, move us toward a more just, peaceful, and sustainable human existence.

## FORMS OF ECONOMIC GLOBALIZATION

Economic globalization takes many forms. It may involve trade between individuals or businesses in one country and those of another. Globalization of this sort is as old as recorded history. Ancient coastal tribes traded with those in the mountains and deserts, each gaining prized goods they could not otherwise have enjoyed. Today, we take for granted that much of what we consume or use originated elsewhere, often in a foreign land.

Or businesses may decide to produce their products not only at home but also in other countries, either to evade the tariffs or quotas of countries where they wish to sell their products, or to cut their costs of production by, say, hiring cheaper labor. Then globalization involves the bundling together of financial capital, technology, and other strategic inputs in order to transfer them as direct foreign investment (hereafter, direct investment) in another country.

Direct investment implies control over the assets transferred abroad. Foreign investments that don't involve control are called foreign portfolio equity investments (hereafter, portfolio investments). They are more likely to be made by financial institutions or investors such as pension funds, insurance companies, or investment trusts, which are interested only in a return on their investments commensurate with the risks they are taking. If returns fall or risks rise, portfolio investment is much less dependable than direct investment as a source of longer-term finance for a country's development.

The activities of transnational corporations are a still deeper form of globalization. TNCs coordinate their activities with many entities throughout the world, producing in many places with complex networks of production and finance. This form of globalization has recently been named "alliance capitalism," in order to stress the growing importance of strategic alliances as businesses search for ways to protect their competitive advantages and global market positions.

Governments also compete for economic advantage globally. They often support private research and development activities, finance worker retraining, protect the environment, and promote interfirm alliances. When governments decide it is in their interest to cooperate rather than compete, they may form supranational organizations, like the International Monetary Fund (IMF) and the World Trade Organization (WTO), or less formal regional bodies, in order to achieve shared objectives, for example, stable macroeconomic conditions, more growth through trade, or "market-friendly" economies.

## GLOBALIZATION TRENDS

*Rapid Growth of Trade*

Since World War II, trade between nations of goods and services has grown much faster than world economic output, primarily for three reasons. First, rapid improvements in transportation and communications made it easier and cheaper to reach new markets. Second, successive rounds of tariff negotiations have virtually eliminated border barriers among developed countries, and many less-developed countries have unilaterally reduced their tariffs and quotas. Third, processing trade—trade involving goods whose components cross borders more than once before reaching final buyers—expanded rapidly. Trade is widespread for almost all nations, and its importance is rising virtually everywhere. A quick review of the labels in one's clothing is a good reminder of the pervasiveness of trade.

Trade between nations also has been transformed in recent years, from transactions over which national governments exercise significant control (international trade, if you will) to a form of globalized trade engineered and managed by large, dominant transnational corporations (transnational trade). Well over one-third of all U.S. imports and exports, for example, take place between the divisions and subsidiaries of the same company. This distinction is important for the reason that it signals a transfer of power and control away from national governments which, for all their failures, can be influenced by the general public. Transnational corporations, on the other hand, are not set up to serve others than their stockholders.

*Even Faster Growth of Foreign Direct Investment*

By latest count, there are at least 39,000 transnational corporations owning production facilities outside their home country. Direct investments by these large firms, which are growing more than twice as fast as trade, are probably the best indicators of the growth of deep cross-border economic integration. In fact, worldwide sales of the foreign subsidiaries of transnational enterprises now exceed the value of all internationally traded goods. The largest one hundred transnational corporations (excluding those in banking and finance) are estimated to control about one-third of the assets held by transnationals abroad.

## *The Flood of Portfolio Investment Across Borders*

Encouraged by "market friendly" policies of developing countries—policies often imposed on debtor nations by the IMF—individual investors, pension plans, and mutual funds increased their stakes five-fold in the equity shares and bonds of Third World companies in the early 1990s. Such rapid growth contrasted sharply with the experience of the 1980s, when equity investments were rare and many poor countries staggered under the weight of external debt.

But by 1997, equity investors suddenly began to reassess the risks of their exposure, and the Asian Crisis was born. In retrospect, the flow of portfolio investments was too fast to be absorbed into productive activities. It created bubbles in stock and real estate prices and encouraged luxury consumption that gave the illusion of prosperity unrelated to real increases in productivity. The faster portfolio investments flowed into Thailand, Malaysia, Indonesia, South Korea, and Hong Kong, the faster money was sucked out of the productive sector to join the speculation. When investors finally sensed their risk, they rushed to pull their money out. Hence, the flood of portfolio investments reversed direction by the end of 1997, ushering in severe recessions in many countries from which none has fully recovered. This sort of instability is very hard to correct in a world free of controls over the floods and flights of money capital.

## *The Proliferation of Business Alliances*

Cross-border agreements between firms based in different countries have become increasingly important complements to traditional trade and direct investment activities, with the range of such agreements growing ever wider. Their rapid growth since about 1985 means transnational corporations are less able to stay competitive without the mutual sharing of knowledge about new technologies, production processes, and distribution techniques. A flurry of mergers and acquisitions during 1998–1999 boosted direct investment flows substantially, despite a slowdown in global economic activity.

## THE INSTITUTIONS OF GLOBALIZATION

As transnational trade and investment soared in the 1990s, so, too, did the regulatory machinery for assuring their continued growth. During this period, the World Trade Organization emerged as the dominant arbiter of trade; the IMF was transformed into a bank of last resort; the IMF and the World Bank sorted out their respective roles in deeply indebted countries; the Organization for Economic Cooperation and Development (OECD) negotiated a Multilateral Agreement on Investment (MAI) designed to restrict a nation's ability to regulate foreign investment; and the sophistication of business alliances between dominant corporate players metastasized throughout the multinational business community.

There is little doubt that these bodies exert enormous influence over the societies and economies of peoples everywhere. They are best described as proponents of trade and investment as a means of encouraging the growth of markets throughout the world. Their stated aim is "prosperity broadly shared." Whether or not these institutions deliberately favor economic over other human aspirations, their preoccupation with economic ends has been widely criticized as "an ideology ordering our thought and action" to the detriment of other individual and social purposes, such as healthy communities and sustainable environments.

## THE CONSEQUENCES OF ECONOMIC GLOBALIZATION

This summary of the spread of economic globalization suggests why it has grown so rapidly. The first reason is the pressure felt by business firms from customers and competitors continually to innovate and upgrade what they produce. As firms discover the limits of their own core competencies, they are feeling the need to combine their skills with those of other firms, often in other countries, in new forms of "alliance capitalism."

The second reason is the spread of market-oriented policies by national governments and regional authorities. In the last eight years, thirty countries have given up central planning and one hundred others have liberalized their trade, foreign exchange, and/or capital transfer policies. The privatization of state enterprises in many countries and the relaxation of government regulations have added incentives for cross-border integration, both within transnational corporations and between independent firms or groups.

There is no doubt that the expansion of transnational trade, direct and portfolio investments, and networks of business alliances has benefited many people. The political changes and technological advances of the last decade have provided a stronger basis for economic growth than at any other time since the mid-1940s. This, it is said by proponents of the system, is because a globally integrated economy can lead to a "better" division of labor between countries, allowing low-wage countries to specialize in labor-intensive tasks while high-wage countries use workers in more productive ways. It allows firms to exploit bigger economies of scale. And with globalization, capital can be shifted to whatever country offers the most productive investment opportunities, not trapped at home, financing projects with poor returns.

In *The Lexus and the Olive Tree*,[2] Thomas Friedman asserts that globalization is overwhelmingly beneficial. In addition to the tangible economic rewards it brings especially to the owners of capital and the technologically skilled, globalized markets also encourage, even compel, governments to adopt "responsible" economic policies because failure to do so will encourage investors to withdraw their funds, imposing huge costs on the country. "Sound" policies, in contrast, attract money and guarantee rapid growth. Countries that trade extensively and invest in one another's economies, moreover, seldom go to war. Trade and investment, and the economic growth they encourage, Friedman argues, are important forces in reducing international tensions.

But globalization also has its costs, and these must be weighed along with its alleged benefits in order to assess its true consequences.

*Heightened Inequality*

Competitive pressures and more market-oriented policies create rapid changes in the allocation of resources among firms, industries, and countries, which in turn create pockets of unemployment not easily corrected in many situations. The structural changes causing unemployment tend to exaggerate the differences between those with the education, skills, and mobility to flourish in an unfettered world market, such as the owners of capital, highly skilled workers, and many professionals, and those without such attributes. Globalization has a way of eroding the bargaining power of groups that cannot move, leading to greater instability in their earnings and hours worked. The apparent "losers," unlike the highly skilled "winners," are made increasingly anxious about their place in an integrated world economy, whether they are blue-collar workers in New England textile factories or subsistence farmers in Mindanao.

The best evidence of this is found in growing income inequalities. The gap between rich and poor countries has long been the major source of inequality among people in the world. Somewhat surprisingly, this gap has, if anything, closed slightly over the past couple of decades. However, income distribution within countries has widened rapidly, and this has had a deleterious effect in many parts of the world. Everywhere in the so-called developed world, despite "social safety nets," the youngest, poorest, and least educated are significantly worse off than their counterparts were twenty years ago.

Many poor developing countries also are becoming less egalitarian in the face of globalization. The rural poor, especially the smallholders and the landless of Asia and Latin America, are being ruthlessly dispossessed and displaced.[3]

What forms of globalization are responsible for these disruptive changes in the markets for workers? Many people blame the changes in more-developed countries on competition from low-wage countries. Most economists, however, blame the losses of lower-skilled workers on technological changes (e.g., computerization) that are biased against the demand for low-skilled labor.

While both of these reasons no doubt have contributed to the widening of income-gaps within countries, the much larger reason appears to be the dramatic policy changes described as "liberalization" that commenced at the end of the 1970s. In the developed countries, these changes included a move from Keynesian toward monetarist macroeconomic policies and a shift from state-provided welfare "from cradle to grave" toward pay-as-you-go social services. At the same time, the public provision of basic services such as water and electricity, frequently at subsidized prices, has been replaced by privatized provision at "economic" prices; industrial interventionism and labor protection have given way to laissez-faire; tax systems whose major purpose was to correct inequalities have been transformed into systems mainly intended to promote incentives and economic efficiency.

There were parallel changes in developing countries, where policy was subject to the same paradigmatic shifts largely as a result of the influence of the developed countries, most directly through conditionalities imposed by the IMF and the World Bank. Their stabilization and structural adjustment programs appear to have hit the poor the hardest, with the urban working class particularly at risk. A still more subtle and effective influence of developed countries on the policies of developing countries was through the dominance of their educational systems, particularly those of the United States, which produced cohorts of so-called Third World technocrats, ready to advocate and "own" the new policies.

*Conflicts over Social Priorities*

Globalization also creates conflicts between national governments over domestic social priorities and the social institutions that embody them. Indeed, it is precisely the convergence of the policies just mentioned that has forced countries into what Thomas Friedman calls a "golden strait-jacket" but others call a "toxic strait-jacket"—a standardization of policies worldwide that vastly narrows the ability of single countries to honor their more unique political and cultural preferences. In Friedman's terms, "your economy grows but your politics shrink." Deviate too far from the new globalization rules and a country soon will see its investors stampede away, interest rates rise, and stock market prices fall.

Put another way, the argument against unrestricted global freedom of trade and movements of financial capital is not primarily an economic one. It is, rather, that the economy should serve the needs of society, not society the imperatives of the market. There is not much doubt that free markets are the most economically efficient type of capitalism. For most economists that ends the matter. Yet what so-called social market economies do, such as those of Japan and most of Europe, is in no sense irrational. Policies in those countries to maintain social cohesion are just as important as efficiency in the allocation of scarce resources.

Consider, for example, the struggle the European Union has had over the harmonization of policies on employment, welfare, immigration, and competition in order to create a common market and a common currency while trying to remain internationally competitive. Social democrats in Britain and other European countries who imagine that the social market economies with which they are familiar can be reconciled with a global free market have not understood the new circumstances in which advanced industrial societies find themselves. In Japan, large corporations have started to dismantle the postwar practice of providing lifetime employment, one of Japan's most distinctive social institutions, in order to adapt to the pressures of globalization. In South Korea, labor unions have taken to the streets to protest the government's relaxation of firing restrictions. Latin American countries are competing with each other to liberalize trade, deregulate their economies, and privatize public enterprises.

Efforts by developed countries in North America and Europe to "harmonize" labor standards are motivated only in part by the fear in developed countries of losing jobs to workers earning much less in developing countries. International labor standards have become a point of contention in trade disputes, not only for economic reasons, but also because low wages and weak safety standards abroad violate the human rights of workers. Even so, the United States and others are finding it increasingly difficult to negotiate worker protections into the charters of multinational institutions such as the World Trade Organization. The failure of the WTO meeting in Seattle in December 1999 was more the result of this policy strait-jacket than of the violent protests in the streets.

Disagreements also are rising over the environmental consequences of globalization. Pollution is generated most often by the processes of industrialization, so the countries that are soon becoming the most industrialized, such as China, Brazil, Indonesia, and India, are the likeliest sources of future global pollution. They are unlikely to throttle back their industrial plans in order to protect the environment, as some in the United States and Europe have suggested. That would raise their costs and erase their comparative advantage. Arguments in Kyoto at the December 1997 Summit on Global Climate Change vividly illustrate the political tensions wrought by globalization.

## *Fragmented Safety Nets*

The so-called invisible hand of the market is acceptable to most people only if the losers from market forces are compensated by the winners. A central function of government has been to assist in this transfer by helping the losers adjust to change—usually by means of unemployment compensation, severance payments, and adjustment assistance. In essence, governments have used their fiscal powers to insulate domestic groups from excessive market risks, particularly those originating in international transactions. This is the way developed-country governments have maintained domestic political support for liberalizing trade and finance throughout the postwar period.

But recently, the idea of giving support to the losers has come under withering attack. Employers no longer grant job security, partly for competitive reasons and also because they are more mobile and less dependent on the good will of local workforces. Governments are less able to help the losers because the slightest hint of raising taxes leads to capital flight in a world of heightened mobility. Moreover, the ideological onslaught against the welfare state has paralyzed many governments and made them unable to respond to the domestic needs of a more internationally competitive economy.

Accordingly, at the very time increased integration into the world economy has raised the need of governments to redistribute tax revenues or implement generous social programs in order to protect the vast majority of the population that remains internationally immobile, governments find themselves less able to raise taxes. The heightened mobility of financial capital has led to competition among nations to attract foreign investment, and a key tool of that competition is to offer a relatively low-tax environment. Tax competition, in turn, threatens to undermine individual and corporate income taxes. The United States and other developed countries have responded, first, by shifting the tax burden from (mobile) capital to (less mobile) labor, and second, when further increased taxation of labor becomes politically and economically difficult, by cutting the social safety net. This is bound to jeopardize social stability. Even governments with significant budget surpluses, such as in the United States under President Clinton, seem less willing to protect the weak against the cruelties of the market.

## WHERE SHOULD POWER RESIDE?

Into whose hands are the powers to set society's goals being delivered as the forces of globalization continue to expand? Virtually everyone concedes that markets are a useful instrument for implementing goals. As mechanisms for delivering goods and services to the people who can afford them at the lowest possible prices, they have yet to meet their match.

But unfettered markets are not the best instrument for setting the goals of society. Unregulated markets often lead to spoiled environments. Nor do markets provide for the national or collective defense. They will not eliminate the scourge of unemployment. They rarely distribute income and wealth in accord with most people's conception of fairness. They are frequently unstable, prone to overshooting as the conditions of demand and supply shift. And they're not usually designed to protect other cultural values. Markets don't care for fairness or community, but only for efficiency.

Who, then, ought to set society's goals? How are today's globalizing communities and nations governed? To what extent do their governance structures hold decision-making powers accountable for the consequences of their decisions? The answers to these questions are rather different according to one's allegiance to one of three schools of thought: the Washington Consensus, the Human Development Consensus, and the People-Centered Consensus.

### The Washington Consensus

This widely held point of view finds its leadership in the business community, the economics profession, and the IMF, World Bank, and WTO. The Washington Consensus supports a top-down structure of global economic governance, as during the debt crisis of the 1980s and more recently during the Asian, Russian, and Brazilian currency crises. Perhaps the best illustration of this has been the habit of these institutions at times of crisis to offer various kinds of debt relief to the nations in economic trouble, but only if the indebted countries agree to adopt some combination of "stabilization" and "structural adjustment" policies that sharply reduce government services, free economies of regulation, and encourage exporting and direct investment. Members of this consensus applaud the growing power of market institutions and the weakening of governments, and favor strengthening key multilateral institutions such as the IMF and WTO. Governments still have important roles to play, especially as providers of a legal framework, education, and stable fiscal and financial policies, but their importance is downplayed.

Because this group says little about non-economic goals, it leaves the impression that it favors policies that place economic growth and trade above other human values.[4]

The Washington Consensus has exerted enormous influence on the processes of change reflected in globalizing economic trends. These trends strongly imply a heightened concentration of economic power in the world, centered especially in large transnational enterprises, a weakening of the countervailing forces of governments and civil societies, and quite probably a further separation of decision-making powers from public accountability for their consequences. Who sets society's goals in its world? It is still a pluralistic world involving enterprises, governments, and civil societies. But the balance of these forces seems now to be shifting in favor of businesses, whose interests are vastly more focused on economic returns than on the health of people and their communities.

*The Human Development Consensus*

This school of thought is best represented by UNICEF and the UN Development Program. It differs from the Washington Consensus primarily by its readiness to highlight the ill effects on human and community life of many globalizing processes. It is blunt about the fact that "market friendly" development strategies usually produce losers as well as winners, and that social cohesion easily is lost when societies fail to find ways to assist the losers with retraining, relocation, and/or income transfers. It rues the growing gap between rich and poor. The Human Development Consensus also has focused attention on the wastefulness of military expenditures and the human destruction wrought by the structural adjustment policies of the IMF and the World Bank.[5]

The Human Development Consensus thinks that an economic system can remain viable over time only so long as responsible governance structures establish mechanisms to counter the abuses of market or state power and the consequent erosion of society's natural, social, and moral capital. This suggests that it believes in a form of democratic pluralism not unlike the framework that guided the post–World War II economic boom of Western nations and resulted in the broad sharing of development benefits throughout their societies. Thus, it supports a process of goal setting which actively seeks the involvement of all parts of society, including the civil society. Even so, it shares with the Washington Consensus a belief in economic growth through free and open markets, and therefore it, too, is hostage to economic power arrangements that produce outcomes especially favorable to business.

*The People-Centered Consensus*

This school of thought finds its leadership in various citizen alliances, such as the People-Centered Development Forum, the Third World Network, and the International Group for Grassroots Initiatives, rather than any official governance structure. It is deeply rooted in the institutions of civil society, including some church organizations. While the People-Centered Consensus acknowledges necessary roles for markets and governments, it insists that the people must take precedence over the interests of either the corporation or the state. It therefore stands in opposition to the patterns of globalization that concentrate economic power in the hands of transnational corporations beyond the reach of public accountability.

Adherents of the People-Centered Consensus favor economic and political decentralization, so that people retain the rights to organize and to participate in the decisions that affect them. In order to achieve this goal, they prefer greater community self-reliance—a drawing back from the deepening entanglements of globalization, not to the exclusion of specialization and trade, but with greater effort to nurture and control the use of local resources. Because the People-Centered Consensus regards the limits of the earth's finite ecosystem as more constraining than do the other schools of thought, it also places greater emphasis on a means of livelihood adequate to assure every person's basic needs. Frugality for the well-off is a sine qua non of this point of view.[6]

The People-Centered Consensus draws strength also from the indigenous communities of developing countries, which resist the westernization of their culture. Their religious roots cause them to perceive their society's goals differently than, say, the elites who have allied themselves with the agents of globalization. For many of them, it is the dignity and sustenance of individual human beings that matters more than growth or even development of the local economy.

Members of these communities wonder, too, if the free market paradigm of the Washington Consensus is not an indirect method of organizing social and political relations and structures in society as well as a means of ordering the economy. It is not enough to have "friendly" economic markets and "socially concerned" business leaders. A society needs a healthy civil society first, lest the economic system be allowed to disrupt harmonious human relationships.

Thus, the kind of democratic pluralism preferred by the People-Centered Consensus probably implies markets with a significant degree of regulation, and trade policies that link national economies to one another within a framework of rules that maintains domestic competition and favors domestic enterprise, employing local workers, meeting local standards, paying local taxes, and functioning within a well-developed system of democratic governance. Foreign competition is not excluded; it simply does not share the preferred status of locally owned businesses that are rooted in place and serve the community in many ways that imported goods and footloose investors cannot.

## THEOLOGICAL AND ETHICAL CONSIDERATIONS

Globalization is not a new concept to the church. It is first prefigured in the Bible by the creation stories. What God has made is a unity; all belongs together. That creation is to be tended, protected, and nurtured by its human participants, who have unique creation responsibilities because of uniquely bearing the image of the Creator. That responsibility involves caring for both "the garden"—the environment itself—and the relationships of the created beings. In the unfolding of the biblical message, a sense of the goodness of community extends to include ultimately all the earth's people and all future generations.

Thus, the moral test of today's globalizing economy is whether it serves adequately the human enterprise and the larger creation. Few would doubt that international exchange has made life easier, more pleasant, and more interesting for those with the resources to participate. But huge segments of the world's population do not have such resources; worse yet, many are further impoverished by the ordinary functioning of the globalized economy.

Community is not encouraged by a competitive market system—even less so by its globalized version. Calls for free trade and free movements of capital, untouched by community constraints, are calls for individual, not community, values. This insistence on social and moral autonomy has caused critics in the church to denounce "the market society in whose logic God's grace and God's justice cannot appear."[7] To acknowledge a sphere of life from which moral scrutiny is excluded is to abridge God's sovereignty and create an absolute that rivals God. Biblical faith acknowledges no such rival.

An economic system in which business profits and high consumption in one society are based on exploitative relationships elsewhere runs headlong into a basic biblical concern. The ability to manipulate people and to play God through money was vehemently condemned by the prophets: "I will not revoke the punishment; because they sell the righteous for silver, and the needy for a pair of shoes" (Amos 2:6). Such words still have a prophetic ring in a time when producers of apparel and sneakers, in the drive to cut costs while protecting market share and profits, search the world over for a labor force that will work for a few pennies less.

Nor can the pain of heavily indebted poor countries be easily dismissed by Christians guided by the biblical witness. In recent years, governments and banks have offered some relief. Still, in dozens of cases, the remaining debt cannot be paid or it can be paid only by imposing enormous human suffering. The biblical message is unambiguous. In the seventh year or the forty-ninth year—"the year of the Lord"—there was to be a time of jubilee. Debts were to be canceled, family land returned, and the impressed and oppressed set free (Lev. 25; Luke 4:18–19). There is debate about whether the law of jubilee was ever formally administered in the life of Israel. Nevertheless, the principle is clear. No economic decision or arrangement must be allowed to impoverish permanently; it must not make the future hopeless. Within history, periodic corrections are to be made that will reestablish right economic relationships and restore freedom, opportunity, and hope. Such a principle has profound implications for the prophetic role of the church in today's global society.

The principle of jubilee is a reminder that biblical faith accords absolute status to no economic system. Nor does it sanction untended economic mechanisms. The biblical tradition assumes that an economy is subject to moral guidance and regular correction. That is no less true of complex international economic relations than of exchanges between individuals.

Facing such realities, the church need not pretend technical competence it does not uniquely possess. It can and should, however, engage in moral analysis of laws and economic proposals, denounce morally unacceptable economic outcomes, name the sin that is causing pain, and insist that more humane policies be sought and implemented. That is an authentic prophetic task of the community of faith in economic life—whether the market is local, national, or global.


## POLICIES FOR JUSTICE IN A GLOBALIZING WORLD


The growth of the world economy could be a great advance for humankind. It could be the beginning of a many-centered world, in which different cultures and regimes could interact and cooperate without domination or war. But that is not the world that is arising around us in the vain attempt by proponents of the Washington Consensus to build a globally free market.

In a world in which market forces are subject to no overall constraint or regulation, justice and peace are continually at risk. Unregulated capitalism degrades the environment and kindles conflict over natural resources. It enriches the educated elites and owners of capital, often at the expense of less able and less mobile populations. By promoting minimal government intervention in the economy, it neglects those in greatest need. And in expanding parts of the world, it locks nation-states into competition not only for markets but for survival. The global market as it is presently organized forces nations to become rivals for resources while instituting no methods for conserving them.

History confirms that free markets are inherently volatile institutions, prone to speculative booms and busts. Overshooting, especially in financial markets, is their normal condition. To work well, free markets need not only regulation but active management. During much of the postwar era, world markets were kept stable by national governments and by a regime of international cooperation. Only lately has a much earlier idea been revived and made an orthodoxy, the idea adopted by the Washington Consensus that, provided there are clear and well-enforced rules of the game, free markets can be self-regulating because they embody the rational expectations that participants form about the future.

On the contrary, since markets are themselves shaped by human expectations, their behavior cannot be rationally predicted. The forces that drive markets are not mechanical processes of cause and effect, as assumed in most of economic theory. They are what George Soros has termed "reflexive interactions."[8] Because markets are governed by highly combustible interactions among beliefs, they cannot be self-regulating.

Thus, thoughtful people are alarmed by the evidence that freer markets are unstable and that all are not prospering from their spread. Whole communities, whole regions, whole nations are being marginalized by the inexorable forces of change brought on by economic integration. Poverty is rising almost everywhere. Yet the power of governments to alleviate the suffering of those who are losing out is slipping away from them.

Nor is an appropriate balance being struck between the economic and non-economic aspirations of human beings and their communities. Indeed, the evidence is mounting that globalization's trajectory can easily lead to the splitting apart of nations along lines of economic status, mobility, region, or social norms. Globalization not only highlights and exacerbates tensions among groups but it also reduces the willingness of internationally mobile groups to cooperate with others in resolving disagreements and conflicts.

What, then, can be done to share the benefits of globalization more widely and to ameliorate its social consequences? The answer is not to disengage altogether from the processes of globalization, as some adherents of the People-Centered Consensus prefer. That would be foolish as well as impossible. Many of the underlying changes that have occurred in the global economy are now irreversible. Rather, the question is how to engineer a new balance between market and society—a balance that will require greater human control over the processes of change and the sharing of its fruit.

The following recommendations are meant to help strike such a balance. They do not conform precisely to proposals generated by either the Human Development Consensus or the People-Centered Consensus, yet they draw from both groups. Nor do they represent a comprehensive blueprint for reform, which surely would include far more radical changes in the institutions of business, government, and daily living than proposed here.

1. *Rehabilitate the modern state.* In Liberia, Albania, Tajikistan, Pakistan, Colombia, Siberia, Chechnya, and Somalia, the threat to peace and economic progress does not come from tyrannous or expansionist states. It comes from the absence of effective government of any kind. The Washington Consensus neglects the many ways in which unregulated world markets threaten cohesion in society and stability in governments. The World Bank's recent repudiation of the dogma of minimal government is welcome, but it falls far short of the need to provide the institutions necessary to assure security from destitution, unemployment, and exclusion.

2. *Develop a regulatory framework for coexistence and cooperation among the world's diverse economies.* As it is presently organized, global capitalism is supremely ill-suited to cope with the risks of geopolitical conflict that are endemic in a world of worsening scarcities. If today's laissez-faire regime is not reformed, it is likely to fracture and fragment as mounting scarcities of resources and conflicts of interest among the world's great powers make international cooperation even more difficult. Free markets are creatures of strong governments and cannot exist very long without them.

3. *Set up more efficient and generous systems of social insurance.* They would allow losers to secure more of the benefits of international economic integration and suffer less of its social costs. Indeed, the social welfare state is the flip side of the open economy; the more exposed is the economy to external shocks, the more certainly it will need a generous system of income transfers. Any movement toward freer trade and movements of financial capital should be accompanied by more generous adjustment assistance policies, including unemployment benefits and retraining and relocational subsidies.

4. *Tax footloose capital movements.* Generous and appropriate systems of social insurance must be financed in some way. If national sources of

taxation are no longer adequate to this task, then it may well be time to consider taxation of footloose factors at the global level, with revenue sharing among nations. The most radical reform would involve outright restrictions on speculative capital transfers, with all their potential for abuse and corruption. A more moderate reform might include measures designed to regulate the timing of capital transfers or ones that increase the cost of speculative transactions. Similarly, a uniform tax might be imposed on intercurrency transactions, for example, the "Tobin Tax."[9] More exchange of information among tax authorities would be another step in the right direction; better still, an international convention to restrict the ability of transnational firms to avoid taxation should be negotiated.

5. *Establish a new system of global safeguards to accommodate important differences in the social, political, and cultural preferences of nations.* Multilateral institutions such as the WTO should permit selective disengagement from the discipline of multilateral treaties, under well-specified contingencies, when countries need breathing room to satisfy domestic requirements that are in conflict with trade policies, for example, to assist labor reallocation or to protect the environment. Similar provision should be made in treaties governing foreign direct and portfolio investment.

6. *Forgive the unsustainable debts of impoverished nations.* Recently the joint IMF and World Bank initiative for heavily indebted poor countries (HIPCs) was launched to much fanfare. Its terms and conditions expect applicants to demonstrate "good policy track records"—a euphemism for policies deemed appropriate by these agencies. Efforts to balance economic goals with other societal objectives are conspicuously absent from HIPC legislation. Recently, a forgiveness initiative for bilateral debts, along the lines of Jubilee 2000, has been announced by several creditor nations.

7. *Encourage partnership relationships with local communities.* All agents of development assistance, including USAID and the multilateral assistance groups, should establish healthier partnership relations with local communities. Partnerships involve mutuality and cooperation and aim at increased self-reliance with respect to essential needs. Self-reliance comes through broad-based local ownership and control of productive resources, land reform (as necessary), and encouragement of sustainable agricultural and locally based business enterprises.

8. *Reform IMF and World Bank conditional lending policies.* These multilateral agencies should replace bankrupt structural adjustment efforts with policies and programs that more adequately meet the needs of

the poor and promote sustainable, participatory, and equitable development. Among the conditions that should be included in loan agreements are:

- Reduction of inappropriate levels of military spending.
- Preservation of spending on basic needs, including education and health care.
- Assurance of a safety net for those most severely affected by adjustment policies.
- Prevention of adverse environmental effects such as deforestation and soil degradation.
- A system for monitoring and correcting (as may be necessary) the effects of adjustment policies.

These agencies also must be more accountable to the people affected by their policies and projects through increased transparency, greater access to information, and greater participation in the development of projects, programs, and policies.

9. *Support legislation that helps end sweatshops.* The garment and textile industries are rank with labor exploitation, here and abroad. There is widespread noncompliance with labor, health, and safety laws, as well as stubborn unwillingness by many large retailers to adequately monitor the labor practices of the contractors with whom they do business.

10. *Redouble individual efforts to support self-determination.* As individual Christians and their congregations contemplate development of covenant relationships with particular nongovernmental organizations or communities abroad, they should seek to support those whose projects are designed by the local community and controlled by its people. By the same token, individual Christians who hold stock in U.S.-domiciled transnational corporations should hold their companies accountable for conduct contrary to just and sustainable human development.

11. *Redouble individual efforts to live frugally and generously.* Christians must lead the way to a basic reconception of the "good life," one that is less materialistic and more frugal. The good life finds fulfillment in a genuinely caring and mutually supportive community in Christ, and through faithful responses to God's call to restore creation and discover the contemporary meaning of doing justice, loving kindness, and walking humbly with our God (Micah 6:8 NRSV).

## WANT TO KNOW MORE?

See the fascinating debate in *Foreign Policy*, "Dueling Globalizations: A Debate Between Thomas Friedman and Ignacio Ramonet" (Fall 1999, pp. 110–127). Friedman, a foreign affairs columnist for the *New York Times*, also wrote *The Lexus and the Olive Tree* (New York: Farrar, Straus, and Giroux, 1999). William Greider argues for more managed globalization in *One World Ready or Not: The Manic Logic of Global Capitalism* (New York: Simon and Schuster, 1997). In *The Post-Corporate World: Life After Capitalism* (San Francisco: Barrett-Koehler, 1999), David Korten stipulates that corporate capitalism could unravel the cohesion of society. Refraining from taking sides, Dani Rodrik reexamines some of the faulty assumptions made on both sides of the globalization debate in "Sense and Nonsense in the Globalization Debate," *Foreign Policy* (Summer 1997). For more about the roles of civil society and nongovernmental organizations, see "The Third Force: Civil Society's Challenge to Corporations and Governments," *World Watch* (November–December 1999).

## NOTES

1. Excerpted from "Who Went Under in the World's Sea of Cash," *New York Times*, February 15, 1999, p. 1; and "Asia Feels Strain Most at Society's Margins," *New York Times*, June 8, 1998, p. 1.

2. Thomas Friedman, *The Lexus and the Olive Tree* (New York: Farrar, Straus and Giroux, 1999).

3. Frances Stewart and Albert Berry, "Globalization, Liberalization, and Inequality: Real Causes," *Challenge* (January/February 2000): 44–92.

4. See the World Bank's World Development Report, 1991.

5. See the United Nations Development Program, Human Development Report, published annually.

6. See David Korten, *When Corporations Rule the World* (West Hartford, Conn.: Kumarian Press, 1996).

7. M. Douglas Meeks, *God the Economist* (Minneapolis: Fortress Press, 1989), p. 37.

8. See George Soros, *Underwriting Democracy, Part Three* (New York: Free Press, 1991).

9. James Tobin, "A Proposal for International Monetary Reform," *Eastern Economic Journal* 4, nos. 3–4 (1978): 153–159.

*4*

# Environmental Movements as Forms of Resistance

## *Heidi Hadsell*

$\mathscr{R}$esistance is an important theme in the Christian tradition. From the prophets of the Hebrew Bible to Jesus' Sermon on the Mount, believers are counseled, cajoled, and even coerced into thinking again, into questioning what has come to seem as unquestionable in our habits and practices and values, and those of the world around us. We are asked to consider and to orient our actions according to such concepts as idolatry, sinful self-interest, openness to and regard for the other, self-sacrifice, concepts that others may find strange or even ridiculous. Thus, we are asked to resist much of the logic of the world around us, both as an act of faith and as a way of loving the world that God has created. In different times and places, such resistance for the sake of being faithful to God and to God's vision for humanity has taken different forms. Today, in a civilization largely characterized by careless disregard for nature, by wasteful and thoughtless consumption, and by the widespread belief that money and material goods are the measure of the person, one of the forms resistance takes is in the active and careful stewardship of all of God's creation. This stewardship is not only one way to care for our natural habitat, of which we are, after all, a part, but also a way to begin to live in relationship to others in ways not determined by such criteria as socioeconomic status, but by values of community. In this way, resistance is faithfulness to the tasks God calls us to.

Leviticus 25 brings together themes that are basic to human relationships with nature, human community, and to life lived in faithfulness. The three interrelated themes are the land, human relationships, and human tasks.

What is the value of the land? How should that value be established? What are proper relationships between people?

55

What is our proper relationship to the land?

What ought we do about divisions of wealth internal to a community?

Are we to care for everyone in our community? In what ways? What about the outsiders?

Why are we here; what is our purpose?

While human communities and individuals ask versions of these questions all the time, we do not often ask them in a fundamental way, probably because most of us are born into societies that are already essentially constructed. The ways in which our communities and the larger society are constructed and the justifications commonly given for those ways are largely taken for granted by those around us, and, especially if we are comfortable and included, we come to take them for granted ourselves.

These questions, however, are classical elements of political and moral thought. And here they are fundamental elements of self-organization, for a people poised on the edge of a new land. They are questions about how best the Jews were to organize themselves once they reached the promised land. This passage is part of a larger whole, which reflects the thought about and the anticipation of how the new society was to be arranged. In it are a number of categories that are clues to what these ancient peoples thought essential in their social organization. Thus, for example, we find a preoccupation with distinguishing between the clean and the unclean, the common and the holy, the insider and literally the outsider, those outside the walls, and outside the religion.

The major question posed here, the question that orients all the other questions, if posed directly, might be put like this: "How are we going to relate to the land that sustains us, to each other inside the community, and to those outside the community in a way that reflects faithfully the overriding and unforgettable fact that God is God, and that God is our central raison d'être?"

These passages are a partial answer to this very basic question. And they reflect strongly the insight that human social organization is a concrete demonstration of basic values and commitments. Thus, human social organization—political and economic life—can and should be intentionally arranged so that it reflects the faithfulness of the people of God to their understanding that God is God.

Since this North American society, more or less like most other societies, is not organized by this basic understanding, but rather by market forces, political parties, and conflicting interest groups, the question "How shall we organize ourselves to reflect our faithfulness to God who is God?" comes to us as unrealistic or quaint. And the answers to the question turn our Western, wasteful, market-oriented sensibilities upside down and provide a healthy occasion for self-reflection.

## THE LAND

After decades of reading these passages, when I finally read them through "green" eyes, I discovered, to my surprise, the overriding role of the land itself: "When you come into the land which I give you, the land shall keep a sabbath to the Lord. Six years you shall sow your field, and six years you shall prune your vineyard, and gather in its fruits; but in the seventh year there shall be a sabbath of solemn rest for the land, a sabbath to the Lord; you shall not sow your field or prune your vineyard" (Leviticus 25:2–4).

In this familiar passage, clearly the land has its own centrality and its own integrity. It has integrity as God's creation, and through its continual relationship to God. In the seventh year, the land needs to rest. It is a sabbath to the Lord—not to people and their own need to rest. Here the first jubilee, the archetype of all jubilees, is that of the land. While the land will provide for the people of Israel, it has its own independent reason for being, its own worth in its belongingness to God, independently of its use for humans.

The centrality of the relationship of the land with God makes the human relationship with the land secondary. It is the independent relationship the land has with God, and the independent relationship the people of Israel have with God, that is to determine the relationship the people of Israel will have to the land. In verse 23, God reminds Moses that the land is his, God's, and that the people are also in relationship with God, and only on the land in the fleeting fashion of a stranger or a sojourner: "The land shall not be sold in perpetuity, for the land is mine; for you are strangers and sojourners with me." Since the relationship with God is the determinant of the human relationship with the land, God insists that obedience in that relationship is the way to insure the land's productivity and therefore its ability to sustain God's people securely. In verse 18, God commands: "Therefore you shall do my statutes, and keep my ordinances and perform them; so you will dwell in the land securely. The land will yield its fruit, and you will eat your fill, and dwell in it securely."

The major statute that God commands in these verses is that of the jubilee, every seven years for the land itself, every fifty years for the ownership of the land. The price paid by the nonobservance of this statute is insecurity on the land and the loss of its productivity. Looking at our own situation, we can conclude that the writer of the text was onto something. For in defining land as private property for the owner to do what he or she will with it, rather than as God's land to be taken care of as God wills, we might well wonder about the price we pay for our disobedience. We get a glimpse of this price when the land loses its productivity, topsoil washes into streams, groundwater is exhausted, and agribusiness dictates overuse. Carrying out such practices that are designed to promote greater short-term productivity and profit, rather than to promote the long-term fertility of the land, are we more secure than we were before?

But if, as God insists to Moses, the land belongs to God, how were the people of Israel to determine its value? The answer is interesting. While the land itself has intrinsic worth and integrity, it has no intrinsic exchange value. The value it has to humans refers to how much it will produce until the next jubilee, when it will most likely change hands again, or, similarly, how much it has produced since the last jubilee. That is, the value is determined not by exchange rates established by the market, which is to say not by human ownership of the land, which is at best transitory and derivative of God's ownership, but by its use value to humans, that is, how much it produces or will produce in the future before the next jubilee or has produced in the past since the last jubilee. "According to the number of years after the jubilee, you shall buy from your neighbor, and according to the number of years for crops he shall sell to you. If the years are many you shall increase the price, and if the years are few you shall diminish the price, for it is the number of the crops that he is selling to you" (Leviticus 25:15).

Brazil is a country well known for its land disputes, largely due to the wide gap between the millions of landless peasants looking for land to farm, and in this way for their own survival, and the relatively few landowners, who often own pieces of land the size of small countries. Over the last several decades, I have witnessed countless landless Brazilian peasants involved in land disputes with owners of large pieces of land. Often the peasants make the same argument that God here makes to Moses. The value of the land for humans, they insist, lies in its ability to produce, to sustain life. The value of land for humans is therefore, or rather ought to be, its use value. The market value, especially in areas and times of rampant land speculation, which in recent years has been the case all over the Amazon basin, negates this use value by making the land a mere commodity to be bought and sold for profit, like any other commodity. Land viewed as a mere commodity makes a few people rich, but prohibits millions of desperate peasants from wresting their own sustenance from the use of the land. Indeed, often the land bought for speculation lies unused or is destroyed through misuse while peasants who could use it well are prohibited from doing so. Land speculation, the peasants argue, negates God's intended use of God's land and it is the peasants who pay, not the land owners, for this disobedience.

Similarly, also in Brazil, I have heard peasants along the Amazon River argue that the small lakes the receding waters of the river leave during the dry season are, and should continue to be for the local communities, a resource from which everyone in the community can fish to supplement an otherwise very meager diet. Such low-impact fishing practices, they argue, are sustainable over many generations, and the lakes and their fish in turn help sustain the communities around them. The peasants do not own the lakes as property, but they depend partially on them, and their fishing practices do not deplete them. This, they argue, is the care for creation God intended. Commercial fishing, which has been increasing rapidly in recent years, however, with huge nets and powerful fishing boats from faraway cities, is unsustainable even in the short run, and destructive of the communities nearby.

The concepts and language of stewardship, care for God's creation, community, and sustainability enable these Amazonian peasants to think about alternatives to what may seem like the inevitable domination and destruction of their lifestyle by those who are stronger and more powerful. Thus, these concepts enable the peasants to resist, and to do so in a way that is grounded in the Christian tradition and in the larger cultural traditions that they share as a community.

## HUMAN RELATIONSHIPS

The second theme in Leviticus 25 is that of human relationships. Human beings are understood and described in terms of their relationships, not only with the land, but also with God, and with each other. God, land, and human relationships, are all intertwined. In this passage, one finds not only brothers, but uncles, cousins, sons, children, kinsmen, Levites, men dwelling outside the walls of a city, strangers and sojourners and servants, both male and female, and both from within and from outside the nation. There are, in short, many people in many different walks of life and in many different relationships.

In our individualistic civilization, it is difficult to perceive perhaps how differently human relationships are portrayed in this text. For the understanding of human identity and human worth is in terms of the web of familial and other social relationships, not in terms of the individual person. And, very importantly, it is this web of relationships that establishes proper economic relationships, and not vice versa. Verse 25: "If your brother becomes poor and sells part of his property, then his next of kin shall come and redeem what his brother has sold." Verse 35: "And if your brother becomes poor, and cannot maintain himself with you, you shall maintain him; as a stranger and a sojourner he shall live with you. Take no interest from him or increase, but fear your God; that your brother may live beside you. You shall not lend him your money at interest, nor give him your food for profit." Verse 39: "And if your brother becomes poor beside you, and sells himself to you, you shall not make him serve as a slave: he shall be with you as a hired servant and as a so-journer. He shall serve with you until the year of the jubilee."

In each of these passages, the human relationships are the independent variables. The human relationships, such as that of being a brother, are what determine the economic relationships, and thus the human relationships are the relationships to attend to. The human relationships guide the economic relationships all the way along, although most dramatically in the year of the jubilee, when land reverts to other owners and servants are set free. The jubilee is important. It is also important for us to understand that all the way along the human relationships, established by kinship, citizenship, religion, clean and unclean, holy and common, are the guides to the economic relationships.

This emphasis on human relationships, which then determines economic status and roles, is almost the complete reversal of our own society in which money, ownership, and other tangible and intangible elements of social class are taken to be the measure of the person, or to be that which is understood as central in the person. Thus it is the case that money, status, and ownership can tear apart families and friendships or, on the other hand, create them. In either case, the logic is that relationships are dependent variables tied to economic independent variables. In contrast, the logic of resistance is one in which the person is valued as part of a larger whole, to which he or she belongs, and thus bears worth that does not refer to monetary value.

In these verses, the market, in fact all of economic life, is subordinate—not unimportant, but subordinate—in that it serves ends that are not its own, it is not an end in itself. Leviticus 25 reflects a profound understanding of how disruptive uneven economic relationships can be to webs of kinship, to community, to all kinds of human relationship. Importantly, the jubilee insures a kind of rough justice. And this rough justice may very well be a necessary precondition for real community. This is an insight shared by varieties of groups in human history, such as some indigenous peoples of the Pacific Northwest who, several generations ago, periodically either destroyed whatever they had accumulated that exceeded the needs of the community or consumed the excess together as a community in the practice known as *potlash*. They did this precisely in order to rid themselves of excess and the concomitant need to distribute it unequally. In this way, they were able to continuously insure a kind of rough equality within their community. Like God, as he speaks here to Moses, they did not want economic inequalities to determine human relationships. In the vision of the jubilee, liberation from slavery, from debt, and from servanthood was good in itself, but perhaps even more importantly, this liberation was a way to nurture and insure the rough justice considered necessary for community.

## TASK

The people God addresses in these texts were people asked to serve ends beyond themselves. God tells them in verse 55: "for to me the people of Israel are my servants." The jubilee arrangements, promoting justice and even forgiveness, are moral in themselves but are not ends in themselves. Rather, they enable other ends. God insists that the people of Israel are there to till the land, to have relationships with each other, but ultimately to have a relationship with God. Therefore the relationship to the land, and the economic and social relationships envisioned, are not autonomous from this relationship to God and should not be allowed to follow their own logic. They are subject to human design in obedience to God, and it is according to this design, this task, that they are evaluated by God.

I am struck by the way good stewardship of land and economy, just relationships, and obedience to God's design come together in this text, and I am challenged by how short our own society and churches fall according to this yardstick. Faithful resistance, as this text suggests, importantly includes careful stewardship of God's land. Such stewardship in turn requires that we begin to view land and the rest of the natural world not primarily as a commodity to be bought and sold for individual or corporate gain and profit, but as God's creation, which as such bears intrinsic worth and integrity that humans violate in disobedience to God and at our own risk. Similarly, resistance requires that we begin to view each other not in relation to how much we have, but in terms of who we are, how much we need, and how faithful we are to God's commands.

Stewardship of creation, relationship in society and with nature, rough justice in community, the centrality of God as God of all creation are values to guide our resistance to materialism, greed, the destruction of the natural world and the commodification of it and of ourselves, and anthropocentric rather than God-centered lives. The tasks are many, but they hold great promise in natural beauty and wild spaces, productive practices that will sustain not only us but our grandchildren and their grandchildren as well as our natural habitat, human relationships and human community sustained by ideals and practices of justice, and faithful relationships to God guided by God's vision for humanity and for all creation.

*5*

# Resistance to Structural Adjustment Policies

## *Laura Stivers*

Before everyone sold their land I worked for small bean and corn farmers and cattle ranchers. Fifteen years ago I lived in the same house as the farmer [with whom I worked]. He gave me a little piece of land to cultivate and we ate together. He gave me seven colones a day, but I could buy things with that. [On the banana plantation] I earn 1,000 colones a day [$7.69], but the truth is I think I could buy more things with the seven colones I earned back then.[1]

$\mathcal{T}$he prevailing model of economic development equates development with growth, modernization, and industrialization. Grassroots groups and others have questioned this narrow interpretation of what development encompasses, proposing that it should instead promote such aspects as human flourishing, environmental sustainability, community, and most of all, justice. Critique in the 1990s and into the millennium has focused on structural adjustment policies (SAPs), defined as economic changes that indebted countries must make in order to continue to receive loans from international banks and development organizations. Most "developing countries" have been forced to make these structural adjustment changes in their economies, and not surprisingly these policies promote the prevailing vision of economic development that emphasizes economic growth above all. Resistance to SAPs and the accompanying ethos surrounding such economic policies has been waged in local circles by people negatively affected by such policies; in international circles by activists concerned about issues of social and economic justice; and in grassroots and academic circles by scholars writing and speaking on such issues.

Resistors argue that economic development should enable people to be capable of functioning and living a flourishing and liberatory life. More specifically, economic development ought to: (1) lessen inequality; (2) promote empowerment; (3) promote gender justice; (4) promote environmental sustainability; (5) make an option for the poor; (6) promote participation from the bottom up; (7) address the roots of poverty; and (8) promote community solidarity and cultural preservation. This chapter will examine whether SAPs have satisfied any of these criteria of *good* development in rural Central America and, if not, what avenues resistors can take and have taken in addressing "maldevelopment."

## ECONOMIC SITUATION IN CENTRAL AMERICA

Most studies have shown an increase in poverty and economic inequality in Central America in the 1980s and 1990s.[2] Estimates from the Facultad Latinoamericana de Ciencias Sociales (FLACSO) and the Comisión Económica para América Latina y el Caribe (CEPAL) in 1990 indicate that 20 million Central Americans live in impoverished circumstances (69 percent of the population). Of those, 46 percent are in a situation of extreme poverty.[3] Although there has been an increase in urban poverty in the last decade, poverty continues to be a rural issue when two-thirds of the poor in Central America live in rural areas and 78 percent of those poor live in extreme poverty.[4] Furthermore, in 1990 over half of the population in Central America lived in rural zones.

One of the rural groups most affected by structural adjustment polices has been the small agricultural producers who, for the most part, produce basic grains (beans and corn). In Central America, 73.9 percent of the agricultural producers are growers of basic grains and 88 percent of them own small parcels of land.[5] In this chapter, I will use the terms "small producers" and "campesinos" to refer to those agriculture producers who have little capital or land (this could be owned, rented, or illegally "borrowed") and mainly rely on the labor of family members to work their land.[6] Women also play an important role in these small familial units of production, although "official statistics" often overlook their work. Official statistics on the participation of women in agriculture fluctuate between 5 and 12 percent for Central America, while other studies register a 25 to 37 percent participation rate of women in agriculture.[7]

## EQUALITY

Liberation and justice entail more than the satisfaction of basic material needs. According to theologian Gustavo Gutiérrez, liberation concerns external liberation from unjust social situations, which implies the elimination of the root causes of poverty and injustice. This entails not only satisfying unmet material needs, but also eliminating oppression in the form of marginalization or exploitation. Liberation is not just about being able to meet one's material needs but is also about living in a society of equality and respect in which each person is treated with full dignity.[8]

Despite the fact that liberation and capability to live a flourishing life are not compatible with deep-seated inequality, SAPs move away from strategies that promote equality, such as land reform or state investment in universal public education. In fact, structural adjustment exacerbates inequality by promoting exports, privatizing public entities, and reducing public subsidies for basic grain agriculture, health care, and education.

State promotion of export agriculture over basic grain agriculture increases inequality because basic grain farmers get lower prices for their products in the free market than they did when the state guaranteed prices,[9] and they receive little or no subsidies, technical assistance, or marketing assistance.[10] Several changes caused basic grain farmers to get lower prices for their products. One was the elimination of controls on exchange rates. Another was the lowering of tariffs on imported goods, including agricultural products. Still another was the elimination of government-regulated buying and selling of basic grains. Previously Central American countries had purposely supported an overvalued exchange rate to make certain imports cheaper. Structural adjustment seeks to reverse this policy. It aims to encourage exports by making them cheaper and discourage imports by making them more expensive. With the elimination of the controls on the exchange rate, each country's currency was revalued at a lower rate. This benefited export agriculture, but not basic grain producers, since imported inputs for agriculture became more expensive, while the prices for basic grains did not go up as fast.

Although the elimination of controls on exchange rates made agricultural input imports more expensive, the lowering of import tariffs made other imports cheaper, especially foreign food. This is a source of competition for basic grain farmers. Advocates of economic growth think this is a positive change because it obliges small producers to become more efficient and, furthermore, creates lower food prices for the consumer. The lowering of tariffs should have meant a decrease in the price of imported inputs such as fertilizers and pesticides as well. The Central American markets, however, are small and controlled by two or three big distributors and, so, when tariffs were reduced, the distributors did not lower the prices but instead pocketed the profit.[11]

In the 1970s and part of the 1980s, Central American governments controlled the buying and selling of basic grains to ensure internal food sufficiency and to provide cheap food to urban areas to keep wages down and placate the urban population. Governments guaranteed the purchase of commodities grown by basic grain producers. Governments also fixed prices paid to producers and sold to consumers. This control gave states a way to subsidize both the producer and consumer—the price paid to the producer was higher than the price consumers paid for the product.[12] The subsidy went mainly to the consumer, however, as prices paid to the producers for basic grain commodities were fairly low.

Many of the governmental organizations that exercised this control were inefficient and ineffective. Producers often preferred efficiency over price and would sell their produce at a lower price to intermediaries. A black market developed. Furthermore, some thought that the government's low prices for the goods were a disincentive to local production.[13] These problems set the stage for the liberalization of prices and the privatization of the state-run organizations. The idea was that small producers would benefit from prices set in the "free market" because the state could no longer set a low fixed price for their produce and because there would be competition between purchasers.

This deregulation and privatization benefited intermediaries rather than small producers. Prices for basic grains might be higher at some times of year, but at the time of harvest they drop drastically. Small producers, desperately needing cash and lacking basic infrastructure to move or store their products, have no alternatives but to sell at low seasonal prices. Consumers also must pay higher prices for basic grains because the government no longer subsidizes the provision of cheap food. This is most detrimental to the poor, who spend a higher percentage of their income on basic grains.

Families are also pushed to the edge financially from declining "real" wages. For example, in Nicaragua, the average salary covered 92 percent of the basic basket of consumer goods in 1990, but only 72 percent in 1991.[14] Furthermore, the number of permanent salaried employees in agriculture has been decreasing. In Nicaragua, there are half as many permanent salaried positions since structural adjustment policies.[15]

The privatization thrust of structural adjustment (minimizing government involvement in the hope of reduced budget costs and increased efficiency) has led to basic grain farmers receiving less credit, technical assistance, and marketing assistance. The problem is that the private sector is not interested in doing research or providing technical assistance to low-profit sectors such as basic grains. Nongovernmental organizations (NGOs) try to fill the gap, but they cannot reach nearly enough of the small farmers who need these services. A few big transnationals are willing to give small producers technical packages for help in dealing with agrochemicals if these farmers produce nontraditional agricultural commodities to sell back to the transnational. The campesino must be literate, however, to use the technological packet correctly. Many small farmers end up selling their land to the big agribusinesses or simply abandoning their land and moving to the urban areas, where there is stiff competition for work.

With SAPs, there is also a push for privatization of state banks. This results in less (or no) credit going toward small basic grain farmers or other small-scale economic development projects.[16] A 1993 study sponsored by the Instituto Interamericano de Cooperacion para la Agricultura (IICA) showed that the proportion of agricultural credit allocated to small production had eroded from 19 percent in 1983 to 9 percent in 1990 and then to an even lower 3.8 percent in 1991.[17] Private banks are more interested in making large loans to corporations, such as agribusinesses, where there is more profit to be made. NGOs have tried to provide nonconventional credit but have been unable to compensate for the contraction in governmentally supported credit for small producers.

SAPS have allowed banks to establish interest rates (active and passive) at levels determined by the competition of the market, which has had the effect of increased interest rates, putting credit out of reach for small producers.[18] Furthermore, the demands that the banks make to qualify for a loan (e.g., property title, proof of no debt, proof of paying taxes) impede small producers.[19] By the time a campesino can comply with all of these formalities (if he can), the loan comes too late. Many cannot provide all of these documents even allowing time.

The reduction of public investment in health and education further exacerbates inequality.[20] The rich can always afford to go to private schools and doctors, while the poor are left to go to an overwhelmed public service or do not get service at all because they cannot afford to pay the newly instituted service fees. There needs to be more, not less, public investment in providing public goods such as education, health care, transportation, and water systems (especially for rural areas), if what philosopher Martha Nussbaum calls "capability-equality" is to be promoted. According to Nussbaum, such investment promotes people's internal capabilities so that they are capable of choosing and taking advantage of external opportunities.[21]

There was inequality before SAPs in Central America. In fact, state intervention, especially when there were dictatorships, ensured inequality in Central America. Nevertheless, in a context of gross inequality, the SAP philosophy of competition in a free market gives preference to those with resources. Cutting public investment, deregulating private-sector activity, and privatizing public entities ends up hurting those on the bottom. There need to be ways to hold both the public and the private sector accountable to the poor. Accountability to the poor has always been extremely difficult in Central America, but it is becoming even more difficult with the changes that SAPs are advocating.

## EMPOWERMENT

Although opportunities should be opened up to all, not all people will automatically be empowered to take opportunities when they are *given*. Empowerment is instead a process that leads people to an awareness that they have the capacity and the right to make decisions. Martha Nussbaum holds that external resources, education, and training are necessary to promote internal capabilities connected to one's body, mind, and character. She is not saying that empowerment can be bestowed on people, but rather that such things as adequate nutrition, early infant development, adult role models, and education help mold how people think about themselves and their internal capability to take advantage of later opportunities. One's internal capabilities can be promoted or eroded by external circumstances.[22]

According to Gustavo Gutiérrez, empowerment is not just personal but collective. It entails communities developing a critical consciousness about their circumstances and turning this critical consciousness into action. The moment of conscientization might happen for a person individually, but the empowerment process is communal. Furthermore, people often come to this critical awareness in situations of deprivation and oppression.[23]

Generally SAPs have not encouraged the provision of external resources that help poor people develop their internal capabilities adequately. On the contrary, SAPs have pushed the poor into situations of increasing deprivation. This is especially a factor in the development of character and sound mind and body in children. Children's capabilities and development are stunted when they do not have access to adequate health care or nutrition. Increasingly under SAPs, children are working rather than going to school. They are either having to assume the reproductive labor of taking care of siblings, cooking, and gathering firewood and water when their mothers are out doing wage labor, or they are joining their parents in doing wage labor.

It is true, however, that such deprivation *can* lead people to bond together communally in resistance, which can lead some toward a deeper critical consciousness and solidarity. Liberation theology and many of the peasant movements of the 1960s and 1970s arose in response to poverty and injustice. This is not to idealize poverty, however. The response of many communities to increased deprivation is an increasing fragmentation and the taking on of a survival mentality of fatalism rather than communal solidarity. Individual resistance might still be occurring in such cases, but it is without the support of group resistance and community solidarity.

In general, resistors agree that SAPs do not provide the external resources necessary for building up people's internal capabilities. This does not necessarily stop people from becoming conscientized and struggling all the harder to transform their society and ensure that such external resources are in place for all. Sustained deprivation disempowers most people, but it *can* at times be a catalyst that spurs communities toward working for social justice.

## GENDER JUSTICE

SAPs have led to the disempowerment of women by increasing their workload with respect to three roles—in the areas of reproductive, productive, and community managing. Due to increasing food prices, and decreasing real wages, women's reproductive labor has been increasing. For example, women spend more time substituting nonmarket goods and services for items they might have previously bought. They also spend more time searching for cheaper food. Basically, women are responsible for coping with fewer resources in the family. *"Vivimos a pura Maria Santisimo"* is a common phrase heard from El Salvadorean rural women that means they just get by. The underestimation of the coping strategies that women have had to employ is common, since traditional measurements of living standards do not take into account the increase in time and intensification of reproductive work.

The cutting of social services also increases reproductive labor. The public provision of such things as water, sanitation, electrification, commuter transportation, and health service can help to socialize the cost of producing a labor force. The SAPs focus instead on decreasing budgets for infrastructure and social services, especially to areas that are not connected to export agriculture. This leaves poor rural women with little support.[24] The more time-intensive reproductive labor is, the less time women have for income earning. Some peasant families end up shifting many of the reproductive responsibilities onto the children, especially girls. This affects girls' access to education. Girls also have less access to education than boys when families must pay for it.

Economist Diane Elson says that by ignoring reproductive labor, SAPs have a built-in bias against women. She says that reproductive labor continues despite the fact that there are fewer resources, hence women's unpaid labor is implicitly regarded as "elastic," or able to stretch to make up for any shortfalls in resources for reproduction. Elson writes: "What is regarded by economists as 'increased efficiency' may instead be a shifting of costs from the paid economy to the unpaid economy." In other words, women become the shock absorbers of the adjustment process.[25]

This increase in reproductive labor happens at the same time that rural women are expected to work longer hours in the fields or find other paid work to help sustain falling household incomes. On the one hand, the market emphasis of SAPs treats women as individuals in their own right who can sell their labor or their products for income. On the other hand, as long as women are solely responsible for unpaid reproductive labor, they are unable to compete with men on equal terms in the market. Women therefore end up with the lower-paid jobs in agriculture or informal work such as selling food in the market.[26] Furthermore, when SAPs decrease the wages and amount of formal employment, more people seek work in the informal sector, which in turn means more competition for the meager income women are making in that sector. SAPs have also decreased rural women's control over resources and their own labor power by placing control of investment in the hands of large-scale agroexport businesses, which are typically in the hands of men. Women are primarily involved in small-scale basic grain agriculture and are receiving no credit or technical assistance under SAPs.[27]

Lastly, with the decreasing provision of governmental services under SAPs, women's community managing role becomes more important. Development assistance from NGOs becomes more important to families. NGOs, however, often require the voluntary unpaid participation of women to receive benefits.[28]

For women to be empowered, development policy cannot be based simply on the market and a narrow concept of efficiency that takes into consideration only "paid" work. Changes must be made in both the private and public sphere. Government assistance in providing services such as sanitation, electricity, health care, and access to water is necessary to lighten the load of reproductive labor. In addition, economic and social policies are needed to ensure that women can compete with men in the labor market or, alternatively, be able to farm. The problems are cultural as well as social. For example, in Central America there are set ideas of what is "men's work" versus "women's work."[29] Cultural views can be gradually changed with social policies. A good example is the move in Central America to set in place policies that make it legal for women to own land. This idea might not be completely accepted culturally yet, but gradually, as more and more women own their own land, cultural perceptions can change.

Empowerment for women requires not only the institution of social and economic policies that address the difference gender makes, but also development processes that help build women's internal capabilities. For example, development programs, through education, can help women overcome their internalized oppression so that they can more adequately participate in program planning and decision-making. Once women are participating in a nontoken manner, the process of empowerment can begin. Often women's groups will first tackle what Maxine Molyneux refers to as "practical gender interests" or immediate needs, such as better health and nutrition, rather than more general and long-term strategic objectives, such as gender equality. As these women's groups continue to deepen their analysis, however, they address both immediate interests and gender transformation.

## ENVIRONMENTAL SUSTAINABILITY

SAPs have had a negative impact on environmental sustainability. With resources increasingly going to export agriculture rather than to small grain farmers, campesino families are being forced off their land.[30] In countries where there is still a frontier of uncut forests, campesinos will burn forested lands to farm. In other countries without this opportunity, campesinos are pushed onto lands with low productivity, such as steep hillsides. Both practices increase the problem of land erosion, a serious problem with Central America's torrential downpours. Flash flooding becomes more likely and dangerous when there is not sufficient land covering and soil to soak up the rain (e.g., as during Hurricane Mitch). Poverty, which is increasing under SAPs, also leads to other environmentally destructive practices, such as overcutting of timber for cooking, polluting of water sources with the cleaning of clothes, and the dumping of refuse. Environmental sustainability requires the promotion of sustainable agricultural practices and economic and social policies that decrease rural poverty.

Campesinos are not the main culprits, however. Multinationals interested in cattle raising and export agriculture destroy more virgin forests by area than do campesinos.[31] This contributes to global warming, soil erosion, and species depletion, the last of which is a major concern, considering that the rain forests of Central America and other tropical countries are very diverse in terms of animal species. The promotion of export agriculture under structural adjustment supports the practice of monocropping, which depletes the fertility of the soil due to heavy pesticide use, intense overuse of lands, and the reduction of plants that regenerate the soil. Decreasing the variety of crops planted also threatens biodiversity of plant species.[32] The pesticides do not simply stay on the crops either. They linger in the air and run off into the streams when it rains. Increasingly more fertilizers are needed to get the same productivity levels, and more pesticides are needed as insects build immunities.

## OPTION FOR THE POOR

A preferential option for the poor is one of the themes most associated with liberation theology. Making an option for the poor means confronting powerful interests. Liberation theologian Gustavo Gutiérrez calls the church to see its mission as one of *serving*, not merely *surviving*. In other words, he thinks the church must make a choice, not be neutral. He claims this is hard for those who prefer not to see conflictual situations, who prefer palliatives to remedies, and who confuse universal love with a fictitious harmony.[33] Social conflict and class struggle is a social fact. Neutrality is neither ethical nor Christian, since it means siding with injustice and oppression. Gutiérrez is not, as some claim, promoting conflict, but is instead trying to eliminate it.[34]

SAPs make an option for the rich and powerful rather than for the poor and oppressed.[35] Placing emphasis on the free market as the way to structure the economy gives an advantage to those who already have more. In a free market, competition is supposed to reign, but how can a small basic grain farmer compete with vertically integrated agribusinesses which have their own packing and shipping facilities, contacts to foreign markets, and a much larger economy of scale?

The free-market strategies of deregulation and privatization have been detrimental to the poor. The deregulation of the financial system has resulted in the rich making huge amounts of money on currency trading and financial speculation, while less money is being put toward investment in sustainable development. The deregulation of the labor market has resulted in lower wages and worsening work conditions for the poor, while the rich make a bigger profit. The deregulation of government-subsidized pricing for basic grains and basic food items has resulted in small farmers' getting lower prices for their produce, yet paying higher prices for food. The privatization of services cuts off access to the poor. Only those who can afford to pay for the service can use it.

Proponents of SAPs argue that long-term economic development requires short-term belt-tightening. An option for the poor, however, would require asking whose belt is being tightened. According to the criterion of an option for the poor, policies that continue to serve the interests of the privileged while the poor are suffering are not morally acceptable. SAP proponents argue that the poor would have been worse off without structural adjustment. Whether this is true or not does not justify privileging the rich over the poor.

An option for the poor will require fundamental change to correct pervasive inequalities. SAPs have instituted fundamental change, but in the wrong direction. An option for the poor means confronting powerful interests, not serving them. Such confrontation entails social conflict and class struggle.

## PARTICIPATION

Fundamental change will not happen by simply preaching an option for the poor to privileged people. The empowerment of the poor struggling for the transformation of unjust structures is more important. Gutiérrez's option for the poor is not about charity, but about becoming a church of the poor or, as Gutiérrez says, recognizing that "the church of the poor *is* the church."[36] This is key to understanding participation. It is not about the privileged including the participation of the poor and oppressed in their programs, but about everyone joining in the struggles that the poor and oppressed have already begun. Often development programs require the participation of the poor (especially women), in order to receive subsidies or program benefits, but the "participants" are not always allowed to participate in planning and developing the type of program that they think would actually lead toward empowerment.[37] Evidence shows that long-term economic and environmental success comes about when people's ideas and knowledge are valued and when they have the power to make decisions independently of external agencies.[38] This means forms of participation that promote conscientization and lead communities toward self-mobilization.

SAPs, however, are instituted with no participation from anyone in the countries that undergo structural adjustment, except perhaps a few political leaders and some local highly paid "technicos" (and even they might not really have a choice). SAPs also make it difficult for rural communities to garner contacts, resources, and technical advice in their self-mobilization efforts because NGOs and other institutions are so overwhelmed by the increasing needs and numbers of the poor. NGOs, even large ones, do not have the size or resources to organize on the scale of governments.[39] Furthermore, development programs that aim to foster functional or interactive participation are much more time consuming and costly. SAPs create a situation of poverty in which the likelihood of time-consuming participatory projects is decreased. Development workers become more concerned about meeting people's immediate basic needs than about long-term sustainable development. This often ends up taking the form of participation for material incentives, which is basically a form of charity that does not help people create sustainable forms of development and self-sufficiency.

## ROOTS OF POVERTY

Economic policies that foster actual rather than token participation will also do more to attack the roots of poverty. Policies that allow or even promote self-mobilization and self-sufficiency are the most helpful. For example, a policy of land redistribution allows small farmers to own and farm small plots of land for family sustenance. Policies that promote access to credit and technical assistance by small farmers encourage self-sufficiency. Without land and such assistance, small farmers usually end up migrating seasonally or moving permanently to urban areas, due to scarce labor opportunities in their own communities. These moves do not end their poverty and tend to fragment rural societies and to destroy cultural cohesion.

Structural adjustment has promoted a "counter reform" in land ownership.[40] From the early 1960s to the late 1980s, all the Central American countries had some form of agrarian reform in which the government redistributed land to campesinos, both in the form of production collectives and individual ownership. In contrast, the theme of the 1990s was *"individual* property rights." In Nicaragua and El Salvador, this meant the break-up of cooperatives and the onset of contentious land titling and conflicts over ownership.[41] These disputes have made for high levels of instability in the rural areas and little long-term investment on disputed lands.[42]

Those in favor of land titling claim that it strengthens tenure security and improves access to agricultural credit. Lack of a land title has been one of the problems campesinos, especially women, face in receiving credit. With so little credit available for basic grain production, however, it is not clear that having a title to land will help. Many claim that securing title to the land *alone* is not sufficient to surmount the many problems that small producers face. For example, since the end of the 1980s in Costa Rica, many small farmers with a title to their land have been forced to sell. There has been a reconcentration of land in the hands of large owners, especially in areas where nontraditional agriculture has grown.[43] Historically in these countries with a rapid expansion of export crops, the value of the land increases and the access of small farmers to the land decreases.[44] In Costa Rican communities today, many peasant families find the prices offered for their land more attractive than trying to eke out a living producing basic grains, especially since government support for basic grain production has stopped and switching to nontraditional agriculture is prohibitively expensive.[45] When these families sell their land, they might buy a smaller, less fertile piece of land in another community, move to the city, or move to salaried work on a banana plantation or other large-scale agriculture.[46]

Attacking the roots of poverty means transforming structures, institutions, and policies that create inequality. This would include SAPs that favor the rich over the poor. Resistors of structural adjustment disagree with proponents that a freer market with less government interference and regulation will in the long run address the roots of poverty. They believe that a freer market will only exacerbate poverty because there is no way that the poor can compete with the rich and powerful without some governmental policies to level the playing field.

Addressing the roots of poverty would require a *transformation* of unjust policies and structures, not simply a *reform*. For example, when countries realized that SAPs were contributing to a deterioration in levels of living for a large proportion of the population, international banks, development organizations, and the governments of several countries instituted what are called "social emergency funds" (often financed by the World Bank and other multilateral and bilateral agencies). In 1991, Honduras and Nicaragua set up temporary institutions (planned for five years) to administer these funds. They had the following purposes: (1) to alleviate the social costs of adjustment, including poverty; (2) to generate employment; (3) to repair infrastructure; (4) to serve as a mechanism for decentralization; and (5) to integrate the poor into the development process. These funds were to be quickly distributed for financing small, simple projects carried out by public, private, and nongovernmental organizations.[47]

Social emergency funds are a reform rather than a transformation of the system. First, they are only temporary. Second, because these funds are short term and need to be distributed quickly, they will not foster the true participation of the beneficiaries. This results in projects that do not encourage empowerment and self-sufficiency. Third, they do not address the roots of poverty, such as the appropriation of fertile land from small farmers, the lack of ongoing credit for small-scale economic development, and the lack of good education and health care in the rural areas. As long as SAPs continue to make these things less accessible to the poor, instituting temporary charity programs will not alleviate poverty. Justice is not about providing charity while keeping intact policies and structures that create poverty and injustice.

## COMMUNITY SOLIDARITY AND CULTURAL PRESERVATION

Promoting community solidarity and preserving culture are seldom the goals of economic development. Community cohesion and cultural preservation, however, not only are important for enabling people to function capably, but they are important goods in and of themselves. A strong cultural identity empowers people and adds to richness and diversity. Cohesive communities are necessary for the preservation of cultural identity and good relationships. Furthermore, many Christians hold that it is in community that true spirituality and hope in God are nourished. In community, faith is celebrated and deepened.

Individualism is one of the most salient characteristics of modern society. Gutiérrez says that in capitalism the individual becomes the "absolute principle of economic activity."[48] Classical economics assumes that the marketplace, through supply and demand, will bring individual interests in line with the general interest. The promotion of a freer market through SAPs, however, has shown otherwise. The general interest is not being served as the interests of an elite few are being promoted over the interests of the majority of the population.[49] Some resistors believe that rather than starting with the individual's interests, we should begin with the interest of the community, especially poor communities. Others agree that community should be promoted but want to be careful not to subsume individual interests to community, since it is women's interests that most often are neglected in an emphasis on the collective.

Structural adjustment promotes individualism and homogenization over community and heterogeneity. One plan fits all is the underlying paradigm of structural adjustment. That is, the promotion of the free market through privatization, deregulation, and liberalization is the solution to the problems of *all* developing countries. The truth is, however, that communities are being broken up and, as a result, cultures are being destroyed. Relying on the law of supply and demand does not ensure that there will be economic development in poor communities. It assumes rather that workers will go where the jobs are. For example, if there is an increasing number of jobs in the urban *maquilas* and less chance for making a livelihood in rural areas, then families will migrate to the urban area. This is regarded as positive development by proponents of structural adjustment. Resistors see this as negative development, since it has displaced people from their geographical, cultural, and community roots. Although there is optimism that communities will form again in the urban areas, there is nevertheless irretrievable cultural loss when people are uprooted and dispersed.

## AVENUES FOR RESISTANCE

Resistance to increasing poverty, inequality, and dislocation in Central America has come in many forms. The most visible has been local and international protest against IMF structural adjustment policies specifically. Less visible has been the promotion of alternative forms of economic development and policy, such as sustainable agriculture, land redistribution, and debt cancellation. Many churches consider social justice to be at the heart of Christianity and are deeply involved in these struggles. Liberationism tends to be the theology of such churches, although they might not identify as liberationist. Such churches claim that profits and possessions take second place to the needs of the people. They are less concerned, however, about the capitalist/socialist debate that was so much the focus of liberation theology in the 1970s. Other churches focus more on members' spirituality apart from social justice. Such an "otherworldly" theology has been on the rise in Central America with the exponential growth of independent evangelical and fundamentalist churches.[50]

International protests of economic globalization have gotten lots of media attention, the most notable being the demonstrations in Seattle at the meeting of the World Trade Organization in November 1999; in Prague at the meeting of the IMF and World Bank in September 2000; and in Washington, D.C., at the meeting of the IMF and World Bank in April 2000. Similar protests have been occurring in countries that are subject to SAPs. In Bolivia, resisters protested the privatization of water and a 200 percent price hike; in Ecuador, 3,000 IMF protesters occupied the legislature, with 10,000 protesting outside; in Paraguay, there was a 48-hour general strike against the privatization of telephone, water, and rail service;[51] and in Costa Rica, resistors protested the government's attempt to privatize energy and telecommunications.[52]

Churches have been more involved in promoting alternative development and working to change economic policies. International coalitions of churches have been very involved in the struggle for global justice. The guiding theme for the World Council of Churches is the "Decade of Overcoming Violence," which includes the distortions of economic globalization. They have held conferences to support churches in seeking out viable economic development alternatives that won't increase suffering and poverty, exploit workers, or destroy the environment.[53] Jubilee U.S.A., a network of organizations including the Presbyterian Church U.S.A., the Episcopal Church U.S.A., the Evangelical Lutheran Church in America, Methodist groups, UCC groups, and others, is calling for immediate unconditional debt cancellation and the elimination of user fees for essential services such as water, and is supporting educational efforts to expose problems of the export-led growth model.[54]

Churches within Central America that are involved in the struggle for economic justice are focusing on local organization. They are involved in the pastoral needs of war-ravaged Central Americans, while also finding effective ways to critique an economy that exploits Central America's people and resources. Guerrilla movements aimed at defeating capitalism are no longer the answer. Churches are involved in empowering people at the local level with small-scale development options for those marginalized by capitalism, health care and education options for those incapable of paying service fees, housing for those displaced from their lands, and more. Although these efforts might seem more a response of charity than justice, organizers hope to involve people in the struggle for a more sustained justice.

## CONCLUSION

SAPs have decreased the ability of families to meet their basic needs and, furthermore, have had an effect on the ability of individuals to be in healthy relationships with one another and with the environment. SAPs do not promote capability-equality or offer an option for the poor. In fact, by making an option for the rich, they exacerbate inequality. The lack of sufficient resources and opportunities in turn has an effect on the development of poor people's internal capabilities. Not only has structural adjustment led to insufficient resources and development opportunities in rural areas, but women have had to pick up the burden of created scarcity. The stress of coping with their triple roles has disempowered women and decreased their well-being.

SAPs do not promote participation. The few programs that claim to promote participation, such as the social emergency fund projects instituted to offset some of the negative effects of structural adjustment on the poor, tend to promote passivity, not self-mobilization. While these programs are an attempt to redress the negative effects of structural adjustment, they do not address the root causes of poverty. Lastly, SAPs tend to fragment rural communities, which leads to the loss of distinct cultures.

Resistors of SAPs do not put a high value on neoclassical economic reasons for structural adjustment in Central American countries. Even if they were convinced that some form of structural adjustment was necessary on economic grounds, they would not concur that shifting to a "freer" market is the answer to the economic problems of Central America. Nor would they concur that it need be on the backs of the poor and women.

## NOTES

1. Excerpt from an interview of a poor campesino. Quoted in Alicia Korten, *A Bitter Pill: Structural Adjustment in Costa Rica*, Development Report No. 7, Oakland, California, Food First (June 1995), p. 22.

2. Alejandro Izurieta and Rob Vos, "Ajuste Estructural y Costo Social en La América Latina: ¿Qué Nos Explican Los Estudios Recientes?" *El Trimestre Económico* 61:241 (January–March 1994): 43. This article reviews studies by CEPAL, the World Bank, and individual social scientists.

3. María Rosa Renzi and Dirk Kruijt, "Los Neuvos Pobres" (San José, Costa Rica: Facultad Latinoamericana de Ciencias Sociales—FLACSO, 1997), p. 7.

4. Helio Fallas, *Centroamérica: Pobreza y Desarrollo Rural ante la Liberalización Económica* (UNA/IICA, 1993); quoted in Rebeca Grynspan, "La Política del Sector Agropecuario Frente a la Mujer Productora de Alimentos en Centroamérica y Panamá," preliminary version (San José, Costa Rica: IICA and the Banco Interamericano de Desarrollo, July 1993), p. 1.

5. Grynspan, "La Política del Sector Agropecuario," p. 2.

6. Studies such as that of Nitlapán in Nicaragua, *El Campesino-finquero y el Potencial Económico del Camesinado Nicaragüense* (1996), have identified eight different groups of agricultural producers. For the purposes of this study, however, I will not go into such a degree of technicality.

7. Grynspan, "La Política del Sector Agropecuario," p. 17.

8. Gustavo Gutiérrez, *A Theology of Liberation*, trans. Sister Caridad Inda and John Eaglesson (Maryknoll, N.Y.: Orbis Books, 1988), p. 20.

9. Ian Walker, Jenny Suazo, Alison Thomas, and Herold Jean-Pois, "El Impacto de las Políticas de Ajuste Estructural Sobre el Medio Ambiente en Honduras," *Cuadernos* (Managua, Nicaragua: CRIES, 1997): p. 89; R. F. Kutsch Lojenga, "Structural Adjustment Programmes and the Environment in Costa Rica," master's thesis, Free University (Amsterdam, The Netherlands, November 1995), p. 71; Adolfo José Acevedo Vogl, *Economia Politica y Desarrollo Sostenible* (Managua, Nicaragua: BITECSA, 1998), p. 194; Adolfo José Acevedo Vogl, "El Campesinado Nicaragüense y Su Difícil Sostenibilidad: Quién de los Que Aún se Llaman Progresistas se Atreve a Agarrar esta Auténtica 'Papa Caliente'??" unpublished paper (Managua, Nicaragua, 1998), p. 6.

10. Acevedo Vogl, "El Campesinado Nicaragüense," p. 8; Rene Rivera Magaña, Pedro Juan Hernandez, Salvador Arias, and Oscar Dada, "Marco General Para Una Estrategia de Desarrollo Agropecuario de El Salvador" (San Salvador, El Salvador: FUNDE, March 1997), p. 11; Lojenga, "Structural Adjustment Programmes," p. 70.

11. Acevedo Vogl, "El Campesinado Nicaragüense," p. 7; Alfonso Goitia, economist, interview by Laura Stivers, 14 August 1998, Concertación Centromericana, San Salvador, El Salvador.

12. Alfonso Goitia and Lisandro Abrego, "Crisis de la Agricultura, Politica Agraria y Ajuste Estructural" (El Salvador: Programa de Formacion en Seguridad Alimentaria, CADESCA and Comisión de las Comunidades Europeas (C.C.E.), July 1990), p. 30.

13. Ibid.

14. Isolda Espinosa, "Mujeres, Politicas de Ajuste Estructural y Flexibilizacion del Mercado de Trabajo," 1994.

15. ATC, 1992; found in Grynspan, "La Política del Sector Agropecuario," p. 13.

16. Carlos Sojo, *La Governabilidad en Centroamerica: La Sociedad Despues del Ajuste* (San José, Costa Rica: FLACSO, 1995), pp. 50–51.

17. Ibid., p. 51.

18. In the post-1990 period in Nicaragua, interest rates were not set in relation to the market but were actually higher than the market rate.

19. Isabel Román and Marvin Acuña, *No Hay Paz Sin Alimentos: Los Pequeños Agricultores por el Derecho a Producir* (San José, Costa Rica: CENAP, 1988), p. 18.

20. Trevor Evans, *La Transformacion Neoliberal del Sector Publico: Ajuste Estructural y Sector Publico en Centroamerica y el Caribe* (Managua, Nicaragua: Latino Editores, 1995), p. 208; Korten, *A Bitter Pill*, p. 50; Victor Gálvez Borrell, René Poitevin, and Carlos Enrique González, *Estado, Participación, Popular y Democratización* (Guatemala: FLACSO, 1994), p. 116.

21. Martha Nussbaum, "Aristotelian Social Democracy," in *Liberalism and the Good*, ed. R. Bruce Douglass, Gerald M. Mara, and Henry S. Richardson (New York: Routledge, 1990), p. 228; and "Nature, Function, and Capability: Aristotle on Political Distribution," in *Oxford Studies in Ancient Philosophy*, suppl. vol., ed. Julia Annas and Robert H. Grimm (New York: Oxford University Press, 1988), p. 164.

22. Martha Nussbaum and Jonathan Glover, *Women, Culture and Development: A Study of Human Capabilities* (Oxford: Clarendon Press, 1995).

23. Gutiérrez, *A Theology of Liberation.*

24. Ingrid Palmer, "Public Finance From a Gender Perspective," *World Development* 23, no. 11 (1995): 1985.

25. Diane Elson, "Male Bias in Structural Adjustment," in *Women and Adjustment Policies in the Third World*, ed. Haleh Afshar and Carolyne Dennis (New York: St. Martin's Press, 1992), pp. 49–50.

26. Manuel Rojas and Isabel Román, *Agricultura de Exportacion y Pequeños Productores en Costa Rica*, Notebook no. 61 (San José, Costa Rica: FLACSO, 1993), p. 50; Laura Gusman Stein, *Politicas para la Mujer en el Sector Rural: Un Balance Critico del Caso de Costa Rica (1980–1990).*

27. Manuel Chiriboga, Rebeca Grynspan, and Laura E. Pérez, eds., *Mujeres de Maiz* (San José, Costa Rica: IICA, March 1996).

28. Caroline O. N. Moser, "Adjustment from Below: Low-Income Women, Time and the Triple Role in Guayaquil, Ecuador," in *Women and Adjustment Policies in the Third World*, ed. Haleh Afshar and Carolyne Dennis (New York: St. Martin's Press, 1992), pp. 110–111. Women's community managing role can be empowering for women if the projects they are involved in are truly participatory and increase the women's skills. According to Moser, however, many projects require participation that does not empower women but instead is an extra burden on their scarce time. Moser claims that with SAPs, women are finding that paid work and unpaid work are increasingly competing for their time.

29. This is true in the United States as well, despite the fact that there are women in "men's" professions.

30. Peter Rosset, "Sustainability, Economies of Scale, and Social Instability," *Agriculture and Human Values* 8, no. 4 (Fall 1991): 33.

31. Walker et al., "El Impacto de las Políticas de Ajuste Estructural"; Cristóbal Maldidier and Tupac Antillón, with Ner Artola, Alfredo Ruiz, and Karla Castillo,

"Deforestación y Frontera Agrícola en Nicaragua," in CRIES 2, Managua, Nicaragua (1997): 77–102; Korten, *A Bitter Pill*, pp. 40–42.

32. Korten, *A Bitter Pill*, pp. 42–43.

33. Gustavo Gutiérrez, *The Power of the Poor in History: Selected Writings*, trans. Robert R. Barr (Maryknoll: Orbis Books, 1983), p. 48.

34. Gutiérrez, *A Theology of Liberation*, p. 159.

35. Proponents of SAPs would argue that this is not the case. They hold that without SAPs, poverty would be worse.

36. James B. Nickoloff, "Liberation Theology and the Church," *Religious Studies Review* 18, no. 1 (January 1992): 158.

37. Lourdes Benería and Breny Mendoza, "Structural Adjustment and Social Emergency Funds: The Case of Honduras, Mexico and Nicaragua," in *Adjustment and Social Sector Restructuring*, ed. Jessica Vivian (London: Frank Cass, 1995).

38. Ibid., p. 172.

39. Sonia Arellano-Lopez argues that not only have NGOs been unable to stem the growth of poverty, but they have often furthered the neo-liberal agenda by serving as intermediaries between the state and grassroots community-based organizations representing poor people, to give structural adjustment a "human face." In effect, they have undermined the grassroots organizations and fragmented movements of resistance. This furthers neo-liberalism's privatization strategy by favoring private charity and self-help over class mobilizations against structural adjustment policies. Sonia Arellano-Lopez, "Non-Governmental Organizations and Poverty Alleviation in Bolivia," in *Neoliberalism and Class Conflict in Latin America*, ed. Henry Veltmeyer, James Petras, and Steve Vieux (New York: St. Martin's Press, 1997), pp. 165–178.

40. Carmen Diana Deere and Magdalena León, "Mujeres, Derechos a La Tierra y Contrareformas en America Latina," unpublished paper (San José, Costa Rica, 1997).

41. In El Salvador in 1989, the state tried to give cooperative lands back to the old owners but could not because there was such a strong political movement against this initiative. Information taken from Alfonso Goitia, economist, interview by Laura Stivers, August 14, 1998, Concertación Centroamericana, San Salvador, El Salvador.

42. In Nicaragua, 71 percent of the area in farms is under dispute. Only 20 percent of the area in farms is titled. The lands in dispute include confiscated land from Somoza and his cronies (40 percent), assignments from the Law of Agrarian Reform of 1981 (26 percent), land bought by the Sandinista government (6 percent), land bought by the Chamorro government (8 percent), and squatter occupations (10 percent). Information taken from "Pobreza: ¿Epidemia Incurable?" *Envio* year 14, number 165 (November 1995): 8.

43. Korten, *A Bitter Pill*, p. 29; Jon Jonakin, "The Impact of Structural Adjustment and Property Rights Conflicts on Nicaraguan Agrarian Reform Beneficiaries," *World Development* 24:7 (1996): 1179–1191; and "El Salvador: Dinámica de la Degradación Ambiental," PRISMA (1995): 23.

44. This was the case with coffee, cotton, and bananas in Central America. Robert G. Williams, *Export Agriculture and the Crisis in Central America* (Chapel Hill: University of North Carolina Press, 1986); and Michael A. Seligson, *Peasants of Costa Rica and the Development of Agrarian Capitalism* (Madison: University of Wisconsin Press, 1980).

45. Rosset, "Sustainability, Economies of Scale," p. 33.

46. Korten, *A Bitter Pill.*

47. Lourdes Benería and Breny Mendoza, "Structural Adjustment and Social Emergency Funds: The Case of Honduras, Mexico and Nicaragua," in *Adjustment and Social Sector Restructuring,* ed. Jessica Vivian (London: Frank Cass, 1995), p. 56.

48. Gutiérrez, *The Power of the Poor in History,* p. 174.

49. Promoters of SAPs argue that the macroeconomic objectives they seek to attain are directed at benefiting the whole community, not just the elites.

50. David Stoll, *Is Latin America Turning Protestant? The Politics of Evangelical Growth* (Berkeley: University of California Press, 1990); and José M. Rodríguez, *Las Sectas Fundamentalistas en Centro América* (San José, Costa Rica: CECODERS, 1991).

51. Brian Kenety, "Report details pattern of southern nations' resistance to WTO and IMF," Witherspoon Society webpage, Presbyterian Church U.S.A., October 16, 2001.

52. Mobilization for Global Justice website, October 16, 2001.

53. World Council of Churches webpage, October 16, 2001.

54. "Jubilee USA Network Is Born!" Witherspoon Society webpage, Presbyterian Church U.S.A., October 16, 2001.

# 6

# Nationalism and International Migration

## Dana W. Wilbanks

The refugee is a powerful symbol of the twentieth century. The forced movement of persons across national borders seemed endless, numbering well into the millions and coming from many different contexts. Following World War I, we saw refugees in the internal minorities of newly constituted European nation-states who were persecuted or driven out because they did not belong to the "national" community. We saw refugees in the Jews who desperately tried to escape from the extermination policy of the Third Reich but who found mainly closed doors when they tried to enter safer nations.

We saw refugees in the massive migrations of persons in post–World War II Europe who were uprooted from their homes and homelands. We saw refugees in the staggering number of persons in postcolonial Asia and Africa who moved inside and across borders established by colonial powers to escape from persecution, war, or economic impoverishment. We saw refugees again in Europe in the 1990s as the Balkans erupted in ferocious conflicts. At the beginning of the twenty-first century, Afghan refugees cascaded into Pakistan to get away from U.S. bombs and fighting between contending forces in Afghanistan.

The twentieth century was also the era of nationalism and the nation-state system of governance. The correlation of nationalism and refugees is not coincidental. The nation-state divides people into territorially bounded spaces that are sharply delineated and tightly controlled. Those who are born in a relatively safe and affluent homeland are very fortunate indeed in this system. The privileged persons in these political communities are likely to value their national membership and understandably have a strong sense of national pride.

But those who are born within a nation-state where they are targeted for abuse or are struggling to survive experience an entirely different reality. They are the abused progeny of the nation-state system[1] who desperately need and want to move but are locked into a bounded space from which escape is blocked in a whole host of only marginally surmountable ways.

Early in the tumultuous twentieth century, political idealists worked vigorously, and successfully, to replace imperial governance with the right of peoples to national self-determination. It is hardly surprising that this was regarded as an emancipatory development. At long last, subordinated peoples were free from externally imposed rule and could now govern themselves. The national idea that took hold in the nineteenth century became dominant in the twentieth.

## EVALUATIONS OF NATIONALISM

At best, nationalism was seen as a necessary corollary to popular sovereignty. Each people should be able to develop its own government and choose its own leaders to represent its interests, values, and hopes. Some early nationalists even hoped that this would be a way that each nation could make its contribution to a cooperative international milieu, obliterating the oppressive rule by outsiders and minimizing the motivations for military aggression.

More recently, the nationalist idea animated the struggles of colonized peoples for independence from colonial rule, which had been maintained by dominant European nations in blatant contradiction to the norm of national self-determination. Even now, long-suppressed minorities (e.g., the Kurds), groups with severe grievances (e.g., Tamils in Sri Lanka), and certain regions in federated nation-states (e.g., Quebec, Scotland, Catalonia) may claim the national designation for themselves to assert rights to self-government.

The nation-state system, however, has not been successful in maintaining or securing the peace, much less in establishing justice. The principle of nation-state sovereignty did not protect vulnerable peoples from the dominance of aggressive and hegemonic national powers. And the system itself has produced millions of refugees, persons who "do not fit" within the definition of a "nation," and whose very life requires moving away from rather than staying within the bounded territory of their birth. Those persons who live in liminal spaces alongside and between national boundaries are exceedingly disadvantaged in this system. In any kind of ethical evaluation of the national political paradigm, the life situation and experience of refugees needs to be brought to the center instead of relegated to the margins.

It is timely for Christians to reconsider our relation to the "national project" as we seek to discern the ways of Christian political responsibility in this new century. Should Christians continue to correlate our faith with nation-centered politics, or should we resist it in response to the historical evils it has spawned and continues to generate? Or, if there is something like a contextually positive nationalism (or aspects of nationalism) in contrast with negative nationalism (or aspects of nationalism), then what is it and how do we sort out the difference?

In making this assessment, we should readily acknowledge that no political system will be without flaws. None will fully reflect or embody the fullness of God's justice and peace. Yet, while we are not looking for perfection, we are called to make concrete historical judgments about which political options are relatively responsive to the love that God has for all peoples and the earth itself, and which options are so fundamentally destructive of life and community that they must be opposed and resisted.

This kind of ethical evaluation does not occur in a vacuum. Nationalism is a timely topic not just because we have seen a resurgence of its appeals and its dangers in the 1990s, but also because there are signs that the nation-state-centered world is losing its dominance in international politics. To many observers, the future no longer seems to belong to nation-state sovereignty but to a myriad of complex linkages between national, transnational, and local institutions and pressures. Peter Marden maintains that territorial boundaries are "no longer commensurate with political authority and absolute control."[2] Vital political challenges such as the environment, security, and human migration are not contained and resolvable within the boundaries of discrete nation-states.

A 1993 World Bank study revealed that over 100 million people live in a different country from the one in which they were born.[3] People are finding ways to move, even though legal options are very restricted and their position is highly vulnerable. The governments of affluent nation-states are in a strange position. They are seeking to control borders more tightly and to admit fewer immigrants and refugees. Yet they are also dependent on international labor and are unable or unwilling to enforce tight controls because the costs in money, energy, and world moral opinion would be too high. Even Japan, which has traditionally prized its cultural homogeneity and closed-door immigration policy, is now beginning to consider recruiting immigrant workers to fill its labor force amid an aging population.

The nation-state does not represent simply the natural evolution and political maturation of long-established communities. It is a relatively new creation, reflecting the historical developments now known as modernity. We can certainly expect that new forms of political community will be fashioned in response to a different set of historical circumstances. Current erosions of nation-state sovereignty suggest that this process may be underway even now.

Nationalism is indeed Janus-faced.[4] It is impossible to discuss it without taking into account both its moral appeal and its destructive practices. In a positive assessment of nationalism, it is closely linked with the project of democracy. In the democratic nation-state, according to its proponents, the person is no longer the subject of rulers, bidden to do their will. Now the person is a member of the political community, the nation. With the membership comes an identity—citizen—that confers dignity, rights, and obligations within the political community.

As just one member of the wider community, the individual must take into account the views and conditions of other members. Yet the individual does have a voice and has the freedom to seek the support of others. Moreover, the individual feels connected with other citizens in a bond that is strong enough to hold the community together, even when members disagree sharply about particular issues. In this political system, the leaders cannot rule simply in their own interest. They must be concerned with the common good, the interests of the many, or they will be replaced. Indeed, since sovereignty rests with the people collectively, they may, as a last resort, replace the government when it no longer exercises authority legitimately.

In democratic versions of nationalism, a multiplicity of nation-states is implied. Nations are construed as particular peoples inhabiting particular territories, aspiring to have their own distinctive state structures. The vision is not one of empire or hegemony but community self-rule in a world containing many nation-states. Each nation-state is important, especially to its own citizens, but its position is relativized by the presence of many other nation-states representing many different peoples.

However, the positive theory of democratic nationalism summarized above has had, in fact, a far more ambiguous history in the nineteenth and twentieth centuries. It is a lofty political ideal rather than a historically actualized project. In nationalism, the cultural solidarity of a people with a strong sense of subjective association is joined to the instruments of the modern state to form a marriage of extraordinarily immense power. The state needs the nation for legitimation and popular support. The nation needs the state for effective governance and international credibility. For critics, this potential for power is the reason that nationalism is so dangerous and has often betrayed its emancipatory promise.

In the latter part of the nineteenth century, nationalism became increasingly intertwined with social Darwinism and pseudo-scientific treatises on race to legitimize explicitly racist structures and policies. Nationalist leaders also came to recognize the effectiveness of mobilizing mass support for the authority of the state by generating feelings of superiority to and hostility toward "others" outside the national community. Nationalism has often been characterized by the readiness to go to war against others as a way to demonstrate the nation's collective spirit, will, and power. Nationalism has so often been characterized by racism, xenophobia, and war that it seems excessively idealistic to believe it can function without them.

In the United States, nationalism generated a readiness to support U.S. foreign policy "right or wrong" as a test of national loyalty, especially in hot wars and in the Cold War contest with the U.S.S.R. "National security" was used promiscuously as a justification for government policies, for keeping many documents secret, and for infringing on the civil liberties of citizens. Economic advantage, new colonialism, and military superiority were the driving forces of U.S. foreign policy, sweeping aside the actual influence of democratic values of freedom, independence, and the self-determination of peoples. The nation and its cause was the object of American civil religion in ways that legitimated growing U.S. domination in the international arena. The hopeful analysis of political realists that a focus on national interest would restrain the use and justification of U.S. power was swept away by the globalizing reach of American national interest and power.

## CHRISTIAN FAITH AND NATIONALISM

What kind of theological and ethical assessment can we make of nationalism, given its radically mixed character? Many scholars have commented on the quasi-religious character of nationalism. Anthony Smith, for example, sees early nationalism as the creation of secular intellectuals "in search of a viable faith."[5] Traditional religion became less and less authoritative as persons turned increasingly to historical and material existence for meaning systems.

Even as nationalism is a political ideology, it functions in many respects as an alternative faith or correlative faith to that of historic religions such as Christianity. The potential for idolatry is very strong. Richard Niebuhr identified nationalism as one of the most influential forms of idolatry in the mid-twentieth century. In his view, the nation frequently serves as the primary center of value for modern persons. It replaces faith in the one God whose love is infinite and inclusive of all with a particular object of loyalty that is finite and exclusive.[6] A non-idolatrous nationalism would affirm the genuine value that the nation has for its members without absolutizing the authority of the nation-state and making it into the primary locus of trust and commitment.

In line with this theological analysis, prophetic Christianity has warned against the dangers of national idolatry and has sought to sharpen the difference between loyalty to God and attachment to nation. Often Christians have been implored to reject the "ism" in nationalism as a dangerous ideology bordering on idolatry while holding up the nation as a valid and important relative good.

Yet, both liberal and conservative Christians have generally accommodated to the era of nationalism, even as they have sometimes maintained a degree of critical distance. Liberals have sought political reform within the national construct as an important way to love their neighbors in the modern world. Conservatives have valued the stability that nation-states may provide while seeking to live the life of faith in the private spheres of life. Even recent Christian revolutionaries in Latin America did not repudiate nationalism but sought the fundamental change of national structures.

On the one hand, Christian thought has sought to resist its dangers and evils while, on the other hand, supporting the moral possibilities of this reigning paradigm. The theological and ethical challenge is how to distinguish between the two, and how to make contextual judgments about when to support correlation or when to advocate resistance. Is the focus on idolatry sufficient for responding to this challenge? Clearly, the analysis of idolatry has been empowering in certain settings. The Barmen Declaration, for example, was a confession of faith in God as God is known in Jesus Christ that challenged the idolatrous claims of Third Reich nationalism. Resistance against the powerful national idol has also inspired many other prophetic protests against repressive governments all over the world.

Because the nation-state and its power are represented symbolically and ubiquitously in our daily life, and because its structures and policies do materially impact people's well-being, it is an appealing and maybe even compelling god for modernity. When nation-states amass vast stores of dangerous weapons that can kill "enemies" but not feed their peoples, or heal the earth, or overcome divisions, its evils must be opposed. Naming and resisting this idol is an indispensable form of Christian political responsibility.

Yet the identification of idolatry as the chief evil is insufficient, or too unspecified. For most Christians in the United States, the critique has failed to convince. Warnings about making an idol of America have generally not helped Christians sort out how faith may require critical tension with American nationalism. In modernity, many nationalist regimes have not asserted themselves directly against religions, even though they may have assumed much of the authority and many of the meanings at the functional level that religions once had. In the West, various forms of alignments and accommodations were made so that adherence to the national project did not require the repudiation of Christianity, or vice versa.

In the United States, nationalism and Christianity were intertwined in the national culture to forge a kind of civil religion capable of generating cohesion for a democratic state. At various times the nation has been construed as a Christian project in which the ordering and even saving work of God can be communally embodied. In Eastern Europe, the tie between religion and nation has often been more explicit than in the West, as Islam, Catholic Christianity, or Orthodox Christianity provided the institutional religious basis for the national culture.

Many persons, therefore, have not experienced a sharp conflict between their Christian faith and the claims of the nation. When they do, they experience it more often with a specific set of policies or political trends than with making the nation and/or the state into an idol. In modernity, religion was increasingly spiritualized and relegated to a nonpolitical area of life. Religion had to do with worship, the individual believer, and the internal life of the faith community, not with politics. It was seen as appropriate and by no means as idolatrous for national attachments to function as the center of value in political life. In this worldview, there could be no basic conflict between being a loyal American and a good Christian. As long as the national government does not require people to close churches and literally worship at the altar of the nation, it cannot really be idolatrous.

Even at Barmen, the critique of idolatry was most persuasive at the time in criticizing the state's encroachments on the life of the church, not on the devastating impact of this totalitarian regime on every aspect of political life. In democracies, it has been especially difficult to sustain a Christian critique of idolatry, because persons are reasonably free to disagree with the government and the national ethos and are not required to substitute the nation-state for God in any official way.

## NATIONALISM AND CHRISTIAN POLITICAL RESPONSIBILITY

For these reasons, the theological and ethical critique needs to move beyond the "ism" in nationalism to identify specific practices that are destructive of the purposes of God for human and ecological well-being. Two destructive defects in the historical construction of nationalism have generated systems of domination that Christians should resist. These are, first, *internal homogenization* and, second, *external exclusion*. Each has implications for Christian social responsibility.

Nationalism has been characterized by two relational dynamics. It presupposed a cultural unity within the nation even when that unity did not really exist. And it sharpened an antagonistic sense of differentness from peoples outside the nation who were separated by territorial boundaries. Presumed or coerced internal unity went hand in hand with national differentiation from and exclusion of outsiders.

The historic drive for the unity of the community through the homogenization of its peoples has been a major force for injustice. The formation of nations usually required that people "fit" with a dominant group's culture. Disregard for and assimilation of group differences by the dominant culture, the "melting pot" approach, was only one strategy. In the United States, other measures involved legalized subordination of those deemed incapable of ever fitting (African Americans and all women), persecution and discrimination (almost all immigrant groups), forced removal and isolation (American Indians), and even extermination (also practiced against American Indians).

Nationalism has been racialized and genderized in such ways that it legitimated racial, ethnic, and gender injustice. Virginia Woolf wrote eloquently and angrily of this exclusion in 1938 on the eve of World War II.

> She will find that she has no good reason to ask her brother to fight on her behalf to protect "our country." "Our country" . . . throughout the greater part of its history has treated me as a slave, it has denied me education or any share in its possessions. . . . Therefore, if you insist upon fighting to protect me, or "our" country, let it be understood soberly and rationally between us, that you are fighting to gratify a sex instinct which I cannot share; to procure benefits which I have not shared and probably will not share; but not to gratify my instincts, or to protect myself or my country. For . . . in fact, as a woman, I have no country.[7]

Many of the refugees of the nineteenth and twentieth centuries were created because they did not belong to the dominant racial or ethnic group. The question about what to do with "internal minorities" went hand in glove with the ascendancy of the post–World War I principle of "national" self-determination. What do "nations" do when there are people within the same boundaries who do not fully "belong" to the national community? The record of Western democracies gives them no warrant for claiming moral superiority over nation-states in other parts of the world now displaying similar injustices.

Now, most nation-states are multiethnic, so the traditional national rationale of cultural homogeneity is often a fiction, albeit still a dangerous one. Many of these nations are being pressured by internal cultural minorities to have their differences respected and valued. The challenge of multiculturalism is an important response to the historical evils of internal homogenization. Where race or ethnicity has been the root of historical injustice, it is appropriate that cultural minorities seek now to represent themselves and their "differences" in a positive light. Charles Taylor calls for the politics of recognition in addition to the politics of equal treatment in democratic societies as a full response to the requirements of justice.[8]

It is now possible to re-imagine a "nation" that values the cultural differences which subnational groups express. Will Kymlicka argues for the principle of group-differentiated rights to provide the political conditions for freedom and equality.[9] In his view, people need a thick culture in order to exercise freedom, and certain specific steps need to be taken to ensure that subordinated groups of persons are able to live as equal citizens in the national polity. Kymlicka believes that in some instances justice supports the claim of minority cultures for relative autonomy. For example, he argues that North American Indians are best recognized as a nation within the nations of Canada and the United States and should have the right to self-governance. They have suffered grievously in the homogenous model of nationalism, which assumes the dominant culture may trump resistant cultures in the name of "national interest."

The second destructive defect is the sharp differentiation between the national community and outsiders. Of course, human groups have always distinguished themselves from outsiders in some way. A major part of the constitution of a cohesive group is its boundary formation delineating who is in and who is out.[10] But in nationalism, this principle of cultural identity is joined with the mechanisms of the modern state to lend overwhelming political power to the national divisions of people and territories. The construction of nations by external exclusion is legitimated by the basic truism of sovereignty: the right of each nation to control its own borders.

In the nationalist paradigm, public moral responsibility is bounded and trumped by the norm of national interest. Outsiders have little positive value unless they are deemed necessary in the pursuit of national advantage. And outsiders may have considerable negative value if they are seen as a threat to national interest or as aliens whose otherness is loathed and demeaned. No matter how enlightened the nation-state may claim to be, the paradigm itself makes it difficult to generate among citizens a positive sense of relatedness to people in other nations. Indeed, it has been in the nation's interest not to do so.

This manifestation of nationalism continues to be highly influential in the United States. In the 2000 presidential campaign, the relation of the United States to other nations and peoples was barely acknowledged, and international responsibility was limited to very narrow notions of national interest. After the September 11, 2001, terrorist attacks in New York and Washington, D.C., the administration of George W. Bush awakened to the need for international allies. Yet, after a burst of alliance building, the administration swung back toward a unilateralism that angers and frustrates other world leaders. Even though U.S. political and economic power has a profound impact on the peoples of the world, U.S. political leaders persist in the moral myopia that this nation does not have substantive responsibilities for the world beyond the nation, and the illusion that the United States does not need to nourish international partnerships to address global challenges.

The construction of nations by external exclusion has produced a system of guarded borders. Even though international law protects the right of persons to escape persecution by seeking safety across national borders, other nations have no legal responsibility to admit them. National borders protect the unjust privilege of the affluent nations[11] at the expense of refugees who are desperate to move, immigrants who aspire to move, and people who remain in impoverished countries. If refugees are to be received at all, they are either regarded as important for national policy goals (for example, refugees from communist countries), or as burdens imposed on the national population rather than persons to whom we are related in wider patterns of human solidarity. If each nation were roughly equal in resources and power, and if the dominant position of some nations were not linked to the subordinate position of many others, this system of national divisions might be relatively just.[12] But since neither is close to the truth, this system perpetuates injustices that cause massive suffering among the world's peoples.

What, then, are the implications for Christian responsibility? In a variety of ways, nation-states are beginning to soften the requirement of internal homogenization. In a number of countries, political struggles to obtain greater racial and gender equality have reduced, though by no means overcome, the alignment of nations with white male supremacy. The status of minority groups in many other nations, however, is still precarious and sometimes dangerous. Nationalism must be resisted when it oppresses subgroups within the national framework. In the United States, it is possible to support the shift from coerced homogenization to a flourishing heterogeneity of peoples who are unified by their common membership and participation in a democratic polity. Jurgen Habermas argues for a similar project in Western Europe in which the connection between cultural uniformity and political unity in traditional nationalism is severed and cultural pluralism is embraced within a political community.[13] The prospects for reformation are promising enough in some settings to work within a revised nation-state paradigm.

The second destructive characteristic of nationalism is more difficult to correct, however. Is it possible to imagine a nationally constituted community that incorporates a thick sense of political and moral responsibility for those outside the nation? The national reality appears to be a too limited field of vision and arena of action for politics today. Resistance to nationalism may be required in the service of wider human and ecological solidarity. The case is clearest when nationalism promotes exclusive regard for national interest and when it demonizes and fosters hostility toward outsiders.

Both of the historical evils associated with nationalism—internal homogenization and external exclusion—require relativizing the authority and claims of the traditional nation-state. A number of contemporary commentators suggest that nation-state sovereignty is eroding and that political authority is relocating up, sidewards, and downwards.[14] Rather than try to shore up the traditional nation-state regime, Christians should support this process of relativization. Concretely, this is the most promising path to guard against idolatry and to correct the historic evils associated with nationalism. What is needed, and indeed is already emerging, is the creation of political institutions and democratic arenas that will enable persons to participate in a wider range of publics, subnationally and transnationally as well as nationally.

Internally, this critique of nationalism is an argument for the value of cultural pluralism, multiracial democracy, and enhanced opportunities for political participation at a variety of government levels. Moreover, governments at each level need to be in more active negotiation with historically marginalized peoples to develop new terms of relationship. Habermas tellingly points out that Western nations were successful as a political construction largely because they benefited a broad and influential sector of the population.[15] But the national construct has not served others well. If marginalized subgroups are to value their relatedness to the nation as well as their own communities, they must have credible reasons to believe this will be beneficial to them. For American Indians, the option of self-government ought to be supported and its terms negotiated.

Outwardly, also, persons are increasingly likely to have personal attachments beyond the boundaries of the nation-state. These may be professional, familial, ethnic, religious, political, and economic. Political responsibility beyond the nation can be imagined and constructed. Human rights organizations, environmental groups, religious organizations, and other nongovernmental groups provide networks of political involvement that reach beyond national politics. This builds cross-border personal affiliations as well as cooperative political activity. In the context of the European Union, Ulrich Beck proposes the formation of "transnational political parties" based on social democratic convictions that could work cooperatively within and across borders.[16]

Ecclesiology is an important place for Christians to make a contribution to preventing and correcting the dangers and injustices of nationalism. Churches already represent this multileveled pattern of relationships. On the one hand, the particularized expressions of the church in local contexts are highly valued. On the other hand, the church has long been a transnational community that at best transcends but in fact has often been captive to national communities. Churches in the United States are beginning to build partner relations with churches in other countries through mutual assistance, visits, and the formation of friendships. There is a great need for Christians to experience the international character of Christianity as a corrective for national exclusivity and as a sign of the wider relatedness that God intends.

But we also need to think in new ways about the way churches should embody local, regional, and international connections. The World Council of Churches has been very important in the post–World War II and decolonization era. But one of its limitations is that it replicates the corporate, bureaucratic model of institutionalization, which relies on a rather small number of professional church elites to organize and plan ecumenical programs and activities. For most Christians, the WCC is remote and unreachable. We need to invent a different kind of international structure for Christians to engage each other more directly in struggling with what our transnational Christian responsibility is in the twenty-first century. We need avenues for engagement and participation to enhance cross-border Christian community and social responsibility.

Nationalism has been a powerful force in shaping the modern world, and it has left a great deal of wreckage for the postmodern world to contend with. The most promising way to resist its domination is to participate in an environment of multiple communal loyalties. National relatedness is most likely to be dangerous when other collective identities are swallowed up in or trumped by the nation. Although the church is an alternative community of loyalty, in the modern era it has too often been grafted onto the nation's projects in the political sphere.

We still have many reasons to value the national community and its institutions, so resistance to the nation-state system itself is too sweeping and too utopian. But, in given settings, nationalism may indeed require resistance rather than critical support; we have specified some of those conditions in this chapter. In this time, Christians should participate in de-centering the nation, correct its historic evils, and seek a greater range of political activity for persons. In Christian thought, theological universalism is inclusive, communal, and personal. Each of us is related in the family of God. Yet particular groupings are valued as well. Each community has responsibility not only for justice in its own particular context, but, at the same time, to welcome the stranger and be a blessing to the other peoples outside its group. This is still "good news" for a suffering and divided world.

## NOTES

1. Joseph H. Carens, "States and Refugees: A Normative Analysis," in *Refugee Policy: Canada and the United States* (Toronto: York Lanes Press, 1991), p. 23.

2. Peter Marden, "Mapping Territoriality: The Geopolitics of Sovereignty, Governance and the Citizen," in *Migration, Globalization and Human Security*, ed. David T. Graham and Nana K. Poku (London: Routledge, 2000), p. 47.

3. Marden, p. 54.

4. Homi K. Bhabha, ed. *Nations and Narration* (London: Routledge, 1990), p. 3.

5. Anthony D. Smith, "The Crisis of Dual Legitimation," in *Nationalism*, ed. John Hutchinson and Anthony D. Smith (Oxford: Oxford University Press, 1994), p. 113.

6. H. Richard Niebuhr, *Radical Monotheism and Western Culture* (New York: Harper Torchbooks, 1960).

7. Jeremy Paxman, *The English: A Portrait of a People* (London: Penguin Books, 1999), pp. 227–228.

8. Charles Taylor, "The Politics of Recognition," in *Multiculturalism*, ed. Amy Gutman (Princeton: Princeton University Press, 1994), pp. 25–73.

9. Will Kymlicka, *Multicultural Citizenship* (Oxford: Clarendon Press, 1995).

10. Fredrik Barth, "Ethnic Groups and Boundaries," in *Ethnicity*, ed. John Hutchinson and Anthony D. Smith (Oxford: Oxford University Press, 1996), pp. 75–82.

11. Joseph H. Carens, "Aliens and Citizens: The Case for Open Borders," in *The Rights of Minority Cultures*, ed. Will Kymlicka (Oxford: Oxford University Press, 1995), p. 346.

12. Veit Bader, "Fairly Open Borders," in *Citizenship and Exclusion*, ed. Veit Bader (New York: St. Martin's Press, 1997), pp. 30–31.

13. Jurgen Habermas, *The Inclusion of the Other: Studies in Political Theory* (Malden, Mass.: Polity Press, 1998), pp. 117–118.

14. Marden, p. 54.

15. Habermas, pp. 118–120.

16. Ulrich Beck, "Democracy Beyond the Nation State," *Dissent* (Winter 1999): 53–55.

*7*

# Resistance and Biotechnology Debates

## F. E. Bonkovsky

*R*esistance is needed. Some directions in American life are wrongheaded, if not evil. The society is wealthy, wasteful, and individualistic. Inequalities among persons are so great that the United States is one of the more unequal of developed societies. Equality, justice, and fraternity are too easily neglected, while only freedom is trumpeted. This chapter reflects critically on American society. Critique of wrong directions is needed. But one also seeks to be constructive in arguing for better use of resources. Biomedicine is a key arena where critical ethical and public perspectives should guide U.S. policy and action.

Good health has been recognized as a signal blessing throughout human history. Today, health care is among the largest American economic sectors, involving more than a seventh of GDP. Health and health care decisions are immensely important. Our values are reflected in how we provide health care and how we make decisions.

At least four models of decision compete in the early twenty-first-century American health care system. They embody and imply differing values and perspectives. Elements of the models resist and oppose each other. The four models emphasize respectively decisions by physicians, by patients, by organizations, and by ethics committees. As we seek to amend society toward greater justice, it is important to understand how decisions are made so that correctives can be properly proposed.

Traditionally, physicians were the key decision-makers about health care and treatment. At first, they shared authority with priests and other community leaders. Then, in nineteenth-century America, physicians gained legal control and sanction over health care decisions. In 1954, Jonas Salk, M.D., was named the Time Magazine man of the year for his discovery of the Salk poliomyelitis vaccine and as representative of the socially preeminent standing of physicians.

The 1960s and 1970s brought dramatic new perspectives into American life. The "baby boomers" challenged their elders and resisted traditions and institutions. In health care, patient decision-making became dominant. Informed consent and patient involvement and control over health care decisions have become the American norm by practice and by law.[1]

In 1993, the Clinton health care reform proposals failed—but they accurately foresaw the problems of spiraling health care costs. Health maintenance organizations (HMOs) and managed care organizations (MCOs) emerged as new centers for decision-making and financial control and monetary gain. By 2001, the balance of power had shifted so dramatically that physicians and patients were complaining and legislatures were considering ways to limit HMOs and MCOs and resist their power in order to give more control back to patients and physicians.

At present, there is conflict between various potential health care decision-makers. But these important agents need to work together. Public policy and "politics as the authoritative allocator of values" (James Easton) will be centrally influential in who decides, what values are affirmed, and what definitions of justice and other virtues shape American health care and biomedicine.

Gaining influence in the 1980s and 1990s, ethics committees (or similar advisory boards) contribute important dynamics and insights to decision-makers. Many advisory committees specify representatives of religious communities and traditions as necessary members. In the United States (perhaps more than in other modern societies), religious communities remain vibrant bearers of cultural mores and norms. Congregations play key roles as culture transmitters and shapers. Thus, churches have unusual opportunities to serve as communities of moral discourse to the benefit of their adherents and the broader society.[2]

Congregations and other religious communities are also places where differing perspectives, conflict, and resistance may surface. At Second Presbyterian Church, physicians see things differently than do MCO executives who are also on church boards. The pastors have been educated about Judeo-Christian traditions, which propose a preferential option for the weak and poor in society. Business and other graduate schools, however, educate for individualism and more freewheeling theories of Adam Smith and Thomas Hobbes. The task of managers is understood to be mainly or even solely to maximize shareholder profits. Many church board or session members are corporation shareholders as well as baptized Christians. So the tensions exist in the session and within persons. How do we resist our own lesser necessities and proclivities and resist the ideas and interests of persons who are friends and societal leaders?

This chapter explores decision-making involving key issues in the promised new medicine and the underlying new biology. These are based on the sciences of molecular biology and new insights about human genetics and the genome. In this discussion, we seek to elucidate a perspective of "constructive resistance" wherein more noble directions are pursued and excesses and errors are criticized. This requires bridging between the languages of high-tech applied science and medicine and the conceptualizations of more explicitly normative and traditional communities.

Such bridging is challenging. Each reader will arrive at combinations of understandings, affirmations, criticisms, confusions, etc., that a personal context permits. Contextualism, not situationalism, is intended by the author and recommended to the reader. The overall context is the early twenty-first century dominated by U.S.-led worldwide biological and medical opportunities and challenges. The application of biological and medical knowledge, and especially its research and technology, is the central concern.

Contextualism emphasizes the importance of the societal setting.[3] Our thinking and policy must be centrally informed both by critically considered principles and by social reality. Context is to be distinguished from situation. By a "situation" is meant a single event (or decision) with no necessary connection to what precedes or follows. Situationalism is significantly informed by existentialist philosophy and its emphasis on a decision at a given moment. Consider the following matter.

Recently refined prenatal diagnosis raises difficult issues. Should a six-week-old fetus with 60 percent chance of cystic fibrosis by age twelve be aborted by Ms. X and Mr. Y? While recognizing that in the contemporary United States Ms. X and Mr. Y (or Ms. X alone) will make a determinative decision on fetus A, contextualism seeks to see clearly and to emphasize the importance of broader societal realities concerning fetal life and abortion. Thus current thinking about disease and treatment and the competing values of the age will be critically examined. Some communities oppose abortion and resist its being societally funded. Broader (contextual) perspectives usually serve as caveats or critical perspectives in an individualistic situational approach. We seek to resist questionable or dangerous spirits of the times in favor of constructive applications of critically examined societal perspectives and religious and ethical norms.

Contextualism emphasizes that a decision is part of human, personal, and societal history and futures. X, Y, and A are not only individuals who may feel alone, abandoned, or isolated. They are part of families and communities and societies. Most importantly, they are part of the human family and of a created order, which is both fallen and good.

So we may affirm the connectedness of our lives. We are challenged to recognize how our lives and decisions participate in fallenness and in goodness. We seek to resist evil and sin. But we are even more concerned to affirm and build upon the good. In many areas, a key challenge is knowing and doing the difference between good and mischief. Moral living requires choosing among lesser and more noble values and purposes.

## SCIENCE AND DEMOCRATIC DECISIONS

We can properly resist or affirm only what we understand. Thomas Barlow notes that American public policy has at least three major problems with scientific information.[4] First, scientific data have become vastly more important in informing policy. In the areas of biomedicine and biotechnology, new human genomics and new gene-manipulated foods are hotly debated. There are scarcely more challenging issues than HIV-AIDS, BSE, and anti-terrorism involving high-tech capabilities.

What sorts of scientific technology and capabilities should be affirmed or opposed for countries such as Iraq, Iran, or North Korea? South Africa and developing countries have recently resisted transnational pharmaceutical interests regarding HIV treatment. Fears of BSE affect the eating habits of millions. In Europe, protesters resist American multinationals' attempts to export gene-modified plants whose products are widely available in U.S. supermarkets, where they are unwittingly purchased. Hence, policy-makers and citizens must understand and utilize scientific information.

The second issue is that the increase in and importance of scientific data have not been matched by an increase in understanding among societal leaders. Estimates are that only 10 percent of leaders are conversant enough with science readily to grasp key issues. This is a particular problem in the United States, which leads in much science and technology but in which natural science education is not readily obtained by persons interested in humanities, arts, and even social sciences.

Thus, there are major difficulties in interpreting scientific information and advice. Shall we oppose proposals for science funding, research, and development? Or is resistance first appropriate only when research and development of new knowledge reach some stage of application? Public policy is most difficult where there are differences of values and goals, and debates about facts. Decisions are hardest but also most effective early in the R and D cycle. Now is the time for regulation of human gene manipulation, for example.

Scientists should be accustomed to disagreeing with each other and to democratic debate. Such challenging lies at the heart of scientific method, and science is supposedly self-correcting. But contemporary science and technology are vastly expensive ventures, demanding much financial support. Money is controlled by vested elites who often seek to impose orthodoxy—including the self-interested orthodoxy that all science and development are good and that unchecked freedom and individuality will inevitably serve society. It may be such orthodoxy and self-interest that causes leading scientific journals *not* to publish negative results and to resist discussion of scientific errors or mischief.

Scientific breakthroughs must sometimes resist entrenched and powerful views. Resistors are not often applauded in their opposition. The most notable example is Galileo's conflicts with established Aristotelian (and church) cosmology. Galileo was forced publicly to recant his heretical (but scientifically correct) views about planetary movement.

Where the sciences involve human processes, scientific laws are often in reality approximations or statistical likelihoods. Proposed research on treatment A for a certain cancer, for example, is promised to lead to an increased twelve months of life in 40 percent of patients. Treatment B may increase life expectations by twenty-four months in 20 percent of patients. Which research should be selected for support? This is a matter very much related to public policy, for (as discussed below) by far the greatest support for biomedical research in the United States comes through the budgets of the National Institutes of Health. These fundings the U.S. Congress has doubled to an annual $28 billion in the past decade.

A third issue is how support decisions should be made. Experts testifying behind closed doors prefer orderly processes as the best way to information and decisions. Where biomedicine is concerned, quick decisions and activity are advocated to provide treatments and to save lives. But educated citizens increasingly favor open discussion in which trust of experts and information is heavily mixed with skepticism, scientific debate, and even resistance to the ideologies of progress and success.

Democratic decision-making requires that the people (demos) have and understand key information and perspectives on all sides of issues. This is very difficult because science is complex and because the issues are sometimes life threatening and extremely controversial. Even top scientists differ in their views and in their policy recommendations. Everyone desires treatment for Alzheimer's disease. Yet, on the basis of proven science, it would be damnably difficult to determine which (if any) embryonic cells should be utilized or destroyed, and at what stage in development, for what achievement or likely increase in knowledge. (It is, moreover, not polite to note that it is unlikely that embryo research will produce an Alzheimer's cure in the next months.)

So this decision (like so many) involves at its heart a difficult choice among competing values that have nobility on both sides but are also quite contradictory. Advocates of contending positions resist the policies of others. At this point in the debate, one cannot both seek an Alzheimer's cure through human embryo research while also treating embryos with the full respect due to human beings. Thus, the biggest challenge is making difficult choices that require the sacrifice of worthy values in favor of others.

## THE CHURCH AS COMMUNITY OF MORAL DISCOURSE

The churches can make important contributions to society and their congregations by serving as communities of moral discourse. Through sermons, education, special events, music, funerals, weddings, written materials, and in many other ways, a church can engage persons in thinking about pressing issues, including the new genetics and the impact it is having on medicine and on more general human understanding and planning.

A community of discourse does *not* have to give final or definitive answers. Rather, it provides a forum for reflection. Leaders can share information and perspectives. Laity and clergy should cooperate. Often church members possess key information and perspectives (e.g., on biomedicine). A possible time for such discussions can be after worship services or at other points when other events are planned. Events of less than an hour are useful and can have the advantage of causing attendees to ask for follow-up. Such limited-time endeavors also have the advantage of not making extraordinary demands on resource persons.

Three great sources of Christian reflection, the Scriptures, Church tradition, and reason, are readily available. Bookshops, journals, daily newspapers, radio, television, and the Internet provide vast amounts of data. But too often what we hear and read are limited or distorted information and perspectives. A community is thus needed to help the citizen deal constructively with the information barrage.

## CHRISTIAN VIRTUES: BETWEEN HOPE AND HUMILITY

Faith, hope, and love abide, these three. The greatest of these is love. St. Thomas Aquinas, the great teacher, added the three theological virtues to the four temporal virtues (courage, fortitude, justice, prudence) taught by Aristotle. Love is the greatest of virtues but, in its agape (self-giving) form, not something to be generally expected in society. How a Christian community recognizes and critically considers its commitment to hope, the second of the theological virtues, is a subject for another essay. Here we focus on how American medicine is committed to hope.

A physician is to affirm and never to undermine a patient's hope. Medicine sees much suffering, disease, and death. But on its public face, medicine wears the expressions of hope. In the past decades, Americans have been encouraged to hope (and even to expect or believe) that modern medicine will bring an end to tuberculosis, malaria, cancer, and a host of other diseases.

Hope has negative as well as positive dimensions. It is needed for a person to continue in difficult circumstances. At the personal level, hope or some kind of belief in a meaningful future is an essential ingredient in the face of difficulties. But hope can have negative consequences that may include family delusions or distortions of public perspectives and of public resources. A patient's hope to live more than twelve months in the face of an advanced cancer must be balanced with more realistic family planning. An admirable personal desire to defeat cancer must be balanced against competing claims for public resources for biomedicine.

Humility is a more difficult virtue for many Americans. Our society is a competitive one. Few of us inherit position or sufficient wealth. So we feel compelled to achieve success in the race of life. Since much of the race is social and comparative, our success involves being thought of well by others, which seems more likely if we put our best accomplishments forward and think (and speak?) well of ourselves.

Much American biomedicine is led by very bright and competitive physicians. Biomedical funding is voted by elected officials who are not allowed to be overly humble or self-effacing. Physicians must seem self-assured and successful in order to bring comfort to their patients and to help assure patient compliance for medical treatments.

American medicine (and perhaps American society in general) thus has difficulties with humility. It is easier to be only hopeful and optimistic. The funders and the public expect promises and news of success in the battles against disease and death. Optimism and hope have for decades been the central themes of information about medicine and the new genetics. Humility, even if appropriate, is easily forgotten, at least in public discourse.

Persons who are theologically informed have an unwelcome challenge in cautioning against excessive hope. Indeed, a faith perspective calls for resistance to arrogance or pride when these become dominant themes in societal interactions. Human pretensions to knowledge, skill and power should be countered even when these claim to be in the service of such noble ends as healing and medical treatment.

## RELIGION AND SCIENCE IN CONFLICT?

Conflict and mutual misunderstanding characterize the modern relationships between some advocates of (organized) religions and natural science. This is particularly problematic when religious and science leaders are ignorant of each other's domains. Some prominent scientists seem to believe that there is inevitable conflict between modern biology and religious teachings and beliefs. They point to evolution as a case in point, arguing that religionists deny the validity of (Darwinian) evolution as a natural phenomenon.

That confusion and disagreement may extend in at least two directions. First some may believe that religious belief in general denies Darwinian evolution. No distinctions are made between fundamentalist and the religious mainstream views. Second, Darwinian evolution becomes a kind of shibboleth. Those who question or doubt evolutionism as a philosophical principle are caricatured as obscurantist and anti-science. Worse, they are seen as opposing reasonable applications of science to modern life.

A liberal mainstream religious response is to confine religion to the private and internal realm. Religion then becomes a perspective by which a person privately interprets life's meaning. Such (liberal religious) interpretations do not have validity beyond private interpretations. The key religious questions become whether and how personal life has meaning, whether there is grace or punishment for oneself, whether there is a God and how one might be related to a God. These are important questions. But privatized perspectives hold that religion has no inevitable impact on and no warrant to speak to "the public square."

In this private religion view, science and religion do not meet—they are on skew lines, as it were. Religious perspectives are excluded in the discussions about whether and how humans are related to other animals through Darwinian modes or through DNA similarities or both. Nor are religious questions of grace or forgiveness raised. Religion is sharply separated, excluded, from the objective world of natural science, which is subject to modern scientific inquiry. The religious sphere has only to do with spirituality and what one believes privately about one's private life.

Traditional Christianity, Islam, and Judaism, however, follow neither the scientific nor the religious separationists or rejectionists. Great religions are concerned to discover how godly perspectives speak to all of life. When it comes to medicine and health care, moral and faith-based inquiry affirms some modern purposes. Faith perspectives resist other proposals and directions. The challenge is to discern what should be affirmed and what should be constructively resisted.

## WHAT DOES IT MEAN TO PLAY GOD?

By definition, no humans should attempt to play God. Thus, resistance appears needed against scientists (or others) who try to play God. But what does it mean to play God? Sometimes this saying seems based on a kind of spatial understanding in which there are areas of knowledge and endeavor where humans have not been involved or remain significantly ignorant. These are proposed to be the spheres of God or the divine.

### *The God of the Gaps (in Human Knowledge)*

These closed or dark rooms (so to speak) are places where humans should not go. They are inhabited by superhuman spirits or demons. For example, in this view, the movements of the planets were God's business. Since Galileo's science culminating in the landing on the moon, humans have been encroaching on God's space or territory. Twenty-first-century astrophysics is seen as knowledge by which the cosmos comes increasingly under human influence. Big-bang hypotheses threaten to take away another cosmic area previously reserved for God. In biology, the world and its life forms were presumed to be created by God.

Until the Renaissance, in the West, only God knew much about the human body. The church forbade human body research. Today, medicine knows a great deal about how the body functions. With the sequencing of the human genome, scientists are learning about DNA arrangements, which shape how proteins, the key building blocks, are organized. Proposed biomedical research could culminate in changes in the make-up of human cell DNA. A realm previously reserved to God's knowledge has become part of human activity.

In the gaps view, as the lacunae in human knowledge become smaller, the realm of God is reduced. Public or scientifically understandable areas increasingly are seen as *not* impacted by the divine.

To address the shrinking gaps problem, some religion advocates recommend privatized religion. Conflicts between traditional religious and social beliefs and the new sciences are solved if religion and beliefs are or should be understood as limited to the realm of the personal and private. This reduces the impact of religion on society and on public discourse. Especially in an age of pluralism, secularism, and anti-authority, privatized religion can often safely be forgotten.

To play God when religion is a private matter is to engage in violations of human rights, autonomy, and religious freedom that impact the individual and the private realm. To play God might mean to use mind-altering drugs or to otherwise coerce how a person believes or thinks. A person can thus play God with one's life. But religious areas remain safely distant from science and technology as well as from areas of most public policy.

## Playing God and Human Pride

In a Biblical view shared by traditional Judaism, Islam, and Christianity, to play God is to try to usurp to particular human control the shaping of the present and future of human and natural life in ways that are inappropriate, given human sinfulness and finitude. Nazi eugenics and the search for a pure, super Aryan race, for example, was playing God, but not because of scientific discoveries, *if* they were valid science. Rather, the evil and immense error came because of the ungodly and inhuman, indeed, monstrous applications or uses of scientific knowledge. Claiming godlike power over other humans, the Nazis became monsters who were neither humane nor divine.

A core problem is that humans are easily self-deluded. We will become wise, knowing good and evil is the ancient phrase dramatically warning against human pretensions. The Nazis believed they were serving higher human values, bringing a purer Aryanism, ridding humanity of undesirables. Claiming to know the good, they did horrible evil.

It is not yet playing God to understand the human DNA or genes or the atom, nor even to understand how nuclear fission and fusion can release vast amounts of energy. However, humans step into dangerous realms when they build and then arm megaton bombs. Use of such weapons on a massive scale would be a terrible instance of playing God—that is, of abrogating to sinful and finite human control massive powers over other humans and over nature in the service of one's parochial understandings.

Nuclear technology was quickly recognized as dangerous by Einstein, Oppenheimer, and others. Hence, domestic and then international public policy was immediately crafted to restrict sharply the possession, applications, and control of nuclear technology and capabilities. For a half-century, such restrictions kept the nuclear genie mainly contained. Today, we fear developments in such areas as the Middle East, the Indian subcontinent, and the former Soviet Union, where restrictions are threatened.

Along with public policy control came sharp democratic resistance to nuclear technology in the forms of weapons and even nuclear power. This resistance was most notable in such front-line societies as West Germany, where the nuclear warheads were stored and most likely to be detonated during the four and a half Cold War decades.

The danger of playing God, of inappropriate human action, is mainly a matter of application or technology, not of pure science. Great scientists such as Newton, Galileo, Einstein, Mendel, and Darwin were amazed, thrilled, and delighted by what they discovered. Newton found profound meaning and satisfaction in his discoveries that he understood to be fathoming God's thoughts. Such gaining of knowledge is a deeply humane but also literally a theological (God's words and ideas) activity.

## GENETIC DIAGNOSTICS AND HEALTH CARE

Where and how shall manipulation of the human genome be regulated? The growing human ability to know and manipulate persons' genetic composition raises many difficult public policy, theological, and ethical issues. Prenatal genetic diagnosis focuses several important questions. Resistance is needed against cavalier preimplantation diagnostics and plans for treatment that would destroy fetuses in order to produce super-children or designer babies. Where and what to oppose is a difficult and demanding matter that must, however, be determined now.

The new genetics in biomedicine has brought deeper understanding of how human DNA constitutes our genes and helps shape who we are. Today, we are increasingly able to alter aspects of human genetics. The rapid development of medical understanding involving genetics creates many new possibilities about which people, physicians, and society must decide.

Starkly putting the matter, some serious persons have proposed that prospective parents have an obligation to have embryonic cells genetically tested so that parents may be able to decide whether or not to abort embryos so that defective human life will not be brought to birth. It is argued that such decisions are entirely questions of a parent's right to choose or of a woman's control over her body. Thus, a parent may decide not to deal with a handicapped or in some way defective or unwanted offspring.

The definition and range of defects can vary from serious neural or cardiac problems to issues of designer babies, where a human designer might only accept a prospective child who would be brown eyed, blond haired, and male with a predicted height of 73 inches and predicted I.Q. of at least 130. "Vicki," a young woman from a small town in Germany, came to her physician with the request for prenatal genetic diagnosis. She was newly pregnant and thought she had become so during Mardi Gras when she cohabited with her boyfriend but also with an African man. If it was their progeny, she and her boyfriend wanted to have and rear the child. They were convinced that neither they nor the small town would accept a child whose genes were significantly influenced by African heritage. So they planned to abort an embryo or fetus with the wrong gene make-up.[5]

There may be many so-called wrong genes that require and challenge the applications of prenatal diagnostics. Biomedical science hopes to provide gene correction or therapy. But where there is no current correction or therapy, the possibility of abortion is considered. Medically defined genetic problems include Down's syndrome (Trisomy 21), Turner's syndrome (XO), which includes mental retardation, and Edwards syndrome, which results in 50 percent mortality during the first weeks of life. Other faulty genes lead to Fragile X syndrome and the most common form of heritable mental retardation. For over a decade, medical genetics has sought to treat or combat cystic fibrosis that becomes increasingly severe and often leads to death in early adulthood. The Huntington's disease gene was discovered some years ago and brought hope for new treatment.

New discoveries are announced regularly as biomedical scientists (successfully) search for the genes linked to breast cancers (BrCa genes), alcoholism, and Parkinson's disease. This is the background from which James Watson, double helix co-discoverer, Nobel laureate, and founding director of the U.S. Human Genome Project, has proposed that some people are obligated to have prenatal diagnosis and further should be urged not to birth chronically diseased or handicapped offspring.[6]

Another response emphasizes treatment through gene therapy. A good model is that of the successful therapy for a handful of children with an inherited severe combined immunodeficiency disorder (SCID). Gene therapy was successful for SCID in a two-year-old child (who is now a teenager) as well as with two infants who are doing well.[7]

I was part of groups that worked toward gene therapy for cystic fibrosis in the early 1990s. One regrets that high hopes and great efforts have not yet been successful. Harold Varmus, Nobel laureate biomedical scientist and then U.S. National Institutes of Health director, noted in 1998 that gene therapy has been dangerously overpromised.

Overall, progress in fully understanding the genome and being able to treat genetic diseases will likely be quite slow and uncertain. Some leading scientists note that only a small percentage of disease is directly gene linked, so even fuller understanding will not lead to cures or certain therapies.

*Responses to the Dilemmas*

The simplistic response is that the woman (like Vicki) must decide. She must, of course. Any prenatal diagnosis inevitably involves her. A tendency in the United States is to end the discussion at this point. In this view, diagnosis of and response to genetic defects are entirely a question of a parent's right to choose or of a woman's right to control her body. The embryo has no standing and no rights. The contrasting view holds, equally dramatically, that the fertilized ovum is already a developing person and must be treated as a human being, with rights.

Despite the sharp clash of opinions, American society will continue to provide resources to biomedical researchers who will develop genetic knowledge and tests. Then the tests will be made available. Presumably tests will be fee-for-service and will be paid either out of private funds or more likely from some insurance system involving private and public funding.

Hence, the broader community inevitably shares responsibility for the context and the parameters of decisions. To be resisted are proposals that consider only individualistic interests and perspectives—even when such proposals are garbed in the language of rights. In modern society's health care, no one is really a singular individual—least of all in so complex and corporate an area as biomedicine and biotechnology. Community resources give us medicine, most especially high-tech contemporary biomedical technology. The community is the source of treatment and resources. Moreover, all humans have a profound interest in the kinds of children we rear and in the kind of human nature we further.

*Some Problems of Public Policy*

Presidents Ronald Reagan, George H. W. Bush, Bill Clinton, and George W. Bush (each in turn) rejected medical science proposals to allow human embryo research and to use public funds for such research. The issues are regularly discussed in relation to the policies and budgets of the National Institutes of Health (NIH) whose more than $28 billion annual budgets set much of the support and priorities for the nation's universities and other biomedical research and subsequent treatment developments.

Public policy shapes the nation's health and biomedical research agenda through the public policy processes that produce the NIH budget. President Richard Nixon (1969–1974) greatly boosted the NIH and U.S. biomedical research when he announced and proposed funding a war on cancer led by the NIH. In the 1990s, the promises of new medicines, possible cures, and successful log-rolling led Congress dramatically to increase the NIH budgets while most other federal departments were held to much leaner increases if not reduced. It is not surprising that members of Congress pay attention to their local biomedical leaders as well as to the NIH. U.S. university-based medical schools very much need, depend on, and work for the support that the NIH provides for university research and overhead.

Public policy may require the NIH and biomedical establishment to engage in genetic research that will impact prenatal diagnosis and intervention. Or public policy can seek to prohibit such activity and research. Or public policy can take stances between the extremes. In the 1970s, the Cambridge, Massachusetts, city council banned certain types of scientific research within Cambridge, which is the home of Harvard University and the Massachusetts Institute of Technology. Some activities then migrated outside Cambridge. Recently, with more supportive public policy, Cambridge has renewed its claims as site of some of the most advanced biomedical research and development enterprises. German scientists have for years protested the strict German federal regulations that sharply limit embryo research in the Federal Republic.

In the United States, the default position has been for public policy to focus on the NIH budget. Some members of Congress champion largely free and well-funded research and biomedical development. Other legislators seek to direct or restrict certain kinds of research and activity—e.g., that having to do with human embryos. To help deal with the issues and public policy controversy, the U.S. president, the secretary of the Department of Health and Human Services, NIH leadership, and biomedical leaders have created various advisory and public policy impact groups such as the National Bioethics Advisory Committee and President George W. Bush's recently created Council on Bioethics.

For public policy, NIH and its related activities are relatively easy targets, since the NIH budget is directly controlled by Congress. This makes it possible for NIH to have a very large budget, but it also makes public policy involvement very easy. A single member of Congress can attach a budget rider that shapes some aspect of biomedical research. Thus, largely in response to one legislator, the NIH has recently greatly strengthened research in the area of alternative medicine.

The default position does not control all U.S. biomedical activity. It is a striking irony that even as Washington-based federal public policy sought to limit embryo research for more than a decade, thriving reproductive medicine specialties and providers became very influential and well known in northern Virginia—within a short drive from the centers of federal power and legislation. Areas such as northern Virginia offer childless couples and others concerned with reproductive medicine the world's leading developments and child choice possibilities.

## The Role of Social Mores

In our individualized pluralistic societies, nondirective counseling has become widely accepted. Nondirective counseling seeks to make clear that the woman shall decide without pressure and certainly without constraints. The counselor helps assure that sufficient knowledge is available and helps clarify the options.

Perspectives differ, however. Do knowledge and options include reference to the possible long-term (largely unresearched and hard to know) effects of a decision? Are the psychological effects not tied to the general social milieu? If an abortion is chosen, subsequent wishes for children never fulfilled, and the society becomes more conservative, one might predict a person's long regretting the abortion decision and even becoming seriously depressed. How much should nondirective counseling address such matters? Some would say not at all; nondirective counseling is to attend only to known matters in the present situation. If nondirective counseling focuses on contextual issues or such long-term potential psychological consequences, its stance is seemingly more conservative than if it considers only the present dynamics.

German law requires mandatory counseling before an abortion is undertaken. After a heated debate in which German Roman Catholic bishops disagreed with the Vatican, the Vatican ruled that Roman Catholic church representatives may not participate in pre-abortion counseling. The Vatican argued that such counseling—whatever its content—was part of the process by which public policy approves or allows abortions. The Vatican holds that, in principle, Roman Catholic representatives must never become part of an abortion approval system.

For American Protestants (and of course for Catholics) the Vatican principles also raise questions. Even nondirective counseling has normative components. For example, nondirective counseling assumes the possibility—perhaps even the likelihood—of abortion.

*Serious Chronic Disease*

More importantly, nondirective counseling requires that the counselor will have thought through and have knowledge and some kind of awareness of principles on the host of genetic diagnostic tests that may lead to an abortion decision. Many would agree that the prospect of serious chronic disease and early childhood death should be avoided. But one has to ask whether the therapy here is for the mother, the potential infant, the family, or the broader society. The easiest decision occurs when all the potentially affected persons have the same interests and the same perspectives.

It is, however, impossible to know whether a still-to-be-born or potential person might rightly or freely choose non-existence over existence with disease or defect. Here one enters the realm of principle or godlike knowledge in which one judges the worth of existence versus non-existence. Here one plays God with human life.

## Cystic Fibrosis

Cystic fibrosis (CF) is increasingly predictable through genetic diagnosis. CF is quite common among the Caucasian middle class and is the result of two recessive genes combining in cell composition. A CF sufferer has trouble breathing because lung cells have abnormal chlorine exchange that results in mucus build-up and in incapacity to clear the lungs. CF patients need constant, difficult treatment. Presently, many such patients die between twenty and thirty years in age. The person experiences the development and dynamic teen years but does not have the opportunity for adult life.

There is hope that gene therapy for CF will be developed soon. But CF prenatal diagnosis currently raises the difficult questions about whether a person should be allowed to be born or whether such existence should not be allowed. That the parents must decide further complicates matters, since they must seek to guess what life would be like for the unborn and also to guess how they and their family would respond to the difficult dynamics of CF in the family.

## Handicaps

Many modern persons expect of themselves high achievement. They also expect this of others. As parents, we hope that our children will be happy and successful. Too often, we may seek to prescribe what happiness and success mean.

We expect of ourselves and our families that we will be normal. Some views of normality exclude handicaps or limitations. If we learn through genetic diagnosis that a child is likely to be less than normal or handicapped, what is an appropriate response?

Citizens and church members throughout Western societies thus face a host of difficult biomedical decisions made possible and pressing by publicly funded and sponsored biomedical knowledge. The range of human choices has been greatly increased to the point at which human nature may itself be altered with unpredictable consequences.[8] Evil as well as good choices are now more possible.

At the personal level much reflection is needed. Even more far-reaching are public policy decisions that shape biomedical research and development. Communities of discourse need to address the public as well as the personal issues. This will mean that some interest groups and tendencies need to be resisted on behalf of the long-term common good.

## AN OPPORTUNITY FOR NIH

One hopes and believes that U.S. biomedical sciences will continue to lead and serve global society. U.S. biomedicine is a very positive dimension of globalization. It is surely desirable that NIH grantees be successful in the search for better treatment for cancers, AIDS, heart disease, diabetes, alcoholism, and the host of other maladies.

With its budget so enhanced, this is a good time for NIH to take on some new directions. They might be called New Health Initiatives. The term "health initiative" is somewhat controversial at NIH, however. In the early 1990s, the first female NIH director, Bernadine Healy, ruffled many feathers by proposing a "woman's health initiative" and more generally challenging the NIH basic research establishment. When President Clinton appointed Nobel laureate Harold Varmus as NIH director, the relief was obvious on the Bethesda campus, and Varmus received strong support in Bethesda and then on Capitol Hill.

A glory of U.S. biomedicine is its technological and pharmaceutical leadership. American research hospitals (throughout the country) provide the latest and most expensive in cutting-edge treatment. Aided by NIH international cooperative grants, American biomedicine leads the world.

A grave problem for U.S. society and U.S. biomedicine is how the politically and socially weak are treated. After a decade of talk, 40 million persons still have no insurance or guaranteed payment for health care. While the upper middle class and affluent Americans are well served, other groups need help. Needy groups include urban Americans, rural folk, and special populations.

### Special Care

Special Care could be the name of a new NIH emphasis. Perhaps the new emphasis could be taken up in an already extant location, such as in the overall programs for Complementary and Alternative Medicine. But there is danger that a new direction might get swallowed by a large historic operation such as the National Cancer Institute if the new is located amongst the established centers.

Urban Health has been a concern for some parts of NIH. In Bethesda, for example, in the mid-1990s, AIDS treatment researchers established initiatives to work with urban centers in Washington, D.C. The Institute on Drug Abuse Clinical Program was (and is) located in urban Baltimore to emphasize a goal of relating NIH activities to urban populations. But the going was tough and challenging. Government rules, regulations, and programs were not always welcomed in urban areas.

NIH has given thought to how one might approach urban persons differently from the way one relates to upper-middle-class patients and their physicians. But neither NIH nor the United States yet knows the answers. Probably we do not even know exactly how to put the questions. Here local communities of discourse and their national representatives might make a contribution through constructive criticism, for local communities understand local needs and perspectives arguably better than do federal bureaucracies in Washington.

An urban program will require knowledge of society and of minority perspectives. We may have to rethink some of our images of medicine. Likely, we will need staff who are trained differently than in the past.

Rural health issues have the faces of North Dakota and the visages of Appalachia. What is common are people who cannot receive high-quality health care where they make their homes. Isolation, remoteness, and thin populations do not attract physicians or hospitals. The emphasis on health care cost-cutting has hurt greatly. It will take the resources and resourcefulness of something like NIH to begin to address the problem of rural health care.

## AN IRONY OF PROGRESS

The promises and hopes of high-technology medicine—including genetic medicine and genetic modification—ironically encourage some Americans to avoid hard issues of life, especially the challenges of death and dying. Genome studies propose new treatments that by being genetically targeted will be far more effective than extant medicines.

Genetics-based medicine (gmed) promises by genetic diagnostics to correct defects or otherwise to lead to healthier persons who avoid chronic diseases. There is even discussion that the aging process can be halted or reversed by gmed. The advocates say that gmed will produce organs and parts for transplantation into humans. As our organs wear out or prove mortal, we can have new organs that have been genetically prepared so our bodies will not reject the transplants. A person of one hundred years could have a significant percentage of new "parts" and so might hope to live longer.

Hence, gmed could renew the age-old search for a fountain of youth—or, at least, for holding off the aging process. Throughout recorded human thought and history—from such theological and cultural beginnings as described in Genesis 3—humans have been perplexed by and fearful of death and dying. Denial has been a common response, particularly in youth-obsessed America.

Our funeral businesses and our nursing homes and hospitals bear heavy burdens of the problems we have with death and dying. Some excellent progress has been made in American medicine in caring for the end of life. The work of M.D. Joanna Lynn and colleagues is exemplary. But the high quality of a percentage of physicians and other professionals who struggle to help us with death and dying must be aided by societal and church assistance. Medicine and society can be corrupted (and led astray) by a widely held desire to avoid death or to seek by any means to escape facing the questions about meaning of life that death and demise inevitably raise.

The churches can be key centers for learning and discourse on these important matters. The meanings of life and death are at heart of the Hebrew, Christian, Muslim, and other scriptures. There are vast resources and many approaches by which congregations can be aided. Heuristic instruments are available. These include sermons and educational materials as well as the music of John Rutter, W. A. Mozart, J. S. Bach, and many great hymns of the churches.

But the churches must resist too simple a trust in the latest promises of biomedical wonders. It will not be easy for congregations to become critical centers of moral discourse about these most important issues. Yet precisely such contentious deliberation is needed in a society that too easily sets aside deep questions of meaning. There is need to resist vast financial interests that have a vested stake in overpromising and in societal funding for pet projects. Distortion is too easy when we all hope against hope.

As centers of critical discourse, our congregations can relearn the more sobering perspectives of such great words as "Guide us, O thou great Jehovah, pilgrims in this barren land. We are weak but Thou art mighty; Hold us by Thy powerful hand. . . . When we tread the verge of Jordan, Bid our anxious fears subside. . . . Strong Deliverer . . . Land us safe on Canaan's side."

## NOTES

1. For a more extensive discussion of these four models and their implications for American health care, see F. Bonkovsky, "Contending Medical Decision Models," *Theoretical Medicine* 22, no. 3 (June 2001): 193–207.

2. The felicitous phrase "community of moral discourse" was learned from James Moody Gustafson, who was professor of ethics and student of H. Richard Niebuhr at Yale and then professor at Emory University. An important book is Gustafson's *Can Ethics Be Christian?*

3. A seminal thinker on contextualism and ethics was Professor Paul Lehmann of Union Theological Seminary, NYC.

4. Thomas Barlow, "The Appliance of Science: There's the Evidence but What Does It Say?" *Financial Times*, June 2, 2001, p. 2.

5. This account is based on information from Dr. Gerhard Wolf of the University of Freiburg Institute for Human Genetics. See Wolf in *Genetik*, Vienna, 1998.

6. See, e.g., the stormy German debate involving Watson's ideas in October 2000, in the leading German newspaper, *Die Frankfurter Allgemeine*.

7. These cases were described by the lead physicians, W. French Anderson, "The Best of Times, the Worst of Times," and Marina Cavazzana-Calvo, "Gene Therapy of . . . (SCID)," both in *Science*, April 28, 2000. See also the discussion by Richard Horton, "How Sick Is Modern Medicine?" *New York Review of Books*, November 3, 2000.

8. See the excellent discussion of this and other issues by Francis Fukuyama, *Our Posthuman Future* (New York: Farrar, Straus and Giroux, 2002).

# 8

# Resistance to Military Neo-Imperialism

## Ronald H. Stone

The maker of heaven and earth has through the teaching and action of Jesus Christ claimed us as peacemakers. God's saving love is adequate to give to humanity power to struggle for the fullness of a just peace in which all interacting dynamically would nurture each other. From our creation we are blessed, but the restoration of that blessedness to our war-torn world requires more serious engagement than we have given.

We are by our nature peacemakers, but in our fallenness we are bent strongly toward war-making and making ready for war. Out of our *yes* to the beautiful creation God has given us for peace, we must now say *no* to the forces that make for war. Our *yes* to God is in gratitude for God's saving love; our *no* to war is said to the forces that deny the reality of that love and its commandments.

The increasing commitment to peacemaking in the Christian churches is antithetical to the deepening militarism of the world. Militarism is understood as a worldwide phenomenon. It is subject to many different definitions. Militarism is viewed by the author as expressed in three dynamic movements that characterize the present:

1. The nuclear arms race, the proliferation of nuclear weapons capacity, and the development of other arms of mass destruction.
2. The trade in conventional weapons, and the spread of military approaches to social problems.
3. The spread of technologies and of training in repression of internal opposition.[1]

These tendencies reinforce a process of the "militarization" of society, but the author's focus is on militarism as it has moved beyond policies of defense

117

or the struggles against injustice or the gaining of independence under the limits of a means of "last resort."[2] Militarism represents the current extreme developments of military power and the too easy reliance upon military power in situations of difficult international relations.

The churches have made bold calls for disarmament and policies of reconciliation through exchanges and negotiations. They have supported the work of international organizations as a move to reduce international anarchy. However, in crisis after crisis, the resort to force has thwarted negotiations. Cynicism about international organizations has been encouraged by the United States, which previously helped develop them. The churches have called for peacemaking emphases throughout their life. The struggle within the church is to find means or patterns of Christian practice that are adequate to the call for peacemaking in the increasingly militarized world.

This chapter builds upon the peacemaking call of the churches in their ecumenical work. It particularly grows out of the Presbyterian tradition represented in *Peacemaking: The Believers' Calling* (1980). Christian peacemaking concerns are very broad. They include the vital preaching of the Word, the proper ministry of the sacraments, the upbuilding of Christian community, and the development of peoples through the service ministry of the church. The equipping of Christians to engage in the public policy formation of their countries and to engage in the politics of peacemaking is central to the vocation of peacemaking; the work of Christians with others in voluntary organizations to struggle for peace is crucial to the task. Peacemaking is naturally an ecumenical task, and the restoration of peace to a divided church is important to the work of peacemaking. In addition to all of the above, more and more Christians are uniting in taking actions, some legal and some illegal, to protest their government's militaristic policies.

Various actions of selective withdrawal from aspects of cooperation with the military system may be described as resistance to militarism. Such decisions are not made without struggle. Likewise, people who are committed to cooperation with government as a necessary aspect of society find civil disobedience and tax resistance difficult modes of action. Resistance has many meanings. Here it is used in a broad sense to include actions against militarism as defined above. Resistance often involves struggles with conscience and with courage. Its modes may include a spectrum from demonstrations, civil disobedience, protests at the School of the Americas, tax resistance, draft resistance, the vocational withdrawal from the military or war-related occupations, and working within one's vocation to oppose militarism. All Christians will not agree about the appropriateness of many of these actions. Moral ambiguity, which often surrounds human actions, is particularly real in questions of this nature. It is hoped that this chapter will help Christians answer the question: What does obedience to God call us to do in this situation? If the direction of governmental policies is to rely more and more upon the threat of world domination and upon the actual use of armed forces, what are we as Christians to do?

Reformed theology and practice is historically activist. It assumes that the Christian life is involved in both personal and social transformation. It has a high respect for the state and says *yes* to the state as a provider of order, the protector of the people, the source of justice for the poor, and the enabler of the weak. It also says *no* to the state when the inevitable temptations of absolutism, imperialism, or militarism are surrendered to by the state. Because the state practice is so necessary to life and because the temptations are so prevalent, Reformed persons should expect at various times in their life to support and to resist the state. The question emerging for many Christians is, should they resist their states? The answer will depend both upon our reading of the situation and our affirmation of our theological-ethical heritage.

## THE PRESENT SITUATION

### *Resistance to Military Neo-Imperialism*

Normally, Americans accept that the United States has enjoyed a role of leadership in the world since World War II. They expect reasonable leadership from their powerful country. So they vote, contribute to political parties, and participate minimally in local and national politics. They recognize that the social-economic opportunities and meaning in America are found in many arenas besides government and its international politics. Power is more accessible to most citizens through nongovernmental organizations or corporations than through government. They ordinarily trust they can leave moral-political decisions to the ordinary processes of politics.

Those normal processes of American politics produced support in the Cold War for the Marshall Plan, NATO, the Korean War, significant military budgets, various counterinsurgency wars, and an activist foreign policy. Only the Vietnam War, the Reagan military budgets, and the Persian Gulf War produced significant citizen opposition to the point of resistance. Resistance here is understood as public demonstrations and activities disruptive of governmental policies (civil disobedience, tax resistance, boycotts, strikes, etc.). The war against al Qaeda and the overthrow of the Taliban in Afghanistan were accepted without massive protest by the American people. The war against Iraq, however, engendered worldwide demonstrations in 2002–2003 against American policy and massive domestic protests in the streets. So, in the early years of the third millennium, protesting resistance against the world hegemony of the United States emerged.

While there was widespread disgust with Iraqi dictator Saddam Hussein, suspicion that there might become dangerous connections between Iraq and terrorism, and worry about the unfinished disarming of Iraq, still the war seemed premature and probably unnecessary to much of world opinion and to significant proportions of the U.S. public. Neither the inspectors nor the UN Security Council completed their work, which was dismissed by the United States.

## Full Spectrum Dominance

The election of George W. Bush in 2000 prepared the way for a group of neo-conservative defense strategists to move into roles of significant power in the United States. These thinkers struggled with others in the administration for dominance. The events of September 11, 2001, allowed them to merge their interests with more traditional conservatives and American nationalists to help shape the president's response. Whereas Presidents Carter, Reagan, and Clinton had only intervened in Afghanistan and Iraq, the neo-conservatives, in the aftermath of September 11, conquered them. The George W. Bush administration expressed its goals for Iraq as liberation from the Saddam Hussein regime, discovery and destruction of weapons of mass destruction, discovery of information on terrorist connections, and destruction of terrorist support. Bob Woodward's reporting on discussions within the administration indicated that many advisors of Bush had hoped to invade Iraq even before the terrorist attacks of 9/11 and had been forced to strike at Afghanistan first.

The bolder willingness to take the United States into war had been announced on May 30, 2002, in the Department of Defense paper signed by Chairman of the Joint Chiefs of Staff General Henry H. Shelton. The document entitled *Joint Vision 2020* is a plan or vision of how the United States will fight wars for two decades. It calls for "full spectrum dominance," which means that the United States will be prepared "to win" any wars across the world, coordinating its actions when possible with other nations and multilateral agencies. It suggests the United States will be prepared to act unilaterally or multilaterally to control any situation. The United States must be able to achieve dominance in any realm—space, sea, air, land, and information—to rapidly project power anywhere.

President George H. W. Bush had built an alliance to attack Iraq in the Persian Gulf War and arranged for other nations to pay the bill; by refusing to conquer the country he had limited his war. The attempt on his life and the later frustrations with Saddam Hussein challenged his son, George W. Bush, to complete what his father had refused to undertake. In 2003, however, there were very few limits. Full spectrum dominance took its role, along with the denunciation of the "axis of evil" and the policy of refusing to be militarily challenged by anyone, to unleash a war deeply resented by a billion Muslims and much of the world. Americans, unenthusiastic about becoming an empire, could use the failure of the war to meet the justifiable war criteria of legitimate authority, last resort, real harm to be corrected, and proportionality as reasons for protests and acts of resistance.

Beneath the issue of a particular war is the question of whether a cultural and economic hegemonic power should also become political director through the use of military power. Fighting al Qaeda is a just cause, but fighting Iraq may not be, and world domination is not a just cause. Massive worldwide protests echoed outrage over a particular war, but also fear of U.S. dominance. Internal resistance to imperial politics is needed to preserve and restore democracy and to return U.S. power to developing life that the world will want to emulate instead of draining the homeland of power for full spectrum dominance of the world. Beyond mass protests and the encouragement of anti-U.S. terrorism, the seeking of full spectrum dominance will engender countervailing alliances.

Neither nation-states nor empires last forever, but the struggle to dominate for security's sake may bleed a country of its resources and its people. Security as a value is very large. But a nation conceived as a republic to be a model for the world can easily lose its soul in striving to become an empire. In that loss may even rest its premature demise as a nation. America cast its lot with freedom, but it does not bear the responsibility to fight all over the world to insure its freedom or to impose its freedom. It simply is not the case that every cruel dictator threatens America. Even every invasion of one country by another does not mean that the United States needs to be involved. We can be responsible Good Samaritans without having to become Roman centurions.

*The Comprehensive Test Ban Treaty*

The Kennedy administration succeeded in banning tests of nuclear weapons in the atmosphere, outer space, above ground, and under water in 1963. Successors to Kennedy through Carter advocated the adoption of a comprehensive test ban treaty (CTBT) that would also ban nuclear tests underground. By March 2003, 166 nations had signed a CTBT, but the U.S. Senate failed to ratify the treaty in 1999 by a vote of 51 to 48. Since that failure, both Pakistan and India (also nonratifiers) tested nuclear weapons. In 1999, Secretary of State Madeline Albright warned of such developments if the United States would not ratify the treaty. Professor Jeanne Kirkpatrick argued on the same day for testing to develop the U.S. arsenal partially as a deterrent against other weapons of mass destruction.[3] U.S. leadership in the weapons of mass destruction has returned full circle with a war in Iraq, with one of its many goals being the destruction of weapons of mass destruction, some biological agents which we sold to Iraq previously. Resistance to government failure to limit such weapons by treaty seems to be a moral option.

The immediate agenda is to persuade through diplomatic means the United States, Russia, China, Pakistan, and India to ratify the Comprehensive Nuclear Weapons Test Ban Treaty, together with the drastic reduction of the arsenals of the United States and Russia. The religious communities have not been leading on this. Some thirty-six years ago, I lobbied conservative Republican Iowa Senator Bourke Hickenlooper on both race relations and the Treaty Against Testing in the Atmosphere. I remember his pounding his desk and saying he never would have voted for the partial test ban if it hadn't been for those "damn Methodist preachers in Iowa." Where are those preachers now?

Of course, it is possible that our efforts to abolish nuclear weapons will fail and that it is our destiny to destroy ourselves through the tensions within our own humanity. If so, meaning is not lost—for ultimate meaning, as perceived in our religious traditions, is not *in* our history, but *beyond* our history.

If we are aware of the self-destructive tendencies in ourselves and in our societies, we are called to resist these suicidal instincts. Life and history have meanings that are worthy to be defended. The resistance against suicidal instincts must be undertaken on all levels: in politics, in economics, in the healing professions, in our communications industry, and in religious life through the finding of serenity and new ways of devotion to the Creator who undergirds our life and transcends our parochial loyalties.

Finally, this resistance to the false gods of nuclearism must be undertaken, as Paul Tillich said forty-five years ago, "in acts which unite the religious, moral, and political concern, and which are performed in imaginative wisdom and courage."[4]

*National Missile Defense*

Despite the failure to establish the technological possibility of a national missile defense after the expenditure of $95 billion, the decision to establish a portion of the defense shield was reached by the George W. Bush administration. This required the abandonment of the Anti-Ballistic Missile Treaty (ABMT) with Russia. Though that treaty permitted two sets of anti-ballistic missiles (ABMs), both Russia and the United States developed only one, which the United States abandoned as obsolete. This is the first abrogation of an attempt to limit a major weapons system since the end of World War II. President Bush defended the unproven ABM system and the abrogation of the treaty as necessary to develop means of defense against "rogue states."[5]

## Biological and Chemical Weapons

The Geneva Protocol of 1925 reacted to the use of mustard gas weapons in World War I by outlawing their use. In 1972, following U.S. leadership, the stronger Convention on the Prohibition of Development, Production, and Stockpiling of Bacteriological and Toxin Weapons and Their Destruction was signed by 144 governments. It went into force in 1975, and about a dozen countries either were seeking the weapons or had achieved them. Most major countries have the capability of producing them, and terrorist groups have used them (Tokyo). In December 2001, the George W. Bush administration blocked further development of the BTW. The United States did not want any enforcement or monitoring legislation to be added.

Chemical weapons, particularly mustard gas, made the greatest impression in the world after German introduction of it at Ypres in 1917. Iraq's reintroduction of mustard gas against Iran in the 1980s and nerve gas against the Kurds received the world's censure and was part of the reasoning for the removal of the Saddam Hussein regime. Russia has admitted violating the Protocol, and the U.S. introduction of Agent Orange in Vietnam was either an avoidance or a violation of the treaty. Agent Orange, conceived of as a defoliant for the jungle, also had nefarious effects on people, animals, and birds.[6]

## Small Arms and Light Weapons

The world is flooded with small arms and light weapons. Kofi Annan estimates that 500 million are available, which is one weapon for every dozen people on earth. The United States has been "instrumental in blocking the creation or development of any instrumentation with the capacity to monitor or control the flow."[7] The United States has been opposed to a ban on sales to nonstate actors, wanting instead to use the U.S. norms of responsible and irresponsible end-users. The United States has not wanted its policies on weapons sales and possession to be influenced by other peoples. It also did not want to "toughen-up" the 1999 treaty or to offend the U.S. gun lobby. There is a lot of profit to be made in international gun sales, and the United States leads the world in exporting $18.4 billion worth of arms and military equipment, which is more than all the rest of the world exported in 1999.[8] These policies reflect the results of an administration elected with the support of the

National Rifle Association and gun lobby support. Resistance may not be the preferred tool of opposition as elections, legislation, and international conventions are at issue.

## THEOLOGICAL SOURCES OF RESISTANCE

### *The Biblical Heritage*

The Bible has shaped our conscience on the questions we are considering. Through its use in devotions, in sermons, in prayers, and in study, it has formed many of our attitudes. However, to throw biblical light on the question of noncooperation with the state, we must take the question to the Bible itself. Not all relevant passages can be considered here, but G. Ernest Wright (formerly professor at Harvard Divinity School) responded to a question about civil disobedience in the Old Testament: "The most significant figures of Scripture all seem to resist established legal authority in some manner."

One of the best tales of resistance is of the Hebrew midwives' resistance to Pharaoh in Exodus 1:15–22. The Pharaoh's attempt to limit the growth of the Hebrew people by putting their male babies to death is thwarted by the chicanery of the Hebrew midwives, whose names are remembered as Shiphrah and Puah. They defied the command of their sovereign and lied to him so that the children might live. In the next chapter, Moses himself is saved by more defiance of the sovereign; this time the resistance to authority involves even the Pharaoh's daughter and his own household. Moses, of course, saved through an act of defiance, is later used by God to defy the state openly and to lead his people to freedom. The author of the Letters to the Hebrews connects Moses' salvation from death and his leadership of resistance against the Egyptians directly to faith.

A case of resistance leading to revolution is in I Kings 12. Solomon's son, King Rehoboam, was urged to lower the taxes that Solomon had imposed for his court and building projects. Rehoboam refused and threatened to increase the tax load. According to the text, the Lord then brought about a "turn of affairs" that resulted in Jeroboam leading the tribes away from allegiance to Rehoboam and founding Israel in Bethel. Jeroboam's own form of worship as an alternative to Jerusalem also received prophetic criticism, but the division of the Kingdom held, with only little Benjamin remaining allied to Judah and the house of David.

Micah represents the figure of the prophet who says *no* to the king. Throughout the Old Testament, the prophet representing God's Word challenges royal authority and is punished for speaking God's Word. Micah in

I Kings 22 warns Jehoshaphat of Judah and Ahab of Israel that their campaign against the Aramaeans will be a disaster. It is not a clear case of a religious spokesman against royal authority, for it is also an intra-religious struggle. All the other prophets promise success. For his negative prophecy Micah goes to prison. In defying his prophetic *no*, Ahab and Jehoshaphat go to battle and to defeat. It costs Ahab his life, "and the dogs licked up the blood" (I Kings 22:38).

Esther's bold breaking of the law began the reversal of fortunes that saved them from a pogrom under Persian rule. Her statement of purpose to save her people represents the best spirit of action against law to save life: "I will go to the king, although it is against the law; and if I perish, I perish" (Esther 4:16).

John Calvin grounded his understanding of religious resistance to governmental decrees in reflections upon the book of Daniel. The young Hebrews under the Persians and the Medes simply refused to follow the orders of the emperor in matters of worship. Shadrach, Meshach, and Abednego refused the command of Nebuchadnezzar to worship and honor the royal idolatry. Similarly Daniel refused to stop praying to his Lord, defying a royal edict. These were rescued from punishment by God's action. This noncompliance when ordered to violate one's faith has been a model for much Christian resistance to religious persecution. The willingness to endure persecution for faith has also, as in Daniel, often been an argument for honoring the faith that has strengthened adherents in the face of persecution.

There is a theme of God requiring resistance to the government in the Old Testament. It is, of course, only one theme. The motif of covenant obligation binding the Hebrews together as a mutually supportive people is a prominent theme. The covenant is made before God; after the Hebrews accept kingship, the ruler is obligated to God. Protestant political thought rests much of its foundation upon the idea of a covenant of the people together, and then the people covenanting with a sovereign who is obligated before God to respect the covenant. The ideas of resistance to the sovereign never disappear. The forms of resistance mentioned in the Old Testament reappear in the New Testament: resistance to save the children, resistance to taxes, breaking of a law to save a people, and religious resistance to idolatry.

The question of the challenge of the Messiah's authority to political authority haunts the New Testament. From the birth narratives of Jesus to his execution as "King of the Jews," political authorities from Herod to Pilate are threatened by Him. His ministry is in the context of Jewish parties agonizing over their relationship to Rome. The gospels reveal the context of their writers struggling with the antagonism of synagogue and church after the Roman destruction of Jerusalem. Paul, writing before the destruction of Jerusalem and before the Neronian persecution, understands the ethics of subordination to the state in one way. The author of Revelation, writing much later, sees Rome's destruction and the victory of the cosmological Messiah over the persecutors of his people.

The New Testament is both more inner and more eschatologically oriented than the much larger Old Testament. Consequently, in political thinking stemming from the Reformed branch of the church, the Old Testament has received more use. But the insistence that the Old Testament is more political does not mean that the New Testament is innocent of political involvement and implications. Much of this less-political character of the New Testament is simply due to the fact that Rome occupied the land. Jews normally were not citizens, they were not subject to military service, and they had little political clout. The state in the New Testament is provisional; it lasts for a while to maintain order. It is not absolute, though Revelation reveals its absolute pretensions.

The central actors of the New Testament all defy the authorities sufficiently to be imprisoned or executed. The New Testament, though focusing on the inner person and focusing on eschatology, is set in a political storm. The ringing statement of Peter, "we must obey God rather than men," is from one who struggled with the political meaning of his beloved Jesus. Peter would not only question Jesus; he would, under pressure, deny him after defending him with a sword. Peter would not only defy the authorities to preach Christ resurrected; he would, with God's help, escape from prison twice.

*Church History*

The New Testament concludes with the struggle between the cosmological Christ and the corrupted Roman state. This struggle has shaped Christianity so that, even today, wild interpretations of Revelation, which neglect the historical context of the book, still confuse Christian political ethics. In this book, only those that have refused the demands of the state are regarded as Christ's.

In response to an inquiry about civil disobedience in the early church, the late Roland Bainton of Yale Divinity School responded: "From Nero to Constantine, any adherence to Christianity was civil disobedience, even though punished only intermittently."[9] The Christians of the early church, until it was legalized under Constantine, prayed for the emperor, paid taxes, and lived lives of exemplary citizenship, but they urged their followers to resist demands for worship or ultimate allegiance to the state's deities. Christian resistance to the imperial cult led to persecution, and to martyrdom occupying a central place in the life of the church. Although they generally refused military service, after 170 A.D. there is evidence of Christians serving Rome in the army. It is of interest to our subject that early Christian resistance is one of the two major reasons for Christian absence from the military in those early centuries. Christian conscience forbade in many cases the honoring of the deities and the worship of the emperor required by military service. That restraint on Christians' serving in the armed forces was removed with the Christianizing of the empire; the ethic of love, however, still restrained many from taking up the sword. The early church said *yes* to the order of the Roman empire, but *no* to the religious practices that legitimated the empire and expressed its claim to absolutism.

The *no* to empire became much more muted after the empire began to be allied with the church. Monasteries and ascetics still separated from the state, but the church embraced it. In the East where the empire was strong enough to survive to the fifteenth century, the rulers tended to dominate the church. In the West where the empire dissolved, the church tried to rally forces of order and to restore civilization. In the emergent church-feudal blended society, the church under strong leaders sometimes said *no* to the princes for the freedom of the church, but the *no* to military practice was very muted and confined to small witnesses. The alliance between the church and militarism reached a zenith in the crusades of the Middle Ages.

Long before the church was involved in the barbaric slaughter that accompanied the crusaders' conquests in Constantinople and Jerusalem, the church's complicity with armed force was established. The same Augustine who out of an ethic of love could reluctantly sanction armed defense, eventually came to excuse the application of armed force against heretics. Crusades approved by the church were carried out against non-orthodox Christian groups, but also against Christian peoples (e.g., the Norman conquest of England). The church sought through the techniques of the Truce of God and the Peace of God to limit violence, but it was too involved in the use of violence to protect its own temporal interests to be an effective peacemaker. Similarly in the European conquest of the world from the fifteenth century until the twentieth, the church complied with the imperial needs of the European powers. It had its own missionary interests, but these were vitally compromised with the worldly motivations for wealth and empire. Here and there a prophetic voice from within the church, like Father Bartolome de las Casas in Central America in the sixteenth century, would protest against the subjection and murder of the native inhabitants. But basically, religious legitimacy in the name of Christ was bestowed upon the European conquest of others.

The uneasy alliance between spiritual and temporal authority that characterized the Middle Ages resulted in many struggles between the spiritual and temporal rulers. But in the eleventh century, the Pope could claim to be, under God, the source of both temporal and spiritual authority. The claim could not hold, however, and the far-reaching claims of the Pope contributed to the conflict that exiled Hildebrand, even from Rome. Secular rulers were limited by custom, by law, and by the power of the church. The church was at least a co-equal, if not the rightful sovereign, in this long, complex period of Western history. The legal thought of Thomas Aquinas (1225–1274) laid the grounds for much of Catholic constitutional theory limiting the role of temporal authority. His claim that positive laws were dependent upon divine law and natural law has, in our own time, been the ground for Christian resistance to unjust positive laws.

The Protestant Reformation tended to pit the new religious movement against the old order. Martin Luther (1483–1546) justified the refusal to obey the commands of the sovereign when they violated God's will ("we must obey God rather than men," Acts 5:29). His high view of scriptural authority also led him to avoid resistance on the grounds of Romans 13 ("There is no authority but by act of God, and the existing authorities are instituted by Him"). Disobedience to the authorities? Yes, when they violated God's law. Resistance to the authorities? No, at least he avoided resistance until very late in life. Finally, he was persuaded that the emperor's move into Germany to persecute the Reformation was illegal, and on the advice of lawyers he agreed that constitutionally resistance to the illegal action of the emperor was legal. Then he could justify armed resistance to the emperor. Later, Calvinist-armed resistance to the sovereign often borrowed from theological arguments developed on Lutheran ground.

John Calvin (1509–1564) tried to restrain his followers from revolution. He also taught that impious commands of the sovereign were not to be obeyed. The authorities were constituted by God and were to be honored, though civil servants had a duty to resist their princes if they acted contrary to the law. His followers in the Netherlands, France, and Scotland were to push the implications of his positive attitude toward government much further. In all those lands, historical forces pushed Calvinists into revolution, and they succeeded in the United Netherlands and Scotland. The early Protestant revolutionaries acted out of the need to defend the true or Protestant faith against blasphemy and idolatry. But by the 1570s, in French Protestant political theory, the grounds of revolution were the supposed original freedoms of the people and their rights under natural law.[10]

Calvinist political theory developed in subsequent centuries until its positive view of the state, grounded in covenantal language with its Old Testament roots and founded in revolution, could be expressed in the U.S. Constitution. It underwent substantial change on its way to supporting popular revolution in John Locke's *Two Treatises of Government* from John Calvin's disobedience to the sovereign in *The Institutes of the Christian Religion*. The Reformed view of the emerging states was positive. The leaders of the states were, of course, sinners and often foolish, but the state was the dike of God against sin. Order was precious and the vocation of a public office holder was, in John Calvin's thought, to be respected above all other vocations. There was no romantic anarchy or idealistic perfectionism in Calvinist political wisdom. Still, in its beginnings, it recognized the duty to disobey on religious grounds. Soon it was driven, in honoring that God is Lord of the conscience, to resist and then overthrow tyrannical-idolatrous regimes. The conception of a covenant between the people and God for the ordering of their lives led to the idea that the sovereign could be overthrown if the ruler violated the covenant. The covenant's meaning was grounded both in the constitutional history of the realm and in the natural rights of the citizens. So the grounds were laid not only to resist unjust laws, but to depose sovereigns. George Buchanan (1506–1582) carried the right to depose sovereigns as far as any Calvinist thinker and, of course, he did it for Scotland, where Calvinists succeeded in deposing the queen in 1567.

The historical material reveals only that Protestant Christians, like their Catholic counterparts, are free morally to resist or to replace governing orders that act against the purposes of the constitution or religious faith.

*A Recent Example*

Resistance to U.S. war policy was well exemplified by Clergy and Laity Concerned about Vietnam (CALCAV). The organization, born in John C. Bennett's living room in the mid-1960s, organized, wrote, lobbied, and demonstrated against the war in Vietnam for a decade until U.S. participation in the war ended. Though dominated by mainstream Protestants, it incorporated Catholic war resisters, including Daniel Berrigan as co-chair until he was exiled by his bishop to Latin America. It provided an expression of protest for Jewish anti-war activists, with Rabbi Abraham Heschel serving as co-chair and a consistently prophetic voice. Its leadership often drawing from Niebuhrian realistic ethics, Richard Neuhaus, Robert McAfee Brown, and William Sloan Coffin encouraged radical actions against the war, including resistance against the draft and many nonsymbolic actions, while CALCAV tried to reach the American middle and to organize the churches against the war.[11]

None of the CALCAV's leadership could be regarded as disloyal, though right-wing opponents including J. Edgar Hoover did so characterize them. John C. Bennett was a consistent leader of CALCAV throughout its decade of work, combining its responsibilities with his editorship of *Christianity and Crisis* and presidency of Union Theological Seminary. Some students at Union were drawn into demonstrations against the U.S. role in the war as early as the fall of 1963. CALCAV's role in reaching the middle of American public leadership undergirded the students' activism, whether in draft resistance and arrest or in political organizing in various campaigns. Reinhold Niebuhr, though too ill to actively lead the movement, had participated in its predecessor organization in September 1963 as the Ministers' Vietnam Committee condemned American tactics in the war as immoral. His address to Union Theological Seminary arranged by John Bennett and the author empowered the student opposition to the war in 1966. The political philosopher Hans J. Morgenthau contributed his political realism to the writings and thought of the group, while Martin Luther King Jr.'s participation represented its commitment to nonviolent tactics of resistance.

Though unable to end the war, its expenditure of millions of dollars and the organization of tens of thousands of anti-war supporters contributed to undercutting U.S. policy, and to the election of more dove-like candidates, and persuaded foreign policy elites to seek to deescalate and eventually abandon the war effort.

King's association with CALCAV symbolized the alliance between the civil rights movement and the anti-war movement, which generally was more natural for whites than for blacks. King led the civil rights resistors to anti–Vietnam War conclusions, but a lot of the black civil rights activists did not follow. The civil rights movement led by black clergy through the Southern Christian Leadership Council (SCLC) of Martin Luther King from the mid-1950s until King's assassination in 1968 is an important successful example of Christian resistance to evil in our time.[12]

The clergy fed by decades of oppression, and a generation of theory of Christian social change, was able when fed by the resistance of Rosa Parks to mobilize masses to change society. In a decade, official segregation was broken and black access to political power was opened. Economic opportunity would remain elusive for millions, though other millions of blacks would gain entry into the middle class.

Leaders of the opposition to the Vietnam War had learned tactics, organization, and theory in Christian social resistance in the civil rights movement. The synthesis of many streams in King and the movement gave it an unusual brilliance.

CALCAV represented mainline, white-dominated resistance, and SCLC represented black clerical-led resistance, with both drawing on broad ecumenical sources for support and participation. Both movements defined clear evils to resist and both expressed religiously passionate community while taking risks to influence society. Neither movement abandoned mainstream politics or American civil society while engaging in tactics of resistance that challenged that society to change.


## PEACEMAKING AND RESISTANCE


In the 1990s, mainline Christianity articulated theories and paradigms of just peace or just peacemaking. These emerging concepts, combined with international interventions to stop genocide, captured Christian thinking in the United States. After the Cold War, military budgets declined as a proportion of gross national product at home. The focus seemed to be to reduce U.S. nuclear weapons while helping to disarm Ukraine, Kazakhstan, and even Russia. Both nuclear weapons and the dangers of militarism in the United States seemed to decline. Globalization, democracy, and human rights were in the minds of some moving toward more international peace. Even Marxists like the authors of *Empire*[13] seemed to think big wars were a thing of the past and imperial power would reduce international clashes to police actions. But the hopes or fears of both liberal and Marxist theorists proved illusory. The arming of the world continued, and the new nuclear weapons of India and Pakistan replaced the denuclearized Ukraine and Kazakhstan in the doomsday club.

Then, with the atrocities of September 11, 2001, the world led by the United States lurched back toward militarism and new uses for nuclear weapons. The realism of Christian neo-orthodoxy seemed more relevant again than the liberal optimism[14] or the Marxian pessimism. The realism about the human tendency toward violence in its international relations[15] combines with several ominous tendencies to highlight the role of resistance combining with enthusiastic political participation to oppose militaristic trends.

While exercising its approved right of self-defense against its attackers, the administration of the United States unwisely tried several other policies. It floated the language of "crusade," a new office of untruthful propaganda, military tribunals, and policies overriding the civil liberties of Mideastern immigrants. These, in the context of releasing studies of new uses for nuclear weapons, abandoning the treaty limiting missile defense, rejecting the land mines treaty, the comprehensive test ban treaty, and the pursuit of the largest-ever military budget, suggested the need for resistance to militarism.

While public criticism drove the "crusade" language and the lying public relations arm of the Pentagon offstage, the other more potent militaristic emphasis remained in place. Minimalist gains toward recognizing the importance of multilateralism, nation building, and peacemaking diplomacy seemed to have prevailed over the hard realism of the administration. But the mid-1980s recognition of the need for resistance against nuclear weapons and militarism through both resistance, by those willing to undertake it, and the extraordinary use of ordinary means of changing policy seem once again appropriate.

Resistance, of course, means opposition to the development of new, threatening military systems through political action, demonstrations, teaching, preaching, noninvestment, and divestment. It calls for occupational withdrawal from and noncooperation with the military when that is used destructively or for domination beyond legitimate self-defense and international order requirements.[16]

Resistance to militarism requires participation in and rebuilding of peace movements within churches and civil society. Clergy and Laity Concerned about Vietnam is a model; more recently, the ecological movement's organizations from Greenpeace to the Sierra Club suggest what needs to be undertaken. One of the more recent studies emphasizing the junction of ecological and anti-militarist concerns on the landscape of the American West is Rebecca Solnit, *Savage Dreams*.[17]

Moral realists, just peacemakers, traditional peace organizations, and churches all have a stake in the never-ending struggle to keep U.S. policy rational and sometimes benevolent. Barbara Green puts the long-term struggle against militarism and excessive armament well in *Church and Society*: "There are some significant characteristics of U.S. military policy that are neither ending nor beginning, but that cry out to be changed. Foremost among these is U.S. over investment in military spending and under investment in alternatives."[18]

The demonstrations against U.S. policy in Iraq were the most significant anti-war protests since the Vietnam War. Peaceful demonstrations around the world were accompanied by some nonviolent civil disobedience leading to thousands of arrests. There were also violent protests against U.S. policy. Many of the demonstrators were mobilized by the churches. However, the elected officials and their advisors could refuse to heed the demonstrators and the civil disobedience. Domestic dissent and even world dissent can be overridden in foreign policy defined as national security. Therefore, the resistance activity needs to be directed toward the desired political goals of winning elections. The policy toward Iraq was decided by an identifiable group of actors who took prerogatives of office under George W. Bush. A different result in the Supreme Court would have produced a different foreign policy. Thus, the church and other nongovernmental peace organizations must plan for positive results at the election booth. The churches can promote para-church peace movements that take direct action while local churches can study the issues, participate in denominational peace activities, support peace-seeking pastors and leaders, and raise financial resources for peace movements.

Finally, changes in foreign policy election results are determinative. Of course, election results are then subjected to bureaucratic politics and the rise and fall of competing ideologies. George W. Bush's philosophy of foreign affairs was changed by his team after September 11, 2001. The competition of ideas, bureaucrats, and lobbyists never ends. Living in a violent world, the church's role of seeking peacemaking never ends either.[19]

## NOTES

1. "The Consultation on Militarism" of the World Council of Churches (Montreux, Switzerland, 1977), in *The Security Trap*, ed. José-Antonio Viera Gallo (Rome: IDOC International, 1979), p. 127.

2. Ibid., p. 117.

3. Dana J. Blackstock, *Trembling Like Trees in the Wind* (Louisville: Presbyterian Church U.S.A., 2003).

4. Paul Tillich, in *Theology of Peace*, ed. Ronald Stone (Louisville: Westminster John Knox Press, 1990), p. 159. In addition to the quote, the preceding two paragraphs represent Paul Tillich's ideas.

5. Blackstock, *Trembling Like Trees*.

6. Ibid.

7. "Resolution on Challenges to Global Security," *Church and Society* (July/August 2002): 80.

8. "Congressional Research Service," reported in Blackstock, *Trembling Like Trees*.

9. Quoted in Richard W. Bauer, Carol Meier, Richard E. Moore, and Henry Carter Rogers, *A History of Civil Disobedience: In Defense of the Reverend Maurice Mc-Crackin*, n.d., mimeographed, p. 14.

10. Quentin Skinner, *The Foundations of Modern Political Thought*, vol. 2 (London: Cambridge University Press, 1978), p. 338.

11. For the history of Clergy and Laity Concerned about Vietnam, see Mitchell K. Hall, *Because of Their Faith: CALCAV and Religious Opposition to the Vietnam War* (New York: Columbia University Press, 1990).

12. The debates about Martin Luther King Jr.'s leadership continue, but there is widespread recognition that the movement for civil rights was clearly its most successful period inspired by King and led by black Christian clergy. See Taylor Branch, *Parting the Waters: America in the King Years 1954–63* (New York: Simon and Schuster, 1988).

13. See Michael Hardt and Antonio Negri, *Empire* (Cambridge, Mass.: Harvard University Press, 2000).

14. Glen Stassen, ed., *Just Peacemaking: Ten Practices for Abolishing War* (Cleveland: Pilgrim Press, 1989), pp. 133–155.

15. See Reinhold Niebuhr, *Moral Man and Immoral Society* (New York: Charles Scribner's Sons, 1952), pp. 83–112. Also Reinhold Niebuhr, *Christian Realism and Political Problems* (Charles Scribner's Sons, 1953), pp. 15–32, 105–174.

16. For further discussion of the pros and cons and means of resistance, see Dana W. Wilbanks and Ronald H. Stone, *Presbyterians and Peacemaking: Are We Now Called to Resistance* (New York: Advisory Council on Church and Society, 1985), pp. 48–57.

17. Rebecca Solnit, *Savage Dreams* (Berkeley: University of California Press, 1994).

18. Barbara G. Green, "Militarism and Arms Control," *Church and Society* (November/December, 1999): 59.

19. Six pages of this chapter are edited material previously published in Ronald H. Stone and Dana W. Wilbanks, eds., *The Peacemaking Struggle: Militarism and Resistance* (Washington, D.C.: University Press of America, 1985), pp. 1–11.

*II*

# BIBLICAL AND HISTORICAL ROOTS OF RESISTANCE

# 9

# The Subversive Kingship of Jesus in Luke

## *Paul Hertig*

*The* Gospel of Luke portrays Jesus as a king on a journey, proclaiming the kingdom of God. "Soon afterwards he went on through cities and villages, proclaiming and bringing the good news of the kingdom of God" (Luke 8:1). Jesus traveled continuously, announcing and enacting this reign. Luke elucidates his journey motif when seemingly out of nowhere in the narrative he suddenly states, "When the days drew near for him to be taken up, he set his face to go to Jerusalem" (9:51). The plot thickens as Jesus and his disciples "went on their way" (10:38) and as "Jesus went through one town and village after another, teaching as he made his way to Jerusalem" (13:22; cf. 17:11). The ultimate destiny of this journey-king is Jerusalem, where he will announce his kingdom. After great anticipation in the narrative, the king finally arrives in Jerusalem (19:28).

Let's look closely at the details. In 19:30 he sends his disciples to find a colt (this could be the colt of a horse or donkey, but Matthew and John explicitly state "a donkey"). Jesus tells them to say, "the Lord needs it" (19:31). For Luke and his readers, "the Lord" refers to Jesus' unique messianic authority.[1] This is illustrated by the subsequent verses in which the disciples declare to the "lords" of the colt that the "Lord" needs it (19:32–33).

What an extraordinary king this is! Why does one calling himself "Lord" *need* it? This king does not even have a colt. He has to borrow it! No royal blanket is laid on the colt; the disciples decorate it with their cloaks (19:35). During the procession, no red carpet is rolled out; they spread their cloaks on the road (19:36).

This is a most unusual manner of asserting authority. The episode is dripping with irony. Barclay perceptively observes that:

> It was an act of glorious defiance and of superlative courage. By this time there was a price on Jesus' head (John 11:57). It would have been natural that, if he must go into Jerusalem at all, he should have slipped in unseen and hidden away in some secret place in the back streets. But he entered in such a way as to focus the whole lime-light upon himself and to occupy the centre of the stage. It is a breath-taking thing to think of a man with a price upon his head, an outlaw, deliberately riding into a city in such a way that every eye was fixed upon him. It is impossible to exaggerate the sheer courage of Jesus.[2]

This journey event was an explicit claim to kingship, one last appeal in fulfillment of Zechariah 9:9: "Even now, will you not take me as your king?"[3] This declaration of kingship was also an act of defiance. The passage is dripping with irony. Kings rode horses in war, but they rode donkeys in peace. Jesus comes not as a triumphant military hero as the crowd anticipated, but as a king of peace. In this sense, the passage has a tone of subversion and defiance. By subverting status-quo kingship, Jesus asserts his authority and proclaims a new form of kingship.

During this grand procession into Jerusalem, a multitude of disciples openly celebrate God's reign, loudly praising God for the miracles they have seen, saying, "Blessed is the coming one, the king who comes in the name of the Lord! Peace in heaven, and glory in the highest heaven" (19:37–38). The Galilean disciples had seen Jesus' mighty deeds and were now streaming in for the Passover, a celebration of God's victory over darkness and death through the exodus. But notice the ironic focus on "peace" during this victory procession (19:38, 42).

The Pharisees tell Jesus to rebuke the disciples for declaring his messianic kingship, but Jesus does not stop them, proclaiming that "even the stones will cry out" (19:39–40). Rather than succumb to the Pharisees' desire to silence his claim to kingship, Jesus openly declares it. Furthermore, Jesus describes this moment as a day of peace, but hidden from their eyes (19:42–44). Therefore, judgment comes into view and will occur "because you did not recognize the time of God's coming to you" (19:44).

Jesus continues to assert his authority, this time visibly, casting out the people selling in the temple and calling it "a den of robbers" (19:45–46). The verb "cast out" is utilized elsewhere of exorcisms, implying that "the money changers are roughly equivalent to unclean spirits who profane the holy place."[4] The temple was a commercial banking center in Jesus' day. Luke's account reminds us that religion is not about money, commerce, or power. "'My house will be a house of prayer'; but you have made it a den of robbers"

(19:46). True worship of God is relational through prayer, not merely trans-actional. Nolland observes that "it is as a royal figure making a regal entry into Jerusalem that the Lukan Jesus acts to purify the worship of the temple."[5] The chief priests, scribes, and leaders respond by plotting to kill Jesus, but they are afraid of the people (19:47). In contrast, the authority of Jesus neither caters to the whims of people nor is motivated by fear, but is authentically from God, leaving people "spellbound" (19:48).

The emphasis of the "cleansing" of the temple passage "lies in the objection to Jesus' authority," indicated by the direct questioning of Jesus' authority in the succeeding passage of 20:1–8 and in Jesus' eviction as the "rejected stone" in 20:9–18 in the parable.[6] In this parable, vineyard tenants reject and kill the owner's beloved son, stating, "The stone the builders rejected has become the cornerstone" (20:17).

## PUTTING CAESAR IN HIS PLACE

Clever spies who are then sent to Jesus inquire into whether it is lawful to pay taxes to Caesar (20:20–22). Perceiving their duplicity, Jesus asks whose image and inscription is on a denarius. They say, "Caesar's." Jesus replies, "Give unto Caesar the things of Caesar, and give unto God the things of God" (literal Greek rendering). Jesus' answer astonishes and silences the people. It is brilliant partially because he outwits the inquisitors, saying neither "yes" nor "no." But far from avoiding their question, Jesus has neither totally affirmed nor totally denied Caesar's authority.

An affirmative answer would have dissociated Jesus from the Jews who deeply resented this tax because (1) the image of the emperor on the silver coin, along with its claims for Roman rule based on divine origin, was forbidden by Jewish law as a graven image (Exod. 20:23; Deut. 7:25),[7] and (2) it signified that the Jewish nation was under Gentile domination. In fact, when the Roman Empire initially brought Palestine under its taxing structure in 6–7 C.E., riots and petitions occurred.[8] A negative answer, on the other hand, would have allowed the spies to charge Jesus with treason for breaking Roman law.

Is Jesus separating Caesar and God into two independent, secular and sacred compartments? This longstanding interpretation represents a misunderstanding. The fact that God created us and gave us life on earth makes us subject to two kingdoms, an earthly and a heavenly kingdom. We are loyal conditionally to one and unconditionally to the other.[9]

Caesar has a right to collect taxes to perform his governmental duties. This is the only particular function of Caesar that Jesus authorizes in the text. But the weight falls on the claims of God. If Caesar were to begin to claim for his own what belongs to God, which is unconditional and absolute obedience, then he has stepped outside his sphere of responsibility. "The effect of introducing the claims of God is to limit the claims of Caesar without attempting to specify where that limit should be drawn."[10] Even Caesar must give to God what is God's. In Acts 12:21–23, for instance, when the crowds shouted that Herod had the voice of a god, Herod was eaten by worms and died because he did not give praise to God!

Luke has actually put Caesar in his place: (1) Jesus recognizes that Caesar needs taxes to perform his functions in his role as a public servant; (2) Jesus limits the rights of Caesar. He has no right to God's domain, that is, to absolute authority. Such is the role attempted by the anti-Christ. In a subtle way, Jesus is asserting his authority over Caesar! Jesus' assertion of authority and defiance of corrupt authority were key issues leading to his crucifixion.

Jacques Ellul points out that an individual mark in the Roman world, much like cattle brands in the nineteenth-century American West, signified ownership. People of the Roman world had their own marks on a seal, stamp, or painted sign. The image of Caesar on this coin was not ornamentation, nor merely a symbol of honor. It denoted that "all the money in circulation in the empire belonged to Caesar."[11] The image on the money would change when the emperor died. The Maccabees demonstrated their understanding of the issue of currency as a sign of kingship by immediately issuing their own currency when Jerusalem was freed from Syrian domination.[12]

Therefore, Jesus' statement "Render to Caesar what is Caesar's" acknowledges that the coin belongs to Caesar. He can have his coin back, but he cannot have God's sovereignty! The verb "render" has the sense of giving back to someone that which belongs to him.[13] Jesus is acknowledging the evidence that the coin bears Caesar's mark. While he has authority to charge taxes for his public duties, this is the limit of his power as well. Paying taxes to him is not paying allegiance to him.[14]

Jesus' response to the spies implies that whatever does not bear the mark of Caesar does not belong to him. "It all belongs to God. This is where the real conscientious objection arises. Caesar has no right whatever to the rest."[15] While God's domain is not limited to coins, Caesar's domain is limited. "The Christian owes Caesar something but not everything. . . . The demands of God are infinitely greater."[16] Those who hold political power receive it from God. While Jesus did not oppose all forms of power, he was suspicious of most forms of power and radically challenged them, but he did not use violent means to destroy them.[17]

In Jerusalem, Jesus relentlessly asserts his authority over all. This text fits its narrative context through Jesus' assertion of power over Caesar and over all of life. Caesar cannot intrude on God's kingship.

During the Enlightenment period, the world was divided into the public world of facts and the private world of ideas. Politics and the state were relegated to the public realm; religion and morality pertained to the private realm. The church gradually withdrew from the complex social world.[18] Its proof-text interpretation of the "give unto Caesar what is Caesar's" text gave reason to avoid the public realm and to compartmentalize Christian faith into a privatized, spiritual realm. A two-kingdom ideology has been widely embraced since the Enlightenment, illustrated by the Christians who were passive during the Holocaust. This ideology depicts the gospel of John Locke, not the Gospel of St. Luke.[19] A strict separation between Caesar's and God's realms of authority would not have surfaced in the minds of Jesus and his Jewish audience, who would have surely presumed that the law of God applies to all of life.[20] This is reaffirmed in the Presbyterian Social Witness Policy Statement of 1974 that "separation of church and state does not mean separation of religion from government or politics, nor the divorce of religion's basic moral and ethical principles from the conduct of public affairs."[21]

Richard John Neuhaus warns of the dangers of religion exiled from the public square. When religion becomes privatized, public moral decisions must still be made. The government that makes laws based on decisions of right and wrong must fill this vacuum. Therefore, the government replaces religion and now sets the moral agenda for the people.[22] The church is on the sidelines:

> It is simply a matter of choosing sides, or like the awkward boy in a game of sandlot baseball, hoping to be chosen by one side or another. Having been permitted to play, the church becomes the team moralizer, offering "homilies and sentiments" in support of its goals and against its opposition.[23]

Christianity becomes delighted to participate as a guest in the public debate and follows the guidelines approved by the host.[24] The church often sanctions a belief that religion has no right to intrude on politics and society, thus justifying its retreat from the world. This passage on Caesar, however, calls the church to resist totalitarian ideologies, whether far left or far right. When governing authorities demand ultimate allegiance from those whom they serve, they have encroached upon God's sphere of sovereignty.[25] Bonhoeffer recognized when this occurred, when the government made itself master over the beliefs of the congregation, and he began asking whether wickedness should be allowed to run its cruel course.[26] Once the congregation poses such questions, it has reasserted itself amid the thorny issues and complex questions of the public arena. Jesus dealt with such issues when confronted with the authority of Caesar, and he wisely announced Caesar's limits but chose not to respond violently.

## Oppressive Religious Practice

In a proceeding passage, Jesus reasserts the public nature of religion while watching the wealthy put their gifts into the treasury. He calls attention to a woman who put in two lepta (small copper coins) and says, "Truly I tell you, this poor widow has put in more than any one of them; for all of them have contributed out of excess, but she out of her poverty has put in all she had to live on" (21:1–4). How could she have put in "more than any one of them" when she actually put in the minimum offering?[27] Jesus introduces a new way to measure an offering. If measured by what is left over after giving, she outgave them all! This supports the concept of proportional giving or a graduated "tithe" that increases the percentage of giving, even above a tithe, as income increases. The concept stimulates generous stewardship, exemplified by some who have given more than 50 percent of their income yet live more luxuriously than others who give 10 percent.[28]

Jesus honors the contribution of the poor with dignity in the narrative, while the rich who are present provide no such model of sacrifice. Jesus' authority has been reasserted; sacrifice and stewardship have been redefined. A poor widow was "almost proverbial for the poorest of people."[29] In this first-century context, widows had a great difficulty acquiring money or means for survival. Jesus has turned the hierarchy upside down by commending the smallest giver for making the greatest sacrifice in contrast to the biggest givers who gave out of their abundance. One in every seven verses in Luke deals with money or material things, and often the pious poor are contrasted with the wasteful rich. Luke highlights that the use of money was a vital social justice issue in an era when wealthy political and religious leaders exploited and distanced themselves from the poor masses, called "people of the land."

In the preceding passage, Jesus had already condemned the oppressive religious practices of the scribes who "swallow widows' houses and for the sake of appearance say long prayers" (20:47). The theme is consistent with Jesus' repudiation of the pious offering of the rich that appears honorable but is dishonorable in light of Jesus' commendation of the sacrificial offering of the poor widow that is tiny only in appearance.

John Calvin urged church leaders in his day to remember the ancient councils which decreed that the bishop should live in a small dwelling near the church with a frugal table and furniture. He accused church leaders of living in "the luxury and the corruption of the times" while ignoring the great needs of the poor. He called this a squandering in disobedience to Christ's commands, accusing the leaders of "building temples, erecting statues, burying plate, and providing costly garments" instead of distributing to the poor. In his *Institutes*, Calvin states that "the daily alms are swallowed up in this abyss."[30] Clearly, Jesus "does not endorse any religious system which supports wealthy institutions or clergy at the expense of poor widows."[31]

Neither does Jesus tolerate discussions about greatness among his disciples. During their dispute about who is the greatest, he reminds them that Gentile kings, that is, those presently ruling, "lord it over" their people and that those in authority are called "benefactors" (22:24–25). The term in the Roman Empire depicted honor among rulers but did not necessarily represent services rendered. Rather than indicating "spontaneous expressions of public spirit," benefaction was primarily "part of a fierce competition for public office."[32] Political leaders are hardly different today.

## SERVANTHOOD AS SOCIAL RESISTANCE

Jesus envisions a counter-community with his contrasting mandate: "But not so with you; rather the greatest among you must become like the youngest, and the leader as one who serves" (22:26). Jesus radically calls for an upside-down community that turns the tables on hierarchy and political power games. Jesus also contrasts himself with contemporary authorities through the declaration "But I am among you as one who serves" (22:27). Jesus explicitly contrasts his style of leadership with the popular style of political authorities in his day. In the shadow of the cross, while the disciples are arguing about their own greatness, Jesus depicts himself as a true benefactor (a kind helper) and contemporary leaders as false benefactors (lording it over others). For Jesus, the true sign of authority is through genuine servanthood. Jesus resists any form of "servanthood" that serves oneself at the expense of others. Benefactors often utilize the language and actions of servanthood in order to control others. True servanthood genuinely benefits others through self-sacrifice. The cross that looms large in this narrative depicts this reality.

Jesus vividly illustrates the call to servanthood by reminding his disciples that he sent them out without purse, bag, or sandals, but that all of their needs were provided (22:35). Then he adds a sobering thought. Now you will need these things, even a sword, for it is written (22:36–37). Suddenly the disciples pull out two swords and Jesus replies, "It is enough" (22:38). How do we explain this strange turn of events? A key to interpreting this passage is Jesus' "But now," implying that everything will now be different from before (22:36). They will have to fend for themselves; they will need to have a purse, bag, sandals, even a sword.

This passage indicates both impending rejection and impending danger. Not only were the disciples' lives in danger, but it follows that people might become reluctant to show them hospitality because it may be dangerous to do so. The disciples will have difficulty in attaining resources. But what about the sword? The statement is surprising, but more so is the reason given: "For I tell you, this scripture must be fulfilled in me, 'And he was numbered among the lawless'" (22:37). This fulfillment citation from Isaiah 53:12 is in reference to Jesus' vicarious suffering: "because he poured out himself to death and he was numbered among the lawless. But he himself bore the sins of many and on account of their sins was handed over" (Isaiah 53:12).

In fulfillment of Isaiah 53:12, Jesus was about to be "numbered among the lawless," condemned as a criminal, and treated as an outlaw. The disciples must now face the same treatment.

## CYNICISM AS SOCIAL RESISTANCE

Josephus reported that Essenes who went on a journey had no need of supplies because they knew they would meet fellow members of their order along the way. However, they carried arms to guard themselves against bandits.[33] In the case of Jesus' disciples, they would not necessarily need protection against bandits, but they would be reckoned as bandits by authorities. In other words, Jesus is being figurative, probably even cynical, about the authorities. But the disciples take him literally and miss the point.

They pull out two swords and Jesus says, "It is enough" or "enough of this" (22:38). A few hours later, when Jesus was arrested, one of the disciples drew a sword and cut off an ear of the high priest's slave, but Jesus said, "No more of this" (22:51), in a similar vein as "enough of this." In the Matthew account, Jesus says, "Put your sword back in its place, for all who draw the sword will die by the sword. Do you think I cannot call on my Father, and he will at once put at my disposal more than twelve legions of angels?" (Matt. 26:52–53). Since violence breeds violence in the Scripture, Jesus is like the noble warrior whose success is not in fighting and winning countless battles, but in subduing the enemy without going into battle.

But in our world, "there are many causes worth killing for but few or any worth dying for."[34] The "good guys" tend not to question what their soldiers do as long as they are not dying in combat. If the enemy incurs casualties, that is the enemy's predicament. The implication is that the lives of our own are more precious than the lives of those in other parts of the world. "This doctrine is perfect for the consumerist age, proposing as it does that there is no reason to feel guilty about sitting at home and watching the war on television."[35] It is no skin off of our own backs:

The nation's religions—particularly the mainstream Protestant denominations—are far too busy worrying about who can marry whom and which songs are too offensive to sing. Why spend precious resources fighting over fighting? It is not, after all, as though any of this warfare affects anybody who actually matters, like a congregant or a member of a favored minority group.[36]

In fact, we tend to pray for our own soldiers and for our own safety, but not for the soldiers on the other side of the conflict or for the safety of civilians of the enemy.[37] How we pray indicates our own distorted viewpoints on violence. Are we really inviting God and God's wisdom into the matter, or are we simply asking God to take our side so that we might be safe at the expense of the lives of people whom we do not know?

Jesus and the disciples were not Zealots with weapons of war. For Jesus to really mean that two swords would be enough for battle against the authorities that came to arrest him would be absurd. "Enough of this" meant that "they had misunderstood his sad irony, and it was time to drop the subject."[38] Jesus had dramatically depicted the far-reaching change that was now occurring among the authorities from the previous missionary journey of the disciples to the present debacle of the cross. Neither the religious authorities nor the disciples understood what was about to occur.

## NAMING EVIL AUTHORITY

During the dark hours of betrayal and arrest, Jesus explicitly names the evil authority of the chief priests, officers of the temple, and elders: "But this is your hour, and the power of darkness reigns" (22:52–53). The term for "power" literally means "authority." The religious authorities were afraid to assert their power against Jesus during daylight hours when he was in the temple, but now they assert their power away from the temple and in the secrecy of the night. Religious leaders are in no way exempt from utilizing their power for evil; in fact, their temptations have often proven irresistible in the course of history. We do not have to go as far back as the Crusades to recognize evil done in the name of Christianity. In recent history, for instance, a church member prayed for an abortion doctor while in church on Sunday and then murdered him during the week.

After Jesus has been mocked and beaten, a cross-examination takes place during a religious assembly. Jesus is asked, "If you are the Messiah, tell us" (22:67). Jesus refuses to answer the council of elders directly: "If I tell you, you will not believe; and if I question you, you will not answer" (22:67–68). There are at least two shades of meaning behind Jesus' elusive answer: (1) he will not respond directly to unbelief; (2) because Jesus and the religious authorities have different definitions of the Messiah, to say "yes" would cause Jesus to be misunderstood. But Jesus becomes more explicit with an additional comment: "But from now on the Son of Man will be seated at the right hand of the mighty God" (22:69). In other words, Jesus declares that his authority is far greater than theirs.

However, they seek a more direct answer. After sending spies and beating around the bush, they now ask, "Are you, then, the Son of God?" (22:70). Jesus again answers indirectly: "You say that I am." This is the literal Greek rendering as found in the New Revised Standard Version. The New International Version translation is unfortunate. Jesus does not say "yes." He cannot reply in the affirmative because Jesus' understanding differs from theirs, yet he cannot deny the term "the Son of God" either. Thus, he must remain vague. In this passage, Jesus clearly rejects the religious authority of the full religious assembly and declares his authority to be greater. The "whole multitude" of religious leaders then bring him before Pilate with several accusations, including that Jesus says he is "the Messiah, a king" (23:1–3).

The council of Jews had asked Jesus if he was "the Messiah." Pilate asks a different question: "Are you the king of the Jews?" (23:3). Naturally, Pilate is concerned about Jesus' political claims. Again, Jesus does not answer in the affirmative. He literally says, "You are saying so" (23:3). The "you" is emphatic in the Greek. Once again, Jesus refuses to answer the question. He was not the king of the Jews in the sense that Pilate meant. Neither was he a Zealot, inciting an insurrection. Nor did he claim to be a political king seeking a throne in the Gentile understanding of the word. "You are saying so" means that you are saying it according to your understanding.

## SILENCE AS JUDICIAL RESISTANCE

Pilate finds no basis for the accusations and sends Jesus off to Herod, who was in Jerusalem at the time. Herod anticipated the encounter with gladness, because he had long desired to see Jesus and hoped he would perform a sign (23:8). Many an evangelist or spiritual leader would have seen this as a golden opportunity to have a spiritual impact on a powerful political leader. Surprisingly, after Herod questions him at some length, Jesus gives no answer (23:9). How could this be? Herod is the only person to whom Jesus refuses to talk during his trial, *and Herod had been eager to talk to Jesus and see a sign*. This is Herod Antipas, earlier depicted as being rebuked by John the Baptist "because of all the evil things" that he had done (3:19), who imprisoned and beheaded John (3:20) and sought to kill Jesus (13:31). Herod committed insidious crimes and lived a life of decadence. His ruthless father had murdered the children of Bethlehem after Jesus was born. Why would Jesus answer to such an evil man? Jesus' non-answer indicates his defiance of Herod's authority. Herod is the only person to whom Jesus says nothing at all! Furthermore, if Jesus had agreed to Herod's request and given a sign, then he would be submitting to Herod's authority on Herod's terms, rather than to God's authority on God's terms.

In fact, Herod and his soldiers then wielded their power by mocking Jesus and placing an elegant robe on him (23:11). Interestingly, Herod and Pilate, former enemies, became friends on that day. Both rulers made light of Jesus' authority, but both rulers would soon stand helpless when darkness came over the land at noon.

Ellul summarizes that, in these passages, Jesus' attitude was "one of total rejection and scorn for all religious or political authority. It seems that Jesus did not regard these authorities as in any way just and that it was thus completely useless to defend himself."[39] Jesus' spoken and unspoken responses to the authorities were subversive in tone. Roman law was considered one of the great justice systems in history. But Jesus was not given a fair trial. Neither Pilate nor Herod felt that he deserved death (23:13–16). But the Jewish authorities had appealed to them with false accusations in order to try Jesus unjustly. After the mob cries out again and again, Pilate finally grants their wish (23:18–24). The mob condemns an innocent man and Pilate goes along with it. Even within the great systems of justice, great injustices take place. The trial of Jesus serves as a great warning of the corruption of power. It is among the utmost of Christian responsibilities to keep justice systems in check.

## JESUS UNVEILS INJUSTICE

Jesus "was the victim of lies and innuendo, frame-ups, and a rigged jury" by supposedly the wisest and most righteous leaders of the land under a great justice system.[40] John Steinbeck once stated that "Power does not corrupt. Fear corrupts, perhaps the fear of a loss of power."[41] Fear of loss of power was clearly at work during Jesus' time in Jerusalem and led to the cross. Self-preservation was the leaders' common objective. By confronting a corrupt religious institution and justice system, Jesus threatened their very existence. In the words of Walter Wink,

> What killed Jesus was not irreligion, but religion itself; not lawlessness, but precisely the law; not anarchy, but the upholders of order. It was not the bestial but those considered best who crucified the one in whom the divine Wisdom was visibly incarnate. And because he was not only innocent, but the very embodiment of true religion, true law, and true order, this victim exposed their violence for what it was: not the defense of society, but an attack against God.[42]

When Jesus was brought before the authority of the government of his day, he was not giving it legitimacy but unveiling a form of injustice disguised as justice.[43] The power of darkness was at work throughout the entire trial.

At noon, darkness came over the land, and the sun stopped shining (23:44–45). These cosmic signs are symbolic not only of the work of darkness that brought Jesus to the cross, but also of Jesus' authority over all creation. The death of the Lord ceased the sun from shining and caused the curtain of the temple to be torn in two. No king or religious leader could match this authority. This cosmic event is a reminder that "all life is from God, the whole universe shares together bane and blessing, life and death, and in the final reign of God: 'the creation itself will be set free.'"[44]

During his trial, Jesus resisted corrupt human authority, was both passively and actively noncooperative, but never called for a revolt. Leading up to his trial, he called for people to recognize "the things that make for peace" but acknowledged that such peace was hidden from their eyes (19:42). Jesus ushered in an alternative kingdom, evidenced in a counter-community that did not operate according to the accepted standards of authority and hierarchy, but one that treated all people with fairness and justice, a servant society that was counter-cultural and lived by principles of love, justice, mercy, and forgiveness. Rather than oppress the poor and suffering as the religious and political leaders often did in his day, the journey-king served those whom he encountered and suffered for all people. Jesus' authentic encounters with ordinary people and political and religious leaders in the public square set an important example for Christians today. Rather than set up counter-communities in the desert, we should "stay in society and set up in it communities that obey other rules and other laws" since it is difficult to change the phenomenon of power.[45]

Stephen L. Carter observes that religion is almost always at its best when it is able to resist. When religion goes against the grain of mainstream culture, both religion and culture are changed in the encounter. Religious resistance becomes a "source of diversity, of dialogue, and, ultimately, of change."[46]

While resistance is a necessary aspect of a religion's survival, it often becomes its strength or its peril. Thus, if the church resists the myriad of temptations offered by the world, including its comforts, tantalizing pleasures, and shortcuts to spiritual and political power, and if the state allows a broad range of religious freedom "to ensure that its own hands are tied,"[47] then the public square will once again become a lively place of exchange and accountability for church and state.

## SOCIAL RESISTANCE FOR
## PRESBYTERIAN SOCIAL WITNESS

The contemporary discussion of a "naked public square" reveals that Christianity has become privatized and thus has lost its meaning, relevance, and power. When religion was exiled from the public square, the vacuum was filled with power-hungry "demons." Rather than comfortably retreat from complex issues in a rapidly changing "postmodern" society, the Presbyterian Church must return to the public square and reengage in public issues. The church must rediscover itself as a transforming agent in an ever-changing context.

When Jesus exorcised those who were selling in the temple (19:45), he was preparing space for a return to prayer and contemplation in the public square (19:46). Likewise, the church today must resist the temptations of consumerism and hypercapitalism. When a dip occurs in the stock market, rather than worry about our own retirement funds, we should pray and contemplate on behalf of those who will be evicted from their apartments the next day and will be on the streets. At a recent Christian gathering, when a drop in the Dow Jones was announced, an unretired Christian scholar replied in anguish, "Oh, my retirement; oh, my retirement." In contrast, consider a poor person facing eviction who might cry out in anguish, "Oh, my God; oh, my God!"

On the global scene, $300 billion in subsidies allows farmers of wealthy nations to saturate the global market with cheap corn, cotton, and other produce. "We call it economic terrorism, because they've wiped out more people with their subsidies than with any bomb," exclaims Uruguayan rancher Juan Carlos Planchon.[48]

There is a time for the church to respond to commercialism with the kind of righteous anger that Jesus modeled. But in order to do so, the church must first cease to be a consumer marketplace in its values and priorities. The church should resist what it ought to resist, rather than resist change. There are glimmers of hope as churches gradually wake up to economic disparities, evidenced in a growing number of churches that now serve fair-trade coffee after their Sunday services. This simple change in the Sunday morning social hour allows an increasing number of farmers from poor nations to make a living in the global market. It also wakes up parishioners to the importance of resisting the norm in daily choices they make when shopping and consuming. It reminds them that they can even make a difference in the lives of the "other" whom they have never met.

In our call to resist global oppression, unjust hierarchies, and power abuse, we are challenged to turn from the assumption that God is on our side at the expense of people we do not know. When the authorities approached to arrest Jesus, his disciples asked, "Lord, should we strike with the sword?" Before listening for an answer to their prayer, one of them struck a stranger, the slave of the high priest, and cut off his right ear. Jesus replied, "No more of this!" and healed him (22:49–51).

When we contemplate or pray about injustice, war, and violence, we must not pray for God to take our side so that we might be safe at the expense of the lives of "strangers." In fact, Jesus hung around with the strangers of society who were already written off by political and religious leaders (Luke 22:36–37, 59–60; cf. 7:34).

One such example is the widow who gave all that she had. The church, when wed to business principles, tends not to make such model sacrifices. It can be cold and calculative in its giving. We must ask ourselves, how are we different from the benefactors of the world of Luke who gave for the sake of their own benefit or in order to control others?

Nearly seventy years ago, H. Richard Niebuhr declared that the problem is not the church in the world but the world in the church. The church "has identified itself too intimately with capitalism, with the philosophy of individualism, and with the imperialism of the West," declared Niebuhr.[49] He challenged the church to revolt against secularization and the system of worldliness by transferring its dependence on the systems of the world to dependence on God. The contemporary church has often been characterized by production and consumption rather than by sacrifice and service to the world. The church is capable of raising huge sums of money and putting on big productions but is often powerless in resisting the injustices of the world. Authentic Christianity resists the world in the church and extends outward to the church in the world.

Resistance of the world in the church demands the reexploration of upward mobility, a social norm blindly obeyed without the blinking of an eye. A new job must have higher pay and status. A new car or home must be bigger or with better features. Churches must increase their membership roles and cash flow, build bigger buildings, and hire more professional staff.

We feel comfortable as long as we are in a somewhat in-between state, moving from our world of privileges to occasional excursions into the world of the less privileged. This relieves our guilt. But if we choose to be "in between" we remain privileged because we benefit from the system of injustice that we seek to elude. To choose both sides means to compromise and to cling to a lifestyle of which we do not wholeheartedly approve.

According to Bryan Stone: "Compassion is not a neutral charity, inattentive to the social arrangements between the givers of the charity and the receivers of the charity."[50] In the words of Desmond Tutu, Anglican bishop of South Africa: "If you are neutral in a situation of injustice, you have chosen the side of the oppressor. If an elephant has his foot on the tail of the mouse, and you say you are neutral, the mouse will not appreciate your neutrality."[51]

However, when we disconnect ourselves from certain loyalties and experience downward mobility, we disunite ourselves from a privileged system of favoritism. To announce his kingship, Jesus rode into Jerusalem on a borrowed donkey. He had no palace, much less a place to lay his head. He was preparing for further downward mobility, a shameful crucifixion arising from unjust decisions of the upholders of religion and law. Already he had stepped off the throne and come to earth as a baby. But the miraculous entry was only the beginning of a series of downwardly mobile acts of the Messiah. A miracle interrupts the normal course of nature. Downward mobility interrupts the accepted norm of upward mobility and thus has transforming power.

Just as it was unnatural for Jesus to step down from his throne and choose downward mobility, it is unnatural for us as well. It takes a paradigm shift to resist the accepted pattern of upward mobility and become downwardly mobile. But such a shift is foundational for the mission of the church and its engagement in the naked public square.

## NOTES

1. John Nolland, *Word Biblical Commentary*, vol. 35c, *Luke 18:35–24:53* (Dallas: Word Books, 1993), p. 925. Murray J. Harris has observed that the concept of Jesus as "Lord" arose during Jesus' earthly life "as a consequence of His authoritative teaching and divine power" and that the church's earliest confession of faith repudiated "their former allegiance to many pagan 'lords,'" reaffirming "their loyalty to the one Lord through and in whom they existed"; in "Lord," *The International Standard Bible Encyclopedia*, ed. Geoffrey Bromiley, 4 vols., fully revised (Grand Rapids, Mich.: Eerdmans, 1990), vol. 3, p. 158.

2. William Barclay, *The Gospel of Luke*, revised edition (Philadelphia: Westminster Press, 1975), p. 239.

3. Ibid., p. 240.

4. Luke Timothy Johnson, *The Gospel of Luke*, Sacra Pagina Series, vol. 3 (Collegeville, Minn.: Liturgical Press, Michael Glazier Book, 1991), p. 299. The uses of *ekballo* for exorcisms abound. See Luke 9:40, 49; 11:14–15, 18–20.

5. Nolland, *Word Biblical Commentary*, p. 937.

6. E. Earle Ellis, *The Gospel of Luke: The New Century Bible Commentary*, revised edition (Grand Rapids, Mich.: Eerdmans, 1981), p. 231.

7. Robert C. Tannehill, *Abingdon New Testament Commentaries: Luke* (Nashville: Abingdon Press, 1996), p. 293.

8. Nolland, *Word Biblical Commentary*, p. 961. "The Jewish historian Josephus reported that in the year 6 C.E. Judas the Galilean had declared it to be treason against God to pay taxes to Rome. It is an atmosphere of anti-Roman revolts, both in fact and in plotting" when Jesus is asked the question about paying taxes to Caesar. Fred B. Craddock, *Luke, Interpretation, A Bible Commentary for Teaching and Preaching* (Louisville: John Knox Press, 1990), p. 236).

9. C. B. Caird, *The Pelican New Testament Commentaries: The Gospel of Saint Luke* (Baltimore: Penguin Books, 1963), p. 222.

10. Tannehill, *Luke*, p. 294; Caird, *The Gospel of Saint Luke*, p. 223.

11. Jacques Ellul, *Anarchy and Christianity*, trans. Geoffrey W. Bromiley (Grand Rapids, Mich.: Eerdmans, 1991), pp. 59–60.

12. Barclay, *The Gospel of Luke*, p. 248.

13. F. F. Bruce, *The Hard Sayings of Jesus* (Downers Grove, Ill.: InterVarsity Press, 1983), p. 216.

14. Ellul, *Anarchy and Christianity*, 60. Lugo argues that the verb "render" implies a moral obligation to pay the taxes as a proper response "to the lawful demands of duly constituted authority" and that this reading calls the Zealot's intent upon holy war into question. Luis E. Lugo, "Caesar's Coin and the Politics of the Kingdom: A Pluralist Perspective," in *Caesar's Coin Revisited: Christians and the Limits of Government*, ed. Michael Cromartie (Grand Rapids, Mich.: Eerdmans, 1996), p. 8.

15. Ibid.

16. David E. Garland, *The NIV Application Commentary: Mark* (Grand Rapids, Mich.: Zondervan, 1966), p. 466.

17. Ellul, *Anarchy and Christianity*, p. 56.

18. David J. Bosch, *Transforming Mission: Paradigm Shifts in Theology of Mission* (Maryknoll, N.Y.: Orbis, 1991), p. 401.

19. This statement is a variation on one made by Lugo, "Caesar's Coin," p. 2.

20. Ibid.

21. Advisory Committee on Social Witness Policy, *Presbyterian Social Witness Policy Compilation* (Louisville: Presbyterian Church U.S.A., 2000), p. 348.

22. Richard John Neuhaus, *The Naked Public Square* (Grand Rapids, Mich.: Eerdmans, 1984), pp. 86–87.

23. Ibid., p. 236.

24. Ibid., p. 142.

25. Lugo, "Caesar's Coin," p. 6.

26. Jean Bethke Elshtain, "Caesar, Sovereignty, and Bonhoeffer," in *Caesar's Coin Revisited: Christians and the Limits of Government*, ed. Michael Cromartie (Grand Rapids, Mich.: Eerdmans, 1996), pp. 55–56.

27. Some Jewish commentators indicate that worshippers were not allowed to make gifts less than two lepta (two copper coins).

28. Donald B. Kraybill, *The Upside-Down Kingdom*, revised edition (Scottdale, Penn.: Herald Press, 1990), pp. 138–139; Gene A. Getz, *A Biblical Theology of Material Possessions* (Chicago: Moody Press, 1990), pp. 99–100.

29. Leon Morris, *The Gospel According to St. Luke* (Grand Rapids, Mich.: Eerdmans, 1974), p. 294.

30. John Calvin, *Institutes of the Christian Religion*, trans. Henry Beveridge (Grand Rapids, Mich.: Eerdmans, 1981), pp. 351, 352.

31. David L. Tiede, *Luke: Augsburg Commentary on the New Testament* (Minneapolis: Augsburg Publishing House, 1988), p. 355.

32. Halvor Moxnes, "Patron-Client Relations and the New Community in Luke-Acts," in *The Social World of Luke-Acts*, ed. Jerome H. Neyrey (Peabody, Mass.: Hendrickson, 1991), p. 249.

33. Bruce, *The Hard Sayings of Jesus*, p. 241.

34. Stephen L. Carter, *God's Name in Vain: The Wrongs and Rights of Religion in Politics* (New York: Basic Books, 2000), p. 132.

35. Ibid., pp. 127, 132.

36. Ibid., p. 127.

37. Ibid.

38. Bruce, *The Hard Sayings of Jesus*, p. 241.

39. Ellul, *Anarchy and Christianity*, p. 68.

40. Garland, *The NIV Application Commentary: Mark*, p. 571.

41. Quoted in Garland, *The NIV Application Commentary: Mark*, p. 571.

42. Walter Wink, *Engaging the Powers* (Minneapolis: Augsburg Fortress, 1992), pp. 139–140.

43. Ellul, *Anarchy and Christianity*, p. 66.

44. Fred B. Craddock, *Luke, Interpretation, A Bible Commentary for Teaching and Preaching*, p. 228.

45. Ellul, *Anarchy and Christianity*, p. 62.

46. Carter, *God's Name in Vain*, pp. 171–172.

47. Ibid., pp. 173, 176.

48. Hector Tobar, Sam Howe Verhovek, and Solomon Moore, "A Scourge Rooted in Subsidies," *Los Angeles Times*, September 22, 2003, pp. A1, A6.

49. H. Richard Niebuhr, Wilhelm Pauck, and Francis P. Miller, *The Church Against the World* (Chicago: Willett, Clark, 1935), p. 11.

50. Bryan P. Stone, *Compassionate Ministry: Theological Foundations* (New York: Orbis, 1996), p. 60.

51. Quoted in Stone, *Compassionate Ministry*, p. 60.

# 10

# Reading Revelation Today: Witness as Active Resistance

## Brian K. Blount

*In* John's work of visionary prophecy, the Revelation of Jesus Christ, the language of witness commends civil disobedience in the form of active, nonviolent resistance. Because it conjures up images of the African-American-led civil rights movement of the 1960s, I use the term "nonviolent resistance" intentionally. Having read Revelation from the perspective of a contemporary African American, I believe that there is a correspondence between John's counsel to witness and Martin Luther King Jr.'s call to march. Both expected their followers to act. Both anticipated hostile reactions from the established powers. Both were certain that the perseverance of their followers would transform the world.

### READING THE BIBLE TODAY: CONTEXT IS KEY

Language is potential. Language creates choice. It provides the persons who draft it and those who subsequently encounter it with the opportunity to decode its audible sounds and visible markers. Words, for example, do not convey meaning but *potential* for meaning. That potential, that opportunity for choice, becomes *meaningful* only when it is performed and accessed in a certain context. One might consider the example "head." Clearly polyvalent, it could refer as easily to the leader of some organization as to the body part occupying the space between your shoulders. In some colloquial settings, it could even be paired synonymously with as unlikely a partner as "bean" or "noggin." An on-duty sailor in search of a particular kind of relief might access it in a different manner still.

155

In such a way, the single word attracts many different, but "correct" decoding choices. The "meaningful" choice depends on the context. Each word, then, is like a prism whose shape allows the refraction of many colors. The color or colors you see will change depending on your position and the position, angle, and source of the light interfacing with it.

If words are by themselves this polyvalent, one can imagine that the potential for meaning will increase exponentially as we collect words into sentences, sentences into paragraphs, and paragraphs into entire texts. The boundaries of choice widen even further in poetic texts, where an author intends that his or her words accommodate a high degree of symbolic elasticity. The language of apocalyptic, John's language in Revelation, is consciously poetic. Symbolic to the core, it invites choice at almost every linguistic turn.[1] The space one occupies will therefore be a critical factor in determining how and what that language *means.* Space matters.

This recognition is as applicable to John's first-century space as it is to our own twenty-first-century space. Context is the key to decoding the choice language affords. We must therefore find a way to reconfigure the context of Revelation's writing and first reading. This will help us reconstruct the interpretive choices its first readers made as they encountered the polyvalence of the text. It will also help establish the interpretive boundaries for our own meaning choice. Saying that a text can mean more than one thing does not imply that it can also mean everything. The linguistic markers provide sociological access for readers and hearers. In order to develop a better sense of how those markers give interpretive direction, we turn to the way that guidance was given to the first reading communities.

And so we start with the context of culture. Here the critical endeavor is a consciously "historical" one. We are looking for the "institutional and ideological background that give value to the text and constrain its interpretation."[2] We are looking, in other words, for the sociological setting in which the text was first formed and performed. John and his audience shared certain cultural markers, many of them unconsciously. One of those markers is particularly important for my own reading of Revelation. The poetic, apocalyptic language that John uses was understood by his earliest readers to be the language of resistance. It is not simply the language of the oppressed and marginalized; it is also the language they used to survive and defy the colonized existence imposed upon them. Jewish apocalyptic writing had already staked out an identity as oppositional literature in works like Daniel and the Maccabees. Indeed, Adela Yarbro Collins observes that the hellenizing crisis brought on by the aggressive efforts of the Seleucid empire and leaders like Antiochus IV Epiphanes stirred the fires of apocalyptic feeling and directly contributed to the Maccabean revolt.

For an apocalyptic thinker, facing such foreign occupation and the real or perceived oppression that was its result, there were only two options: accommodation, which would ultimately lead to assimilation, or resistance. The apocalyptist chose to resist.[3] So, apparently, did Jesus. "[His] preaching, deeply inspired by apocalyptic, stands in radical opposition to the wise and learned who rule over the people."[4] Christian apocalyptic writings followed Jesus' lead.[5] John's choice of apocalyptic language and imagery to convey his prophecy is therefore significant. He knows what kind of language he is using, and so do those who hear and read his words in their shared context at the close of the first century. He is using the language of resistance; it should be accessed accordingly.

But exactly what kind of resistance is John's apocalyptic word of prophecy conveying? Was it a passive endurance that awaited a supernatural moment of historical engagement in which human disciples played absolutely no constructive part? Or was it an active operation that anticipated such a forceful synergism of human and divine challenge that the defiance of the believer, and the persecution it provoked, actually *contributed* to the success of God's transformative cause?[6] The language must, therefore, determine how the first readers would most likely have accessed the text.

Each text is a performance. The circumstance in which that performance first takes place—what M. A. K. Halliday calls the context of situation—critically influences how meaning is both vested in, and accessed from, that text. The problem is that John's first-century performative context is difficult to reconstruct. Halliday believes that because the context of situation is embedded in the text, formulas of appraisal can be developed that will ferret it out. He therefore devised a theoretical tool to evaluate the various modes of language in order to ascertain, through the language of the text itself, the context of situation in which that language took its shape.

His method operates through an analysis of three primary types of linguistic discourse. The first is the field of discourse: what is happening in the text. The second is the tenor of discourse. The tenor concerns the characters whose identities, personalities, motives, and role relationships determine the flow of the narrative and also give useful hints about the make-up of the world in which their realities were constructed. The third is the mode of discourse. All language is functional. The mode of discourse considers how a text's language impacts the characters caught up in its narrative world. It also, I would argue, considers a text's attempts to shape the motivations and behavior of its "flesh and blood" hearers and readers. Mode of discourse asks the question: "What does a reading of Revelation *do* to someone who submits to its world of vision?"[7]

An appeal to these three types of discourse and a careful consideration of the data they yield help an investigator begin the process of reconstructing the situation in which the text was first performed. This information, combined with the results gleaned from the study of cultural context, offers the researcher a fuller picture of the lens through which the text and its primary symbols should be read. Using the results of such an analysis, I want to consider how John's first-century communities in Asia Minor most likely engaged the text of Revelation, and how that engagement can influence our own interpretive work in our own very different contextual locales today.

## READING "WITNESS" IN REVELATION TODAY

Specifically, I want to demonstrate that "witness" in John's Revelation has enough meaning potential that someone in the African American community reading in the twenty-first century could, like someone hearing or reading the same apocalyptic imagery at the end of the first, access it as a commendation of active, nonviolent resistance. Persistent demonstration of this resistance would complement, and even contribute to, God's own effort to transform the world.

### Revelation 1:1–3

This is an action text. These verses script a delivery sequence for the revelation of Jesus Christ that moves quickly from God's heaven to John's Patmos. "The means whereby this revelation was given can be depicted in the analogy of a chain whose main links are God–Jesus–the angel–John–his readers."[8] The language John uses to build this chain suggests a literary equivalence between the term "revelation" and the formula "word of God and witness of Jesus Christ." What started with God ended up with John. Verse 3 adds another dimension; it represents the same revelation as John's written prophecy. A literary equation has developed. The Revelation of Jesus Christ is "the word of God and witness of Jesus Christ," each of which is also the written prophecy that John's hearers and readers are to keep.

But what does that equivalence mean for our consideration of John's language of witness? *What*, actually, are they supposed to be keeping? H. Strathmann pushes us in the right direction: "The Word of God and the witness of Jesus Christ are inseparably interwoven."[9] But what are the parameters of that relationship? What can we determine about either the word or the witness from the fact that they are so integrally connected? David Aune observes through his translation—"the message from God, that is, the witness borne by Jesus"—that, in this particular context of situation, Jesus' witness specifies the exact nature of God's word. "The *kai* here is epexegetical rather than correlative, so that 'the word of God' and 'the testimony of Jesus' are not two different things, but rather the second is an aspect of the first."[10] There lies the crux of the problem for John's first readers (hearers) and for us. The testimony of Jesus Christ cannot clarify the word of God unless we know what that testimony is. So what exactly is the witness of Jesus Christ?[11]

We can say that it is not a believer's witness about Jesus, but, as Aune translates, a witness "borne" by Jesus himself. The genitive in the clause is subjective. In fact, early use here sets the pattern for use later on. John is consistent; when he talks about the "witness of," he is referring to the "witness borne by."[12] In most cases, it is borne by Jesus Christ.

Of all the players in the tenor of discourse for these three verses—God, Jesus Christ, "his" angel, "his" servant John, and "his" servants—the one who plays the most critical role for my reading is Jesus Christ. In this context of situation, however, the flow of action is more meaningful than the characterizations caught up in it. I therefore want to focus on concerns that, while acknowledging the symbolic importance of the portrayals, take their cue from the field and modes of discourse. What does the flow of the text movement *mean* for how characterizations in the text and readers and hearers of it are to orient their lives? What does this text want them to *do*?

The answer lies not in *what* he tells them but *how* he tells them; in verse 3, he uses the language of commendation. The commendation takes the specific form of a blessing.[13] John discloses that he, along with God and Jesus Christ, will celebrate particular people who do particular things. Not surprisingly, those particular things pertain to the revelation of Jesus Christ, which is, as we have seen, the witness borne by Jesus Christ and proclaimed as prophecy by John. The person who reads this witness aloud so that others may hear it and the persons who hear this witness and keep it are those whom John considers blessed. This is the action he is commending, the action he wants both his implied and "flesh and blood" readers to perform. It is so important that before he closes he will pronounce the commendation again at 22:7. Indeed, he encourages them throughout to realize the importance of this "keeping"[14] and promises eschatological victory to those who do.[15] He wants them to proclaim and keep the witness that is borne by Jesus Christ, a witness so powerful and true that it is, for them, in their circumstance, the word of God. They may not yet know what it is, but right from the start they know what to do with it.

## Revelation 1:4–8

With its immediate reference to "the seven churches that are in Asia," this liturgical field of discourse invites consideration of its cultural context. The scholarly consensus that the book was written during the last decade of the first century, probably during the emperor Domitian's reign, gives us a place to start. What would life have been like in the eastern part of the empire for communities who believed in Jesus as the Christ? What assumptions would John and his hearers have shared about their common circumstance?

One might start with the presumption of general religious tolerance. Rome encouraged the demonstration of fidelity that subject peoples wanted to pay to their gods and goddesses as long as their worship also included appropriate recognition of Roman deities. Since acknowledgement of Roman religious figures and practices also carried with it an explicit claim of loyalty, or at least obedience, to the Roman political infrastructure, refusal of cultic participation attracted suspicion and hostility. In such a circumstance, religious fidelity and political homage were one and the same.

Christians were bound to have problems. As was the case with their Jewish forebears, they were beholden to the first commandment's prohibition against the worship of other gods. Christians were, by definition, religiously intolerant. In their context, this made them politically suspect. Under the Flavians, particularly Domitian, "the Asian provinces strongly promoted the imperial cult."[16]

While there is debate whether Domitian demanded that the populace acclaim him in worship as Lord and God,[17] there does seem to be a growing consensus that the requirements of the imperial cult in general and the demands of Christian faith were mutually exclusive social and religious positions. "According to a tradition which probably represents the actual situation, they were required to make the two-word acknowledgement of Roman sovereignty, 'Kurios Kaisaros' ('Caesar is Lord'), an exact counterpart to the basic Christian confession 'Jesus is Lord' (cf. Rom. 10:9; 1 Cor. 12:3)."[18]

While there is little evidence to suggest the kind of comprehensive and systematic persecution that took place in the 60s during Nero's reign, it does seem clear that this perceived religious intransigence and political disloyalty put many Asian Christians in social, economic, and in some cases even mortal jeopardy. A letter from Pliny, a governor of one of the eastern provinces during Trajan's succeeding reign, makes the case for just how precarious circumstances for Christians could be.

> In the meanwhile the method I have observed towards those who have been denounced to me as Christians is this: I interrogated them whether they were Christians; if they confessed it, I repeated the question twice again adding the threat of capital punishment; if they still persevered, I ordered them to be executed. . . . Those who denied they were, or had ever been Christians, who repeated after me an invocation to the Gods, and of-

fered adoration with wine and frankincense to your image, which I ordered to be brought for that purpose, together with those of the Gods, and who finally cursed Christ—none of which acts, it is said, those who are really Christians can be forced into performing—these I thought it proper to discharge.[19]

The observations thus far are suggestive. John is writing to churches located in an area of the empire famous for its attraction to the emperor cult. He is writing in a symbolic language noted for its characterization as resistance literature. And he chooses his words carefully. He brackets this small section with a provocative characterization of God: "the one who is, who was, and who is coming." Boring points out that, in the Greek-speaking world, a threefold formulation like this one was a commonplace way of celebrating a deity's eternity and immutability. "It was said, for example, that 'Zeus was, Zeus is, and Zeus will be' (Pausanias)."[20] John testifies that this notoriety belongs to God, but with a twist. God is not only the eternal one, but he is also the coming one. And God is coming for a purpose. John hints at that motive when he follows up on the formulation in verse 8 with the term *pantocrator*. God, the eternal and coming one, is also the Almighty. God is the true and supreme power in the cosmos. In the eastern provinces of John's seven churches, where Rome was also making precisely this claim, God's coming, as the Almighty, was bound to make headlines. And conflict.

John heightens the probability for that conflict by the way he describes the second key figure in this tenor of discourse, Jesus Christ. He does not use proper grammar. Of course, John's problems with Greek are legendary; many have argued that his flawed speech is the work of someone who thinks in Hebrew or Aramaic. But Allan Callahan makes the important observation that John operates this way intentionally. Because "most of the grammatical rules violated are flawlessly observed elsewhere in the work,"[21] he believes that John *chooses* to write in a Greek that is heavily influenced by Semitic principles. He does so because he wants his use of language to be a representation, a working symbol as it were, of the social and political resistance his people must wage.

John intentionally mismanages his characterization of Jesus Christ, for "the connection of the three titles with the name 'Jesus Christ' is grammatically incorrect."[22] Since "Jesus Christ" is in the genitive case, operating as the object of the preposition "from," the titles that follow should also be in the genitive. Instead, John puts "the faithful witness," "the first born of the dead," "and the ruler [of the kings of the earth]," in the nominative case. As Callahan might say, John isn't making a mistake; he's making a point. G. K. Beale notices that John is following the same pattern he initiated in verse 4, where the threefold formula about God is in the nominative case, even though its function as the object of the preposition "from" should have it in the genitive. There, as here, Beale argues, John stays with the nominative because he wants to direct attention to an allusion he is making to Psalms 89:37 (88:38 LXX), where the controlling moniker, "faithful witness," also occurs in a nominative formulation.[23] But it occurs there with a specific orientation, as does "firstborn" in 89:27 (88:28 LXX). The context of the two references in their Old Testament location is one of kingship, "the unending reign of David's seed on his throne (cf. likewise Ps. 88 [89]:30 [29]). John applies the phrase directly to the Messiah's own faithful witness, which led to establishment of his eternal kingship."[24] Indeed, the reference to "firstborn" in the psalm is directly associated not only with kingship, but with the highest kingship on the earth. That is exactly the kingship John envisions for Jesus Christ.[25]

The initial access that John wants his hearers to make of Jesus Christ as faithful witness, and even firstborn, is that of kingship. If Callahan and Beale are correct, John has skewed his grammar in order to shepherd his hearers toward this pointed connection. Now the actual content of the titles can have the force the visionary intended.

Witness is key, not only because of its lead position in the chain of three, but also because it follows John's opening three verses, which convey his entire work as the witness borne by Jesus. We already know Jesus is the central witness, so here John is not telling us something new. It is also not surprising that Jesus Christ would be described as *faithful*, since his witness is the word of God for this particular cultural circumstance.[26] The strikingly new element is that this faithful witness is the firstborn of the dead and (in a phrase he highlights by appealing to it only here) the ruler of the kings of the earth. At a key moment, *kai* ("and") connects two of John's key descriptive components. Here, as in verse 2, it is epexegetical rather than correlative; a better translation would be "the firstborn of the dead, who is the ruler of the kings of the earth." Not only does the entire phrase clarify what it means for Jesus to be a faithful witness, but the image of universal kingship clarifies what it means for Jesus to be firstborn of the dead.

John has intentionally mishandled the Greek in order to draw attention to a particular psalm reference that has a primary interest in the establishment of secure and abiding kingship. He is using warped grammar to straighten out his readers; he is telling them how to access the reality of Jesus Christ. Christ has a witness to make; he is the firstborn, the ruler of all the kings of the earth. As God is ruler of all, *pantocrator*, Jesus is ruler of the entire human realm. *This* is the revelation of Jesus Christ.

In a cultural context in which Rome already lays claim to ultimate kingship, this is also a revelation bound inevitably for trouble. Indeed, as Beale points out, this awareness is already present in the language John uses. "Kings of the earth" points "typically elsewhere in Revelation to antagonists to God's kingdom (6:15; 17:2; 18:3, 9; 19:19; cf. 16:14). This includes not only the kingdoms and peoples represented by the kingdoms but also the satanic forces behind those kingdoms."[27] Jesus' kingship, by claiming to be the one abiding and universal kingship, necessarily *resists* the already established kingdoms that are making the same claim. In John's cultural context there is only one, Rome.

What does such an interpretive perspective *do*? The answer lies again in the language John uses. The tone of his writing commends his characterization of Jesus as the faithful witness. "The phrase 'the faithful witness' points to Jesus, not only as the revealer from heaven but as the one who also, like the Christians in John's churches, once stood before the Roman authorities. He had borne his witness, even at the cost of his life (cf. John 18:33–19:16; 1 Tim 6:13)."[28] Indeed, this is the one part of the description that Christians can emulate. They cannot be the firstborn of the dead, nor the ruler of the kings of the earth, but they can, like Antipas, and like John himself (1:2), be faithful witnesses to the witness that Jesus himself bears: God is the Almighty, and Jesus Christ is his coming king. In their cultural context, to bear such witness is also to broker a dangerous form of political as well as religious resistance.

### Revelation 1:9–11

John's appeal to the formula "the word of God, that is, the witness borne by Jesus" (1:9) acts as a bookend to his use of it in verse 2. But what is most interesting is John's *causal* point. He says that he is on the island of Patmos "because of," "on account of," that witness. Boring points out that the phrase "on account of" is "always used in Revelation for the result of an action, not its purpose. John has been banished to Patmos because he had been preaching the Christian message."[29] That message is Jesus' own witness to his universal and abiding kingship.

In this tenor of discourse, John is the primary player; his own actions are commended and lifted up as a model to be imitated. Therein also lies the text's mode of discourse. John calls himself the partner of his hearers; in doing so, he also challenges them to live up to the expectations of the partnership. As he held to the witness borne by Jesus, despite the consequences, so must they. This suggests a kind of active resistance. To harbor the view that Jesus Christ is king in a world that actively proclaims the lordship of Rome and its Caesar is to act obstinately. It is to resist, to refuse to fit in. Even more—since John believes God is coming soon to inaugurate that kingship and make a kingdom of Christ's followers—it is to invite "tribulation." Endurance in such a context of situation cannot mean passive waiting in spite of what Rome is doing. It suggests instead a continued resolve to keep to that witness even though, by its very nature, it provokes an angry Roman response.

*Revelation 2:12–17*

In a place like Pergamum, a hostile response to the witness of Jesus' universal and exclusive lordship would be expected. The capital of the entire Asian province, the city was a hotbed of pagan cults and interest in the cult of the emperor. Fiorenza calls it a "citadel of Hellenistic civilization in Asia" which, even more importantly, claimed to be "the official center of the imperial cult."[30] Beale notes that the city referred to itself as the "temple warden" of a temple devoted to Caesar worship.[31] No wonder Richard claims that it was "the center of imperial worship for the entire region."[32]

Not every believer in Pergamum resisted accommodation to the institutions that proclaimed imperial lordship. Not only did some accept the rites and expectations of foreign cults; prophetic leaders like Balaam and prophetic communities like the Nicolaitans even argued that such behavior meant holding to the witness borne by Jesus Christ.

The particular issue at hand was the eating of meat sacrificed to foreign deities. Participation in feasts where such food was available was one of the ways in which members of a community integrated themselves into the fellowship of the larger populace. John believed that such "integration" came at too high a price. He believed that followers of Christ needed to make a stand. If they truly believed that Jesus was the Lord of history, then they must live in a way that showed it. He therefore demanded that they refuse to participate in any rite, or eat any food, consecrated to another person's or power's lordship—no matter what the consequences.

Through his portrayal of Antipas as the key characterization in this discourse field, John commends an opposing action, resistance. He commends Antipas by the way he describes him. He is *like Jesus*. Once again John uses what appears to be a grammatical error to make his theological point. Beale points out that "witness" here should be in the genitive case, as should the adjective "faithful" and the noun "witness" that follow it. John, however, against rule, forces them into the nominative. "Again, the awkward nominative is a device directing attention to the [Old Testament] allusion in order to make clear the identification of Antipas' witness with that of Jesus."[33] That not only suggests that he witnesses to what Jesus witnesses to, the kingship of Jesus, and then dies because of it; it also makes his tragic character one worthy of emulation.

The tenor of Antipas' character also provides John with the foundation for his mode of discourse. He is counseling his readers and hearers to be like

Antipas. Indeed, he already commends those who have behaved like Antipas (2:13) and condemns those who have not (2:14–16).[34] He celebrates those who have held fast even though such defiance in such a place can lead to the very end that claimed Antipas.

The directive that develops is clear. The community at Pergamum, despite the consequences, must be what Antipas has been, a faithful witness to the kingship of Christ. But that will also require them to do what he has done: resist the temptation to acquiesce to the demands of the Roman cultic and political infrastructure, demands that stem from the foundational belief that Caesar is Lord and Rome is the universal kingdom. This activity is bound to be seen as contrary and treated as provocative in *this* context. In other words, the language of witness, whether it is related to Jesus Christ, John, or one of John's fellow believers, suggests active resistance to contemporary cultic and political expectations. In fact, it is so controversial a resistance that it can lead to death. John is not commending passivity, then, but active resistance to what *this* context desires, namely, celebration of, and devotion to, the lordship of Rome and its many client deities. He is asking hearers to testify to the lordship of another, and, in so doing, to put themselves in harm's way.

*Revelation 6:9–11*

The formula "the word of God, which is the testimony borne by Jesus" is reaffirmed.[35] This time John uses it to clarify his causal connection; it *is* because of their witness to Jesus' lordship that believers have suffered. Aune's grammatical investigations confirm the point.[36] He notes that the overwhelming occurrences of the expression "because of" in Revelation deal with either cause or reason, even to the point of conveying the sense of instrumentality. As prominent examples, he includes 6:9 and also 20:4, which speaks of those who have been beheaded "because of" their testimony. Witnessing to the lordship of Christ *causes* their physical deaths.

This is why the souls are crying out for justice. They want God to vindicate their testimony that Christ is king. For as long as justice is delayed, those who deny that witness will continue to believe and promote Rome's lordship instead. So now the martyrs wait beneath the heavenly altar for action. But their waiting passively in heaven does not imply that they also waited passively on earth. They are in heaven, as slaughtered souls (or as beheaded ones in 20:4), precisely *because* they *actively* witnessed to Jesus as the ultimate Lord of human history in a world where Rome laid vicious claim to ultimate authority.

Ironically, this oppositional witness, which has caused their deaths, also participates in the transformation that it seeks. Even as the souls cry out for

God to act, John's description of their situation leaves one with the impression that the efforts of their earthly compatriots continue the transformative effort they had begun. He implies that the souls in heaven have but a little while to wait for the justice they seek, just until the deaths of witnesses like themselves have come to a completion (v. 11). Their deaths, in this way, contributed to the coming of God's vindication and justice, God's kingdom. But again, we must clarify that John is not commending death. In none of the contexts of situation that revolve around "witness" has this been the case. He has instead been commending witness, even though he knows that such witness, given its content and the cultural context of his hearers, will inevitably lead to tribulation and perhaps death.

A narrative formula lies beneath this descriptive symbolism. Yes, the deaths of the witnesses lead to the coming of God's kingdom. But it is the active witnessing that causes the deaths. The witnessing, not the dying, holds the primary position of activity. It is the witnessing that believers can control. They cannot control Rome's response, be it censure, appropriation of property, denial of social privilege, exile, or death. But they can control whether they witness to the lordship of Jesus Christ. The more who witness, the more intolerable will become the word that is witnessed, and the more belligerently Rome will be forced to act. The witnessing, the provocative activity John has been commending all along, will set up the circumstances of Rome's response. It is the witnessing, then, that leads to the coming of God's justice and vengeance, God's kingdom. Dying is a result; witnessing is the cause. For it is witnessing that plays a synergistic role with God's own efforts to accomplish the universal and abiding lordship of Jesus Christ. *This* is the revelation of Jesus Christ.

## FINAL DISCOURSES: COMPLETING THE CASE

The study thus far provides the access points we need to read the witness material that follows. Having acquainted ourselves with the contexts of culture and situation of the first six chapters, we are better prepared to access the language in the final sixteen. I select two discourse fields from those chapters as cases in point. The language that encompasses 11:3 and 11:7 is a good place to begin. John's narration highlights the two witnesses presented here as positive role models for those aspiring to be true witnesses. The intent of prophecy becomes clear. The witnesses are not given a gift to hold passively; they are given a mandate to prophesy for a specified period of time. They are, in other words, to be active witnesses by spreading a particular prophecy.

But John also repeats the warning he has issued before. Rome, in the symbolic guise of the beast, will make war upon them and kill them. We now see that it would be perfectly reasonable for a reader or hearer to conclude that John is making a causal point. The beast is not simply killing two witnesses who prophesy the lordship of Christ; it kills two witnesses *because* they prophesy the lordship of Christ. Still, Rome's response, the slaughtering, is not the focus; the activity of the witnesses is the focus. Their deaths are a result of their witnessing, and are thus secondary to that primary activity that John wants to commend.

What they do will have a transformative effect. The language in 12:1–17 makes this clear. Verse 11 is crucial. The key characterization is not the divine child, or the supernatural woman, or the aggrieved dragon. It is instead the almost anonymous "them" of 12:10 who become the active "they" of v. 11. "They" are the people who do what John has been commending since 1:3. They *keep* the word of God, which is the testimony borne by Jesus (v. 17). The relationship between witnessing and suffering remains causal. Because they keep witnessing, they are continually hounded by the power that denies that testimony. However, 12:11 says something more, something that on the surface seems startling but is really only a confirmation of what has been claimed before. They will conquer the dragon. They will break the back of the force that backs Rome. They will shatter its claim to lordship.

Once again John uses the language of instrumentality.[37] The relationship between witnessing and transformative victory is causal. "They" will conquer "because of" the blood of the Lamb. Here, of course, they are dependent upon divine action that they themselves cannot emulate. Though their blood, too, will spill, it cannot have the redemptive and victorious effect of the blood of the Lamb. But John does not stop here. He continues with another statement of instrumentality ("because of") that places them in partnership with God. They will conquer because of their witness.

John's language leads to a particular contextual conclusion: by obstinately proclaiming the lordship of Christ, they help effect it, even in a world that believes in and prosecutes for the lordship of Rome.

> We must not fail to observe the implications of this. If it is right to say that the basis for a new order of society is God's word of judgment pronounced in Christ, then it follows that the witnesses who proclaimed that word to challenge the prevailing political order were not acting antipolitically at all, but were confronting a false political order with the foundation of a true one. We must claim John for the point of view which sees criticism, when founded in truth, as genuine political engagement.[38]

This is witness not only as active resistance but also as triumphant cultic, social, and political transformation. *This* is the revelation of Jesus Christ.

## A CORRESPONDENCE OF RELATIONSHIPS: THOUGHTS OF MARTIN

Reading Revelation's language of witness through a contemporary African American lens has already deeply influenced the way I reconstruct the contexts of culture and situation and then draw meaning through them. Even as I read "behind" the text, I am consciously reading "in front of" it. The end of this "exegetical" exercise, however, is not the end of the endeavor. These "historical" findings also correspond to and give meaning for my present circumstance. From where I stand in front of Revelation, the witness language corresponds in a powerful way to Martin Luther King Jr.'s call to nonviolent resistance. Like King, John asked his followers to act on his criticism of society. Thus, his witness language not only connects; it also cajoles. With each reading, it urges continuance of the oppositional effort. It commends confrontation with the powers and forces of our age that demand ultimate loyalty. It demands persistent proclamation of the contrary message that Jesus Christ is Lord. As followers obstinately practice the message they preach, they cooperate in God's program of effecting the new reality that message envisions. In this way, the witness John commended to his readers and hearers corresponds to the witness King pressed on his followers.

I am reminded that King's "enemy" also claimed total allegiance to the reality it proclaimed as truth. The truth of the segregationists against which he and his fellow witnesses marched was this: the white race is genetically and spiritually superior to all others. That "truth" was the dragon. The beast it used to put its truth into societal effect was the institutionalized system of segregation.

King fought back with oppositional witness. To be sure, his truth was not precisely the same as John's; the change in circumstance warranted and even demanded a change in the way truth was expressed. But King was also convinced of the ultimate lordship of Christ and the movement, the ultimate—the *apocalyptic*—bend of human history toward God's justice. God's justice demanded human justice, and human justice demanded the equal treatment of all God's people. So King pushed for what John had desired, a witness to an alternative and transformative truth that would obstinately resist the truth of the present, segregationist age. He, too, called for a resistance that existed as an oppositional, contrary witness.

Again like John, King also knew that such active resistance could entail persecution, suffering, and even death. For he knew that the twentieth-century dragon would, like its first-century counterpart, protect its truth with fierce hostility. He even desired it, in a public way. For only in this way would all of America see how bestial the system of segregation really was, see the hideousness of the evil that lay behind it. Enraged at what they saw, Americans, King believed, would then move to change it, to transform it.

This witness, though inviting, guaranteeing, and even needing the vitriolic response of the bestial institution, participated in the institution's ultimate destruction and society's ultimate transformation. To be sure, King did not focus on the suffering or the dying, just as John had not. They were evils that *accompanied* the witness. This witness, in King's case manifesting itself through sermons and marches (in John's day through preaching and prophesying), effected the positive societal change King and his civil rights compatriots sought. The Book of Revelation commends, and Martin Luther King Jr. exemplifies, bold witness—active resistance to powerful, deeply entrenched forces of institutional evil. This courageous witness may issue in suffering and even death but also, as King's example shows, in the transformation of society.

## NOTES

A previous version of this chapter was published as Brian K. Blount, "Reading Revelation Today," *Interpretation* 54 (October 2000): 398–412. Reproduced with permission.

1. M. E. Boring, *Revelation*, IBC (Louisville: John Knox, 1989), p. 54; E. Schüssler Fiorenza, *The Book of Revelation: Justice and Judgment* (Minneapolis: Fortress, 1998), p. 185.

2. M. A. K. Halliday and R. Hasan, *Language, Context, and Text: Aspects of Language in a Social Semiotic Perspective* (Oxford: Oxford University Press, 1990), p. 49.

3. A. Yarbro Collins, "The Political Perspective of the Revelation to John," *Journal of Biblical Literature* 96 (1977): 241–242.

4. P. Richard, *Apocalypse: A People's Commentary on the Book of Revelation* (Maryknoll, N.Y.: Orbis, 1995), p. 18.

5. Ibid., pp. 18–19.

6. Collins, "Political Perspective," 243. Collins argues, for example, that Daniel represents the passive type and the Assumption of Moses the active.

7. E. Schüssler Fiorenza, *Revelation: Vision of a Just World* (Minneapolis: Fortress, 1991), p. 3.

8. Catherine Gonzalez and Justo L. Gonzalez, *The Book of Revelation* (Louisville: Westminster John Knox, 1997), p. 13.

9. Hermann Strathmann, "martys, martyreó, martyria, martyrion," *Theological Dictionary of the New Testament*, ed. Gerhard Kittel (Grand Rapids, Mich.: Eerdmans, 1994), vol. 4, p. 500.

10. David Aune, *Revelation 1–5*, Word Biblical Commentary 52a (Dallas: Word, 1997), p. 6.

11. One could always point, of course, to 19:10c, where John declares that the witness of (borne by) Jesus is the spirit of prophecy. That clarification only *appears* to help. In fact, it tells us no more than what the opening three verses have already revealed. Jesus' revelation is Jesus' witness, which John inscribes as a literary prophecy.

12. Aune, *Revelation 1–5*, p. 7: "The phrase [martyria Iesou] occurs five times in Revelation (1:2, 9; 12:17; 19:10; 20:4). In most instances in which a gen[itive] is dependent on [*martyria*] in Revelation, the gen[itive] is subjective (1:9; 11:7; 12:17; 19:10 [2x]; 20:4)."

13. Boring, *Revelation*, p. 67: "That John has exactly seven beatitudes (1:3; 14:13; 16:15; 19:9; 20:6; 22:7, 14) is an indication that he considers the form itself important."

14. Revelation 3:3, 8; 14:12; 16:15; 22:9.

15. Revelation 2:26–29; 3:10.

16. Fiorenza, *Revelation*, p. 54.

17. Fiorenza, for example, makes just this claim. Yarbro Collins maintains that the evidence is incomplete and that no firm determination of Domitian's demands in this regard can be made. A. Y. Collins, *Crisis and Catharsis: The Power of the Apocalypse* (Philadelphia: Westminster, 1984), p. 104.

18. Boring, *Revelation*, p. 18.

19. See Fiorenza, *Revelation*, p. 193; Boring, *Revelation*, pp. 14–15. Boring includes a full citation of the translated Pliny letter of note.

20. Boring, *Revelation*, p. 75.

21. A. D. Callahan, "The Language of the Apocalypse," *Harvard Theological Review* 88 (1995): 457.

22. Fiorenza, *Vision of a Just World*, p. 41.

23. G. K. Beale, *The Book of Revelation: A Commentary on the Greek Text* (Grand Rapids, Mich.: Eerdmans, 1999), p. 192.

24. Ibid., p. 247.

25. "And I will make him firstborn, highest among the kings of the earth" (translation mine); cf. NRSV, "I will make him the firstborn, the highest of the kings of the earth."

26. John will reaffirm this designation of Christ as faithful, and also true, witness at 3:14.

27. Beale, *Revelation*, p. 191.

28. Boring, *Revelation*, p. 76.

29. Ibid., p. 82.

30. Fiorenza, *Vision of a Just World*, p. 54.

31. Beale, *Revelation*, p. 246.

32. Richard, *Apocalypse*, p. 57.

33. Beale, *Revelation*, p. 247.

34. His choice of language, *kratein*, "to hold," makes it clear that he is contrasting the two characterizations. Those who "hold" to Jesus' name (2:13) are commended; those who "hold" to the teachings of accommodation and acquiescence (2:14, 15) are castigated.

35. A. A. Trites, "*Martys* and Martyrdom in the Apocalypse: A Semantic Study," *Novum Testamentum* 15 (1973): 71–80. The fact that "Jesus Christ" is missing is inconsequential. "The reference is plainly to the testimony of Christ to God which they 'had' [*eichon*], that is, had received, and for which they were prepared to die" (p. 75).

36. Aune, *Revelation 1–5*, pp. clxxvii–clxxviii.

37. Ibid.; cf. Beale, *Revelation*, pp. 663–664.

38. O. O'Donovan, "The Political Thought of the Book of Revelation," *Tyndale Bulletin* 37 (1986): 90.

*11*

# Nature, Resistance, and the Kingdom of God

*John C. Raines*

The idea of domination has received robust attention in postmodern thinking. But less attention has been given to the idea of resistance.[1] This is directly related to the fact that most of social science, like most of theology, analyzes human behavior as if we humans were all born twenty-six years old and male. It is this adult world that is everywhere represented to us as "real"—on television news, in movie scripts, and also in religious reflection. And in this adult world it is males who are portrayed as the significant actors. Power, the struggle for power, and the exercise of power, in short the arts of domination, occupy both our near and distant horizons of attention.

But this is a gender-biased way of thinking and a gender-biased way of representing reality. It ignores the work assigned by men (in almost all cultures and in all times) to women, and the unique moral excellence women display in that work—namely, the nurture of young children. The first world we learn to live in is a world constructed largely by the work of women. Becoming accomplished at living in this first world lays the foundation for all later worlds—of political economy, of the academy, or the writing of social science and theology. To ignore the centrality in the way of human dwelling of the work of infant nurture betrays not only a lack of gratitude but leads to a powerfully skewered grasp on the nature of human behavior.

It is popular these days to be cynical. And those who write cleverly and cynically about the human condition become popular. But cynicism is the self-indulgence of the comfortable and gives us excuses about what we can and cannot expect of ourselves and others in terms of moral behavior. We don't need more excuses. In an age of cynicism and suspicion, to be radical is to be persuasively optimistic about the moral possibilities of our human condition and, therefore, have demanding expectations of our self and others. I

173

intend to do that here by pursuing an analysis of the work of women in infant nurture, and the resources established in that work for persistent resistance to all that degrades, denies, and seeks to destroy human dignity.

## RESISTANCE AND THE WORK OF WOMEN

The first world we learn is not the Nietzschean world of "the will to power," nor is it the world of the Manchester School with its rational selves maximizing utilities in the market. The face we look into first is a welcoming face, a face that celebrates our presence and beckons us forward. It is a woman's face, and mediates that reflexive distance into which I actualize and build my self as self. It is the face of my caregiving adult—the face I see, the voice I hear, the touch I feel, the smell I smell . . . as one who is just awakening into life.

The truth is that the first world we learn is a world established between the infant and the caregiver. Notice I said "between," not by. True, the adult caregiver is something of a senior partner in the relationship, but it is a genuinely two-way relationship. And it founds a world that happens in the space of reciprocity.

Social psychologist G. H. Mead asked us to ponder the human cry. What is it? An instinct? A desperate gesture of dependency? Clifford Geertz in *The Interpretation of Cultures* argues that "human behavior is more like a wink than a blink." The blink has a purpose—to wash the eye. But it arises as an unconscious, inside-the-skin or instinctual response. The wink, however, is consciously purposeful; it is intentional. And it happens not from inside out but in the in-between. What Geertz did not see and should have seen is that a wink becomes a wink only when it is seen as a wink and not a blink. Which means that a word like "agency" or "intention" is wrongly conceived if seen as something originating all by itself, inside an individual consciousness or will. All behaving is a behaving together, intentions becoming repeatedly intended only because of ongoing, successful co-intentionality.

We cry at birth. But that is still a blink, an instinctual response. If Mead is correct, and I think he is, this cry as blink must become and does become in and for the infant the meaning-filled gesture of the cry as wink. It is from the responding gesture of the caregiving adult that the infant learns the meaning of the gesture called cry, giving that gesture, when used by the infant, the capacity to predict accurately the response intended. What that cry announces is not a naked need or desperate dependency but a confident expectation of comfort. In and through the cry is an emerging sense of self and of self-esteem. The self begins to learn itself as a self in experiencing its capacity and competence and, therefore, its "distance" from all that is out there, but a distance that welcomes us back and invites us into its possibilities.

The cry announces more than capacity and confidence. It announces a deservedness. It says, first, "I deserve to be acknowledged," and second, "I do not deserve to hurt!" It is here, in the co-production called self, that I find the foundation for that persistent and persisting *resistance*—the "I do not deserve this" to all that denies and degrades us. (Later in life there will be much that denies and degrades and therefore needs resisting.) It is a sense of confident expectation that voices itself in the infant's cry. Usually, this chronic bias of expectant expectation that underlies all human behaving is confirmed. Alfred Schutz speaks of this chronic bias as "the taken-for-granted-world-of-everyday-reality." We live and have to live, he claims, in a world of routine, a world of unproblematic and shared expectations. Yes, sometimes we cry uselessly; no one comes, and there are no answers and there is no comfort. But we did not learn to cry (to repeat the predicting and expectant gesture) by failing at our first crying. The first world we learned, a world taught to us by the work of women, and the world upon which all subsequent worlds would be built, was a world that paid attention to us, and pretty much gave what we asked for—a smile for a smile, a breast for a cry, a song in rocking arms for a babble.

Theological language that speaks of us as "resident aliens" is bad theology. It is bad for two reasons. First, as Charles Darwin would remind us, if we humans were in any serious way aliens we would never have become residents on planet Earth in the first place. Second, it is bad theology because it is the world—this world!—that summons us into our *imago Dei*. It is because we learn we belong here that we blossom as competent selves, as those who display agency and an expectant hope that the future will correspond to our intentions for it. It is our mother's coming when we cry that mediates our potential *imago Dei*[2] into actuality. That is why I like natural theology. It thinks about God by beginning with this world and what we learn about the Divine from living here, as humans on planet Earth. There is, of course, the danger of naturalizing the socially constructed. But that is a less important danger than the danger of forgetting all that we owe to the positive moral resources of our everyday existence.

As a species, how did we learn to prosper? The world we first learned in our early human nurturing was not something individual or esoteric. It was the shared world of our given culture, with its routine of competencies that we learned in the expanding repertoire of the back-and-forth of the infant/caregiver discourse. To be sure, this was a socially constructed discourse, but a discourse in which power (adulthood) welcomed fledgling power (infancy) into a space made open and awaiting. The infant learns to expect to be expected, a point of initiative upon the world that welcomes and invites initiation. This is how we learned we belonged, and became ever better at the arts of belonging.

Out of our early successes at crying, of smiling (together), of cooing and babbling (in all cultures adults babble adult language to infants in order to actualize their brain's hardwired potential for language)—out of these fledgling accomplishments would be built the whole world of our cultural competencies, including that most important competence called language. We learn language by talking together. If we pay close attention, we can see what marvelous co-performers we are. We gesture as the other expects us to, our gestures getting to our intended meaning almost always before our words get there. In speaking, we voice our voices, so that it is more like singing and dancing together than some flat surface of talking.

But the language competence we learn as infants also introduces us into "the fallen world." Yes, we must follow for a while now the trajectory we Christians call "the Fall."

Concerning language, I like how Pierre Bourdieu corrects the formalism of F. de Saussure and the grammatologists. Language is best understood not as a system of signs but as a practice, a social performance. It is largely an unconscious or preconscious performance, a performance less embedded in mind or will than in the body. For Bourdieu, language is part of habitus—"a structured structuring disposition." It is a disposition lodged in the deployment of tongue and teeth and lips and cheeks—displaying itself, for example, in the degree of nasalization or pharynxization. And all of this is socially inscribed. Our "mother tongue" gives voice to our social location of birth, to our place in the gendered social hierarchy. At the level of speaking and of hearing, language is socially constructed and totally arbitrary as to its "correct" or "legitimate" usage. It both reflects and reinforces how power constructs and mediates hierarchical social relations in the everyday world. It is hierarchs, obviously, who are thought to speak the correct or legitimate language. Power uses dictionaries and schools to "naturalize" the (arbitrary) system of deference and deferment that displays itself in everyday speech acts.

In the adult world, power and privilege inscribe themselves behind and before words—in the dispositions that shape verbalization, in the dispositions that guide gesturing and shape voicing, or in the dispositions that position heads and eyes and torsos in that vast choreography of socially inscribed bodies talking.

Bourdieu is brilliant in unveiling the "unsaid" in the said. He deciphers how adult bodies in their deployment and deportment are embodied enactments of hierarchy, eliciting the complicity we call authority. We may use the example of the authority we call "Priest." Disposed to display the social magic of symbolic power, the priest elevates the host (just so) and intones the words of institution (just so) and thus invites in the congregants what Bourdieu calls "the mis-recognition that allows us to recognize." Sacredness is produced by the congregation which recognizes in the priest's gestures and words their very own sacred, their very own holy. Symbolic power—exercised by priests and politicians and others in authority—is accomplished only by the complicity of those who in receiving that authority authorize it as authoritative for them, but cannot, for Bourdieu, recognize that it is they who must do the recognizing if the alchemy of "ritual magic" is to work.

(There is an interesting opening here for theology to reflect upon the church as "the body of Christ" and the congregation as an extension of the Incarnation. Beyond Bourdieu's one-sidedly cynical and manipulative reading of community and ritual is the lived reality of reciprocity in worship. In worship we affirm transcendence together—a going beyond the self—and experience together that beyond. Transcending, going beyond is a co-production of the congregation. It is something we do together in worship. The ritualization of transcendence is not a self-deluding, a fake social magic, except for those who stand outside and decide to see it that way, which raises the question of where they stand and why.)

Whether it is Bourdieu's unveiling of that everyday veiling which "naturalizes" the arbitrariness of social position, or Michel Foucault's analysis of panopticism and the dominant and dominating gaze that gets internalized by the prisoners (women under the male gaze, blacks under the white racist gaze, the rest of the world under the gaze of the West)—we who would pursue progressive political agendas must find space—a persistent and enduring ground—for resistance. Both speaking and seeing are political. They happen in the space of seeing-and-being-seen, of hearing-and-being-heard. And that space is occupied by power, made all the more powerful by being both invisible and silent.[3] What is our hope?

Resistance has its grounds established in a world that precedes the fallen world. So let us go back again to that first world, behind the adult world, the world upon which the adult world, deeply inscribed by power/domination, has necessarily had to construct itself, the world of the infant with its work of women where we were not reduced to passivity, subservience, or dependency. That world was not and could not have been a world of lies or of mirrors.

The world in which we learned to speak spoke back to us as we had been taught to predict. Behind the friendly face we saw was the intention usually of a real not simply a simulated friend. Power operated in that world to empower, not as a euphemization of force. This is where the critical powers of postmodernism become uncritical and overgeneralized. It is a reading of society and of social relationships that misreads the possibilities of collective and effective resistance—possibilities lodged in an other world, behind and below our adult worlds, where dissimulation and mirage seem so often and so subtly to rule.

Let us think clearly about the first world we learned. It was a world where power (adult caregivers) used their power to empower. It was a world of reciprocal delight, a delight where we first learned to delight in ourselves. Think of the empowering it takes, the confident sense of learned deservedness it takes, the expectant expecting of trusted responses proved trustworthy it takes, for the two-year-old, with eyes blazing, to announce "No! I do it." Think of what this says about our first learned sayings of "I" and "do." Or think about the game that three-year-olds in all cultures play. I will call it the Suzy game.

Suzy, noticing that her mother is noticing, pretends to sneak outside the door, which she partly closes behind her. What is mother supposed to say? What is this game about? It is about the relationship of dependency and independence. It is a deep lesson in reciprocity that gives the lie to all those who would set in binary opposition freedom and dependency. Suzy waits behind the door and her mother—voicing her voice to display her worry, her not knowing, her dependable dependence—asks "Where is Suzy?" and waits. Suzy also waits, enjoying immensely the power delegated to her, an empowering sense of her own independence from her mother, and of mother's dependence upon her own, Suzy's action. At last, full of a sense of her independent dependence, Suzy throwing open the door announces "Here I am!" and runs into her mother's awaiting arms.

Is there a winner and a loser in this game? Is it a zero-sum game, where someone gains power only at the expense of another losing power? No. We find here a different politics, a different polity, where both are empowered in and through the power of the other. The first polity we learn is not the polity later taught to us by university political science departments, a polity where freedom means my freedom to pursue my self-interest so long as I grant you the same freedom, and equality means (at best) equal chances to become unequal. No, the first politics we learn is the politics of reciprocity, the mutual delight that characterizes the back-and-forth of the infant and the caregiving adult.

The world we learn first, the world upon which all subsequent worlds are built, is a world of fundamental mutuality. It founds in us a sense of "how things in fact should be." It shapes our anticipated anticipation of that just dwelling we Christians call the Kingdom of God. The Kingdom of God is a remembered anticipation, a future promise we first learned of here in this world. How can we understand our understanding of the Kingdom of God except as a remembered foretaste that allows us to expect the (un)expected?

How could we possibly *come to know* something that we had not already, in part, experienced? "The Kingdom of God is within you" because that is where we first learn to hunger and thirst for that kind of future.

## TRUST AND COMMUNITY

We learn more than reciprocity in the world that the infant and adult caregiver build together. We learn we live and can only live by trust. "False consciousness," "complicity," "mis-recognition in order to recognize"—all of these depend upon an endowment they did not create, and in plain fact could not create. To modify a saying of William James, we trust because we must, and would trust everything if we only could. The world we first learned taught us we were safe enough to trust. It was not without blemish; mistakes were made; signals got crossed or ignored. We wanted more love than we could get in the crowded space of our family of origin. Mother, in despair or desperation, said "no" instead of "yes" to our "no." Older brothers and sisters made fun of us, which was no fun for us at all. And different cultures have different ways of valuing or dis-valuing a newborn (for example, the third daughter born to a Hindu family that has no sons). And societies can and do treat poor families or families of the "other" in ways deeply disrespectful and injurious.

Family-in-society was not and is not in any simple way "safe." But it was safe enough for most of us. This thing we call human got started there. We learned to cry. We learned to smile. We learned to babble and then to speak. We got our rise there, our boosting into our boasting of "I want" and "I will." The image of God was summoned forth in us there, born in us by that first world that usually proved itself trustworthy enough for our trust. We learned to dance our bodies and to sing our voices, without second thought, in that elaborate choreography displayed routinely in human bodies talking, equally expert in the elaborate converse of conversing in everyday conversations. Theology gets it right when it insists that the consequences of the Fall are always limited by an imago Dei that persists and perseveres even under terrible assault.

To understand that the *imago Dei* is nurtured and energized in a space of trusting reciprocity is to understand why later in life *community* is so important in mounting and sustaining resistance. There is no better example of that than the resistance deployed by black slaves in North America. In one of the songs of sorrow we hear: "I got shoes, you got shoes, all God's children got shoes. And when we get to heaven we'll walk all over God's heaven, heaven; when we get to heaven we'll walk all over God's heaven."

These words were sung in unison as shoeless black slaves worked the cotton fields of the deep South. Note that the announcement of protest and resistance is voiced as "*I* got . . . *You* got . . . *all God's children* got . . . when *we* get to heaven." It is the language of community as it celebrates and sustains the shared intentionality of resistance. Misunderstood by the slave masters who found comfort in such singing, "heaven-talk" was not simply the talk of resignation, talk about a place in the sky bye-and-bye. As sung by the community of resistance, "heaven-talk" is about how things should be right now, and someday will be. It is a song of shared deservedness. And "God-talk" is the statement of common faith and trust that, against all material evidence, this is the *really real*.

Successful intentionality arises in the space of trust-worthy reciprocity actualized in the infant/caregiver interaction. It is in this space of "common grace" that gradually the whole repertoire of successful adult behavior is built up. It is the generative space that later in life will sustain the cry of protest and resistance.[4] Because no matter the counterlessons we learn (and how powerful those lessons become!), we never forget our first world. Trust is not a foolishness we foolishly give to others. Trust is not first of all or last of all that self-deluding that solicits and elicits a comforting (but false) complicity in the alchemy of authority. Trust is what allows us to use a world together in a taken-for-granted and unreflective pragmatism that simply employs that world we find at hand, to whatever task. We get up in the morning, dress, eat breakfast, get on the bus, and go to work—without once wondering whether the bus driver is a mass kidnapper in disguise. We do not live and indeed we cannot live by way of suspicion. We trust because we must, because it is the only way we humans can live side by side in this world, and get on with it.

## RESISTANCE AND JUSTICE

The world that we find at hand today, ready for our everyday trust and use, is a world of radical inequality and global injustice, a world that fundamentally contradicts the recognition and reciprocity we first learned to live and to trust. It is a world where the cry of the poor is ignored in the stampede for global profits. It is a world where financial speculators at computers in New York or London or Frankfurt can in a moment reduce to shambles economies that had induced the poor to trust their future to the promises of top-down development. It is a world where the International Monetary Fund can admit to "a slight miscalculation" that causes the infant mortality rate in places like Indonesia to triple in one year! Here at home, we are again as unequal in terms of wealth distribution (and therefore how power works) as we were one hundred years ago in the Gilded Age, before there were labor unions or graduated income and inheritance taxes.

In face of such a world, the trust we learned in our infant world, the trust we learned from women's work, can and must become a radical trust, a trust that mistrusts those whose explanations defend the world we find at hand. To be radical, we know, means going to the root. The root of protest and resistance against all that degrades and demeans is rooted, I claim, as deep as human nature. All that betrays trust, all that misuses trust to advantage power and disadvantage those less powerful—all of this "fallen" world—lives off an endowment it did not create, could not create, and constantly depletes by its betrayal but cannot destroy.

To be radical in an age of cynicism like our own is to be persuasively hopeful. It is a trust which distrusts that in us which would give in to hopelessness. Why? Because we have been taught that when we get hurt we do not have to remain silent; we can cry (out).

The Kingdom of God is not just a utopia ahead of us; it is an anticipatory memory. It is not a stranger to this world, any more than we humans are strangers here. We literally could not be here, and together here, if we were in any fundamental sense strangers to this world or to each other. It is this experienced reality that allows us to glimpse a shadow of ourselves in the others that are not our selves—the gender and racial and religious and global others. Yes, we humans do Bosnia; we do Holocaust; we do Sri Lanka and Rwanda. We also do Thailand and Indonesia and Brazil and North Philadelphia. But we humans betray what we are, or at least what we can and therefore should become, when we do that.

Sometimes we humans resist the horrors we see, and would resist even better, I think, if we could only see the horrors we do not see—the horrors we mis-see as holy wars, or mis-see as the undeserving poor at home or abroad who only need a little more development from above, or mis-see by seeing in the other's determined otherness to our sameness a threat to our settled sense of ourselves (as the West, modern and model for the rest). Resistance is deeper in us than domination can make us forget. It is always there, always ready to break out into action, turning the past into a future that those who were writing history, just yesterday, did not foresee or even think possible.

The struggle for justice always looks impossible the very moment before it becomes possible. Resistance generates a community of insistent insistence because it is born in that still-remembered co-conspiracy of hope that is infant nurture, the gift and legacy of the work of women. Like a cry, it is an insistent reaching out to others that makes possible what had seemed impossible. Take, for example, the rebellion that so unexpectedly overthrew that so solid-looking world of Jim/Jane Crow. Looking back, we see the success of black resistors. But if we look not back but rather forward from 1960, how bleak the way ahead appeared. Yes, it took a certain moment in time— including an activist Supreme Court, the right president (Johnson), and a northern news media (especially television) open to the cause. But those four black students who decided in early February 1960 to sit down at the segregated Woolworth's lunch counter in Greensboro, North Carolina, couldn't possibly have known, ahead of time, that the time for successful rebellion was "now!" The future surprised everyone—those who welcomed it, and those who deplored and fought against it.

That is my point. No one knew then, and no one knows now, what tomorrow may bring for those of us who hold out progressive hopes for the future. What we can know is that resistance needs persistence, a patience rooted in expectation, rooted in the memory of an anticipation that makes the promises of the Kingdom of God as real and as insistently generative as a baby's cry. It is that radical trust that mistrusts the power so fascinatingly powerful in its (seemingly endless) degrading and demeaning of others less powerful. It is a trust that has learned to expect the future in unexpected places. It holds to a truth we learned at the beginning of our existence, when we did not yet know there was a world ahead of us that would welcome us.

## NOTES

1. Ever since Karl Marx announced his idea of "false consciousness" and the Frankfurt School theorized a new velvet-gloved domination that becomes domesticating, the analysis of persistently dominating power has become exceedingly persuasive. Add postmodernists like Michel Foucault (see *Discipline and Punish: The Birth of the Prison* [New York: Vintage Books, 1979]), with his theory of power/knowledge that organizes our new disciplinary societies within its subtle arts of "normalization," to Pierre Bourdieu's analysis of the complicity from below that "naturalizes" the hierarchical relationships of socially constructed patterns of privilege (see *Language and Symbolic Power* [Cambridge, Mass.: Harvard University Press, 1982]), and you have in modern cultural studies, in critical theory, and in postcolonial analysis an intellectual deployment of power/domination that leaves, it seems, little space for theorizing resistance. Even James Scott, in *Domination and the Arts of Resistance: Hidden Transcripts* (New Haven: Yale University Press, 1990), where he works to privilege resistance over against domination, has only the most precarious theoretical foundation upon which to build his observed practices of resistance.

2. The contemporary Roman Catholic Church is considering the elevation of Mary to the position of co-redemptor. My argument here argues that we Protestants should give this more serious intellectual attention than we do.

3. When we see bodies, we do not see light waves, we see the socially constructed meanings projected upon those bodies that allow us to re-cognize what we see (literally, cognize a second time). It is that socially constructed unseen in our seeing that allows us to see.

On women under the male gaze, see Anne Marie Hunter, "Measuring the Hairs on their Head: Power and Myth of the All-seeing God," *Journal of Feminist Studies in Religion* (Fall 1993). On blacks under the white racist gaze, see Cornel West, *Prophesy Deliverance! An Afro-American Revolutionary Christianity* (Philadelphia: Westminster Press, 1982). John C. Raines, "The Politics of Religious Correctness: Islam and the West," *Cross Currents* (Spring 1996).

4. Perhaps here on earth, common grace or the grace of creation is what we have to cling to, a grace which swirls down from the beginning of cosmic process, and from there on through all that is still becoming from that beginning.

## 12

# Citizenship, Resistance, and St. Augustine

### Frances S. Adeney

$\mathcal{I}$knew I had a problem when by day I was teaching my daughters, Jennifer and Rina, to love their country and by night I was being arrested for demonstrating against my country's policies on nuclear arms. What was going on?

Whatever it was, it had been going on for a long time. During the 1950s I attended the integrated public schools of New Jersey. Every morning I said the Pledge of Allegiance to the American flag, my hand covering my heart. I learned that America was the haven for persecuted people from all over the world, a place in which all people were equally respected. I saw that demonstrated in my racially and culturally diverse classroom. I sang "America the Beautiful" with gusto, believing that my country lived up to all of those ideals.

By the 1970s I was participating with Pacific Life Community in demonstrations against nuclear arms development at Lockheed Corporation in California. Along with friends from my congregation and two small daughters, I poured ashes on the road at the Lockheed gate on Ash Wednesday, held candlelight vigils at the doors of the building on dark winter mornings when the day shift arrived, and was arrested more than once for civil disobedience by crossing the dreaded blue line.

What had happened to the loyal fourth grader who pledged allegiance so fervently to the flag? I had been taught that citizenship entailed loyalty and service to one's country. I still believed it, but the actions of protest and resistance that I took then seemed inconsistent with that ethic of loyalty to my country.

I began to wonder how I could raise my children to be patriotic citizens while resisting the policies of the government. Could my children learn to love and serve their nation while they participated with their parents in resistance activities? Was civil disobedience compatible with good citizenship?

I gained some insight into this dilemma on a trip to Nicaragua in 1985. As part of a National Women's Delegation sent on a fact-finding tour during the civil war between the Contras and the Sandinistas in that country, we visited factories, communities, and war-torn areas. We spoke with soldiers, mothers of the disappeared, women's groups, and Christian base communities. We marched along a road near the northern border, planting crosses at sites where people had been killed. We interviewed political figures, religious leaders, and representatives of the American government in Nicaragua, listening to their views on the conflict.

It was at the U.S. Embassy that I gained an insight into loyal resistance. The Embassy was the most guarded building in all of Nicaragua. Walls, barbed wire, and guards greeted us upon arrival. Our group of twenty American citizens was searched and questioned before finally being admitted into the building that represented our nation.

Shocked at the inhospitality and military presence of our own government, the women were enraged by the time we boarded the bus at the end of the interviews. There was anger, but there were also tears. When I inquired into the meaning of this response, some of the women told me that they hated their government for what it was doing in Nicaragua. That explained the anger. But it didn't explain the tears. I began to suspect that, beneath the declarations of hatred, the women loved their nation. I know that I did. I think that their tears showed not only frustration but disappointment and embarrassment with the nation they loved.

## CITIZENSHIP, LOYALTY, AND RESISTANCE

As a result of experiences of conflict and ambiguity around the issue of how to serve one's country even when disagreeing with its policies, I began to do research on citizenship and ethics, turning to classic Western thinkers to attempt to sort out the dilemma. That process included defining *citizenship* and its relation to moral action. Who is the citizen, what is the good, and how are those related to one another in different historical situations?

That process also included understanding the obligations of *loyalty*, both to the state and to other institutions that demand loyalty, especially religion. Loyalty is commitment to a group, idea, or entity that results in actions that support and further the interests of that entity even when actions that may individually serve one's interests run counter to that support. Loyalties form a basic part of human life as the individual, shaped by society and influenced by group values, nonetheless acts as a moral agent.

My study further showed that the struggle with conflicting loyalties to the state and the good, as one understood it, were not uncommon. Policies developed in nation-states, I also learned, sometimes go against deeply held convictions.

*Resistance* is noncompliance, such as complaint, public demonstration, or other forms of action that make public one's dissatisfaction with and intent to change social norms or government policies. Political resistance comprises intentional individual acts usually organized and performed by groups and movements. Depending on the centrality of those convictions, individuals may organize to resist and thereby change those policies.

These studies led me to the conclusion that resistance can be a form of loyal and responsible citizen action, a conclusion I will support by appealing to Augustine's thought on citizenship and loyalty. In the contemporary era, I will show that the mutual exclusivity of loyalty and resistance set forth by Augustine need not be continued, and that resistance can be an expression of the loyalty to God that Augustine outlines. Today, loyal resistance can form a nexus for a responsible citizenship ethic.

## RECONNECTING CITIZENSHIP AND ETHICS

Citizenship today is often seen in terms of individual rights rather than civic interdependence. Political theorist Jean Bethke Elshtain claims that the American experiment in democracy is failing due in part to a focus on individual rights that erodes helpful structures of authority.[1] William M. Sullivan describes an individualistic notion of voting for one's self-interested advantage as "fundamentally to misconceive the actual interdependence of citizens in a commonwealth."[2] By conceiving the political process as a system of protections for individual rights, the citizen fails to understand that "the maintenance of private liberty depends on active citizenship and that in turn upon public virtue, a shared moral order."[3]

According to some, that shared moral order is under threat. Charles Taylor describes a separation of moral sources from modern values of liberty, equality, and universal benevolence. The enlightenment project itself began to conceal moral sources in order to insure free choice of ends, he argues.[4] The reasons for acting well in the public sphere become obscure as citizenship action focuses on choosing individual goods. As citizens become separated from the very notion of moral citizenship, a clear understanding of public virtue in a shared moral order disappears. Loyalties shift from responsible action to protection of individual rights and opportunities to consume.

Emphases on individual rights and free choice of individual goods can easily eclipse citizenship ethics in the modern world. Yet without a clearly articulated ethic, citizens may fall into apathy about their role in public life. How can the problems of (1) conflicting interpretations of the role of the Christian citizen in public life, (2) the size of nations and corresponding inaccessibility of the decisions of government, (3) the focus on individual rights rather than moral responsibilities for citizens, and (4) the loss of clear moral sources for ethics be addressed?

Augustine's focus on a personal attitude of loyalty to God, combined with the stress on individual choice and action in modern society, can be a point of entry for articulating a cogent citizenship ethic. Charles Taylor suggests that a modern turn inward opens a new moral source in which inner yearnings unite with outside events, the Christian story for instance. Deep personal resonances unite with spiritual resources that can provide reasons for ethical behavior.[5] Sullivan, while lamenting the loss of civic community, also recognizes the primacy of the individual and his or her attitudes in today's society. He states, "The contemporary starting point for understanding the classical conception of the citizen must be the recovery of a sense of civic life as a form of personal self-development."[6] Both Taylor and Sullivan connect action to personal sensibilities and practices; loyal resistance fits well into this frame for modern citizens.

Augustine's radical notion of reflexivity emphasized individual response to God's love as the source and criterion of ethical action. The theological controversies about how the Christian should relate to the public realm and the separation of citizenship from ethics in modern society can be informed by attention to Augustinian thought. Viewing citizenship ethics from a standpoint of responsibilities and responses to God and others, rather than from the standpoint of rights and personal freedoms, requires reflection on practices that are important to participation in public life. Including attitudes and motives in making ethical decisions brings loyalties to God and the nation into focus.

## AUGUSTINE: CITIZENSHIP AND LOYALTY

Those loyalties were operating in my own life as I participated in resistance activities when my children were small. As I struggled to integrate those loyalties with each other and to relate them to my own Christian ethics and my actions as a citizen, I discovered the writings of St. Augustine.

In the classical tradition that precedes Augustine's writings of the fourth century C.E., human reason and intentionality in developing habits that shaped one's character were central themes. While important facets of ethical reflection, those emphases did not help me to explain the seeming contradictions in my own behavior. Although practices of resistance did not appear to be acts of a good citizen, I felt that those practices were rational, intentional, and developed habits that shaped my own character in positive ways. Moreover, those acts of resistance arose from deep convictions that motivated me to interact with decisions of the nation as a citizen who identified strongly *with* the nation. I did not practice resistance only as a Christian but as a U.S. citizen. And that resistance did not imply a rejection of the nation. It seemed more like a calling to accountability or a loyal protest. The classical thinkers did not address this aspect of citizenship.

I found in Augustine an emphasis on loyalty as a mark of the good citizen. In contrast with modern or other classical views of citizenship, which emphasize rights or virtues respectively, Augustine places wholehearted love of God at the center of citizenship.[7] Rational thought, intentional choice, and the development of habits were here augmented by the affective areas of human life—loves, motives, relationships, and commitments. Augustine's focus on acting in loyal response to God became the basis for developing an ethic of loyal citizen resistance.

Exploring Augustine's thought on loyalty to God and its relation to citizenship revealed four insights:

1. Placing *love for God* at the center of citizenship presents a basis for ethical action and a critical standard by which actions are evaluated. Actions toward the common good grow out of loyalty to God and are performed in service to God according to Christian understandings of the good. This moral source unites one's personal experience and action in the world with God's wisdom as understood from revelation and experience.

2. The *ambiguity of moral situations* and the impossibility of avoiding moral conflicts come to the fore as the loyal Christian attempts to act rightly in a fallen world. Understanding the limitations of reason and the mixture of good and evil aid the Christian in sorting out conflicting interpretations of citizen action and moral order. Freed from the search for moral purity, Christian citizens may act toward the good of their country in loyalty to God in ambiguous situations.

3. Augustine's *emphasis on responsibility* for action provides an antidote to excessive emphasis on the rights of citizens in the United States today. Loyalty to God makes demands upon individual Christians and congregations that may go beyond society's expectations for the good citizen.[8] Loyalty to nation and loyalty to God do not necessarily conflict, but loyalty to God is more demanding,

motivating the citizen to go beyond minimal civic duty to more demanding acts of justice.

4. Loyalty to God *places the Christian citizen squarely in an affirming community* of accountability. Individual acts are made within a community of identity that supports and gives meaning to those acts.

Socrates, who chose death rather than be barred from Athens, showed group loyalty to be an integral part of his identity. For Socrates, to be a person was to be a part of the community; exile was a worse fate than death.

Augustine saw things in a rather different light. For him, there were two loyalties that the citizen held: loyalty to the heavenly city as a Christian, and loyalty to the earthly city as a citizen. Accountability to each was required.

## AUGUSTINE ON POLITICAL ETHICS

Augustine inherited and reshaped the Christian revolution.[9] During a time of chaotic change and spiritual hunger, his creative mind blended elements of Greek philosophy, Roman culture, and Hebrew/Christian faith into an interpretation of life and a vision of hope that has had a lasting impact on Western civilization.

Augustine's early writings drew heavily on Greco-Roman philosophy and language. The idea of a universal order accessible to the mind through reason lent an intellectual optimism to Augustine's quest for wisdom.[10] But after 393 C.E., Augustine slowly abandoned his high estimation of human intellectual and moral capacity.[11] The order of the universe did not change, but because of the fall, Augustine came to believe that humans could not relate properly to that order. The need for grace and the idea of the corruption of the human will became central concerns in Augustine's thought.

Those emphases led Augustine to combine an understanding of citizenship with an inward reflexivity and an emphasis on personal growth. Because reason was fallen, it could not be the arbiter of moral decision-making. Augustine, instead, emphasized the limitations of reason and the reality of conflicts among moral goods.

The inability to comprehend God's order through reason led to Augustine's division between the eternal and the worldly orders. The Greco-Roman emphasis on reason and virtue through obedience became incorporated into the path to earthly peace. But the true, eternal end of humans, love for God, was realized not through reason but through *caritas*, love, a gift related to an entirely different order of reality. The Christian sojourns on this earth but retains true loyalties in heaven. Peace, the goal of the earthly life, can be established through order and reason but not without the help of God's grace. The true eternal end (*telos*) is love of God, and relates to that spiritual kingdom which develops alongside the earthly city but is vastly more important and lasting.

But separation in Augustine's view is not as neat as might be implied above. Augustine's focus is on well-ordered loves of God and earthly things, and his orientation is toward the whole personality rather than on the merely rational. This puts motives and loves at the center of Augustine's ethic. Whether addressing affairs in the heavenly or the earthly realm, ordering one's life according to what one loves results in a dynamic focus on habits, values, and qualities.[12] One's loyalties determine one's actions. By transposing the classic virtues into well-ordered loves, Augustine unites the Greek ideal of citizenship with a notion of citizenship that revolves around loyalty to God.

## THE ROMAN CONTEXT FOR CITIZENSHIP

The tumultuous changes in Augustine's beliefs and attitudes reflect on a personal level the increasing insecurity and chaos of the surrounding culture. Augustine defined citizenship not in the Greek *polis* but in the context of an overgrown, failing Roman Empire.

In his younger years, the alliance of church and state in Africa, combined with Augustine's classical heritage, led him to emphasize loyalty to the state. He utilized the biblical imagery of Nebuchadnezzar and the Babylonian captivity to underscore the Christian duty to support the state.[13] "The earthly city, which does not live by faith, seeks an earthly peace, and the end it proposes, in the well-ordered concord of civic obedience and rule, is the combination of men's wills to attain the things that are helpful to this life."[14]

As tensions in society and in his public life increased,[15] Augustine's thought became increasingly characterized by a fundamental tension: the final end of humans—true peace—could never be achieved in this life. Augustine became "acutely aware of being caught in an existence that denied him the fullness for which he craved. He is defined by tension towards something else."[16] Augustine's sermons began to emphasize the yearning of the Psalms and a love for the future. "Augustine gradually realized that the final solution of tensions endemic in the human situation could never be achieved in life on earth."[17] True peace could only be realized in a heavenly future.[18] At the same time, his yearning for what could never be realized in human society resulted in a dual vision: the earthly city and the city of God.

Augustine's concept of the two cities divided the world into two types of people: those who strove to love God totally and those whose interests were temporal and earthly.[19] One's *dilectio*, the fundamental orientation of the entire personality, determined the locus of one's citizenship.[20]

Using this emphasis on a deep personal element of loyalty, Augustine redefined a republic as a group of people oriented toward a common loyalty.[21] A true republic was centered around love for God. "The fact is," he stated in refutation of Cicero, "true justice has no existence save in that republic whose founder and ruler is Christ."[22]

## RESISTANCE TO AUTHORITY

Nonetheless, citizens of that true republic must live on earth, serving the partial justice made possible through political structures.[23] One must cooperate with government because the kingdoms of the world were in God's providence, set up by God to curb the evils of a disordered humanity.[24] To obey the state was somehow to follow the hidden ways of God.[25] A Christian's loyalty to the earthly city was a mark of a deeper orientation: love for God. Inner freedom was not lost in such a situation.[26] Only if the state's commands were absolutely opposed to God's ordinance (e.g., idol worship) should state edicts be disobeyed.

Rarely would a citizen make such a decision, however. Augustine's scheme depicted citizens "not as mature, rational persons who have the right to be consulted about their wishes, but as willful passionate children."[27] The ruler was depicted as father of the people ruled; those in his care obeyed.[28] In that appraisal, Augustine reflected both Plato and Aristotle. Resistance was not an option.

Unlike Plato and Aristotle, however, Augustine did not believe that political institutions were natural, but they were established to keep a check on human greed and to prevent society from collapsing into anarchy and chaos.[29] Even though earthly regimes were permeated with evil, the all-powerful God could use their evil deeds to accomplish God's purposes. Through wicked rulers, God chastised the wicked and tested the fidelity of the good.[30] Every action was caused both by human will and by God's providence. So God used even wicked behavior to bring about God's will. That view of predestination plus human agency left Augustine a wide berth for human authority in the political realm but little room for citizen resistance.

Augustine's strong view of state authority rose partly from his growing conviction that biblical prophecy was being fulfilled in history.[31] Although history would not result in final peace, it was moving toward the day of judgment. Interfering with state authority could be interfering with God's plan to fulfill prophecy. On the other hand, suppression of paganism might hasten that day.[32] An active, powerful state could enforce morality, thereby attacking the inward enemies of vice and heresy.[33] In Augustine's eyes, those were the real enemies because they thwarted devotion to God.

## LOYALTY, VIRTUE, AND CITIZENSHIP

The dual nature of Augustine's ethics resulted in a complicated connection between virtue and citizenship. Augustine's central principle for living was not reason or fate, but love. As a complex combination of the rational, emotional, and circumstantial elements of life, Augustine's concept of love was nuanced. Predestination by God, reason, will, and feelings each played a part in determining one's true loyalty. Loving God by one's own effort was impossible. A work of grace was necessary. God initiated that work and called a person to respond. In order to respond, one must be predestined to heavenly citizenship, understand the Christian message, and act on that basis. Becoming a citizen of heaven involved the total personality.

The resulting transformation changed one's life. Once defined by that love for God, the center of sin, egoism, self-centeredness, and self-deification, must be rejected.[34] Temporal goods were not to be sought, although they were not evil per se. Rather, orientation to the concerns of heaven emphasized their unimportance in the grand scheme of things. But the citizen of heaven still must seek the peace of the earthly city. The treasure of heaven could not be stored up while the earthly city was in chaos.

Therefore, the Christian was to order actions according to love of God, acting in the world according to what made for peace, or lessened tension in the temporal city. Those acts by Christian citizens were performed out of loyalty to God. The Christian emperor, for example, was to act in justice because his loyalties were toward God. Were a pagan emperor to do the same thing, but without orienting his motives toward God, that action was not truly an act of justice.[35] Loyalty to God acted both as the standard for right action as a citizen and as a criterion for just acts.

At times the duties of rulership seemed to conflict with the Christian ethic of love. In such situations Augustine characteristically emphasized the motive of the public official and the importance of doing what must be done in a spirit of love. Virtue in the public realm consisted of both acts and attitudes: the acts chosen in accord with pragmatic considerations, the attitude related to love of God.

Augustine's lengthy discussion of nature and custom in Book 3 of *Confessions* resolves into a nonabsolutist ethic of the fitting response. One's experience and understanding of both nature and custom, directed by a love of God, resulted in choices that harmonized with the whole. "Any part which harmonizes not with the whole is offensive."[36] The specific act was not nearly so important as how it fit with the harmony of the earthly city as guided by the loves of the heavenly city.

Despite the dualism inherent in Augustine's division of the earthly and heavenly cities, loyalty to God as a central focus of life unifies his citizenship ethics. One acts toward God, doing all one can to harmonize the goals of the heavenly city with actions in society. Conflicts inevitably arise, and Augustine struggles with many of them, but one's orientation to love of God provides an overarching rubric for action in the world.

Problems arose when it seemed that God's commandments went against custom. True justice then would be served by following God's commandments. "Can it be at any time or place unjust to love God with all his heart, with all his soul and with all his mind; and his neighbor as himself?"[37] No, that was the essence of justice. God's eternal law revealed to humans what was just.[38]

In practice, however, desire to love and obey God, for Augustine, seemed to mean simple obedience to the state. "To obey the king cannot be against the commonweal of the state, nay, it were against it if he were not obeyed, for to obey princes is a general compact of human society."[39] True virtue, ordered by love of God, would motivate the citizen to perform his function in society well and be obedient to the king.

## FROM AUGUSTINE TO LOYAL RESISTANCE

Just as Augustine could not transfer Greek citizenship ethics situated in the *polis* directly to Christian action under a Roman emperor, one cannot simply appropriate Augustine's citizenship ethics today. Neither could I transfer Augustine's views directly to my dilemma with my daughters' training. Although I had discovered a moral source that embraced loyalty to God as a part of ethical reflection and articulated the application of that loyalty in morally ambiguous situations, resistance found no place in Augustine's ethic. I found, however, that a separation of Augustine's view of loyalty from his convictions about the actions that such loyalty required in the context of the Roman Empire uncovers a usable dimension of Augustine's work.

Although the Christian's life was organized into two spheres (heavenly and earthly), and although Christ's followers had to deal with the temptations of sin and self-aggrandizement (light vs. darkness), the orientation of the Christian was singular. One must act always in love of God. Helped by God's grace, this unified focus became a total orientation of the personality and informed all of one's actions. Responding to God in love led to a fitting response in a particular situation.

The Christian citizen was not thereby shielded from conflict. Actions required by loyalty to God often seemed to conflict with what appeared to be a loving response in a particular situation. For example, Augustine, not without sorrow, persecuted heretics because he believed that their work was delaying fulfillment of prophecy.[40] Ultimately, for Augustine, loving God meant punishing or destroying some of God's people. Augustine's decisions on behalf of loyalty to God included not only punishment of heretics but unquestioning obedience to the state. How to act in loyalty to God was not always clear. Following the eternal law of God seemed incompatible, at times, with unquestioningly obeying the state.

Those contradictions and the different contexts for contemporary citizenship ethics necessitate a separation between Augustine's emphasis on loyalty to God as a basis for citizenship ethics and how that loyalty was carried out in Augustine's concrete situated decisions.

Biblical examples of acting toward earthly institutions in loyalty to God show a diversity of behaviors, each appropriate to a particular situation. Ruth's loyalty to Naomi's people led her to unquestioningly follow the marriage customs and laws of the Hebrews. Loyalty was primary; unquestioning obedience was the means to express that loyalty. Esther's loyalty to God and the Hebrew nation was exhibited by a courageous, nuanced, and flattering appeal to bastions of power. Loyalty was primary—behavior was pragmatically chosen to protect that loyalty. Peter's loyalty to God meant a direct defiance of governing authorities. He faced a conflict of loyalties and decided that his loyalty to God meant disobedience to the state.

One can accept Augustine's holistic emphasis on loyalty to God and reject his advice on how to act according to that loyalty. Augustine brings the biblical injunction to love God with all of our heart, soul, and mind to the realm of action in public life. But Christian citizens today need not accept Augustine's responses to conflicts of goods. A place for loyal resistance can be found.

## APPROPRIATING AUGUSTINE'S INSIGHTS

Using Augustine's notion of loyalty to God as a basis for citizenship ethics today allows us to go beyond narrow constructions of reason, utility, or self-interest as a basis for citizen action. His use of loyalty as a central motif in citizenship ethics has three advantages:

1. The *whole person* is involved with what one loves. Putting love of God at the center of ethics in the public realm knits together the project of seeking the public good with inner resonances and loyalty to God.
2. That loyalty also provides a *critical standard* for evaluating actions taken by government. While not always in agreement with one another, Christians come to conclusions about the good and the right through understandings of God's word in text, tradition, and community. Those assessments can be used to critique state action and declarations of morality and advocate actions more suited to human flourishing.
3. A third advantage of using loyalty as a central idea in citizenship ethics is its *relationality*. Rather than delineating a static or rule-oriented public ethic, loyalty to God encourages Christians to seek the good in relationships between individuals, groups, and the larger society.

Loyalty provides the common link between the citizen and those relationships. Josiah Royce spoke of a common loyalty as the link that bound a person with the universal human community.[41] A common loyalty to the nation, centered in loyalty to God for the Christian, binds us to other citizens as we seek the common welfare.

For Christians, this may be a way to break through the current apathy in civil society. Loyalty to God, expressed through loyalty to others in a common quest for peace and goodness, motivates Christians to act toward the common good. Congregations that feed the homeless, help the elderly fill out tax forms, volunteer in local fire departments or elementary schools, or provide other services to the community are acting as good citizens. Many find the motivation to act in those ways energized by their loyalty to God.

For Augustine, loyalty to God was linked to obedience to the state. Not only does our context call for a different response, but different theologies today remove the reasons Augustine paired loyalty with obedience to the state.

A deterministic view of predestination gave Augustine the impression that even wicked rulers and evil acts should not be tampered with by mere humans. Because reason itself was fallen, people could not depend on their moral evaluations. A belief in God's predestination of rulers and understanding of all that they would do, combined with that low but absolutist view of human reason, led to Augustine's injunction to obey at all costs.

An urgent understanding of the fulfillment of biblical prophecy also kept Augustine from advocating an active stance of resistance. Any action that interfered with the movement toward the day of judgment was against God's will. Hastening that day through suppression of paganism by the Christian state itself, however, was laudable. These interpretations sound strange to our modern ears because they are not applicable to our situation. We live not in a decaying totalitarian regime, but in a republic that rightly expects citizen input and responsible action.

Different understandings of theology, human reason, biblical prophecy, and Christianity's relation to the state combined to bring Augustine to the conclusion that it was wrong for the citizen to resist actions or policies of the state. None of those understandings apply to Christians today. Theology has come to be understood in ways that allow for human freedom as well as changes in God. Current understandings of reason as historically situated and socially constructed allow us to understand it as a mixed blessing and a human activity. We need not fear reason because of its total "fallenness" or worship it as the ultimate path to knowledge. Finally, we live in a pluralistic society that has carved out a sphere for self-governance and freedom for people of many different religious traditions.

## RESISTANCE AS LOYALTY

The last forty years has seen a change in North American understandings of the role of resistance in the public realm. Although people are still arrested for civil disobedience, demonstrations as peaceful public declarations of resistance to government policies are much more acceptable, whether or not they influence government policies.

Those demonstrations have become a new way for U.S. citizens to express opinions on public policies. Environmental groups enter international waters to protect dolphins against net harvesting of tuna. People concerned about poverty in the two-thirds world carry placards at international free trade conferences. Christian scholars outline resistance procedures and their rationale for denominations and churches.[42]

A theology of loyal resistance to government can become a conscious part of citizenship ethics for Christians in the United States. H. Richard Niebuhr's radical monotheism insisted that putting any cause or object at the center of one's values and paying allegiance to it before God was idolatry.[43] Ronald Stone and Dana Wilbanks take up that stance when they declare that "Christians may find it necessary on occasion to resist government policies as a decision of faith in the Lord of history."[44] Here resistance is supported on the basis of loyalty to God but is not directly related to loyalty to the nation as a citizen.

Some suggest that loyalty to the nation is not needed to achieve the good ends that resistance seeks. Loyalty to the nonviolent ethic of Jesus requires for some a "political atheism" that obliterates political and ethnic boundaries for the Christian.[45] Here, resistance as a loyal citizen drops out of view.

Martin Luther King Jr., working out of a Christian framework for civil rights, called the nation to live up to the Constitution—to cash the constitutional check of promised freedom written by our founders. While leading the most powerful resistance movement of the twentieth century, he consistently demonstrated his loyalty as a citizen of the United States. That loyalty, for King, was based in loyalty to God.

King demonstrated that Augustine's concept of loyalty can be linked with resistance against structural evils of our society as they are enacted through law or custom. Envisioning resistance not as antithetical to good citizenship but as its expression moves us toward breaking down Augustine's eternal divide between the heavenly and the earthly cities. Loyalty to God can be enacted wholeheartedly in the public sphere as resistance to policies that inhibit human flourishing or allow the perpetuation of evil.

Uniting loyalty to God and loyalty to nation enacted as resistance also gives citizens a voice in national affairs in between voting every two years for Congress and every four years for president. In a large and complex nation, resistance gives citizens a way to express their views and convictions about government actions or pending decisions in a public way. Although one may not be able to evaluate the overall impact of off-shore drilling or mining in national forests, for example, concerned citizens can see the damaging effects of those activities on wildlife and vegetation. Public outcry and sustained resistance gives those citizens a voice in future public policies that affect the environment.

Understanding resistance as an act of loyalty to the nation rather than solely an act of loyalty to God brings ethical issues into critical dialogue from the perspectives of Christian ethics and national ideals. Rather than conflating national and religious loyalties, citizenship as loyal resistance maintains the distinction between state and religious obligations modeled by Augustine. But the two are brought together when action in the earthly sphere is informed by Christian ethics rather than state dictums. Unthinking patriotism on the one hand and apathy on the other are avoided. Critical assessment of issues on the basis of Christian ethics leads to specific action in the public realm based on loyalty to God and an appreciation of the role of the state in civic life.

Maintaining a space for legitimate loyalty to both spheres opens the way for integrating without conflating loyalties to God and nation. The danger of religiously sanctioned state violence is avoided by the separation of those loyalties. At the same time, one also sees the possibility of loyal resistance as a citizen if government policies run counter to Christian ethics.

While working with the Christian community and using Christian ethics to critique the unjust treatment of African Americans in the United States, Martin Luther King called upon the nation to be true to its own constitutional and republican principles. Loyalty to the United States, for good citizens, required resisting the failure of the nation to live up to its own ideals.

Civil rights resistance was Christian resistance for some—their loyalty to God led them to resist. It was citizen resistance for others—their loyalty to the ideals of the nation spawned resistance. For King and still others, it was both. As a Christian and a loyal citizen, I resisted my nation's failure to live up to its ideals, invoking both my heavenly and earthly loyalties.

## CONCLUSION

As my view of citizenship ethics as loyal resistance developed, I could explain to my children how I could love God, love my country, and participate in acts of resistance. Establishing loyal resistance as a basis for citizenship ethics uses Augustine's strengths without separating actions toward the heavenly realm from action in the world. This rubric provides a way to link loyalty to God and reflection on citizen contributions to public life. It offers a way for citizens to voice opinions and act on convictions in a huge state. It provides motivation for citizens to band together in concerted action, thus strengthening civil society.

Augustine's emphasis on the inevitable moral ambiguity of situations allows for citizen action that does not require total purity or perfection. The expectation of human failure applies to the state—we expect the state to fail and occasion the need for resistance. Making a space for critical loyalty to the state centered in loyalty to God, based on well-ordered loves, and resulting in loyal resistance enhances the moral order, stimulates civil society, and motivates citizens to act for the common good.

## NOTES

1. For further analysis see Frances S. Adeney, "Jean Bethke Elshtain: Political Theorist and Postmodern Prophet," *Religious Studies Review* 27, no. 3 (July 2001): 247.

2. William M. Sullivan, *Reconstructing Public Philosophy* (Berkeley: University of California Press, 1982), p. 166.

3. Ibid., p. 214.

4. Charles Taylor, *Sources of the Self: The Making of the Modern Identity* (Cambridge, Mass.: Harvard University Press, 1989).

5. The inner depths "may take us beyond the subjective" (to the transpersonal), "but the road to them passes inescapably through a heightened awareness of personal experience." Taylor, *Sources of the Self*, p. 481.

6. Sullivan, *Reconstructing Public Philosophy*, p. 157.

7. For an analysis of Augustine's view of the good and his critique of classical virtue, see Frances S. Adeney, *Citizenship Ethics: Classical Virtue Theory and Responsibility Ethics* (Ann Arbor, Mich.: UMI, 1989), ch. 2.

8. See John A. Coleman, "The Two Pedagogies: Discipleship and Citizenship," in *Educating for Citizenship and Discipleship*, ed. Mary Boys (New York: Pilgrim Press, 1989).

9. See Dorothy H. Donnelly, "Augustine and Romanitas" (Ph.D. diss., Graduate Theological Union, Berkeley, California).

10. F. Edward Cranz, "The Development of Augustine's Ideas on Society Before the Donatist Controversy," in *Augustine: A Collection of Critical Essays*, ed. R. A. Markus (New York: Anchor Books, Doubleday, 1972), p. 339.

11. Ibid., p. 352f.

12. Peter R. L. Brown, "Political Society," in *Augustine: A Collection of Critical Essays*, ed. R. A. Markus (New York: Anchor Books, Doubleday, 1972), p. 326.

13. *The City of God* 19.26, p. 529, Great Books of the Western World, vol. 18, trans. Marcus Dods. All further references to this work will be abbreviated DCD and will be taken from this edition.

14. DCD 19.17, p. 522.

15. Peter R. L. Brown, *Augustine of Hippo: A Biography* (Berkeley: University of California Press, 1967), p. 314f.

16. Brown, *Augustine of Hippo*, p. 156.

17. R. A. Markus, *Saeculum: History and Society in the Theology of St. Augustine* (New York: Cambridge University Press, 1970), p. 173.

18. DCD 19.27, p. 529.

19. Herbert A. Deane, *The Political and Social Ideas of St. Augustine* (New York: Columbia University Press, 1963), p. 239.

20. Peter R. L. Brown, *Religion and Society in the Age of St. Augustine* (New York: Harper and Row, 1972), p. 42.

21. DCD 19.24, p. 528.

22. DCD 2.22, p. 162.

23. DCD 19.17, p. 522f.

24. DCD 5.11, p. 216.

25. Brown, *Religion and Society in the Age of St. Augustine*, p. 35.

26. Deane, p. 52.

27. Ibid., p. 153.

28. DCD 19.14, p. 520.

29. Deane, p. 96.

30. Ibid., p. 69.

31. Brown, *Religion and Society in the Age of St. Augustine*, p. 267f.

32. Ibid.

33. DCD 2.23, p. 164.

34. Deane, p. 57.

35. DCD 19.21, p. 524.

36. Augustine, *Confessions* (New York: Collier Books, 1961; reprint ed., 1966), 3.8.

37. Ibid.

38. DCD 19.14, p. 520.

39. Augustine, *Confessions* 3.8.

40. Brown, *Religion and Society in the Age of St. Augustine*, p. 267f.

41. Josiah Royce, *The Problem of Christianity* (New York: Macmillan, 1913; University of Chicago Press ed., 1968), p. 41.

42. See Ronald H. Stone and Dana W. Wilbanks, *Presbyterians and Peacemaking: Are We Now Called to Resistance?* (New York: Advisory Council on Church and Society, 1985).

43. See H. Richard Niebuhr, *Radical Monotheism and Western Culture* (New York: Harper and Bros., 1960), pp. 16–18, 65–68, and Frances S. Adeney, "Niebuhr's View of an Ethic of Citizenship," in Adeney, *Citizenship Ethics*, pp. 166–172.

44. Stone and Wilbanks, *Presbyterians and Peacemaking*, p. 46.

45. Daniel L. Smith-Christopher, "Political Atheism and Radical Faith: The Challenge of Christian Nonviolence in the Third Millennium," in *Subverting Hatred: The Challenge of Nonviolence in Religious Traditions*, ed. Daniel L. Smith-Christopher (Maryknoll, N.Y.: Orbis, 1998), p. 145.

## 13

# "Is God Dead?":
# The Complexity of Resistance

## Scott C. Williamson

$\mathcal{A}$frican American Christians have creatively used resources internal to their traditions to resist white-racist ideology in the culture at large and among allies in the reform effort. Resistance against the oppressive social relationships born of this ideology has been an enormous task, made all the more difficult because white racists were counted among friends and colleagues as well as adversaries. Though the object of resistance has been self-evident, *how* to resist white racism has proved quite complex for black Christians. The complexity of black resistance to white racism is discerned in three overlapping spheres of concern: (1) how to interpret Christian resources for resistance; (2) how to resist the racism of white colleagues in the struggle; and (3) how to choose between the various modes of resistance, including but not limited to moral, political, nonviolent, and violent approaches.

Nineteenth-century black abolitionists posed the very challenge: to use Christian resources in resistance against racism, not only in its vulgar manifestations, but also in the milder paternalistic form it took among fellow abolitionists. Frederick Douglass is an appropriate representative here. Douglass took up the challenge against racism and developed a nuanced strategy of resistance. He prophesied against promethean forms of racism that were institutionalized in the national culture. He confronted the racism of white friends. He also agonized over the most effective mode of resistance, changing his mind to the chagrin of the moral suasionists with whom he was associated.

In his early years under the tutelage of William Lloyd Garrison, Douglass addressed the first horn of this dilemma, namely, how best to resist the vulgar forms of white racism that authorized slavery and dehumanized blacks.[1] Following Garrison's lead, Douglass argued that nonviolent noncompliance and moral suasion were sufficient responses to God's will for emancipation. Later, in his post-Garrison years as a political abolitionist and editor, Douglass rejected the sufficiency of these responses. He championed political abolition instead and stressed human effort over divine providence in the struggle for black emancipation. Douglass even defended violent resistance as a morally justifiable tactic in the struggle.

His earlier trust in God's provident direction of history confirmed nonviolent noncompliance and moral suasion as necessary and sufficient modes of faithful resistance. As he matured, however, Douglass accepted that the work of abolition was accomplished less by faith in divine sovereignty and providence than by aggressive political action and tactical compromise. Men and women won the war against slavery with their blood and sweat. Douglass's theological foundations shifted to accommodate new ideas about God and human responsibility for immediate outcomes in human history. Instead of waiting patiently upon God for the fulfillment of ultimate ends, Douglass urged his audience to fight, and he understood the good fight against slavery as a moral duty that was necessary to the unfolding of God's eschatological aims. In terms more familiar to Douglass, God sanctioned resistance and took no delight in pious complicity with slavery.

Resistance took yet another form in Douglass's work. Beside the cooperative effort to end slavery and to subdue the more public and trenchant forms of white racism, Douglass also resisted the paternalism of his white coworkers. Douglass found that prejudice against blacks was an enduring obstacle, even among northern white sympathizers. Curiously, the white defenders of black humanity were not necessarily advocates of black equality. From the start, Douglass resisted both types of racial prejudice: promethean and paternalistic. Tired of the paternalistic assumptions that underscored his role in the Massachusetts Anti-Slavery Society, Douglass eventually broke from Garrison's guild of abolitionists to pursue an enlarged agenda independent of white superintendency.

His decision to found a newspaper, over the fierce protest of former colleagues, was not an easy one to make. Douglass had to assess the benefits of being independent, of having a forum for his thoughts, and of demonstrating black excellence against the liability of promoting separate racial institutions. The benefits were more compelling, and Douglass withdrew his allegiance to old friends. He preferred to broker his own agenda than to underwrite Garrison's.

Though he acknowledged an immediate need for separate racial institutions to empower blacks and to begin the work of racial elevation, Douglass was leery of creating permanent black institutions. The material goal of elevation was inclusion in the white mainstream and participation in middle-class pursuits. Douglass did not doubt that a separate black America was a mistake. Ever the practical strategist, Douglass feared that separation from whites would leave blacks vulnerable to white domination. He supported racial integration for its benefit to blacks and whites alike, but Douglass's negative reason for integration, or his assessment of likely consequences in the absence of integration, was original and compelling. Douglass cautioned his peers that blacks were safer intermixed among whites than separated from whites. The history of slavery in the United States provided ample evidence that not even the Atlantic Ocean could forestall white lust in a black homeland.

The story of Douglass's protest against slavery and inequality raises intriguing issues for students of Douglass regarding his moral and religious convictions. The topic of resistance in Douglass's thought invites questions about his views on God and the work of sanctification, about moral warrants for suasionist and political abolitionism, and about cooperation in pursuit of shared goals. These questions not only reveal the rich antecedents and mature formulations of Douglass's thought but also inform current conversations about resistance. Douglass sorted out these matters in public forums and left behind an invaluable contribution, a glimpse into a nineteenth-century mind at work on issues of race and justice that trouble us still.

## FROM MORAL SUASION TO POLITICAL ACTION

"Frederick, is God dead?"[2] With characteristic aplomb, Sojourner Truth put the matter straightforwardly and penetrated the veneer of eloquence that Douglass cultivated so carefully. They shared the stage in 1852 at an abolitionist rally in Salem, Ohio. Her question had more to do with the efficacy and sufficiency of nonviolent noncompliance in the abolitionist crusade than with divine ontology per se. His reply was unsettling. Douglass affirmed both divine providence and the justifiability of violence in defense of freedom. These ideas were not more radical than similar sentiments advocated by the fathers of the American Revolution, but they were more inflammatory when juxtaposed by Douglass on behalf of black equality.

His reply is remarkable beyond the controversy it generated. In 1852, Douglass was betwixt and between his earlier indebtedness to Garrisonian moral and religious precepts and his later indebtedness to German "freethinking." In earlier writings, while under the tutelage of Garrison, Douglass expressed his conviction in a personal God and what he called the "Christianity of Christ."[3] By the mid-1850s, however, Douglass was exposed to new interpretations of religion coming out of Germany. He was particularly drawn to the writings of J. G. Fichte, D. F. Strauss, and Ludwig Feuerbach. In an undated speech from this period, for example, he credits the laws of the universe for teaching that humanity is to be its own savior or its own destroyer.[4] Between these positions, in the late 1840s and early 1850s, Douglass attempted to interweave a waning trust in evangelical notions of divine omnipotence, beneficence, and providence with a growing confidence in the moral authority of human reason.

## WHERE IS GOD?

The efficacy of moral suasion, the sufficiency of nonviolent noncompliance in the abolitionist crusade, and the meaning of trust in God were at issue for Sojourner Truth and Frederick Douglass on that summer evening in 1852. Truth pressed Douglass either to affirm the seemingly ludicrous proposition that God summoned the faithful to bloodshed in order to bring about peace and justice, or to acknowledge that he conceded no authority to God. Douglass argued a third alternative, that God inspired the oppressed to fight for their God-given freedom in any number of ways, including violent resistance. Truth took a different tack.

Like Douglass, Sojourner Truth was introduced to Christianity while enslaved. Her experiences confirmed that slavery and patriarchy were evil, but her commitments to nonviolence and moral suasion issued from her Protestant Christology, the teachings of Quakers and Spiritualists among whom she counted many friends, and the ideology of the Garrisonian abolitionists with whom she labored for emancipation. God was, for Truth, powerful and merciful, compassionate and just. God also spoke directly to her, as she reported to audiences and friends on numerous occasions.[5] Her trust in God's providential care issued in an optimism that resonated in her question to Douglass. God was neither dead nor gone from the scene of human crisis and, therefore, the faithful received divine, supernatural guidance even during tumultuous times. Experience of God's other-centered love was a prompt for Truth to do likewise. Having accepted God as her "last master," Truth accepted an obligation to respond to divine love with trust and mutuality. Nonviolent noncompliance and moral suasion, then, were consistent with Truth's veneration of God, trust in God's providence, and duty to neighbor-love.

Douglass had once shared these views, albeit with some difficulty. He, too, was converted to Christianity in younger years, during which time he was overcome with love for all people. But, unlike Truth, Douglass held resolutely to the conviction that the person who succeeded in whipping him would also succeed in killing him. After his epic battle with the slave-breaker Edward Covey in 1834, Douglass resolved to fight to the death in self-defense.[6]

The brutal persecution suffered under Covey occasioned a moral and religious transformation in Douglass. An observation from his second autobiography illustrates the nature of the moral baptism[7] occasioned by this epic fight: "A man without force is without the essential dignity of humanity. Human nature is so constituted, that it cannot *honor* a helpless man although it can *pity* him; and even this it cannot do long if the signs of power do not arise."[8] Defiance and noncompliance were not regarded as virtues for blacks in the standard morality of his era, yet Douglass recognized their significance as indicators of human dignity. He authorized these alternate virtues, not by appeal to God, but by appeal to an essential human nature.[9]

The Covey experience occasioned the beginning of a religious transformation as well. Before he vowed to resist Covey, he believed to great measure what he was taught. He believed in a personal and benevolent God; he believed that salvation was the mysterious work of God, and that physical resistance against his master was at odds with trust in God. But his trust waned under Covey. The severe treatment he received, despite his pleas to God, led him to doubt the efficacy of prayer and the soundness of religion. Douglass's faith was not great, but it endured. In a revealing passage, Douglass equated his victory over Covey with Jesus' victory over death. He wrote: "After resisting him, I felt as I had never felt before. It was a resurrection from the dark and pestiferous tomb of slavery, to the heaven of comparative freedom."[10] Douglass held that slavery, resistance, and freedom correlated, respectively, to death, resurrection, and heaven. Physical resistance occasioned a resurrection for Douglass. He was raised from a state of coerced self-denial to a state of conscientious self-regard.

Vis-à-vis slave owners, conscientious self-regard was simultaneously life-threatening and life-affirming for slaves. Douglass knew that violence could cost him his life, yet the alternative was less attractive. Better to fight, Douglass thought. In the act of direct psychological and physical defiance, regardless of the outcome, the slave saved her humanity, claimed her dignity, and savored but a taste of the freedom that was her right by nature. This revelation undermined the efficacy of nonviolent noncompliance in his thought. Though he preached its virtues under Garrison well into the 1840s, his hands were not "tied by [his] religion."[11] For slaves to affirm nonviolent noncompliance while held in a state of coerced self-denial was tantamount to complicity—complicity with the dehumanizing standards of their enslavement. Douglass discovered that physical resistance against slavery imported its own brand of deliverance from evil and mediated divine justice.

Salvation for Douglass was not merely a religious matter, the supernatural and mysterious working of a transcendent God to deliver the faithful from evil. Douglass had in mind a more social-political salvation, inspired by God but accomplished through human vision, commitment, and initiative. In this way, by holding in tension two modes of salvation, Douglass appealed to men and women to accomplish God's will for emancipation. God did not intend slavery. Douglass was confident in this belief because God endowed the slave with reason and a capacity for self-expression and self-direction, both of which were denied in slavery. Nor did God require the faithful to relinquish responsibility for social reform. On the contrary, God's righteousness inspired the hue and cry for justice, and God's wrath energized the slave to avail herself of all resources in resistance against her chains.

Assumptions about God's creative relations with the world are couched in these positions. Douglass held God's realm as being distinct from the human realm. This distinction accorded latitude to humans in fulfilling God's aims for life and liberty. Religious beliefs that circumscribed this latitude, such as the beliefs that authorized nonviolent noncompliance, promoted trust in God but compromised the effectiveness of social reform.[12] Douglass feared that waiting patiently upon God for deliverance occasioned a pious apathy among blacks, and a politics of conformity. Nevertheless, Douglass shared in a Millennialist expectation that God would cleanse the land of slavery. The complexity of this viewpoint underscores Douglass's commitment to both divine and human spheres of influence in the abolitionist movement. Douglass's position illuminates his struggle to understand how God is present in human crises, and how the divine mind enlists human action to direct outcomes in history.

Assumptions about the character of God and the efficacy of religion are also couched in these positions. Douglass did not subscribe to traditional notions of God as a supernatural person, the majestic object of reverence through bended knee and extravagant ritual. In accordance with the liberal bent of his closest friends in the abolitionist movement, Douglass thought of God more in terms of creative power than personhood—an intentional and inspirational energy that set, animated, and stabilized the created order. This divine activity was accomplished through the work of nature, including human relationships. Douglass grew frustrated with an orthodox reliance upon prayer and miracle to effect supernatural occurrences. Reason simply did not support divine intervention. On the contrary, a belief in the supernatural intervention of a divine person undermined confidence in reason. In later years, Douglass favored a saying to illustrate his lack of confidence in divine intervention: "All the prayers of Christendom cannot divert a single bullet from its course."[13] Divine inspiration, however, was a different matter than divine intervention. Inspiration was consistent with reason, and Douglass preached a faith in God that was informed by reason.

Douglass's conception of God and God's relation to humanity held significance for his ethics. If a belief in God's sovereignty authorized the pacifism of Garrison, then Douglass's anthropology authorized his political abolition. William Lloyd Garrison was categorically opposed to violent resistance on the authority of scripture. Although he argued for nonviolent noncompliance, Garrison was not uncompromising in his view. He once argued that he would rather see slaves violently resist their masters than succumb to the soul-crushing effects of chattel slavery. Garrison thought, however, that a better alternative was available to slaves and to those who opposed slavery. He made an eloquent case for what he called nonviolent conscientious noncompliance by appealing to the authority of Christ.[14] Douglass, for his part, was less concerned than Garrison about religious authority and more concerned with the Christian's responsibility for the social and political outcomes of action. Douglass never advocated unlimited or reckless violent resistance, nor did he believe that God was irrelevant to resistance. Rather, Douglass interpreted "active" resistance in a way that balanced God's will with human initiative, moral protest with political reform, and that tempered reverence with reason. Faith in God and a calculus of probable outcomes posed no ethical dilemma for Douglass. On a continuum of Christian responses to evil, Douglass and Garrison differed mainly about how "active" the Christian could be.

## COOPERATION AND INDEPENDENCE

Given the volatile nature of the personalities involved, it is a wonder that bloodshed did not ensue from Douglass's break with Garrison. The break was a contentious one, and personal attacks were volleyed back and forth. Garrison labeled Douglass an ingrate and egomaniac. Douglass denounced the attack against him and questioned the motives of former friends who did not support his budding independence. .

The break was indeed necessary. Douglass tired of his scripted role, a role that encouraged him to tell his story in vivid detail but discouraged him from arguing the abolitionist case against slavery. Other minds could handle the philosophy, but who better than Frederick Douglass could narrate the horrors of slavery? Douglass needed to speak his mind and to set an agenda free of white superintendency.

Though the break was necessary, Douglass's tenure as a Garrisonian lecturer was highly successful for both parties. Within the fold, Douglass achieved international acclaim as a lecturer. The publication of his first narrative in 1845, while a fugitive from slavery, was followed by a European tour. Speaking engagements in Ireland, Scotland, and England introduced Douglass to a new audience of white sympathizers and to environments that were more conducive to black success than were those in the United States. With a published book and a polished style to his credit, Douglass developed self-confidence as an abolitionist lecturer. He also gained new contacts and offers of financial support from benefactors who did not share Garrison's misgivings about Douglass's intention to found yet another abolitionist journal.

The Garrisonians found in Douglass a captivating speaker, a tireless worker, and a receptive mind. His experience as a slave, his personal charisma, and his eloquence as a speaker were unmatched; no other lecturer brought that combination of gifts to the stage. Douglass opened audiences to Garrison's message, but that role came at a high price.

Recommendations that he stick to narration did not sit well with Douglass. He perceived the issues at stake as well as any white abolitionist, he understood the platform and its underlying philosophy, and he was quick to rebuttal, for he could find the deficiencies of contrary arguments with great skill. Given his talents, Douglass correctly perceived that his race was a stumbling block for his white colleagues. They welcomed him for what he could contribute to the society and to the cause for which they labored, but they welcomed him to a limited role. Not even praise for excellence as a lecturer offset the discontent that Douglass experienced within that prescribed role.

## THE CHALLENGE OF COOPERATION AND THE PROBLEM OF WHITE SUPERINTENDENCY

A particular species of discontent befalls those who are kindly belittled by their peers. Douglass wrote that he expected his friends in Boston to be "favorably disposed"[15] toward his idea to found a journal. He was sadly mistaken. On the contrary, his colleagues listed four reasons why Douglass should not start an abolitionist journal: the paper was not necessary; it would interfere with Douglass's valuable work as a lecturer; he was more proficient as a speaker than as a writer; and, finally, the paper could not succeed. Douglass acknowledged the soundness of each reason; still, he questioned whether his white friends had reached the limits of their faith in his abilities. More significantly, he was uncomfortable with abandoning this pursuit on their say-so. Being wrong was less costly than being manipulated. A healthy self-estimate and the support of friends outside the fold enabled Douglass to resist Garrison's advice and to redefine his role as an abolitionist.

Beyond his discontent at a limited role within the American Anti-Slavery Society, Douglass also felt strained relations with Garrisonians over several matters of principle. Nonviolent noncompliance, as discussed above, was one Garrisonian principle that simply stuck in Douglass's craw. It came at cheaper cost for whites than for blacks in the context of white racism and privilege. Blacks who chose nonviolent noncompliance relinquished other potentially beneficial strategies for racial uplift, or empowerment. White Garrisonians renounced violence, but they benefited nonetheless from the privilege attendant to race.

The exclusiveness of moral suasion was another principle that caused stress for Douglass. Garrison held moral suasion as a fundamental principle. Regardless of the outcomes, moral suasion was inherently right because of the trust that it placed in God's sovereignty and providence. Douglass valued moral suasion not as an end, but as a tactic used along with political means of reform. Moral suasion failed on three counts: it provided no tactical direction; it steered no course beyond emancipation; it was held in needless tension with political measures that increased the effectiveness of the entire campaign. Here too Garrison's insistence on nonvoting came at cheaper cost for white males than for blacks. Educated white males could choose to refrain from voting for moral reasons; blacks did not have the voting rights necessary to make such a moral choice. Furthermore, black abolitionists wanted citizenship rights for blacks—rights that were undermined by a nonvoting stance.

Douglass was also troubled by Garrison's insistence on disunion. Douglass believed that Garrison's pledge to have "no union with slaveholders," either religious or political, issued at best in a Pyrrhic victory for blacks. Even if the Union was dissolved and its fundamental documents of incorporation were scrapped, the problem of slavery still persisted in the South. Douglass believed that abolitionists had a responsibility to emancipate the slaves in the South and not merely leave them enslaved in a confederacy of southern states, should the Union dissolve.

Moreover, Douglass grew weary of arguing along with the apologists for slavery that the U.S. Constitution was a slaveholding document. To take this line was to concede that slavery was protected by the law of the land. Under the influence of New York landowner and philanthropist Gerrit Smith, Douglass rejected his former position and argued that the U.S. Constitution was "in its letter and spirit" an antislavery instrument. By taking this position with other political abolitionists, Douglass argued that structural change on the matter of chattel slavery was authorized throughout the country on political grounds. Douglass claimed further that the Constitution demanded the abolition of slavery "as a condition of its own existence."[16] To be consistent with its preamble, Douglass held, the Constitution had to authorize abolition. The document, like the nation, could not simultaneously defend both liberty and slavery without contradiction.

Beyond these specific reasons for discontent with his role as a lecturer for the Massachusetts Anti-Slavery Society, Douglass was hampered in his service to the Society by four tangential factors. First, Douglass was chagrined that his white friends did not support his desire to "handle the philosophy," beyond narrating the same basic facts of his days in slavery. This little slight undermined Douglass's confidence that he was esteemed as an equal by white Garrisonians. His response was essentially the same as it had been when his "mistress," Sophia Auld, broke off his reading lessons; Douglass committed himself to self-improvement. He did so again in his waning years as a Garrisonian. Douglass developed those capacities for philosophic comprehension, critical critique, and effective composition that his friends had failed to appreciate.

Second, Douglass faced the problem of white superintendency. Although he gladly accepted offers of assistance from whites, setting the agenda was a different matter. As he matured in his roles as an abolitionist and black leader, and as his confidence grew, Douglass wanted to set his own agenda. Having control over how best to utilize his budding talents reinforced Douglass's estimation of his own "manhood" or character. It also lent greater authenticity to his public appeals, and it heightened trust in his capacity to direct an abolitionist front.

Third, Douglass realized that black abolitionists had a responsibility to blacks that was not and could not be shared by whites. This additional responsibility, as he referred to it, entailed fostering character and modeling success so as to advance the cause of black elevation. Whites could fight for abolition, but elevation had to be a black affair. Douglass argued that freedom could not be given; it had to be taken. Sympathizers could fight for human rights and material equity if they were so disposed, but one cannot claim empowerment for another. That work is necessarily internal.

Finally, Douglass received very generous offers of assistance from white friends outside the Garrisonian fold. Several prominent British abolitionists fanned his desire to become an editor and to redefine his role as an abolitionist. With financial assistance and encouragement from these white benefactors, who had already raised money to buy him from master Hugh Auld, Douglass purchased the second installment of his freedom; he acquired the liberty to set an agenda, to speak his mind, and to be independent.

Among his reasons for leaving the Garrisonian fold was an expectation of gain. Douglass envisioned benefit for himself, for the abolitionist cause, and for African Americans generally in the role of editor. First, he needed to be his own boss. By editing a journal and coordinating his lecture schedule, Douglass controlled the terms of his employment and the use of his narrative. He was finally his own master. As an editor, he did not have to recite his narrative on cue, nor did he have to turn his audience over to another agent to explain the philosophy of abolition. Rather, editing a journal required that Douglass use his experience and learning to *define* arguments and not merely defend them.

Douglass as editor was also able to pursue a trajectory of self-realization that he set in childhood to develop his mind and character on his own terms. Whereas learning was a boon to his understanding, so, too, the exercise of social, intellectual, and economic power was a boon to Douglass's character. The role of editor afforded Douglass an opportunity to mature and to deepen on both counts. His learning enabled him to understand with greater nuance the nature of the racial problems that befell his era. With the power of the pen, Douglass scripted an agenda of reform to address those problems.

Further, editing a journal enabled Douglass to cooperate with white abolitionists on terms of independence rather than indenture. The significance of an independent editorship for Douglass was twofold. He exposed the lie that blacks were not well suited to the creative, organizational, and pecuniary rigors of editing a journal. Douglass also challenged his own limits, and by so doing he disproved Garrison's observation that he was better suited to lecturing than to editing. Moreover, the Douglass editorials added a fresh and critical perspective to an array of abolitionist critiques. The running commentary on the nation and its ills posed by his editorials illumined not only an abolitionist take, but also an African American perspective on the pressing issues of the day.

Finally, in the role of editor, Douglass promoted his agenda of emancipation, elevation, and material equality with whites through self-help and protest. In this arrangement of means and ends, the reformer achieved not only originality as a leader, but also a representative voice among African Americans. The gamble to break from Garrison and start a journal paid off richly in a figurative if not financial sense. Douglass did not make much money as a lecturer and editor. Nevertheless his work during the antebellum and Civil War years earned a different sort of currency. Though he possessed no ecclesiastical authority whatsoever and his views on religion were largely disavowed by blacks, Frederick Douglass became the undisputed representative voice of black America in civil matters.

His years in slavery and efforts as an agitator for human rights leveraged his reform agenda against criticism and authorized his platform for the elevation of African Americans. Unlike his white peers in the reform movement,

Douglass's message to blacks was free from the taint of white supremacy, paternalism, and hypocrisy. Though he did not successfully court a significant black readership, blacks trusted Douglass. He was the object of trust and esteem among blacks largely because of his outspokenness and indefatigable drive to self-realization. He won trust because he suffered their experiences of oppression but nonetheless steeled himself for a more just America. Douglass also demonstrated care for African Americans. His reform platform in the antebellum years was broader than abolition because his concern for black well-being went beyond emancipation. At war's end, Douglass wanted to build character and engender success among a generation of blacks who he feared would fall back into quasi-servitude if they did not rise to the challenges of emancipation. In accordance with this aim, he defended the prerequisites for success. Vocational education, public schooling, voting rights, thrift, sobriety, pragmatic religion, and protest against injustice everywhere were among the positions that filled out Douglass's columns and speeches.

## LESSONS FOR THOSE WHO RESIST

Douglass wrote his manifesto in the fall of 1852, only months after his Salem, Ohio, encounter with Truth.

> I have one great political idea. . . . That idea is an old idea. It is widely and generally assented to; nevertheless, it is very generally trampled upon and disregarded. The best expression of it I have found is in the Bible. It is in substance, "righteousness exalteth a nation—sin is a reproach to any people" . . . this constitutes my politics, the negative and positive of my politics and the whole of my politics.[17]

The theological categories of righteousness and sin framed Douglass's political thought. Social sinfulness authorized resistance. Whether it took the form of an active hostility to blacks or a passive but equally aggressive paternalism, the sinfulness of social institutions occasioned three modes of resistance. Each mode of resistance seeded righteousness and engendered hope that justice would prevail.

Self-possessed agency was at the core of a moral resistance against social sinfulness. Douglass believed that self-possessed action patterned virtuous character among the disenfranchised and set a foundation for solidarity with white allies. Conversely, disempowerment and complicity followed closely upon an acquiescent adoption of agendas that were not of one's own deliberation and express consent. Exercising authority in matters of one's own well-being was the hallmark of a self-possessed agency.

Trust in divine inspiration was at the core of a religious resistance against social manifestations of sin. Douglass believed that divine activity was manifested in human productivity, and that God inspired men and women to be agents of righteousness. The faithful found God in the struggle and did not wait for God to orchestrate the struggle.

Lastly, commitment to the cause of reform was at the core of a political resistance against social sinfulness. In an oft-repeated phrase that characterized his position on politics, Douglass quipped, "I am a Republican, but not 'a Republican right or wrong.'" Of more importance to Douglass was the outcome than the method, the platform than the party. And his commitment to any political organization was tempered by an assessment of progressiveness and the likelihood of success in shared pursuits. His loyalty to a particular guild, party, or affiliation was ancillary to his loyalty to the causes of emancipation, human rights, and material equality.

Resistance served moral, religious, and political purposes in Douglass's thought. Given the nature of the case to which it was applied, the means of resistance morphed to the demands of the challenge. The goal of resistance, however, remained constant. Resistance "revived" the "lines of eternal justice." Sometimes nonviolence was sufficient to revive those lines and resistance took shape around nonviolence. On occasion, however, the lines of eternal justice were so "obliterated by a course of long continued oppression that it [was] necessary to revive them by deepening their traces with the blood of a tyrant."[18]

# NOTES

The autobiographical accounts to which I refer in this chapter, *My Bondage and My Freedom* (New York: Miller, Orton and Mulligan, 1855), and *Life and Times of Frederick Douglass, Written by Himself: His early life as a slave, his escape from bondage, and his complete history to the present time* (new rev. ed., Boston: DeWolfe, Fisk [1892]), are found in one volume: *Frederick Douglass: Autobiographies*, ed. Henry Louis Gates (New York: Library of America, 1994). The pagination I cite refers to the Gates volume.

1. Douglass subscribed to Garrison's weekly, *The Liberator*, in 1839, the year following his escape from Maryland to New York, and his relocation to New Bedford, Massachusetts. He was well acquainted with Garrison's views on abolition and emancipation when the two men met in August 1841 at a meeting of the Bristol County Anti-Slavery Society in New Bedford. Douglass addressed the convention and occasioned an impassioned speech by Garrison. Later, Douglass accepted a three-month trial membership as a salaried agent of the Massachusetts Anti-Slavery Society. The Society favored moral suasion, immediate emancipation, disunion, and the civil equality of blacks. It opposed the colonization of freed slaves, political abolitionism, and

union with slave holders, either religious or political. Douglass was a twenty-three-year-old laborer, fugitive slave, husband, father of two, and African Methodist Episcopal Zion licensed preacher when he accepted the trial membership as an agent of the Massachusetts Anti-Slavery Society.

2. Carleton Mabee, *Sojourner Truth: Slave, Prophet, Legend* (New York: New York University Press, 1993), pp. 83–88. Compare the Oliver Johnson account in Mabee, p. 88, to Douglass's autobiographical account in *Life and Times*, p. 719. Johnson writes: "Mr. Douglass stood for a moment in silence and seemed fully conscious of the force of the question; and when he replied he could only affirm that God was present in the mind of the oppressed to stimulate them to violence." Douglass writes a different account of the fabled story some thirty-seven years later: "I expressed this apprehension that slavery could only be destroyed by blood-shed, when I was suddenly and sharply interrupted by my good friend Sojourner Truth with the question, 'Frederick, is God dead?' 'No,' I answered, 'and because God is not dead slavery can only end in blood.'" Johnson captures better the essence of what Douglass actually said, whereas Douglass presents what was, on reflection, an amplification of his intent.

3. Douglass wrote in the Appendix to his 1845 narrative: "I love the pure, peaceable, and impartial Christianity of Christ. I therefore hate the corrupt, slaveholding, women-whipping, cradle-plundering, partial and hypocritical Christianity of this land."

4. Douglass writes: "It seems to me that the true philosophy of reform is not found in the clouds, in the stars, nor anywhere else outside of humanity itself. So far as the laws of the universe have been discovered and understood, they seem to teach that the mission of man's improvement and perfection has been wholly committed to man himself. He is to be his own savior or his own destroyer. He has neither angels to help him, nor devils to hinder him. It does not appear from the operation of these laws, nor from any trustworthy data, that divine power is ever exerted to remove evil from the world, how great soever it may be." From "It Moves," *Frederick Douglass Papers*, Washington, D.C.: Library of Congress, Manuscript Division.

5. Mabee, p. 45. Truth recounted, for example, that God changed her name from Isabella Van Wagenen to Sojourner Truth and set her upon her life's work. When she asked God for a new name, to signify a new direction and purpose in life, God named her "Sojourner" in recognition of her new work as a traveling evangelist, and "Truth," for the message that she would bear.

6. Douglass was not quite sixteen years old when he was sent by his master Thomas Auld to work for a poor man with a rich reputation as a "slave breaker," a farm-renter named Edward Covey. Auld grew tired of Douglass's bold self-defense in response to charges of impudence and decided that Douglass needed "to be broken" in order to become a more compliant slave. Covey did his work well and Douglass wrote that he was indeed broken in mind and body by Covey's "savage persecution." Nevertheless, Douglass refused to be whipped by Covey on one occasion, and chose instead to fight back. Douglass wrote in his second autobiography: "The fighting madness had come upon me, and I found my strong fingers firmly attached to the throat of my cowardly tormentor." During the epic battle of slave against overseer that Douglass estimated at two hours, the defiant slave emerged as victor and vowed that the man who succeeded in whipping him would succeed in killing him.

7. By "moral baptism" I mean a recognition that one's moral beliefs have been transformed in a fundamental and profound way, and an awakening to a new way of being in light of that transformation.

8. Douglass, *My Bondage*, p. 286.

9. Unfortunately for his readers, Douglass does not organize his criteria for power. Unresolved questions remain pertaining to the extent that power endorses either virtue or vice. Nevertheless, it is consistent with Douglass's fundamental principles to argue that power is virtuous minimally to the extent that it animates character and discloses autonomous action. Power becomes abusive, however, when it is used to deny or unjustly restrict another's self-expression, or when it is used to pirate her self-direction.

10. Douglass, *My Bondage*, p. 286.

11. Douglass, *My Bondage*, p. 286.

12. Kathryn Tanner, *The Politics of God: Christian Theologies and Social Justice* (Minneapolis: Fortress Press, 1992), p. 15. Tanner writes: "beliefs that bifurcate the spiritual and the material, the heavenly and the earthly, make indifference to the exercise of political power seem reasonable."

13. Douglass, *Life and Times*, p. 913.

14. Texts such as Matthew 5:39 ("But I say to you, Do not resist one who is evil. But if any one strikes you on the right cheek, turn to him the other also") were foundational to Garrison's ethics.

15. Douglass, *My Bondage*, p. 389.

16. Douglass, *My Bondage*, p. 392.

17. Douglass, *Frederick Douglass' Paper*, October 22, 1852.

18. Douglass, *Frederick Douglass' Paper*, August 20, 1852.

*14*

# Korean Women's Resistance: "If I Perish, I Perish"

*Young Lee Hertig*

Several visits to Korea from 1996 to 2000 compelled me to revisit the stories of courageous early Christian women pioneers. It saddened me that their spirit of resistance, which could have offered theological wholeness and anchoring to desensitized Korean churches, had left no trace in contemporary Korean Christianity. Anesthetic cocacolonization numbs the spirit of the country as a whole. Korean society, at the whim of globalization, is floating in midair, lacking serious resistance, yet Korean history is full of resilient resistances against more than 400 foreign invasions.

Early Korean Christians provided crucial and sacrificial leadership toward nonviolent resistance against Japanese colonization. Forgotten are the stories of the powerful Christian women whose nonviolent resistance against a fully armed Japanese army eventually brought independence to Korea. Due to limited space, I chose to focus in this chapter on two key leaders from among the many who gave up their lives for the emancipation of the people. The first one is Maria Kim, a Presbyterian, and the second one is Yu Kwan Soon, a Methodist. In their lives of resistance against Japanese annexation, a dialectic truth of *yin* and *yang* is exemplified. Their fearless resistance (*yang*) against torture and violence is derived from their spirit of surrendering to death (*yin*)—"If I perish, I perish."

My own social and cultural locations impact in the way I interpret such historical figures as Maria Kim and Yu Kwan Soon. I am a Korean, Korean American woman, an ordained Presbyterian clergy, bilingual, bicultural, and a scholar with both an insider's and an outsider's perspective in relating to both Korea and North America. My academic discourse is also interdisciplinary due to the multiplicity of my existence. I utilize a case-study methodology.

The main thesis of this chapter contends that the Korean society faces another form of colonization—cocacolonization. The term cocacolonization here refers to the global domination of mega-corporations such as Coca Cola and Wal-Mart that hinders any room for competition from small businesses. On the verge of wholesale seduction of cocacolonization, Korean society is in serious need of consciousness raising. We need to tap into the spirit of resistors such as Maria Kim and Yu Kwan Soon once again in order to rally against readily available and seductive mammonization.

What are the factors that rendered such a disconnection? Why is it crucial to revisit their tenacious spirit in the twenty-first century? What relevance do they have in today's setting? Is the level of resistance dependent on the level of the brutality of oppression? Although the type of colonization between the turn of the century and twenty-first century differs—the former with a brutal force, and the latter with a seductive force—a call for resistance against such domination remains the same. Relentless resistance demonstrated by Maria Kim and Yu Kwan Soon has been regretfully discontinued due to an otherworldly theology, thus confining Korean Christianity within the four walls of the sanctuary. Bridging the discontinued spirit of resistance will provide theological identity to this current generation confronting cocacolonization. By reconnecting with the silenced historical consciousness, "the mass" (*daejung*) will be transformed into "the people" (*minjung*) who resist the mass culture of cocacolonization.

## THE ROLE OF CHRISTIANITY AND THE KOREAN INDEPENDENCE MOVEMENT

The start of the twentieth century was one of the most turbulent times for Korea. After 500 years, the Yi dynasty was waning and the opportunistic Japanese grasped their moment to colonize the Korean peninsula. The Korean people demonstrated fierce nonviolent resistance against the fully armed Japanese colonizers.

One of the most remarkable resistances in Korean history is the Korean independence movement. This movement is particularly significant because it united people beyond religious and generational boundaries in order to work toward the common goal of freeing the motherland. The four major groups that consolidated for the independence movement were *Chundokyo*, Christians, Christian student groups, and Buddhists.[1]

Several concrete domestic and international events prompted leaders of the March First Independence Movement of 1919. First, a comprehensive eight-year land survey snatched many Korean farmers' lands, religious temples, shrines, and other public property. These were sold to Japanese settlers at low costs. Second, King Kojong died suddenly, apparently murdered from food poisoning. The March 1 event occurred two days prior to the king's funeral.

On the international scene, President Woodrow Wilson wrote a Declaration of Self-Determination in January 1918, and it spread globally. With the whirlwind of Woodrow Wilson's doctrine of self-determination, Korean Christian leaders also wrote a Korean version of the Declaration of Independence, which inflamed the resistant movement. The peace conference held in Paris in April 1919 became a target for Korean Christian leaders to draw international attention to the brutal conditions of Korean people under siege by the Japanese imperial military.[2]

Frustrated with ailing Confucianism, Korean intellectuals found Christianity appealing. They pursued Western education as a primary vehicle for social change. Christianity provided new impetus for Korean people under the Japanese regime. Unlike in other two-thirds world countries, Christianity came to Korea without the direct baggage of Western colonization but instead fueled a resistance movement against the Japanese occupation. Inspired by the biblical narratives, key leaders dedicated their lives to the emancipation of the motherland from the torture of the Japanese armed forces. The Declaration of Independence was instrumental in mobilizing the people's nonviolent movement.

The Korean independence movement marked a turning point for Korean women's status. Steeped in the patriarchal Confucian confinement of the women's role, Korean women were basically "male supporters" behind the scene. Female status had been reduced to simply being a vehicle of progeny. Christianity, however, revolutionized women's consciousness, awakening them from their deep-seated internalized sexism and oppression. This is not to say that Korean women throughout history had never made a social impact. Under Buddhism prior to the Confucian take-over, Korea had several female queens. It was the Neo-Confucian social organization that later reduced women to second class.

Undoubtedly, the gospel message of Jesus Christ touched many women's *han* (affliction) and provided them with a channel to recover their dignity as human beings. Through the opportunities of education at the start of the twentieth century, women's eyes were open and they began to see beyond the Confucian boundary. Christianity, therefore, was widely embraced by Korean women from the beginning as they soaked up the message of liberation, dignity, and justice. The independence movement became the impetus that energized women to pour out unyielding resistance against Japanese annexation.

Ironically, the crisis caused by Japanese annexation gave birth to the Korean women's social and political leadership. During the crisis, no one had the luxury to debate about women's roles. Maria Kim and Yu Kwan Soon among many others led the resistant movement and transformed women's role beyond the traditional privatized role. They actively organized and instilled the vision of emancipation to the people in darkness. They became symbols of hope for the Korean people under siege.

## MARIA KIM, BORN TO PIONEER CHRISTIAN PARENTS

Maria Kim was born on June 18, 1892, in Sorae village (*sorae* means "a clear stream and full of pine trees"). Her parents were already exposed to Christianity and thus baptized their daughter within a month of her birth. They supported the American Presbyterian missionary, Horace G. Underwood, by providing food, clothing, and living expenses. Maria's parents and uncle, deeply touched by the gospel, released their servants. They also established a school and planted the first Korean church, Sorae Presbyterian Church. Deeply committed to women's education, they enrolled their daughter Maria in an elementary school run by the Sorae church.[3]

When Maria was five years old, her father died from sickness. Her uncle, Yoon Oh Kim, raised Maria in his house, which was the center of the famous Korean elite reformers. In fact, Maria's mother often talked about sending Maria to college and put it in a will even on her deathbed. Kim's mother passed away when Kim went to Seoul to attend Jeong Shin girls' mission school. She was only thirteen years old when her mother died.

Everyone who was around Maria recognized her extraordinary leadership qualities. She permeated a very peaceful presence combined with sharp consciousness. She was always the top student in all her classes. In a society where education existed exclusively for males, girls' mission schools granted women's rights for education and thus produced women pioneers like Maria Kim, Yu Kwan Soon, and many others.

From her childhood, Maria, for a girl, had unusual educational opportunities. She continued to study in a girls' mission school in Sorae and also moved to Seoul to attend a famous girls' mission school, Jeong Shin. Upon graduation, she taught at Sophia and then at Jeong Shin, where she graduated. Through the recommendation of Principal Lewis of Jeong Shin, Maria decided to go to Tokyo for further study in 1914.

At the age of twenty-two, Maria went to Japan, where Korean students were deeply concerned about the motherland's independence from Japanese rule. At Tokyo Women's College, Maria Kim met an American missionary, Miss London, who mentored her closely. Miss London provided spiritual guidance for Maria Kim.

On January 22, 1919, Korean students in Japan heard the news that the Japanese official had fatally poisoned the Korean king, Kojong. Song Gye Back and Pak Kwan Soo composed a Declaration of Independence. On February 8, 1919, Maria and 500 Korean students in Tokyo gathered at the Korean YMCA and demonstrated against the Japanese murder of Kojong and the annexation. They read the Declaration of Independence and shouted for the liberation of Korea. Due to this demonstration, Maria Kim was arrested by the Japanese police and was tortured for eight hours before release because of her student status.[4]

Upon her release, Kim copied the Declaration of Independence secretly and took the responsibility of bringing it to Korea despite a tight vigil by the Japanese. Kim's role in the Korean independence movement is crucial in several ways. She not only led the preamble of the March First Independence Movement on February 8, 1919, in Tokyo, but she also was instrumental to the movement for carrying the secret documents of the Declaration of Independence that fuelled the March First movement.

The March First movement in 1919 took place in 212 cities for sixty days consecutively. More than 1,100,000 people participated 1,214 times. According to the Presbyterian General Assembly in October 1919, it was reported that Korean male Presbyterian prisoners numbered 2,125, and female 531.[5]

After the March First Independence Movement, Kim was caught by Japanese soldiers at gunpoint on March 5, at Jeong Shin, where she taught. As in all cases of colonization, Japanese policy utilized Korean traitors who aligned themselves with the Japanese power structure. It was a Korean traitor who tortured Maria Kim during the inquisition in the prison basement. As she was dragged down the stairs, the screaming of many Korean prisoners filled the eerie torture chambers. The following describes the actual prosecution of Maria Kim by the soldier:

*Soldier:* "Are you Maria Kim?"

*Maria:* "Yes."

*Soldier:* "You must know why you are here?"

*Maria:* "I don't know why you capture innocent people and torture them."

*Soldier:* "Is that so? I will explain it. You ignored the emperor's decree and committed an anti-empire crime. Isn't that a crime?"

*Maria:* "The emperor is your emperor not Korean. Why is it a crime to recover sovereignty of my country? You'd better admit that you are the one who is committing a crime by taking over my country by force."[6]

Kim withstood Japanese torture bluntly and bravely. Before she even finished her incrimination against Japanese rule, the soldiers assaulted and whipped her with a leather rod. The Korean traitor kicked Maria with his boots. Despite torture that ripped her clothes and scarred her whole body, Kim did not yield. This cruel torture almost took her life. After five months of torture in the prison, she was finally released on August 4, 1919, at the age of twenty-six.

The flame for liberation from Japan's atrocity was burning even stronger within Maria following her release. During the celebration party of her release, Kim was able to unite various women's patriotic groups. She was elected president. The previous version of the group focused on raising funds for the male leaders of the independence movement. Under Maria's leadership, the Patriotic Women's Group moved into a new phase. The following quote from Maria Kim's inauguration reflects the transition of the organization:

> An old saying urges us to love your country as your household. Even a foolish husband and wife understand that as a family member if we don't love our family, that household cannot be well, as a people if we do not love our country, the country cannot be preserved. Ah! We wives are also part of the people. Toward recovering the national and human rights we must only move forward with no retreat. I urge you to be courageous women and unite for this noble cause.[7]

Her inaugural address stresses the mission of the Patriotic Women's Group as the "recovery of the country" and "recovery of human rights." Under such strong leadership, the membership grew quickly. They were able to accomplish miraculous achievements. The group also sent 6,000 won to a Korean government in exile in Hawaii. However, in November one of the members betrayed the group and reported the movement to a Japanese official. Immediately more than 1,000 women, including the staff, were arrested. By then Maria's health was very weak due to her rigorous work since her first imprisonment and torture. Yet her spirituality rooted in fervent prayer sustained her through a relentless spirit of courage and perseverance. She led prayer meetings in the prison cell. Early-morning and late-night prayer meetings became so strong that the flame of prayer inflamed and the sound of praise echoed in the prison.

The crueler the torture became, the calmer Maria was. They plugged a hose into her nose and poured water. She was sentenced to five years in prison, but thanks to the endless advocacy by missionaries and friends, Maria was released early from the hellish torture of the prison cell. On July 10, 1921, missionary George S. McCune helped Maria take refuge in Shanghai. During her physical recovery time in Shanghai, she joined the national independence movement through the government in exile in Shanghai.

Unlike Bible women who sold Bibles and evangelized door to door, Maria Kim had an opportunity that was rare for Korean women. In 1923, she came to America, and in 1924, she was enrolled in Park University and studied sociology for two years. In 1928, she studied at the University of Chicago and earned a master of arts in sociology. In the 1930s, she studied theology at the Biblical Theological Seminary in New York. While in New York, she also organized the Patriotic Women's Group and continued the independence movement. Her constant learning and organizing kept her going in exile.

In 1933, after thirteen years of life in exile, Maria Kim returned to Korea, which was still under Japanese siege. She taught at Martha Wilson Bible College. Her Jeremiah classroom was flooded with tears from her lecture.[8] The weeping prophet's message addressed the condition of Korea under siege.

Because of her strong opposition to Shinto worship, the Japanese shut down the school. Maria never recovered from the shock. Regrettably, one year prior to independence, she went to be with the Lord on March 13, 1944. She was only fifty-three.[9] In Kim's life, we can see faith in action and theological education embodied. Her calm endurance before the cruel torturer exemplifies courage, spirituality, and authentic power. Her unyielding stance for truth and courageous resistance against evil made the forces of evil timid and powerless. In fact, the oppressor could not shake the depth of Kim's spiritual well within. The theological dispute during post-independence, which split Korean Presbyterian churches into many pieces, cannot be found in Maria Kim's life. Her life speaks the wholeness of the gospel with unyielding spirituality.

## YU KWAN SOON, JOAN OF ARC IN KOREA

Another woman resistor was a young girl, Yu Kwan Soon, a Methodist and the Joan of Arc in Korea. Her heroic story is passed down to every Korean from early childhood. But one wonders how the current generation relates to her life story. Yu's life also parallels the early Christians under the Roman Empire.

Like Maria Kim, Yu Kwan Soon was educated in a mission school. Both women's parents were pioneer Korean Christians who embraced Christianity and Western education as a solution for the Korean national struggle.

Yu's father, Yu Joong Kwon, started a school and planted a church in his village, as did Maria Kim's. He sought reformation through education and protection in God's grace. He instilled in Yu the vision for the liberation of

Korea even when she was very young. Under such a spiritual father, Yu's vision and leadership for the emancipation began. Her father stressed, "Be diligent in learning and become a leader. Do not forget about the labor of emancipation of the lost country."[10] A female Methodist missionary in the village visited Yu's parents and requested permission to send Kwan Soon to Seoul to study at the Methodist Girls' School, Ewha. Her parents gladly approved.

At the age of thirteen, Yu followed the missionary to Seoul, leaving her parents and friends behind. During her school years, Yu was inspired by the biographies of Joan of Arc and Florence Nightingale. Strongly identifying with these two women, naturally Yu was inflamed with a vision of liberating the motherland as Joan of Arc and sought to have an angelic heart like Florence Nightingale.[11] She embodied both women in her fierce resistance against the Japanese annexation. The horizons of time and space are bridged as Yu Kwan Soon identified her life with the pioneer women's inspirational life stories. Joan of Arc and Nightingale sharpened Yu's calling and sense of destiny in a different time and context.

Within three years of her study in Seoul, the March First Independence Movement began. She could hear the thunder of liberation from the crowds outside her dorm. When she heard that her village was left out of this independence movement, Yu headed down to her village to organize people.

Yu demonstrated unusual leadership qualities for such a young age. Traveling from village to village, she informed people of the planned demonstration and asked for representatives to participate in planning meetings. She announced the signal would be a torch relayed from the mountaintop. The night before the scheduled demonstration, she personally climbed the mountain and ignited the fire to signal the gathering the following day at the Aunae Market. Yu addressed the crowd, read the declaration, and led a march through town. The Japanese responded with brutal force, killing many people, including Yu's parents, and arresting many others.

Although she initially met with resistance because of her youth and the fact that local police were watching carefully, she eventually won the support of the local people. With the help of local church-group elders, she planned and organized a mass demonstration similar to the one in Seoul, this one scheduled for March 1 by the lunar calendar, which happened to fall on April 1. The following is her prayer.

> Oh! Oh! God now time has come nearer.
> May you grant us freedom by removing the
> enemy, the Japanese. Tomorrow, grant your
> courage and strength onto the key
> representatives so that this land may
> become a happy land of our people. Lord,

may you grant courage and strength unto
this girl as well. Viva Korean independence!
Viva Korean independence!¹²

## HOPE BEYOND TORTURE

Both of Yu's parents were shot to death by the Japanese during the independence march, and Yu Kwan Soon was arrested. As in the case of Maria Kim,
the flame of the independence movement in Yu Kwan Soon burned even
stronger in the prison cell:

> Yu was first sent to Ch'onan prison where she was tortured for many days
> before being transferred to Konju prison. She was tried and sentenced to
> three years in prison. Prison life was extremely harsh; her last words spo-
> ken were, "Japan will fall." The Japanese guards then reportedly tore her
> limbs from her body into many pieces. She died in Sodaemun Prison in
> Seoul on October 12, 1920. She was sixteen years old.¹³

In the prison cell, Yu organized a special March First Independence
Movement anniversary and all the prisoners cried out in unison, "*Dae Han
Dok Lip Man Se*," which translates into English as "Victory for Korea."

Richard Saccone writes: "This extraordinary young woman with an indefatigable spirit accomplished much, in her short life, to inspire the Korean
people. Her actions gained the admiration of everyday people and helped
them to persevere when they needed hope most."¹⁴ Saccone also called Yu the
"Joan of Arc" in Korea, and praised Yu's "ability to organize and incite people
to action during the March First Independence movement in 1919."¹⁵

Yu brought hope in a crisis situation. Mary C. Grey describes hoping beyond hope in her book *The Outrageous Pursuit of Hope*, quoting from a Ghana-
ian woman theologian, Mercy Amba Oduyoye: "wear hope like a skin." Grey
stresses, "The more desperate a situation is, the stronger the hope. . . . Hope
stretches the limits of what is possible."¹⁶ Ironically, Japanese colonization released Korean women from the patriarchal rules. Under unusual circumstances, Korean women went out to the public space for their active participation toward emancipation.¹⁷ Grey spells out resistance:

> Resistance is a far deeper concept than simply activism. Because, in the
> depth of our hearts, we have said "no" to injustice and oppression on a
> global level, something has been liberated deep within us and in the soli-
> darity of the groups with whom we are in relation. We can recover our col-
> lective soul. Resistance springs from the centrality of compassion. This

compassion is more than a feeling or emotion. It is rooted in the mothering, womb-like compassion of God.[18]

Demonstrating hope beyond hope, Yu Kwan Soon became like a human torch. Yet, researching the document about her life can be one of the most frustrating experiences. "Her tomb is not well taken care of," laments Rev. Jae Hoon Park, a Korean church music pioneer who composed an opera about Yu Kwan Soon and directed its premiere opening in Seoul, Korea, in March 2000.[19]

Paulo Freire describes the oppressed's struggle for liberation:

> In order for the oppressed to be able to wage the struggle for their liberation, they must perceive the reality of oppression not as a closed world from which there is no exit, but as a limiting situation which they can transform. This perception is a necessary but not a sufficient condition for liberation; it must become the motivating force for liberating action.[20]

The deep resonance with the biblical narrative of struggle for liberation equipped Yu with hope in the face of unbearable violence and torture in prison. Prayer without ceasing, morning and night, and social organization and resistance against evil eventually emancipated the Korean people. Her courage and extraordinary leadership at such a young age transcended all of the Confucian taboos concerning gender and age. Remember that her parents died during the initially peaceful independence gathering when the Japanese killed people to disperse the crowds. Imagine the pain of losing parents, leaving younger siblings as orphans, and undergoing imprisonment and death.

## RESISTANCE LEADERSHIP

From the lives of Maria Kim and Yu Kwan Soon, we can draw key principles of resistance leadership formation. Totally unarmed, these women resistors maintained a spirit of "If I perish, I perish" that threatened the fully armed colonizer. Guns could not defeat their courage and relentless faith in God. Their fearless leadership emerged from the combination of divine providence, unusual parents, a uniquely historical moment, their faith in God through Christian education, and character formation.

Both Maria Kim and Yu Kwan Soon were raised by devout first-generation Korean Christian parents. Both women's parents recognized extraordinary leadership qualities in their daughters. They both had access to education through mission schools established by Presbyterian and Methodist missionaries. They dedicated their whole life to the emancipation of the motherland.

Both were women of fervent prayer and action. Inspired by the gospel of justice, liberation, and human dignity, they both demonstrated contagious leadership and the spirit of "If I perish, I perish." Their freedom from death brought life to Korean people in darkness. They were able to inspire and mobilize people to resist the evil empire. Just as Stephen was stoned to death but truth prevailed, and the good news spread, these women's courageously resistant spirit deserves to be passed on to today's spiritually desolate generation. They were murdered for resisting injustice. The gospel took on the political, social contexts of Korea and imbued hope for liberation despite violent torture.

Their life-giving example through life-relinquishing sacrifice provides a model for liberating the schismatic trap of Korean Christianity. In the Christian witness of these two women, we do not find the division between proclamation and social action that plagues post-independence Korean Christianity.

What we do find is a still-divided Korean peninsula. The leadership examples of these women are once again in great demand as Korea faces a crisis in a less visible, far more subtle economic force of cocacolonization. The names Maria Kim and Yu Kwan Soon carry the meaning of a powerful embodiment of the Christian teachings of courage, strength, and redemption of a crisis-ridden country. Paradoxically, under crisis, the infant-stage Korean Christianity showed the greatest maturity. Korean Christianity at the beginning exemplified integrity with courageous leadership.

As the word "crisis" in Chinese characters connotes both danger and opportunity, during one of the darkest moments in Korean history, numerous men and women demonstrated courage and strength. Their zeal and courage inspired the nation and provided a unified spirit toward independence. But the precious spirit and action of Korean women have been buried. How regrettable it is that today's Korean Christians do not remember such stories.

How absurd it is to see the churches fighting against the old sacred cows of conservatism versus liberalism, splitting the gospel into many pieces. How absurd it is to see the churches lacking vision, mission, and a sense of history and justice. Korean Christianity, which once bore such powerful Christian witness, stands almost timid when it experiences the Korean version of Constantinization with the increase in number. The stories of patriotic women and their unyielding spirit of "If I perish, I perish" need to be transmitted to generation after generation.

## YINISH SURRENDER AND YANGISH RESISTANCE

The lives of two courageous women—Maria Kim and Yu Kwan Soon—exude a paradoxical duality of *yin* and *yang*. The first dynamic is a dialectical duality of pacifistic inner surrender to death (*yin*) and subversive outer social resistance (*yang*). Out of such inner tranquility flows the yangish subversive resistance of the two women. The outer resistance (*yang*) without being grounded in the inner surrender (*yin*) does not endure brutal oppression from without. The second dynamic is the dualistic intergroup dynamic of *yin* (the oppressed) and *yang* (the oppressor). The oppressed here are Maria Kim and Yu Kwan Soon, who have consciousness (*yin*), and the oppressor, the Japanese colonizers (*yang*), who lack consciousness. The oppressor, lacking power flowing from within (*yin*), asserts power by domination (*yang*). The redemption for such oppressors can only begin when they are willing to journey within and discover the oppressed within (*yin*). From the false dichotomy of *yang* versus *yin*, the oppressor needs to shift toward a duality of *yin* and *yang* as demonstrated by these two Korean women resistors.

Without freedom from fear of death, such fearless resistance against fully armed Japanese soldiers cannot even be imagined. Our own Lord Jesus Christ embodied the authentic courage emerging from the total surrender to death. The Gospel of John contains the paradoxical duality of both *yin* and *yang* as Jesus deals with Jewish authority through godly authority. Jesus says, "The reason my Father loves me is that I lay down my life—only to take it up again. No one takes it from me, but I lay it down of my own accord. I have authority to lay it down and authority to take it up again. This command I received from my Father" (John 10:17–18, NIV).

Jesus, an innocent man, carrying the cross of slaves and criminals, subverts perverted power. The cross, used for violent punishment, was redeemed for the purpose of life-giving replenishment. Because he was so centered on God's will within, Jesus was able to contradict the Roman culture of punishment with a redemptive replenishment. The yinish subversion of yangish perversion of Jewish and Roman power is embodied in Jesus' crucifixion.

There is a purifying power in subversive resistance against evil forces. The external force, although it may break the human body, cannot break the internal human spirit as long as one is willing to drink a bitter cup of death. Death no longer has power over those who let go of life. In the dialectic duality of *yin* and *yang*, death no longer is the opposite of life. They are paradoxically one.

Jesus' total obedience to death exemplifies the subversive power of the cross. He invited his disciples to take up the cross, as they had to continue the ministry that he imparted. "If you lose your life, you will gain your life" (Luke 9:24, NRSV) expresses two Korean pioneer women. Their readiness to die for the cause of liberation did not allow any room for fear. The power of domination and control persists as long as people, in fear of death, conform rather than resist evil. Freedom from fear of death leads to courage; courage leads to action.

## FROM DAEJUNG TO MINJUNG

The inside-out spirituality can transform "the masses" to become "the people." Kwon Jin-Kwan differentiates "the masses" (*daejung*) from "the people" (*minjung*). He defines the people as

> those whose social consciousness is critical, and consequently, whose readiness to undertake new historical tasks is intense. The term "the people" emphasizes the state of a people who are self-conscious and critical of their own political situation by distancing themselves from the situation. . . . The masses are not conscious of their own situation. They live *within* the situation where they happen to find themselves. The masses are not self-conscious of their collective interests, and do not act upon the structure that binds them in bondage.[21]

Both Kim and Yu conscientized *daejung* and transformed them into *minjung*. Their ability to transform the masses into people with a collective consciousness stems from the deep spirituality of prayer. The holistic spirituality of both Kim and Yu reveals one of the most important contributions of Western mission—dedication to women's education when Korean society only offered educational opportunities for men. Despite such solid examples of holistic faith, Korean Christianity pushed aside such historical movements and thus is on the verge of spiritual starvation. Conforming to the status quo, Korean churches are busy reaching the masses, not the people, and thus continue to fail in their prophetic role. A large number of Christians remain silent as objects of the status quo, with their eyes and ears closed to the crucial historical developments of today.

Korean Christianity started among the *minjung* and for the *minjung*, identifying with the *minjung's* struggle. Where had all the spirit of courage and truth gone? Do all the martyrs who shed their blood deserve the heritage of such division of the nation? The external crisis turned inward, torturing one another as if the colonizer's chain still binds. Where are women's passions today? With what are they consumed? Do we need another crisis in order to recover our lost consciousness?

## ANESTHETIZATION OF CONSCIOUSNESS
## DURING POST-INDEPENDENCE

Unlike the earlier colonization, the current cocacolonization numbs human consciousness, leaving it vulnerable to the economic prey. As the Constantinization of Christianity desensitizes the spirit of resistance under persecution, the resistance of the early Korean Christian against the Japanese was also domesticated to the expansion of the Korean church.

Aloysius Pieris rightly critiques comfortably mammonized Christianity, which hinders the church from its role as a *messianic* people.[22] Mammonized Korean Christianity resulted from the lack of theologizing during critical moments in Korean church history. Whereas the emphasis of indigenized Christianity in Korea through the Nevius mission policy shows its strengths, a negative aspect is the minimizing of pastoral education. The consequence of keeping pastoral leadership at a minimal level kept the Korean churches on the back burner when the radical paradigmatic global changes began during the 1920s and onward. Unlike the church that was at the forefront of the March First Independence Movement in 1919, the latter Korean church lagged behind the societal demands while floating in midair with an otherworldly revival emphasis. It lacked theological backbone even to respond, let alone lead, while faced with complex challenges from within and without. Sadly, there were two separate branches of Korean Christianity at this time: the church-centered, otherworldly revival church and the church of the sociopolitical gospel that sought to continue the March First Independence Movement spirit.[23]

The American Presbyterian denomination's mission policy for the Korean peninsula after Korea's independence set the course of Korean Protestant Christianity. Affected by the emergence of the liberal voice in America, a staunch conservative camp, with its dualistic split—conservative against liberal, and this world against the other world—represented mission work in Korea. Regrettably, the spirit of the independence movement was quickly renounced rather than honored. Once the external force of oppression was lifted, there was no forum for processing pain and hurt. The painful *han* from the thirty-six years of oppression was simply denied. A country in deep need of recovery from external wounds and internal pain turned to an otherworldly theology imposed by the missionary policy, burying the tension and unresolved issues at hand.

Elevating revivalists, the mission policy of the Presbyterian Church offered no room for the sociopolitical activists who firmly grounded their actions in the biblical narratives. Christian thinkers with a deep consciousness could not quench their thirst within the church, and many who could have provided leadership in giving birth to theological identity left the church. Many young and inspirational leaders could not find any niche in the otherworldly churches and thus turned to communism. Therefore, regrettably, the marvelous Christian leadership demonstrated during the crisis discontinued.

Consequently, Korean Christianity quickly resorted to the revival track and became fixed on the otherworldly, dualistic theology and culture, splitting denominations and churches into many pieces. The post-independence Christianity under the rise of fundamentalism in the American context broke a once holistic gospel that bore a powerful witness into an otherworldly one. Under the otherworldly mission endeavor, the transmission of the pioneers' resistant consciousness was obstructed, leaving lasting implications for Korean Protestant Christianity:

1. Anti-intellectualism permeated Korean Christianity and remains today. The result was a split between the spiritually oriented group and the social action-oriented group, bitterly dividing the Korean body of Christ.
2. Once losing the golden opportunity to build theological identity, Korean Christianity became dogmatic and busy with hair-splitting doctrinal arguments.
3. Before the division of the 38th parallel, doctrinal and denominational divisions were drawn along the 38th parallel.
4. Christianity, once an inspiration for unified movement of independence, was polarized. In the south it was characterized by otherworldly revivalists, and in the north by atheistic communism. The divided Korean peninsula symbolizes a divided Christian theology of the left and right wings.
5. Still today, Korean Christianity, despite its numerical growth, is greatly hindered in its role in society and in the mission of transformation. It is as if one is expanding a house without checking the beams and structures that support the house.

The result of the divided gospel between social and spiritual is the deadening of consciousness and anesthetized Christianity to the world of cocacolonization. Despite powerful examples of Christianity that transformed *daejung* into *minjung*, the current Christianity exhibits depoliticized and privatized practice. Aloysius Pieris critiques Korean Christianity: "collusion between the neocolonialist Christianity and developmentalist ideology conspires to keep the unshepherded masses (*daejung*) from leaving their chains and exercising their role as a messianic people (*minjung*)."[24]

A cold war in the Korean peninsula, more than half a century old, also mirrors a deep-seated theological split as well. The difficulty today lies at the death of consciousness due to the death of education under hyper-materialism. The visible long-standing cease-fire, however, can paralyze the consciousness of the people and cause them to be vulnerable to materialism instead of resistant. The challenge lies in the fact that many people have to come out of their comfort zones and see the urgent need to bring reconciliation between the two divided governments. Those who suffer most, the separated family members, are reaching their last years on earth. This task demands sacrificial leadership such as Yu Kwan Soon and Maria Kim demonstrated. Politicizing unification issues has been pervasive among the politicians and Christian leaders.

However, Protestant Christianity confines the gospel into the four walls of church buildings and thus dichotomizes faith and the world. Sadly, the power of the gospel remains relatively invisible in society despite the expansion of Christianity. Meanwhile, Korean society as a whole is seduced by wholesale globalization, and its people are in desperate need of authentic inner transformation. Once again, numerous prophets in action are needed as the country confronts an unavoidable crisis, national humiliation from the financial corruption that led to national bankruptcy. Christianity without the cross perverts it into mammonism.

## IMPLICATIONS FOR THEOLOGICAL EDUCATION

Although Korean Christianity has reached remarkable growth alongside the speed of modernization, theological growth has not accompanied it. The internalization of the gospel and the sense of history diminish. As Korean Christianity hits the declining phase, this may be the time to examine our Christian history rigorously.

The very structure and content of theological education have to be challenged and transformed. A mass production of theological education in general lacks personal contact. Education in this scenario functions as delivering knowledge in isolation. A true education that is Christian embodies the nature of discipleship. Both prophetic and institutional leadership must co-exist and create a symbiotic organism of constantly evolving and maturing theological education.

From the two women's lives we can see the impact of education which awakened them to confront the reality and hope beyond hope. Regretfully, such stories are exempted in the westernized theological education curriculum in Korea. Students spend more time copying Western theologies and graduate with no theological identity rooted in Korean contexts and history. Korean theological education needs educational reform, instead of teaching Xerox-copy theology from the West.

We can draw universal principles of resistance for the particular contexts of today, just as Kim and Yu connected with biblical contexts of early Christians under siege. Weeping prophet Jeremiah's stories were their stories. If the stories of Joan of Arc and Florence Nightingale inspired a Korean girl like Yu Kwan Soon, then the stories of Yu Kwan Soon and Maria Kim should all the more inspire the current generation in identity crisis. Despite unimaginable obstacles, the authenticity and integrity of humanity demonstrated by these women transcend time and space, collapsing cultural, geographical, and historical horizons. Their life examples intersect our life today. Such stories shape identity and conscientize *daejung* (the masses) to become *minjung* (people). For such conscientization to take place, educators themselves need to be awakened from the struggling effect of materialism and step into the long-awaited indigenizing process.

Amid a titanic impact of mammonism, consumerism, and expansionism, the Korean society once again confronts the challenge of reformation. The severe moral decay in all segments of the society calls forth the radical processes of internal purification. In reshaping the Christian identity, reconnecting with the forgotten stories of such women pioneers as Maria Kim and Yu Kwan Soon is crucial.

Lack of Christian identity tarnishes the marks of our female saints who offered their lives so generously. It is a dry season now waiting to be soaked. Theological educators today need to provide students with a sense of history and identity rooted in Korean history, so that they may catch the vision grounded in the accurate perception of the reality.

The challenge of today's resistance movement is to drink from our own theological well and rediscover the holistic duality of *yin* and *yang*. By lifting up the courageous women's spirit, the current and forthcoming generation of women may once again lift the spirit of justice and liberation for all people. It is our responsibility to carry on what they demonstrated so fiercely and so purely for equality, justice, and salvation for all people.

Parker Palmer describes the authentic leadership that Korean Christians need: "The power for authentic leadership, Havel tells us, is found not in external arrangements but in the human heart. Authentic leaders in every setting—from families to nation states—aim at liberating the heart, their own and others', so that its powers can liberate the world."[25]

An inside-out journey of resistance may flow like "streams of living water from within" (John 7:38). The holistic duality of *yin* and *yang* offers a rich theological lens through which we can theologize and indigenize. Revisiting Maria Kim and Yu Kwan Soon is a ritual of retelling the self-giving, life-giving stories. Their lives embody resistance rooted in the womb-like compassion of God, conscientized by the liberating messages of Jesus Christ. Many Korean Christian pioneers like Maria Kim and Yu Kwan Soon transcended immanent torture for all time.

## NOTES

1. Kyung Bae Min, *Hankook KidookKyo KyoHyeSa* (Korean Church History) (Seoul, Korea: Yeonsei University Press, 1993), p. 340.

2. Wei Jo Kang, *Christ and Caesar in Modern Korea: A History of Christianity and Politics* (Albany: State University of New York, 1997), pp. 51–52.

3. Suk Ki Chung, *Han Kook Ki Dock Kyo Yeo Sung In Mul Sa* (Korean Christian Women Leaders' History) (Seoul, Korea: Qumran Publisher, 1995), pp. 105–123. (English translation by the author.)

4. Yeon Oak Yi, *Yeo Jeondohyo Hak* (School of Women's Mission Committee) (Seoul, Korea: Korean Presbyterian Women's Association, 1993), pp. 106–118.

5. Ibid., p. 112.

6. Suk Ki Chung, pp. 116–117.

7. Ibid., p. 119.

8. Ibid., pp. 121–122

9. Ibid., p. 119.

10. Kang Hoon Lee, *Chung Sa Ae Bit Nan Soon Kook Sun Yol Dul* (Korean Martyrs) (Seoul, Korea: Yok Sa Pun Chan Hyo, 1990), p. 640. In Bock Yeo, *Han Kook Eui In Mul* (Korean Leaders} (Seoul, Korea: Yeo Moon Sa, 1972), p. 182.

11. Hyo Sop Chung, *Yu Kwan Soon, the Korean Joan of Arc* (Seoul, Korea: Yeo Sung Dong Ah, 1971), p. 67.

12. *Kook Ga Bo Hoon Cheo, Purun San, Got Eun Sol* (Green Mountain and Straight Pine) (Seoul, Korea: In Ruk Jeong Bo Center [Human Resource Information Center], 1995), p. 158. (English translation by the author.)

13. Richard Saccone, *Koreans to Remember: 50 Famous People Who Helped Shape Korea* (Elizabeth, N.J.: Hollym International Corp., 1993), p. 233.

14. Ibid., p. 234.

15. Ibid., p. 230.

16. Mary C. Grey, *The Outrageous Pursuit of Hope* (New York: Crossroad, 2000), p. 6.

17. Ibid., p. 35.

18. Ibid.

19. I visited Rev. Jae Hoon Park in Toronto. He is retired from his ministry with the Divine Light Presbyterian Church. A conversation with him affirmed frustration with the Korean government and the Methodist denomination in their negligence of Yu Kwan Soon's memorial site.

20. Paulo Freire, *The Pedagogy of the Oppressed* (New York: Seabury Press, 1970), p. 34.

21. Jin-Kwan Kwon, "Minjung Theology and Its Future Task for People's Movement: A Theological Reflection on the Theme of Religion, Power and Politics in the Korean Context," *CTC Bulletin* 10 (May–December, 1991): 17.

22. Aloysius Pieris, S.J., *Fire and Water: Basic Issues in Asian Buddhism and Christianity* (Maryknoll, N.Y.: Orbis Books, 1996), p. 72.

23. Institute of Korean Church History Studies, *A History of the Korean Church* (Seoul, Korea: Christian Literature Press, 1989), pp. 301–302.

24. Ibid.

25. Parker Palmer, *Let Your Life Speak: Listening for the Voice of Vocation* (San Francisco: Jossey-Bass, 2000), p. 76.

*III*

# THEOLOGICAL ETHICS
# OF RESISTANCE

*15*

# Resistance, Affirmation, and the Sovereignty of God

*Mark Douglas*

## REFORMING RESISTANCE

*O*ver the past forty years, the language of resistance has become idiomatic to the vocabulary of socially active churches. As these churches clarify and defend their own ideological spaces, they feel not only the need to distinguish themselves from the surrounding cultures, but also the threat that such cultures can impose on their continued existence through antipathy or apathy. This emphasis on resistance should be neither surprising nor, in itself, troubling. Not only is there a clear biblical witness for the church to distinguish itself from the larger culture, standing over against whatever rulers, systems, powers, or principalities in that culture promote injustice or threaten the church, but there is a growing and increasingly sophisticated body of literature on resistance. From how-to books on organizing political demonstrations and practicing civil disobedience to more theoretical work by Christian theologians and ethicists as diverse and sundry as Martin Luther King Jr., Daniel Berrigan, Stanley Hauerwas, and Ralph Reed, the cry "Resist!" reverberates not only from the streets, but from the bookshelves as well.

Lost amid the cries for resistance is the possibility that Jesus did not come preaching resistance at all.[1] While the matter is far from closed, a strong case can be made that the Christian faith ought to advocate nonresistance rather than resistance. From Jesus' teachings in the Sermon on the Mount[2] and Paul's teaching in Romans[3] to Jesus' willingness to endure the cross and his silence before Pilate and the powers of the state, there are repeated calls toward and visions of nonresistance in the New Testament.

Yet these passages about nonresistance do not settle the issue. There are, after all, also repeated references to resistance in the New Testament,[4] and Jesus' life as it is recounted in the Gospels certainly suggests that he was willing to actively resist the religious leaders of his day. Moreover, a larger set of questions about Christian perspectives on justice and responsibility suggest that nonresistance can be so problematic as to render it immoral from those perspectives. What the existence of the language of nonresistance in the Bible does suggest, however, is that we cannot be content simply to cry "Resist!" and feel comfortably justified in our cry. Instead, the very ambiguity about the place and meaning of resistance in the Bible (and thus in Christian faith) ought to encourage us to think more carefully about whom and what to resist, as well as how to resist.

Other chapters in this book explicitly address those first two questions about whom and what to resist. In this chapter, I explore the third question: how do we resist or, more properly, how do we think about what we are doing when we resist? Within it, I hope to develop a vision of resistance that springs out of some of the central theological doctrines of the Reformed tradition as it began in sixteenth-century Geneva (e.g., God's sovereignty, sin's ubiquity, and the importance of political action).

Toward that end, I will analyze a recent site of Christian political resistance: the challenges posed by the Jubilee 2000 movement to the International Monetary Fund (IMF). While the debates between Jubilee 2000 and the IMF extend far beyond the goals of this chapter, my use of this example will, hopefully, serve a three-fold purpose within the context of answering the question "How ought we resist?" First, it will provide a basic background about an issue of worldwide concern: namely, the crisis of Third World debt and the variety of responses to it. Second, it will provide a way of theologically analyzing that crisis and those responses. Finally, it will serve an openly apologetic function by suggesting that Jubilee 2000's resistance to the IMF can helpfully be couched in a larger set of theological ideas about resistance which lend nuance to a mass movement that sometimes pursues its ends with insufficient thought given to its means.[5]


## THE IMF AND JUBILEE 2000: A BACKGROUND


At the conclusion of World War II, various members of the international community came together to develop several systems by which to regulate the movement of capital around the globe, principally in order to promote worldwide employment and world trade and to smooth market fluctuations before they damaged economically fragile countries.[6] Perhaps the best-known program associated with these efforts was the Marshall Plan to redevelop Europe after the war, but several other programs were born at roughly the same time, including the International Monetary Fund. The IMF was initially conceived to be under the authority of the United Nations with the purpose of serving as a resource for addressing currency matters. Though it never actually existed as a program of the UN, the IMF kept broadly to its initial purposes during the worldwide economic boom from the 1950s into the early 1970s.[7] From the 1950s onward, the IMF has functioned something like an international economic cooperative, with member countries (including many wealthy Western countries and all countries who would take out loans from the IMF) putting money into the IMF, which the IMF then loans out to countries in need.

During the economic boom period, many less-developed countries borrowed heavily from international banks in order to develop their own economies so that they could keep pace with and prosper in the new world economy. However, in the wake of rising inflation worldwide, the oil crisis of the mid-1970s, and the West's preoccupation with the Cold War, these poor countries found themselves paying increasing amounts of interest on those loans at the same time that they were less able to earn money through exports in order to cover the terms of those loans. Starting especially in the 1970s, countries faced growing debt as their economies slowed, rather than being able to pay down their loans as their economies grew.

The problems these countries found themselves in were then exacerbated by the neo-liberal economic policies of Reaganite America and Thatcherite Great Britain. Deeming economic intervention, management, and cooperation unnecessary and unhelpful, these powerful countries focused on managing their own inflation in spite of the fact that their macroeconomic policies triggered further global recession and the collapse of prices on the very commodities being exported by developing countries. Simultaneously, they cut foreign aid.[8]

In the face of anxious and powerful creditors, economically fragile countries were put in the position of having to borrow money just to pay off the interest for their prior loans. At this point, the IMF stepped in and began a program of lending money at reduced interest rates and lengthy maturities in order to stabilize these struggling countries. Toward the end of stability, the IMF tied its loans to various economic reforms (or "Structural Adjustment Policies") that it demanded of these countries, principally the tightening of their fiscal and monetary policies and the further opening of their borders to trade; this connection of loans to reforms is called "conditionality." In principle, short-term pain would produce long-term gains as these countries became economically stable by adhering to IMF conditions.

The problem with IMF conditionality is that it has been fairly severe, and in order to achieve the demands set by the IMF conditionality, debtor countries have often faced the choice of making draconian cuts to social programs (health, education, welfare, etc.) or defaulting on their debts. Moreover, there was little empirical evidence that the IMF-mandated reforms would be successful in the face of desperate need. By 1993, for instance, only six of twenty-nine sub-Saharan IMF-aided countries had achieved any improvements in their economic situations. Many were worse off, in part because they could not pay down the interest on their IMF loans.

When the failures of its concessional lending programs became apparent, the IMF took steps to modify its lending practices in order to compensate for those failures. Initially, these steps involved payment rescheduling and new loan packages. As these steps also failed, the IMF took more aggressive action, including debt reductions in the early 1990s, the development of the HIPC (Heavily Indebted Poor Countries) Initiative in 1996, and the enhancement of that initiative in 1999.[9]

At the same time that the IMF was changing its lending programs, a variety of religious and social organizations were becoming increasingly concerned with debt crisis. In June of 1997, during a G-8 summit (a meeting of senior representatives of the eight most powerful countries in the world) in Denver, a coalition of over forty Roman Catholic and Protestant agencies came together to form the Jubilee 2000/U.S.A. movement.[10] Taking their name from the command in Leviticus 25:10 that every fifty years Israel would hold a jubilee year in which slaves were freed and debts were cancelled, the Jubilee 2000 movement called for the cancellation of poor countries' debt, particularly that owed to the IMF and its sister institution, the World Bank. A grassroots advocacy campaign, Jubilee 2000 has since produced a series of publications designed to inform the public of the moral and economic problems of debt, set up prayer services, coordinated letter-writing campaigns to Congress, the president, and the IMF and World Bank, actively protested various meetings of international lenders, and developed a means of reaching out to the media by attracting celebrities to its cause. Its strategy in all this—like that of many other activist campaigns—has been to so focus unwanted attention on international lenders as to embarrass them into forgiving their loans.[11] Along the way, it has attracted millions of people and thousands of churches to its cause and has influenced Congress to forgive billions of dollars in loans—as well (probably) as influencing the IMF to revise some of its loan procedures. Moreover, by positioning itself as an agitating influence opposed to what it sees as First World economic tyranny, it serves as an excellent prototype for the type of responsible resistance that bears closer examination in this chapter.

# JUBILEE 2000, THE IMF, AND THE SOVEREIGNTY OF GOD

It is not the purpose of this chapter to explore the various merits of or criticisms leveled against either the IMF or Jubilee 2000; such work has been done elsewhere.[12] In what follows, I hope to tease out some of the threads of rhetorical and structural relationship between Jubilee 2000 and the IMF and to use those threads as an example of how we might—or might not—think about resistance from within the Reformed tradition. Said differently, I hope not so much to describe IMF and Jubilee 2000 relationships as to re-imagine them through a particular theological perspective.

Jubilee 2000's strategy relies on the fact that the IMF is at least partially driven by moral considerations. After all, that strategy turns largely on Jubilee 2000's ability to shame the IMF into changing its policies. Political shame, which functions as a type of moral persuasion—albeit a persuasion that often expresses itself in confrontational ways—is the only means available for Jubilee 2000, which has no other strong cards to play (e.g., economic or military force, or the coercive power of blackmail or threatened legal action) in order to express power. Yet for moral persuasion to be effective, it must assume that the opponent is open to change not only because of outside pressure, but because the opponent has certain internal values that are congruent with the goals and values of the persuader. Were this not the case, the opponent could simply ignore the actions of the persuader. This is especially the case in regard to the IMF/Jubilee 2000 relationship, since there is some evidence that Jubilee 2000 has actually convinced the IMF to change its position on occasion.[13]

This is not to say that the IMF and Jubilee 2000 share precisely the same set of values. They do not. Nor is it to say that Jubilee 2000 can't exercise a form of secondhand coercion by trying to persuade other moral agents to use their coercive power to change the IMF's mind—as in the instance of convincing the U.S. Congress to challenge the IMF. They do. Nor is it to say that this set of common values ought to be seen as either somehow more basic than any of the other values that drive each organization or as the only basis for conversation between the two organizations. They may not be. Nor, finally, is it to say that there is a conceptual confusion between the rhetoric and methods of Jubilee 2000 (or the IMF, for that matter). That could be, but it wouldn't necessarily make the arguments less compelling or fruitful. It is, however, to suggest that Jubilee 2000 cannot treat the IMF and its goals as expressions of evil in need of abolition; instead, they must, by virtue of their own strategy, treat the IMF as errant and in need of correction. It follows that the two organizations must share something morally in common, and that whatever that thing is, its existence creates the initial rhetorical space needed not only for persuasion-as-resistance, but for progress in overcoming whatever needs resisting. This, perhaps, is the beginning of wisdom.

Two observations follow from this one. First, if Jubilee 2000 and the IMF share some moral common ground, it will be important to discern *what* that ground is, not only to serve as a basis for future conversation,[14] but to more accurately specify the disagreements between the two in order to clarify what, within the IMF and its processes, needs resisting. Second, if we hope to generalize from the Jubilee 2000/IMF case to some more general guidelines for thinking about resistance, it will be important to think about *why* they share common ground. Indeed, it is at the level of this second observation that we might best develop for this case-analysis the very type of theological substructure which also serves as the primary aim of this chapter: a Reformed conception of resistance. Moreover, exploring *why* common ground exists may even—if counterintuitively—further clarify *what* that common ground is. For that reason, I will turn to the "why" question first.

## ANSWERING "WHY": THEOLOGY MATTERS

At least four Reformed theological tenets are immediately pertinent to the question of why Jubilee 2000 and the IMF share common ground. They concern particular visions of creation, sin, politics, and God. For our concerns, we might designate the first two theological tenets as broadly anthropological, the third as political, and the fourth as dogmatic, undergirding the other three at the same time that it contributes something in itself. Though none of them is unique to the Reformed tradition, all of them are dominant within it. I will take up each of them in turn[15] and, though such a discussion can hardly do justice to the depth and range of thought on these tenets, I will at least suggest how each of them is applicable to the question at hand.

The first anthropological tenet grows out of a Reformed vision of creation. Within Reformed thought, God has created all that has been, is, or will be, what God has created is good, and its purpose is individually and collectively to glorify God.[16] These statements, though brief, are packed with pertinence. If God has created all things and all that God has created is good, it follows that the Reformed tradition takes a radically anti-dualistic view of the universe and all that inhabits it. Evil has no separate, alternative existence over against that which God has created but can only exist as a perversion or privation of what God has created. It follows not only that we ought to treat what we are resisting as somehow related to God—even if that relationship has been significantly warped—and capable of being redeemed by the same God that created it, but that no person or group is ever in the position of declaring its opponent either wholly evil or, for that matter, wholly wrong. Reformed resistance is tempered by the humility that comes with thinking of one's opponents as created by God, no matter how far from their creator they may appear.

Moreover, the Reformed vision of creation is one in which all aspects of creation are radically interconnected with God and each other, and humans, in particular, are created in the image of a God who perpetually interrelates in the Trinity. At our core, we are relational creatures who cannot make sense of ourselves or our purposes apart from our connection with God and others in God's creation. This emphasis on interconnection expresses itself in several ways. On the one hand, it means that we are reliant on others in ways that can even be hidden from us; therefore, we must take care to engage our opponents in ways that do not cut us off from them and do not cut them off from others. On the other hand, this very emphasis on interconnectedness drives the need for us to resist in the first place. Resistance is, after all, a combination of challenge and connection; it is a particular way of relating to another that challenges them to relate to the world in different ways.[17] Thus, it is the Reformed emphasis on creation-as-relational that simultaneously makes resistance possible and moderates how we go about resisting.

The second anthropological tenet follows from the first when it is combined with the recognition that, in spite of the goodness and interrelatedness of creation, things are not as they ought to be. It is the doctrine of sin.[18] The Reformed tradition has always had a strong doctrine of sin; it is usually associated with John Calvin's claims about "total depravity." His meaning was that sin existed not as a modifier for certain types of actions, but instead as a condition that is endemic to all persons and expressed in all actions. This emphasis on sin as pervasive in each part of all of our lives has many implications: that none of our relationships—even with those on whose behalf we are resisting—are expressed as they ought to be, that we cannot claim a natural righteousness on our side over against a natural unrighteousness in that which we oppose, that we have within us the potential to become like those we oppose, that none of our actions is ever wholly pure—and the list could go on. Indeed, just as resistance is premised upon the relationality of creation, so it is made necessary by the destructiveness of sin. Said differently, we would not be able to resist if we were not intrinsically relational, and we would not need to resist if we were not sinful.

One of the most complicated notions to tease out of the doctrine of sin is that we participate in the very thing we resist. Obviously, we would prefer not to think of ourselves in this way—especially when we are attempting to "fight the good fight" of resistance. Nevertheless, combining the emphases of intrinsic relatedness and sinfulness opens us up to the possibility that we do just this. How is this so?

A first step in thinking out how this could be so is to reflect on the dynamics of suffering when that suffering is caused by someone or something. One of the primary motivators for resistance is the desire to overcome suffering. We see suffering, we empathetically feel the pain of the sufferer, we seek a means to overcome the pain we feel and the suffering of the other, and we choose resistance as the means toward those ends. That second clause—we empathetically feel the pain of the sufferer—turns not only on what is best in us (our relationality), but also what is worst in us (sin). For our empathy not only connects us with the other but also highlights both our separateness from the other (else we would simply feel suffering rather than empathy) and our recognition that what the other is going through is suffering. Yet if we are separated from the other, then our recognition of suffering turns on some prior understanding of suffering that already resides in us: "I feel your pain because I can imagine what it would be like to be in your place. But I can only imagine that because I have some experience of suffering—which means there is already something wrong in me as well."

The second step follows from this recognition that "there is already something wrong in me as well." This is not a normative judgment (at this point, anyway) about something *bad* in me; rather, it is a descriptive evaluation about something *unsettled* or *disordered* within me. My own life can be perfectly whole only if the lives of those around me are perfectly whole as well. Since they are not, mine cannot be, either. Moreover, if I wish my life to be perfectly whole, I must work toward the perfect wholeness of those around me.

It follows—the third step—that in seeking wholeness for the other, I must explore what keeps me from being whole, since in this context, what keeps me from wholeness is preventing the other's wholeness as well (else we would feel something other than empathy). When I do so, I will discover that what unsettles me is inside me—and it is bad. Moreover, if my empathy is authentic, what is bad in me—what causes my empathetic suffering—is the very thing that is also causing suffering in that other person. Even my most humane impulse implicates me in the very expressions of inhumanity that injure the other. In his letter to the Romans, Paul describes this in his plaintive cry: "for I do not do the good I want, but the evil I do not want is what I do."[19]

This is not, of course, to say that we need take on the entire responsibility for the suffering of another. Indeed, the attempt to do so turns out to be just another cause for suffering.[20] It is to say, however, that to make sense of moral responsibility—or, more accurately, moral accountability—we must first register our own connections, both for weal and for woe, with the other.

Nor is it to assume that all forms of suffering are the same and that resistance is, therefore, always an appropriate response to suffering. Some forms of suffering—e.g., from natural disasters such as hurricanes, earthquakes, and floods—need response; however, a response of resistance would, in such cases, be counterproductive and nonsensical. Working backward from the previous paragraph, we might even conclude that resistance is an appropriate response precisely to those occasions of suffering in which we recognize that we, ourselves, are implicated in its causes. So envisioned, our participation in that which we resist does not so much distract from the possibilities of resistance as help constitute the very conditions by which we recognize the need to resist.

The third theological tenet of the Reformed faith—a distinctive vision of the political sphere[21]—further refines a Reformed conception of resistance. In Reformed thought, persons cannot separate various aspects of their lives into distinct sacred and secular spaces. Instead, all human activities are broadly directed toward the same end, which is to glorify God by pursuing the work She has called each of us to do in our own lives and in the community around us. It follows that our political engagements must, themselves, be thought of as arenas in which to give witness to the glory of God.[22]

This sets all political activities—including acts of resistance—within a framework that allows its patterns of relationship to be directed by the grandest of ends. The negative practical expression of this is that we ought never treat resistance as an end in itself, but instead ought to treat it as a means for pursuing God's ends in the world. We do not resist for the sake of resisting, but only because our resistance is a faithful expression of our larger calling to glorify God. The positive practical expression of this is two-fold. First, by ordering our resistance to our greater calling, rather than vice versa, we not only clarify our reasons for resistance, but we do so from within a position that demonstrates our faithfulness to the world and our accountability before the God who calls us. Second, the confessional recognition that all persons have been called by the same God toward the same ultimate purpose carries within it the implication that the number of potential resistors is as expansive as the number of people in the world. That is, the ranks of resistors need not, in principle, be limited to a few select people but instead are open to all—including those who do not currently favor resistance and even those who are being resisted. It follows that resistance must have explicitly apologetic and pedagogical components within it by which potential new participants have their consciences trained. Moreover, these apologetic and pedagogical components are based not so much upon the strategic advantages of gaining new recruits as upon the more profound theological conviction that resistance must be an expression of witness to the God whom we seek to serve and an opportunity for training others to pursue their own callings through their participation in resistance.[23]

Undergirding all three Reformed formulations of these major doctrines is a more basic emphasis on the sovereignty of God. The Reformed vision of creation is premised upon it.[24] Sin cannot undermine it.[25] Political activities are limited expressions of it.[26] In all cases, the church's earliest confession, "Jesus is Lord,"[27] claims that ultimately all things—resistor and resisted, oppressor and victim, even time, space, and language—exist inside the providence of God's creative, sustaining, and culminating will as it is uniquely and *gracefully* expressed in Jesus Christ.

At first blush, strong claims about God's sovereign will seem to lead toward quietism rather than resistance: if God is working out God's purposes regardless of whether we pursue those same interests, then we might as well just stay out of the way and wait for God to finish. However, such a conclusion misses the more basic conviction that God's sovereign action extends into our lives—that we cannot isolate ourselves into a part of the world where God is not acting in order to stay out of the way. Moreover, it misses the very point of the earlier claim that we participate in that which we would resist. If we are always already implicated in that which causes the suffering we resist, then doing nothing is tantamount to giving tacit agreement to the cause of suffering. Indeed, in the Reformed vision of the world I am describing, such quietism can only be seen as an expression of sin; it is attempting to set oneself apart from God and God's actions, attempting to be a type of creature different than we were created to be. Instead, we must be continually open to God working through us.

At the same time, however, we cannot confuse God's work with our work; nor can we confuse God's work through us with the whole of that work. The former inevitably blurs the parts of the primary and secondary actors in the divine drama of God's providence; the latter refuses to engage the other actors on the stage. Rather than looking at the negative expressions of such confusions, however, it may be helpful to explore the positive implications of keeping these roles straight. Positively, strong claims about God's sovereignty remove from us the onus of making history come out right. That is, whatever our responsibilities are when we engage in acts of resistance, they do not include controlling all the variables, known and unknown, that contribute to or inhibit the success of our goals. Given the intransigently complex world we live in, such a task would be impossible for us, anyway, and could only lead to frustration and despair. Positively, strong claims about God's sovereignty open us up to the possibility that God is using people other than ourselves to pursue God's ends. We may be surrounded by compatriots we do not recognize—including some who do not recognize their actions as falling within God's providence. The isolating burden of thinking "If I don't, no one will" is lifted from our shoulders.

None of this is to dismiss our responsibility to resist those who oppress or destroy. Instead, it is to reenvision the nature of that responsibility. Building from H. Richard Niebuhr's claim, "God is acting in all actions upon you. So respond to all actions as a response to his action,"[28] the strong claim for God's sovereignty is that God is acting in all actions—upon us and otherwise. Obviously, this is not to say that God is the immediate cause of all things; such a claim is not only morally repulsive but theologically incoherent, removing both human will and intellect from what it means to be human. It is, however, to place God into the middle of history and ask us to discern how God is acting, including how God is acting in the lives of those whose actions we resist. If God could use the Persian king Cyrus to save Israel, God can use modern rulers, rebels, and systems—even those we resist— toward salvation as well.[29]

What follows for pursuing faithful resistance? At a basic level, one conclusion to draw from these strong sovereignty claims is that those of us who would resist must, nevertheless, always attempt to discern the way God is acting not only in our actions, but in the actions of those persons and projects we resist. Said differently, we are always in the difficult but faithful position of listening for how God might be speaking to us in the words of those with whom we disagree. It follows from this not only that faithful resistance is premised on disagreement, but that we need to treat disagreement itself as an opportunity for growth rather than division.[30] Not all disagreement is productive, but when it is placed within the theological context I have laid out above, it can be remarkably fruitful.[31] After all, disagreement often marks the initial period of ferment out of which spring new understanding and vision. Thus, the type of disagreement I wish to affirm exists as a sign of hope for the future—and it is ultimately our hope in the future that undergirds faithful resistance.


## COMMON GROUND AND FUTURE DIRECTIONS


While I have hardly exhausted the Reformed meanings of creation, sin, politics, and the sovereignty of God, I hope that I have at least given some reasons and resources not only for why we resist, but for what that resistance might look like. What remains, then, is to bring these reasons and resources back into the context of the IMF/Jubilee 2000 relationship. Let me merely lift up five proposals for that relationship which grow out of the previous section:

1. While they do not agree on strategies for addressing the problem, it is important for the IMF and Jubilee 2000 (and, for that matter, everyone else involved) to notice that they share a common starting point and vision: namely, the desire to relieve debt in the world's poor countries. Forgetting this common starting point risks not only maligning the other's motives but confusing one's own.

2. The differences between the IMF and Jubilee 2000 highlight the degree to which neither functions with a clear mandate from God over against the other. Both positions have strengths and weaknesses, and it is always the task (no matter how hard) of all involved (no matter who) to discern what all those strengths and weaknesses are (no matter how many) in order to develop better ways of engaging debt.

3. In light of (1) and (2), part of what the IMF and Jubilee 2000 share is a need for their vision to be corrected as they continue to interact with the way God is acting in the world. Jubilee 2000, in particular, must be explicit in this effort as it recognizes, at least to a nominal degree, that its vision is directed by a mandate that springs from God's will for the world. However, even where the IMF does not explicitly interpret history as the stage within which God acts, it still needs its vision to be corrected by its interpretation of what is going on around it.[32]

4. In light of (1) and (3), it follows that the IMF and Jubilee 2000 need to be particularly responsive to each other. Their common starting point and vision suggest that they, more than many other organizations, are attuned to the problems of international debt. Their respective resources in collecting and analyzing data could be invaluable not only to each other, but to those countries whose debt they are attempting to address.

5. The IMF and Jubilee 2000 need each other. This is not to say that they need to share the same strategies, nor even all the same motives. Indeed, they need *not* to share them, precisely so that their differences challenge each other. The IMF needs Jubilee 2000 to keep it honest to its stated goals and to challenge its strategies where they do not achieve those goals. Jubilee 2000, on the other hand, needs the IMF not only to supply economic resources that would otherwise be unavailable, but to constantly remind it that debt is only one part of global poverty. What both need is to promote the types of disagreement that are fruitful rather than counterproductive. Given the current political and economic structures in the world, Jubilee 2000 is best able to promote that type of disagreement precisely by engaging in resistance of the kind I've suggested above.

## AN INVITATION

This chapter is, I suppose, an act of resistance in itself: it is an attempt to resist those forms of resistance that promote opposition at the expense of service and the symbolic value of resistance at the expense of seeking to benefit those on whose behalf they resist. This is a tenuous position to develop. On the one hand, if we always participate in the thing we resist, this chapter is full of unfair oppositional language and unhelpful symbolism. On the other hand, by resisting those things, it risks aligning itself with those who resist resistance generally, thereby promoting the very thing I wish most to resist, namely, the inability to develop strategies for effective resistance to the causes of suffering in the world. Where the former might promote unproductive disagreement, the latter might inhibit productive disagreement. I cannot resolve those tensions; I thus find myself in the altogether paradoxical position of resisting aspects of my claims about resistance and using those claims themselves as tools for doing so.

There are some claims in this chapter that many may resist, and many claims that some may resist. This, however, is as it should be—and my paradoxical reflexive position recognizes this. What such resistance indicates may only be the need for further thoughtful action: more vigorous and helpful disagreement, more shared conversations, more movement from disagreement and conversation to action. Ultimately, however, the question at hand is always whether our methodological conversations will lead us to work toward alleviating suffering in the world. Thus, the conclusion of this chapter can and ought to be seen primarily as an introduction or, rather, an invitation to a larger discussion about faithful resistance, but only if that discussion leads to faithful resistance. The chapter fails if it does not invite us to move beyond it and out into a world in which there is much to resist and much to learn about faithful resistance in the process.

## NOTES

1. Indeed, the witness of the earliest witness of the earliest gospel is that Jesus came preaching repentance, not resistance: "Now after John was arrested, Jesus came to Galilee, proclaiming the good news of God and saying, 'The time is fulfilled, and the kingdom of God has come near; repent, and believe the good news'" (Mark 1:14–15). All biblical citations are taken from the New Revised Standard Version.

2. "You have heard that it was said, 'An eye for an eye and a tooth for a tooth.' But I say to you, Do not resist an evildoer" (Matthew 5:38).

3. "[W]hoever resists authority resists what God has appointed, and those who resist will incur judgment" (Romans 13:2).

4. E.g., "Resist the devil, and he will flee from you" (James 4:7).

5. The Reformed tradition is no more single-minded than any other rich tradition. I make no claims toward developing *the* Reformed vision of resistance. Indeed, I suspect many of my Reformed colleagues in this volume would challenge some of my assertions here. More modestly, then, I hope to advance a particular way of thinking about resistance that is broadly coherent from a Reformed perspective. I take my colleagues' disagreement with the vision I advance not only as further evidence that none of us ever gets it wholly right (certainly a conviction near the heart of Reformed faith!), but as the opportunity for us all to develop better ways of thinking about Reformed resistance in the future. Disagreement is often the very site upon which progress builds.

6. For a history of the development of the so-called "Bretton Woods" institutions (including the IMF and World Bank), see Michael Edwards, *Future Positive: International Cooperation in the 21st Century* (London: Earth Scan, 1999). For further information on the IMF, in particular, see their website, http://www.imf.org.

7. During this time, there was a 400 percent increase in world trade and a 300 percent increase in real income around the world.

8. In 1979, the United States gave roughly $80 billion in foreign aid. By 1985, the United States was actually getting money (via debt repayment) to the tune of about $15 billion per year.

9. As of the writing of this chapter, the IMF is considering further revisions, including programs to protect debtor countries while they appeal the conditions of their loans.

10. The Jubilee 2000 movement is an international movement, with active chapters all over the world. For the sake of convenience, I will concentrate on Jubilee 2000 in the United States. For further information on Jubilee 2000/U.S.A., see their website: www.j2000usa.org.

11. For an excellent examination of the "strategy of embarrassment" used by activist campaigns, see Jarol B. Manheim, *The Death of a Thousand Cuts: Corporate Campaigns and the Attack on the Corporation* (Mahwah, N.J.: Lawrence Erlbaum, 2000). The grounds for this embarrassment are the focus of the next section of this chapter.

12. My own inclinations tend toward those of the IMF's critics. These inclinations are born, primarily, of the sense that the IMF has done too little too late to correct its own failings and address the problems of international poverty that it is nominally fighting—and that its delays and rigidity are expressions of certain interests and values that are unsupportable in light of the sheer volume of suffering incurred as a result of world debt. I do not, however, doubt the IMF's claim that it is pursuing the alleviation of that suffering by the means at its disposal.

13. See, e.g., Michael Edwards, "Edwards Urges Building Constructive Dialogue Between IMF and Nongovernmental Organizations," *IMF Survey* 30.8 (April 16, 2001): 121.

14. I take it simply as a truism that Christian engagement with an opponent must be based upon an accurate description of that opponent, and that such a description

must be rendered in such a way that the opponent recognizes himself or herself in that description. This truism flows out of both the demands of justice and the central Christian virtue of charity. In this instance, recognizing common moral ground is one aspect of accurate description.

15. Systematically, Reformed theology would tend to begin with the doctrine of God in order to emphasize other doctrines' dependence upon it. In this instance, I have located it last not to deemphasize it, but to emphasize its particular contribution to the case at hand. I leave it to the reader to remember the caveat at the middle of the paragraph: the doctrine of God undergirds the other three. To separate any of the other three from the doctrine of God would be to misunderstand them all.

16. Think, for instance, of the answer to the first question of the Shorter Catechism: "Q: What is the chief end of man? A: Man's chief end is to glorify God and to enjoy him forever."

17. One could develop a strong argument that the very things that most need resisting are things that warp, inhibit, or destroy relationships, whether with persons in other parts of the world, the environment, or whatever. In such an understanding, the very goal of resistance would be to reform those relationships. To make this argument convincingly, however, would engage one in answering a series of complex philosophical and empirical questions about the dynamics of relationship, oppression, and suffering that move far beyond the scope of this chapter.

18. For an insightful and contextually sensitive vision of sin, see Charles T. Mathewes, *Evil and the Augustinian Tradition* (Cambridge: Cambridge University Press, 2001).

19. Romans 7:19.

20. Our inability to take on the entire responsibility for the suffering of the other also and simultaneously reveals our need for a grace that is alien to us and the miracle that such grace has been expressed in the gospel.

21. "Politics" has taken on an overly narrow and generally negative meaning in contemporary society—roughly "using the resources available to you—including those around you—to pursue ends advantageous to yourself and those you favor." Though that definition may reveal an undeniable aspect of political life, we need to keep a broader definition in mind, namely, "the range and processes of relationships between persons and groups who work to pursue specific ends." This latter definition is the one that pertains to my use of the word.

22. This should not, I would hasten to add, be understood as equating our political engagements with the glory of God, which can only be seen as a common and vicious form of idolatry.

23. While it requires further development than I can give here, I would argue that the idea that we participate in that which we resist as described above is readily exemplified within the context of a Reformed political vision. Such a vision leans toward a broadly democratic system of governance in which all citizens take on part of the responsibility for the actions of their country by virtue of the fact that theirs is a government constituted "of, by, and for the people." Given the morally ambiguous places in which governments often necessarily find themselves as they pursue goods in tension with each other (such as order, equality, and liberty), a democratic system will simultaneously reveal the complicity of its citizens and promote opportunities for their resistance.

24. See, e.g., Colossians 1:15–17.

25. See, e.g., Romans 8:18–25. (Indeed, see most of the Epistle to the Romans!)

26. See, e.g., Romans 13:1–7.

27. Romans 10:9. For a thoughtful exploration of the early church's high Christology and how the church's confession connects it to a larger vision of the cosmos as ordered and directed by God, see Richard Baukham, *God Crucified: Monotheism and Christology in the New Testament* (Grand Rapids, Mich.: Eerdmans, 1998).

28. H. Richard Niebuhr, *The Responsible Self* (San Francisco: HarperSanFrancisco, 1963), p. 126.

29. See Isaiah 45:1–7.

30. In light of the church's long history of internecine bickering, many have criticized the church for its failure to understand how to agree. In light of the claims of sovereignty, we might wonder, instead, if the church needs to learn how to disagree.

31. Having affirmed the value of disagreement, I would nevertheless hasten to add that we must be constantly vigilant in recognizing and restricting the ways various forms of power inhibit productive disagreement. In this regard, we have much to learn from those who have been injured by the dangerous combination of ideology and power that treats disagreement as a battleground upon which it will wage war until victorious.

32. I take the IMF's continued modifications of its work with debtor nations to be precisely this.

## 16

# Fundamentalism and the
# Big Picture Bible

*Robert A. Chesnut*

*M*any of us may remember having a special child's Bible. If yours was like mine, it was probably an oversized book with pictures in it—a big picture Bible. I distinctly remember seeing in mine, for the first time, a picture of Christ on the cross. It made an indelible imprint on me, an image that remains vivid to this day.

The big picture Bible. What indelible imprints do you carry around with you from the Bible? What Bible stories or verses stick with you over the years? The Exodus and the parting of the Red Sea? The Ten Commandments? David and Goliath? Jonah and the whale? The twenty-third Psalm? The nativity story? The crucifixion? The resurrection? The miracles of Jesus? The Golden Rule?

The Bible is a large, diverse, and possibly confusing collection of various types of literature, written by individually unique authors with their own personal and cultural viewpoints, and coming out of a span of history covering almost a millennium and a half. With all that complexity, we really cannot make much use of the Bible unless we begin to formulate some framework of interpretation, some big picture concept of what matters most in this book. The Bible is a mixture of very human, fallible viewpoints on the one hand and, on the other hand, the eternally enduring word of God.

One example of what I'm talking about is the issue of slavery. You will find in the Bible no explicit condemnation of slavery. You will find some passages that assume slavery as a given, even some passages that condone it. On the other hand, if you look at the big picture in the Bible, you will see clearly that slavery is absolutely inconsistent with the pervasive and enduring themes of fairness and justice, mercy and compassion that run throughout the Scriptures.

Today, Christians have a solid consensus that slavery is a horrible evil utterly inconsistent with the essential tenets of our faith. But we wrestle with other issues of human worth, dignity, and equality in our time. One of the big ones for us now, of course, is sexual orientation.

As we try to sort out current issues in the light of our faith, we should keep in mind that not all that long ago, many, many Christians—particularly those who read the Bible literally, without the big picture in mind—justified slavery as an institution allowed, even condoned by the Bible. Not all that long ago, my own maternal grandfather grew up in a household where there were slaves.

Here's a crucial question that we ought to ask ourselves again and again: Is the way I interpret the Bible and understand its authority today compatible or incompatible with the way those in the past—and some even to this very day—used the Bible to justify slavery, racism, second-class status for women, persecution of gays?

I think that much of the mission of Jesus can be understood as an attempt to move the people of his time—especially the religious people and the religious leaders—to focus on the big picture of their Jewish faith. This is exactly the point he was making to the Pharisees when he said: "You strain out the gnats and swallow the camels." "You tithe everything, right down to the mint and cumin, but you neglect the weightier matters of the law." In other words, you can't see the forest for the trees. You can't see the big picture. The big picture is to love God with all your heart, mind, soul, and strength, and your neighbor as yourself. The big picture is fairness and kindness, mercy and compassion. The big picture is doing unto others as you would have them do unto you. The big picture is to love mercy, to do justice, to walk humbly with your God.

Without the big picture in mind, the kind of religion that we end up with—in the time of the Pharisees and in our own time of resurgent fundamentalism—is a religion that abandons the big picture Bible for a religion that is its very antithesis. That antithesis is a religion of legalism, judgmentalism, self-righteousness, a religion of exclusion rather than inclusion. It is a religion that, as Jesus said of the Pharisees, lays heavy legalistic burdens on people, a religion that boards up the gate that leads to life in God's realm of mercy and fairness and welcome to all.

The book of Jonah provides one of my favorite examples of how easy and how pervasive is our inclination to misread the Bible, to miss its central messages. For those who grew up going to Sunday school, this is probably one of those key Bible stories learned in childhood.

Many of us could probably retell the story, at least its basic outline: God calls Jonah to go on a mission that is repugnant to Jonah, namely to go and preach repentance to the city of Nineveh so that its people might be spared God's wrath. Jonah, trying to flee God's call, boards a ship that gets caught in a storm. Jonah goes overboard, is swallowed by a great fish, survives in its belly for three days, and finally gets spit out on dry land. Whereupon, God calls Jonah again on that mission to save the people of Nineveh. This time, a sadder yet wiser Jonah obeys.

Jonah is a very effective, successful prophet. The people of Nineveh, from the highest to the lowliest, heed Jonah's warning, repent, and are spared God's righteous wrath. God is pleased, but Jonah is anguished and sinks into a deep depression.

What is the central message here? About all that has stuck in most people's minds is the big fish story. In my experience, that is where the fundamentalists tend to focus—on the miraculous, literal element. So they insist that if you're a true Bible believer, you have to take it all—hook, line, and sinker—as literally true, as something that actually happened just as it is told.

So the big picture in Jonah is lost; the essential message is obscured. The reason Jonah fled from his mission was because he hated Nineveh and wanted it destroyed. Nineveh, you see, was the capital of Assyria, a nation that was the hated enemy of the Jewish people, a nation that had a long history of cruel and brutal oppression of Jonah's people. That's why Jonah was such a reluctant prophet, why he sank into such despair when his God-given mission was successful. He could not rise above his hatred of his enemies. And there is the key message of the story: God loves even your enemies, seeks their redemption, and calls you to do the same.

The book of Jonah precedes Jesus by several centuries, offering the same message that Jesus taught: love your enemies and pray for those who persecute you. That message, I would say, is really a lot harder to swallow than the big fish story. The essential message of Jonah really has nothing to do with whether or not the events of the story actually took place—no more so than whether Jesus' parable of the Good Samaritan is about events that actually ever took place. Focusing on the question of literal truth here is really a distraction, and a dangerous one at that. It is in the central messages of these stories that we find the word of God, the enduring and eternal truth.

One big implication of all this, then, is to reinforce the absolutely essential importance of reading the Bible in the right way so that we come to it with the right questions, so that we are not distracted from its essential truth. We must not turn the Bible into something it is not—into a legalistic code book that provides comprehensive and infallible answers to every moral dilemma of our time; or into a scientific account of exactly how the earth was formed; or into an objective historical record of events that actually took place in every detail as reported; or into a soothsayer's guidebook predicting every stage of the future and exactly how and when the world will come to an end. All of these approaches to the Bible can be distorting and dangerous distractions from its essential and enduring truth, its big picture messages.

There is every good reason *not* to read the Bible ourselves and *not* to teach its stories to our children unless we are keen to focus on its essential and enduring messages, unless we are sure to teach the big picture Bible. Otherwise, unless we are careful to avoid the distractions and the distortions, the Bible can be a very dangerous book. We can make it a tool of prejudice and oppression, even as it has so sadly been misused in the past and even to the present day to put down women, gays, people of color, people of other faiths, divorced people.

Fundamentalism of any stripe imprisons its adherents in the past, just as it has the Taliban who are trapped in medieval worldviews. To be thoroughly consistent, both Muslim and Christian fundamentalists must declare that women are inferior to men, that nothing in their scriptures directly prohibits slave holding, that our planet is flat, and that the sun revolves around the earth. Such literalism allows for no new beginnings, no thinking of new thoughts or coming to new insights. Everything is fixed, absolute, and ultimately authoritarian, for there is no room for independent thinking, freedom of thought, or individual questioning.

So we look for the big picture in the Bible, not the jots and tittles of isolated verses here and there, but the constant and enduring message. This is also why our own Presbyterian tradition of biblical interpretation is very sound and wise in insisting that we must look first and last to Jesus, who is the living Word of God, the central figure in the big picture. We must test everything else we find in the Bible against Jesus, *his* life and *his* witness. If we Presbyterians did not approach the Bible in this way, we could never justify ordaining women to ministry and other positions of leadership in the church.

When we look to Jesus on gender issues, I think we get a pretty clear message. Jesus never ever said or did a single thing to put women down. On the contrary, he went out of his way to affirm women in ways that were sometimes radical and controversial. He used feminine images and symbols in speaking of God. He took women seriously as persons who were entitled to discuss serious questions of faith with him. He spoke with women in public, something strictly forbidden to a righteous, observant Jew of the time.

New Testament scholars observe that the earliest church was more like Jesus on gender equality, but that by the time we get to the later writings of the New Testament, it is clear that the church was reverting to a more conservative, patriarchal stance. A lot of the blame for this often goes to Paul, but in his defense we can say that not all the New Testament writings attributed to Paul were actually written by him. In any case, we do have that wonderful verse from Paul affirming that in Christ all distinctions of gender and race and social status are transcended, for our baptism and our faith make us all one in him (Gal. 3:28).

The Bible is full of the invitation to "Sing to the Lord a new song." The Bible is full of God's declaration, "Behold, I do a new thing." Christians believe that Christ represents the new thing that Jesus did with the faith of Israel. Paul's vision of Christ being for all people, not just for Jews, was a radical new thing, as was Peter's conversion to that vision. Christians who began to conclude a couple of centuries ago that slavery was not compatible with Christianity believed that God was doing a new thing in their time.

James Russell Lowell wrote a poem about that new vision as it pertained to slavery. His poem was then set to music as a powerful hymn that makes this bold affirmation:

> New occasion teach new duties;
> Time makes ancient good uncouth.
> They must upward still, and onward,
> Who would keep abreast of truth.

In contrast to fundamentalism's basic thrust, the big picture Bible tells the story of an ever broadening divine movement to challenge and overthrow—as Jesus did—all those systems and powers and dogmas that repress, exploit, or demean any of God's beloved children; to liberate the oppressed; to include all people, without regard to human distinctions or barriers, as equally loved, honored, and empowered by God. This is truly good news!

*17*

# Is This New Wine?
# Resistance Among Black Presbyterians

## *Ronald E. Peters*

$\mathcal{I}$n African American communities across the nation, harsh realities confront people's lives daily, including disproportionately high instances of infant mortality, substance abuse, HIV-AIDS, incarceration, racial profiling by police, unemployment, troubled school systems, and high rates of crime in neighborhoods. Meanwhile, the preoccupation of the Presbyterian Church U.S.A. (PCUSA) with procedural and theological technicalities that do not seem to touch upon these realities in any meaningful way is a circumstance that many African American Presbyterians believe must be resisted at all costs. These Presbyterians believe that they must address the need for healing ministries in their African American communities rather than be consumed by denominational maneuverings. They are determined to resist cultural hegemony that passes itself off as theological rhetoric and liturgical correctness and results in deflation of ministry in black Presbyterian churches.

In 1993, resistance to denominational insensitivity to African American concerns became the point of focus for a group of American Presbyterians[1] who lifted a challenge to the church in a discussion paper entitled *Is This New Wine?* This group evolved from the denomination's African American Advisory Committee (AAAC) and worked with the national church's office of Racial and Cultural Diversity. The AAAC had been meeting since 1990 on ways to strengthen new church development and communal outreach activities in African American communities. At its December 1992 meeting, several committee members began raising questions about the inconsistency of attempting to forge ministries uniquely targeted toward African American concerns from denominational structures (presbyteries, synods, and General Assembly councils) that were out of touch with the core needs of these communities and did not appreciate the African heritage. It was from these initial discussions that the group began to refer to itself as *Presbyterians for Prayer, Study, and Action.* I agreed to pull together a document based upon our discussions that could be later shared with wider constituencies of African American Presbyterians. By March 1993, the draft was completed and adopted by the group.

Presbyterians for Prayer, Study, and Action essentially were frustrated with the large number of vacant pulpits in black Presbyterian churches and what they saw as the denomination's benign neglect of social injustice and spiritual issues. The aim of the document was to spell out the group's rationale for considering withdrawal from the denomination as an option for black Presbyterians. The New Wine Paper essentially called for the focused attention to community outreach in African American communities. At issue were the social mores and theological bickering of the Presbyterian Church U.S.A. that frequently resulted in the sidelining of concerns central to the spiritual effectiveness and physical survival of African American congregations.

In an April 1993 cover letter to the sessions of African American Presbyterian congregations introducing the New Wine Paper, the group outlined its intentions in the following manner:

> As we approach the 21st century, how will African American Presbyterians create viable ministries in their respective communities? . . . This is not to suggest that we are unconcerned for the welfare of our sisters and brothers among other racial/ethnic groups, including our White sisters and brothers. We are also not unaware of the current crisis of spirit that is currently forcing the denomination to make drastic cuts of staff and programs that can only result in the further marginalization of African American concerns. This focus on the African American community merely reflects our realization that it is inappropriate for us to: (1) attempt to suggest what others should do in their respective communities; and (2) place denominational politics as a priority over the welfare of our own children and communities.
>
> The aim of this paper is to challenge African American congregations to action concerning the most viable way we, as Presbyterians, can most effectively address the urgent needs of the African American community. Our aim is only to present this matter for the prayerful reflection and debate of all Sessions of predominately African American congregations and their congregations. The goal is for "grass roots" African American Presbyterians in our congregations to deliberate this matter for themselves: God, alone, is Sovereign of conscience.[2]

Presbyterians frequently pride themselves on being rooted in scripture and giving serious attention to the theological analysis. While all God-talk (theology) evolves around the human response to Divine initiatives, accurate analysis of the moral obligations of the believer resulting from this encounter is impossible without attention to the social, political, economic, cultural, environmental, and spiritual context defining people's lives. Indeed, it was because John Calvin took seriously the social and political realities of his day that he was able to do profound theological analysis (i.e., *Institutes of the Christian Religion*). In the opinion of the Presbyterians for Prayer, Study, and Action, the denomination has fallen well short of its historical theological orientation on the issues of import to its African American members.[3]

The New Wine Paper suggested that African Americans should consider withdrawal from the PCUSA as a means of achieving more effective ministries within African American communities. The paper offered a brief chronicle of historical reasons for its bold suggestion. It posited that a new *re-forming* spirit of Presbyterianism that embraced *Afrocentric* models of ministry was needed for black Presbyterian congregations to be effective in community outreach.[4] Moreover, the paper lifted up a vision of what an idealized "African Presbyterian Church in America" could look like in the year 2052 should black Presbyterians opt to embark upon the establishment of a denominational alternative to the existing PCUSA. Finally, the paper called on African American Presbyterians to engage in a seven-year period of prayerful discussion of the issues. This document is remarkable because it challenges African American Christians in the PCUSA to resist being taken for granted and being co-opted into participation in a religious structure that is not spiritually nurturing or empowering.

Consistent with genuine resistance efforts, the paper created a storm of controversy among black Presbyterians, who largely divided into three major ideological camps. One group consisted of those who were disturbed by the apathy of the denomination to their issues but were not ready to consider withdrawal as an option. A second group was willing to debate the issue but not sure if an alternate denominational structure was the answer. For many in this camp, the solution was merely to exit the denomination and affiliate with some other that was more spiritually rooted in the ethos, needs, and spiritual strivings of the African American community. Others in this group seemed to favor remaining within the denomination, if change became a realistic option. A third and small but vocal contingent, mostly young clergy under the age of forty, was decidedly interested in pursuing withdrawal as a practical option.

Over time, the focus shifted from the "whether we stay or go" debate toward finding ways to address black community issues through existing structures. Although there are no clear figures as to the actual numbers of African Americans in the PCUSA, estimates generally place the total somewhere around 2.5 percent of the whole (about 50,000 persons). There are several vibrant and growing black Presbyterian congregations with strong community outreach ministries. Nationwide, however, large numbers of black Presbyterian congregations still struggle without pastoral leadership, with several facing the possibility of closure. Presbyterian new church development activities in African American communities are quite rare. For many black Presbyterians, however, consideration of the viability of the PCUSA for ministries of reconciliation, evangelism, and nurture within the African American community is still a matter that is very much open for discussion. As such, it remains to be seen how the bulk of African American Presbyterians will respond to the challenge lifted in the New Wine Paper.

The following is the text of the original discussion paper circulated among black Presbyterians in 1993.

## IS THIS NEW WINE?

A paper for discussion among African American Presbyterians presented by Presbyterians for Prayer, Study, and Action, April 1993.

> "No one uses a piece of new cloth to patch up an old coat, because the new patch will shrink and tear off some of the old cloth, making an even bigger hole. Nor does anyone pour new wine into used wineskins, because the wine will burst the skins, and both the wine and the skins will be ruined. Instead, new wine must be poured into fresh wineskins." Jesus (Mark 2:21–22)

## THE CHALLENGE FACED BY THE AFRICAN AMERICAN CHURCH

> Nobody knows de trouble I've seen; nobody knows but Jesus.
> Nobody knows de trouble I've seen! Glory! Hallelujah!
> (African American Spiritual)

In the paper "A Call to a National Dialogue," produced for the recent Kelly Miller Smith Institute on African American Church Studies at Vanderbilt University Divinity School (October 1992), the challenge faced by the African American Church is clearly outlined as follows:

> The African American Church is in crisis. At a time in history when we are about to enter a new millennium, the African American Church stands

at the crossroads of decision. Its traditional role as the conservator of Black culture and the conscience of the Black community is at stake. It must choose either life or death, blessings or curses. Whatever choice it makes will determine whether or not we and our descendants will live as a redeemed and redeeming community in this land where God has befriended us. The signs of the crisis we face today are unmistakable:

*Witness*—the social and economic descent of more than a third of the Black population into a burgeoning and permanent underclass.

*Witness*—the children of our impoverished, drug-infested neighborhoods coming to the point of birth, and yet dying in the womb of human possibility.

*Witness*—the rate of incarceration of young Black males which has 23 percent of those aged 20 to 29 (almost one of every four) in prison, on bail, on probation or parole.

*Witness*—the turning of thousands of our young people toward illegal drugs in a vain, hedonistic escape from reality, or an attempt to enter a degrading, criminal career.

*Witness*—the unprecedented assault on Black family life by urban violence, poverty, homelessness, and teenage pregnancy on one hand, and on the other, the demands of an upwardly mobile, materialistic lifestyle that is scornful of God and has no place for the church of Jesus Christ.

*Witness*—the reversals in the public arena of hard won policies ensuring affirmative action for minorities and women.

*Witness*—the rampant individualism, the loss of community, and the decline of the Black Church as an effective agent for justice and liberation among all poor and oppressed people. The list goes on.[5]

Unfortunately, the above information is common knowledge in our society. It is also, unfortunately, common knowledge that, overwhelmingly, black Presbyterian Christians lack the ability to address themselves to this crisis in their communities. At a time when human suffering in urban areas where high percentages of African Americans are found has dramatically increased, frequently black Presbyterian congregations are experiencing dwindling numbers, decaying physical plants, and vacant pulpits with the result that many Presbyteries are closing more and more black congregations and starting none. It has been noted that an upsurge in the initiation of new churches is reflected nationwide throughout the Presbyterian Church U.S.A. in every racial group, except among African Americans. Indeed, while there are several examples of new church development, growth, and vitality regarding effective urban ministry among African American churches in other denominations, the nationwide record of African American new church development within the Presbyterian Church U.S.A. over the past ten years has been effectively written off by the denomination.[6]

This is not to suggest that merely the initiation of new congregations is needed. Also needed are efforts that will enable existing African American congregations to more effectively address critical issues of economic blight and educational, social, and political disenfranchisement of their parishioners. Many black Presbyterian congregations, however, view themselves as being so "middle class" in their orientations, and imitative of what they view as proper "white Presbyterian" liturgy and ethos, that they do not relate effectively to other blacks. Many black Presbyterians expend so much time and energy perpetually trying to relate to the structures of white Presbyterians that they are unable to relate to their own heritage or to others within the African American community, a characteristic Gayraud Wilmore (*Black and Presbyterian*, 1983) documented long ago:

> Let us put the matter squarely. Some of us have been so anxious to prove to our white brothers and sisters that we too are Americans and that we too 'belong' that we have deprived them of the gifts God has given to us as a people. . . . We have been so busy learning how to be "human beings in general" that we have paid little attention to the special qualities of Black humanity that we have to bring when we are true to our own history and traditions.[7]

Wilmore further suggests that this identity crisis among many black Presbyterians has engulfed them in a situation of dual penalty wherein they are frequently not taken seriously by their white Presbyterian sisters and brothers nor by members of the wider African American community: "Black Presbyterians have been criticized by other Blacks for remaining in a predominantly white church where they were under the double jeopardy of having to fight both class consciousness and racism."[8]

Is it possible for African American Presbyterians to reclaim, unapologetically, their cultural and spiritual African heritage? Is it possible for black Presbyterian churches to truly reclaim what Wilmore[9] described as the *five resources of the black religious heritage* and suggested as the means to more effective relationship of black Presbyterianism to the African American community? These five resources are defined by Wilmore as (1) Personal and Group Freedom from White Control; (2) The Image of Africa as the Land of Origin; (3) The Will of God for Social Justice; (4) Creative Style and Artistry; and (5) Unity of Secular and Sacred (avoiding the Euro-American sharp and artificial divisions of reality).

In light of the challenge faced by the African American community today, the Rev. Marsha Snulligan Haney has described the challenge faced by black Presbyterians this way:

Because of our professed belief in the "one, holy, universal, apostolic church," we join committed Christians throughout the world (be they in Africa, Brazil, the Caribbean, or Australia) in asking key questions concerning discipleship and ministry. . . .

1. What shape will our Christian obedience take?
2. What kind of theological reflection is appropriate to this obedience?
3. How do we (as African American Christians) understand the command to follow Christ into the 21st century?[10]

This New Wine Paper is especially directed to Presbyterians of African descent. This call, however, is also issued to any and all persons (Presbyterian or not) who, regardless of ethnic or cultural considerations, are concerned with the welfare and future of African American communities as part of their concern for the future of humankind. *It is a call to take whatever steps are necessary to empower black Presbyterians toward a more clearly Afrocentric proclamation of the gospel in the African American community as the essential means of addressing the social and spiritual crisis in that community from a Christian perspective.*

## A CALL TO PRAYER, STUDY, AND ACTION CONCERNING FORMATION OF AFRICAN PRESBYTERIAN CHURCHES IN AMERICA

> Sing a new song to the Lord!
> Sing to the Lord, all the world!
> Sing to the Lord, and praise God!
> Proclaim every day the good news
> that God has saved us.
> (Psalm 96:1–2)

As Moses was called to lead the people of God out of bondage into freedom and out of the wilderness into the promised land, and as the Ethiopian official was called to return to Africa and proclaim the Good News to his people, and as John Gloucester and Lucy Craft Laney were called to address the unique needs of African peoples in America, we are called by God to acknowledge the sovereignty and Lordship of God in our lives and affirm dignity and respect for all humankind by the following:

*Whereas,* we are a communal people with a rich African heritage and background acknowledging the triune God and the imperative of justice and love as the prerequisites of real unity and peace; and

*Whereas*, we as persons of African descent and members of the Presbyterian Church U.S.A. for the last 185 years of laboring within its bounds, give thanks to this denomination for its attempts, at many points, to stress inclusion and to proclaim justice issues, we yet recognize that its behavior has been and continues to be inconsistent with its stated objectives; and

*Whereas*, the various governing bodies, ministry units, committees, and task forces of the denomination formed to address the constitutional aims of inclusion and justice have failed to do either adequately with regard to its sisters and brothers of color; and

*Whereas*, African American membership in the Presbyterian Church U.S.A. has been dually penalized in that we are neither fully embraced within the denomination and, as a result, viewed with some skepticism by our sisters and brothers in the African American community beyond the church; and

*Whereas*, African American Presbyterians can no longer be held back by denominational structures of the Presbyterian Church U.S.A. which prevent our immediate and ongoing responsiveness to the pain, suffering, oppression, and hopelessness that characterizes the community inhabited by our African sisters and brothers worldwide;

*We, therefore, appeal* to our African American sisters and brothers within and without the Presbyterian Church U.S.A. to join together with us in fulfillment of our common hope and divine destiny to become a community wherein God's love, our respect for the dignity of all people, and the rich diversity of God's creation will be cherished, honored, and preserved.

*Let it be known* that, while it is our hope that all Presbyterians of African descent will join us in this noble undertaking should events require, we will respect the decision of those who choose to remain within the Presbyterian Church U.S.A. beyond our period of prayer, study, and action; we will continue to love, respect, honor, and be in partnership with them; and

*Let it also be known* that this call extends to sisters and brothers who are not of African descent, but who seek to embrace the African Presbyterian Church in America which, of necessity, includes the adoption of an Afrocentric perspective which binds us to love, respect, and value all people as human beings and as our sisters and brothers under Almighty God.

*Be it resolved, therefore, that we*, the people of African mothers and fathers, daughters of the dust and brothers of the earth, Call for the immediate initiation of a seven-year period of prayer, study, and action that may require formation of an *African Presbyterian Church in America*. This period of prayer, study, and action will conclude not later than seven years following its initiation and may result in the formation of separate corporate denominational entity. This period of prayer, study, and action is called to begin during the year of our God 1993. May the Love of God, the Grace of Jesus Christ, and the Power of the Holy Spirit undergird and bless this undertaking.

## REFORMED, REFORMING, AND THE CHALLENGE TO BE TRANSFORMED BY AN AFROCENTRIC PERSPECTIVE

> When the Israelites saw the king and his army marching against them, they were terrified and cried out to the Lord for help. They said to Moses, "Weren't there any graves in Egypt? Did you have to bring us out here in the desert to die? Look what you have done by bringing us out of Egypt! . . . Moses answered, "Don't be afraid! Stand your ground, and you will see what the Lord will do to save you today." . . . The Lord said to Moses, "Why are you crying out for help? Tell the people to move forward." (Exodus 14:10–15)
> Do not conform yourselves to the standards of this world, but let God transform you inwardly by a complete change of your mind. Then you will be able to know the will of God—what is good and is pleasing to God and is perfect. (Romans 12:2)

While a very grave step, the formation of a new African Presbyterian Church in America would not be as radical a departure from the historical tradition of black Presbyterianism in this country as it might appear to be at first reading. Indeed, this is not the first time black Presbyterians have considered such action.[11] This movement, in essence, represents an evolution of the spirit of previous generations of Black Presbyterians to address the needs of the wider African American community and to engage in "uplifting the race" not only spiritually, but also educationally, economically, socially, politically, and culturally. In this sense, an Afrocentric approach to worship, evangelism, Christian education, nurture, mission, and stewardship only implies a more focused and less racist approach to addressing the concerns of the African American community.

## WHY BLACK CHRISTIANS OR WHITE CHRISTIANS?

Discussion of this topic, with any semblance of integrity, would carry us far afield of the aims of this paper. Yet, for many Presbyterians (whether black, white, Native American, Hispanic, Korean, or any other of the multitude included in God's mosaic called humanity), this issue surfaces as paramount prior to any serious consideration of the merits of Afrocentricity as an enabler of the Christian proclamation of the gospel among African Americans. Wilmore addressed this issue in his book *Black and Presbyterian*:

> Sometimes one hears the question: "What does the Bible have to do with a Black Christianity or a White Christianity?" ... The word "Christian" appears only three times in the Bible (Acts 11:26; 26:28; and I Peter 4:16) and "Christianity"—with or without a modifier—never. It is a term used to describe the religion that developed around the person and work of Jesus of Nazareth, long after he and those who knew him in the flesh had passed off the scene. When you and I use the term "Christianity" we are speaking ... as sociologists of religion—that is to say, as persons interested in the belief systems, practices, and social structural aspects of this tradition.[12]

According to Wilmore (and many others, including Cone, Felder, Grant, Mays, Roberts, Thurman, West, or Woodson), the reality of black Christianity and the uniqueness of the black historical, cultural, social, and *theological* frame of reference in distinction from white mainstream reality in America hardly needs elaboration here. In addressing the matter within the context of the black Presbyterian Christian perspective, Wilmore writes:

> To speak of a Black Christianity is simply to refer to a social and cultural fact of life. It just happens to be a fact that for the more than four hundred years of Black history in the New World, eighty-five to ninety percent of all Black Christians have worshiped with people of their own race in all-Black congregations. As we might expect, certain realities and characteristics of faith and life are attached to that simple fact. To recognize them and take them seriously in a discussion about the Christian religion is neither to condemn nor to commend it. ... Like it or not, there *is* such a thing as Black Christianity and it is neither unbiblical nor unchristian to acknowledge its existence.[13]

## THE VALUE OF AFROCENTRISM

During this 500th anniversary of the Columbus event, there has been much discussion concerning its impact upon cultures outside of Europe. There is widespread agreement that one of the most harmful cultural effects of this era has been the distortion of history. It is in this area of historical and, therefore, cultural perspective that one of Afrocentrism's greatest contributions to black Christianity can be made. Molefi Asante (one of the most prolific writers on Afrocentrism) defines the aims of an Afrocentric approach to reality this way:

My work has increasingly constituted a radical critique of the Eurocentric ideology that masquerades as a universal view in the fields of intercultural communication, rhetoric, philosophy, linguistics, psychology, education, anthropology, and history.

Yet the critique is radical only in the sense that it suggests a turnabout, an alternative perspective on phenomena. It is about taking the globe and turning it over so that we see all the possibilities of a world where Africa, for example, is subject and not object. Such a posture is necessary and rewarding for Africans and Europeans. The inability to "see" from several angles is perhaps the one common fallacy in provincial scholarship.[14]

Asante argues that when persons of African descent are able to perceive the world from an African-oriented center (as for Asians, an Asian-oriented center; or Europeans, a European-oriented center) a new awareness or consciousness of one's own humanity is fully achieved.[15] This movement toward an Afrocentric consciousness enables persons of African descent to achieve, from within an African center, what Jesus talked about when he articulated the great commandments: first, love of God, and second, love of neighbor as one loves self (Mark 12:31).

## AFROCENTRISM AND BLACK PRESBYTERIANS

By their very historical definition and current expressions, African American congregations in general and the black Presbyterian congregations in particular are (in their best and most authentic expressions) informed by an Afrocentric perspective. While the term *Afrocentric* is relatively new, the historical reality of black Christians, corporately and individually, whose perspective of the gospel message has been oriented within the context of the issues and needs of an African-centered worldview is well documented. Numerous writers on the subject of the black church have affirmed this position from a variety of differing perspectives, including Cannon, Cone, Grant, Lincoln, Mays, Mitchell, Paris, Woodson, and Wilmore to mention a few. Specifically, the history of black Presbyterianism that has been guided by what would now be considered an Afrocentric worldview is also rich with examples (see Inez Parker's *The Rise and Decline of the Program of Education for Black Presbyterians of the United Presbyterian Church 1865–1970*; *Periscope 1, 2, and 3*; Wilmore's *Black and Presbyterian: The Heritage and the Hope*; Wilson's *Black Presbyterians in Ministry*; and *Black Presbyterians in History*, vols. 51–52, among others).

One of the worst legacies chattel slavery has left to many African Americans has been self-hatred. There is an old adage, well known within the African American community, that betrays not only the values of society at large regarding black people, but the internalized values of oppression and self-hatred among blacks. The adage says: "If you're white, you're right; yellow, you're mellow; brown: stick around; but black, get back!" The internalization of this warped value system is supported by the systemic relegation of the concerns of blacks and other non-Europeans to the periphery of conscious thought in Western society while lifting up the cultural, aesthetic, and social values of Europe as central and portraying them as *universal* values. Christianity has figured prominently in this distortion of reality.

The white institutional church in America and many of its imitators among black churches have been part and parcel of this deceptive misuse of the Christian faith. The national dialogue on "What It Means to Be Black and Christian" has suggested that this misuse of Christianity must first be addressed by black Christians, if they are to be able to truly address the needs of the broader African American community:

> It is not possible to be a Black Christian . . . without recognizing the deep ambiguity and paradox that are at the conjunction of these two ways of being. Malcolm X described Christianity as the "perfect slave religion" because he saw how White people invented a religion calculated to keep Black people passive in slavery and subservient after emancipation. Therefore, the first requirement for understanding what it means to be Black and Christian is to admit that Christianity has been used to subjugate Africans and African Americans. Too many [persons of African descent] lack the spiritual and intellectual courage to make that admission. But only after we have made it can we begin to see how Blackness [Afrocentrism], as a state of mind . . . and as a theological and cultural demystification of Anglo-Saxon religion and culture, can correct the distortions that modern racism induced into the message and mission of Jesus.[16]

The Rev. Warren Dennis has assessed the origins of this situation as it pertains to Presbyterians of African descent and suggests how an Afrocentric perspective provides a means of remedy:

> The last five hundred years of world history have been devastating for the acquisition of knowledge about other than European culture and history. Thus, we need to reclaim the negative and the positive of our African past prior to our converting to the Presbyterian system of belief as further response to the conditions of racism that have maligned, omitted, and distorted our images and culture as important contributions. As Black Presbyterians, we no longer have to view ourselves from the cultural perspective and history of the majority of Presbyterians.[17]

According to Dennis, Afrocentrism is one method by which African American Presbyterians can reclaim their cultural, historical, and spiritual heritage as a means of more effectively relating the gospel of Jesus Christ to the challenges faced by the wider African American community today:

> As a method of inquiry [Afrocentrism] asks the question, how do we gather meaning out of African or other existence? . . . Afrocentrism becomes the source of regeneration for our true values and beliefs grounded in a method of inquiry and discernment. . . . By lifting up Afrocentrism as a method of exploration, the centrality of African ideas, beliefs, and values as valid frames of reference for acquiring and examining historical and Biblical data for truth and accuracy is established. Afrocentrism then is a picture of the way things are actually represented in our most comprehensive ideas of nature, self, and society. It is the composite montage of specific ways of thinking, feeling, and acting, which is peculiar to African Americans in general, and African American Presbyterians in particular as distinguished from other groups.[18]

## A VISION: THE HALF-CENTURY ANNIVERSARY OF THE AFRICAN PRESBYTERIAN CHURCH IN AMERICA

The year is 2052, and the African Presbyterian Church in America is celebrating its fiftieth anniversary. Seven years before its founding a small group of African Americans, who were then members of the Presbyterian Church U.S.A., captured a vision for a new Presbyterian church free of the tenacious grip of racism. We are gathered in the sanctuary of the First African Presbyterian Church of Philadelphia. For all who know, this represents a phenomenon in human history. For this was the first congregational expression of black Presbyterianism in the older Euro-American Presbyterian Church U.S.A. Today, at almost 250 years of age (First African was founded in 1807), it is the first church of the fifty-year-old denomination whose anniversary we are assembled to celebrate today.

As an overflowing crowd fills the pews and chancel, a speaker emerges from the gathered community and approaches the pulpit. She is the daughter of one of those who ventured to dream sixty years ago, and she was one of the first persons ordained to ministry in the African Presbyterian Church. As she begins her prayer, she recalls how good God has been to this community of believers. She recalls the early struggles: how some African Americans resisted the call toward an African-centered proclamation of the gospel, but how the faithful were the continuing recipients of God's love, mercy, and grace.

Other speakers followed. Among some of the points being made was the recognition of how the "new" church began with one hundred congregations following a seven-year-long planning/education process; how the denomination has 575 congregations with 1.75 million members; how its communion reflected every African grouping in the world: Afro-Brazilians, Jamaicans, Afro-Brits, Haitians, Ghanaians, Kenyans, and so many others. And of course, there were African Americans who hold special place, since it was the fathers and mothers of those present today who were the bearers of a dream first realized fifty years ago with no real notion of what God would have wrought.

The Presbyterian Church U.S.A., out of which that first group of blacks emerged, is still in existence, through barely. Currently, it numbers less than 250,000 members, many of whom are white, male, and over seventy years old, for this denomination, toward the end of the last century, so successfully alienated women, people of color, and others who were determined not to be suitable for membership that the current church is almost a homogenous group, racially, generationally, nationally, and in gender. While there are residual representatives from communities of color and other formerly marginalized people, they enjoy no real access to the corridors of power within the PCUSA.

It is remarkable, notes one celebrant, that in the 1990s African American males were considered an "endangered species." Now, as the speaker surveys the participants crowding the sanctuary, he notes how the room is a balance of men and women, many of whom appear to be arranged in family groupings with as many children and young adults as older believers. Young men now are rarely seen idle on urban streetcorners, since most work long hours in family-owned businesses or have formed partnerships and other business organizations with what tends to be members of the church.

Most congregations within the APCA have founded elementary parish schools where young pupils are taught the typical grammar school curriculum as well as APCA church history and PCUSA history since 1807. The required languages are Spanish and at least one primary African language. Some schools offer Korean where there are large numbers of Korean people residing in close proximity to APCA neighborhoods. Musical instruction as well as art appreciation are also significant components of the curriculum. Early on in the education of the young is fostered the belief that a college education is an absolute minimum for preparation for the world. The APCA child is taught that they have been called by God to lead the world. Education is believed to be a principal means of preparing for this responsibility.

There were many, many more expressions of joy testifying to the power and love of God as reflected by the successes of this community of God.


## WHERE TO FROM HERE?

> God of our weary years, God of our silent tears,
> Thou who hast brought us thus far on our way;
> Thou who has by Thy might,
> Led us into the light,
> Keep us forever in the path we pray.
> (James Weldon Johnson, *Lift Every Voice and Sing*)

Mere consideration of the establishment of an entirely new denominational structure is an awesome task, one involving risk and a strenuous test of faith. It is significant that the Presbyterians for Prayer, Study, and Action would even seriously consider recommending that African Americans consider such an option. This fact clearly represents the high degree of frustration and alienation many third- and fourth-generation African American Presbyterians feel within their denomination. The aim of this call is not to be schismatic. On the contrary, it calls on African American Presbyterians and others concerned with the welfare of the black community to be more unified and focused in addressing the crisis of survival facing African Americans today.

The crisis faced by the African American Church in general and the African American Presbyterian in particular demands the response of faith, if it is to be seriously addressed. Indeed, the task would be awesome. Yet, when demanded by circumstances, neither the awesomeness of the task nor the risk involved prevented persons such as Moses, Ruth, Mary of Magdalene, the Apostle Paul, Martin Luther, John Calvin, John Knox, Richard Allen, Harriet Tubman, John Gloucester, Samuel Cornish, Henry Highland Garnet, Lucy Craft Laney, Mary Mcleod Bethune, Mahatma Gandhi, Martin Luther King Jr., Edler G. Hawkins, or Nelson Mandela from doing what they felt their faith required of them.

While the task may not be easy, the late Rev. James Cleveland reminded us that we "don't believe that God brought us this far [along our faith journey] to leave us" alone and unattended now. As God has been with African Americans in the past, it is clear that the "God of our weary years, the God of our silent tears, . . . who has led us into the light" is able to "keep us forever in God's path" as we journey toward a new century and a new reality: a witness to the gospel of Jesus Christ in African American communities by

Presbyterians that is truly Afrocentric: "And I will be with you always, even to the end of the age" (Jesus, from Matthew 28:20).

## RECOMMENDATIONS

In order to initiate dialogue about the concepts presented in this chapter, some very practical and strategic recommendations are in order. The following are submitted for consideration of all who wish to pledge themselves anew to a witness to the love and liberation found in Jesus Christ which seeks to be oriented within the unique needs, history, culture, and aspirations of the African American community rather than viewing these as peripheral. This is a call to an Afrocentric proclamation of the gospel.

*Recommended Actions*

1. Distribution of this chapter to African American Presbyterian sessions for the education of their congregations through prayerful study and dialogue. It is recommended that African American Presbyterian sessions and congregations should, as soon as possible, arrange for the prayerful study and dialogue within their respective Presbyteries and Synods of the issues raised in this chapter.
2. Arrange a national meeting of African American Presbyterians to discuss this matter. A national meeting to which all African American Presbyterians would be invited should be arranged as quickly as possible to consider the issues raised in this chapter. This would allow for dialogue around ideas presented and/or for the development of appropriate alternatives aimed at accomplishing the goal of empowering black Presbyterians toward an Afrocentric proclamation of the gospel.
3. Initiation during 1993 of a seven-year period of prayer, study, and action regarding concepts outlined in this chapter. It is recommended that a seven-year period of prayer, study, and action be initiated by August 1993 concerning the proposals outlined in this *Call to a New Reality*. During this period, pragmatic steps will be outlined and undertaken with a view toward creation of an African-centered Presbyterian witness to the gospel of Jesus Christ. These steps should include but not be limited to the following: (a) development of appropriate theological reflection regarding concepts raised in this paper; (b) the adoption of a national goal calling for the establishment of at least five new African American Presbyterian congrega-

tions annually over the next seven years; (c) the setting aside of funds ($500 annually) by all existing African American Presbyterian congregations for support of new church development in African American communities as well as by individuals able to do so; (d) the establishment of New Church Development Leadership Teams (a paradigm for new church development that includes the pastor, secretarial support, and a musician with skills in Afrocentric musicianship); and (f) the outlining of regional organizational and administrative structures.

## NOTES

1. This was actually a conversation group (a chat room) of approximately twenty persons nationwide who were active in the Black Presbyterian Caucus and working with the late Mildred Brown, then staff person to the PCUSA's national staff on Racial and Cultural Diversity. Frustrated with the denomination's benign neglect of critical social-justice issues in African American communities and congregational needs in black Presbyterian churches, the group assumed an ad hoc committee posture in order to identify themselves and their positions with the wider body of black Presbyterians and chose to call themselves *African American Presbyterians for Prayer, Study, and Action.* They identified their position with the following words: "We join together in Prayer (for the guidance of the Holy Spirit concerning these matters), Study (of options that will assist in alleviating the negative situations now gripping our communities nationwide), and Action (to create Afrocentric ministries to uplift and liberate the oppressed)." The group saw their goal as seeking an Afrocentric Proclamation of the Gospel and undertook activities to distribute and defend this methodological approach to congregational ministry via the *Is This New Wine?* study paper.

2. Letter forwarded to black Presbyterian congregations April 1993, signed by the late Mildred Brown (then PCUSA national church staff for Associate for Racial and Cultural Diversity), Rev. Robert Burkins (pastor, Elmwood Presbyterian Church, Orange, N.J.), Professor Ronald Peters (Pittsburgh Theological Seminary), Professor Warren Dennis (New Brunswick Theological Seminary), Rev. Phyllis Felton (Harambe, Baltimore) Dr. Johnnie Monroe (Grace Memorial Presbyterian Church, Pittsburgh), Rev. Jerry Cannon (CM Jenkins Presbyterian Church, Charlotte, N.C.), Rev. Curtis Jones (Madison Ave. Presbyterian Church, Baltimore), Rev. Amitiyah Elayne Hyman (New York Avenue Presbyterian Church, Washington, D.C.), Professor Marsha Snulligan Haney (International Theological Center, Atlanta), Dr. Lonnie Oliver (New Life Presbyterian Church, Atlanta), and Marjorie Ward (then Manager, General Assembly Committee on Representation, PCUSA).

3. See Gayraud Wilmore (1983 and 1998), *Black and Presbyterian: The Heritage and the Hope* (Philadelphia: Geneva Press, 1983).

4. By Afrocentric worship in the United States, I refer to an approach to the ordering of congregational life (celebration, education, nurture, outreach, and stewardship) in such a manner as to emphasize the centrality of African people's needs in America that does not begin only with the heritage of American slavery, but with the heritage of precolonial black Africa as well. Many black churches, while proud of their history, shy away from discussions of Afrocentrism because so many of its leading proponents have been critical of Christianity's role in black oppression globally and do not define themselves as Christian. For the most part, Afrocentrism has been criticized in academic circles as historical and cultural romanticism rather than substantive scholarly endeavor. However, I believe that we must be careful not to "throw the baby out with the bath water." Seminaries and churches should at least be aware of the Afrocentric dialogue which finds emotional affinity, if not serious critical examination, in many quarters along "city streets." By affirming the preslavery period of African heritage, we move beyond the antebellum period as the origin of African American culture. This process embraces information about African antiquity in the same fashion as Europe looks to ancient Greece and Rome or Chinese culture draws its current focus from its antiquity.

5. The Kelly Miller Smith Institute, *What Does It Mean to Be Black and Christian* (Nashville: Vanderbilt University Divinity School, October 1992), pp. 1–2.

6. Mildred Brown, Associate, Evangelism and Church Development Ministry Unit (PCUSA), noted that as a result of consultations with Congregational Development Committees of several Presbyteries, there was little or no manifested interest in initiating new congregations in areas of significant African American populations. Report on "African American New Church Development" given to the African American Advisory Committee Meeting, December 10–12, 1990, Longboat Key, Fla.

7. Wilmore, *Black and Presbyterian*, p. 35.

8. Ibid., p. 55.

9. Ibid., pp. 93–100.

10. Haney, Marsha Snulligan, "Missiological Reflections on the Ministry and Work of the African American Advisory Committee," unpublished paper presented to the December 1–5, 1992, meeting of the African American Advisory Committee, Presbyterian Church (USA), Montego Bay, Jamaica, p. 2.

11. While it is beyond the scope of this chapter to examine such issues, it should be noted that at various times throughout the history of black Presbyterianism, the matter of withdrawing from the predominately white denomination has been debated (see Wilmore's *Black and Presbyterian*, pp. 69–70). At the December 1–5, 1992, African American Advisory Committee meeting in Montego Bay, Jamaica, it was informally reported that in at least two separate meetings of key African American clergy leaders within the denomination (one in 1968 and the other as recently as 1990), serious discussion was given to withdrawal from the denomination.

12. Wilmore, *Black and Presbyterian*, p. 37.

13. Wilmore, *Black and Presbyterian*, p. 39.

14. Molefi Kete Asante, *The Afrocentric Idea* (Philadelphia: Temple University Press, 1987), p. 3.

15. Molefi K. Asante, *Afrocentricity* (Trenton: Africa World Press, 1988). See chapter 3, Analysis and Science, particularly the discussion of "The Way of Newness, Levels of Transformation, Consciousness, and Relationships." Asante presents a radical critique of the limitations of a Eurocentric presentation of the gospel for the African and what movement toward an Afrocentric consciousness can do to enable a "victorious" perspective (pp. 47–52).

16. The Kelly Miller Institute, *What Does It Mean To Be Black And Christian?* Nashville: Vanderbilt University Divinity School, October 1992, p. 11.

17. Warren Dennis, "Afrocentrism," an address delivered November 13, 1992, to the African American Presbyterian Heritage Colloquium 2 held at Johnson C. Smith Seminary, Atlanta.

18. Ibid.

*18*

# Spirit and Resistance: A Theological Perspective on Lillian Hellman

## Lora M. Gross

*R*ecently I attended a theatrical production of Lillian Hellman's play *The Little Foxes*. Having read the play years ago, I was struck once again with its searing social, critical analysis and its brilliant literary creativity. Revisiting Hellman's play stimulated my interest in her life, in particular her actions and motivations for social and political resistance.

While I was acquainted with some highlights of her life as a famous and talented playwright, I was curious about the woman herself. Why did she choose to place herself at the front of major events of the mid-twentieth century: Germany during the rise of Nazism, Russia during the purge trials, Spain during the Civil War, the Russian front during World War II, Yugoslavia soon after Tito broke with Moscow, and the McCarthy trials? What motivated her to confront the social and political injustices embedded in these events with persistent and dignified resistance?

In my experience as a Christian, I am well aware of the religious motivation that inspires countless heroes and heroines of faith to "lay down their lives" in circumstances of oppression. In doing this, they embody the central Christian message of justice, compassion, and freedom. Lillian Hellman, however, was not a Christian, and although she was Jewish by birth, nothing in her three memoirs or biographies indicates that she actually embraced Judaism.

The inquiry I pose is two-fold. First, what values, beliefs, relationships, and personal experiences motivated Hellman to refuse to insulate herself with fame, wealth, and power? What led her to use her considerable intelligence and creativity to relentlessly engage the social and political tyrannies of her day, often at substantial risk to her own comfort and safety and to those she valued most in her life?

Second, how do Christians theologically interpret and celebrate the lives and actions of people like Hellman who live lives of resistance to social and political injustice, but who do not attribute their actions to Christian theological categories for motivation? Are there other theological and secular traditions that can be enriched and expanded to create new meanings and depths within the Christian paradigm in its dialogue with the world? Is it important, even essential, for Christians in today's world to strengthen critical conversation with secular voices that can both challenge the community of faith to embrace more fully its prophetic role in the world and to focus more intently on its task of self-critical analysis?

This inquiry is hardly a new agenda for Christian theology. Paul Tillich, for example, eloquently articulated this dialectic as a method for doing theology after his experience of World War II. He saw that unless Christians address the widest ranges of human experience in light of the Christian faith, the relevancy of the Christian message and the obligation of the church to live under the Protestant Principle would be greatly diminished.

The religion-culture dialogue is especially important at the current time for three major reasons. First, we are faced with an unprecedented environmental crisis that poses an enormous opportunity and challenge to Christian theological and ethical response. Second, Christian faith is challenged to resist the increasing influence of religious fundamentalism, which seeks to privatize the Christian message. Such attempts isolate Christianity from society and culture and consequently undermine its powerful prophetic voice. Third, Christian action in the world calls for an astute response and challenge to the view of growth and progress in a capitalistic society.

To make this inquiry, I will use the notion of Spirit as a theological category from which to interpret resistance as vocation and lifestyle for those who stand both within and outside the Christian paradigm.

## LILLIAN HELLMAN: AN UNFINISHED WOMAN

When a lifetime friend of Lillian Hellman heard that she had died, his response was: "Lilly didn't die, someone reached down and grabbed her by the throat."[1] This impression of Lillian by a devoted friend serves to characterize the life of resistance and the creative literary genius she used to stand over against the political, social, and economic oppressions of her times. In confronting what she saw to be violations of personal and collective freedoms and of common decency and compassion, she made a decision to fight, to stay alive, and not to let go.

She was by no means a saint, however, which is why she is so compelling as a resistance fighter. Known for her ability for searing critique, those around her considered themselves fortunate to be counted as her friends and not her enemies. When asked as a young woman what she was made of, she answered: "Pickling spice and nothing nice."[2] In a day when women were expected to be sugar and spice and everything nice, Hellman set the stage for the social-critical analysis of gender that eventually formed the basis of the second wave of the feminist movement in the early 1970s.

Lillian Hellman was born on June 20, 1905, in New Orleans, and although she moved to New York at the age of five, she frequently returned to the South, which often was the geographical setting for her plays.[3] She studied at New York and Columbia Universities, after which she worked in publishing, first writing advertising copy and later serving as a play reader. She also wrote for the *New York Herald Tribune* before moving to Hollywood in 1929. It was there she met the hard-drinking but talented novelist Dashiell Hammett, with whom she had a thirty-year, tough-loving relationship that in no way resembled a *Father Knows Best* marriage. Hammett, whose own writing career was formidable but short-lived, contributed to Lilly's talent by becoming her best critic.

In 1937 she visited Europe, attending a theater festival in Moscow and accompanying Ernest Hemingway for a firsthand view of the Spanish Civil War. In 1944 during World War II, the Soviet Union invited her on a cultural mission as a journalist with the advancing Russian armies until ill health did not permit her to continue.

In 1948 she returned to Europe, where a sympathetic interview with Tito in Belgrade added to unsubstantiated suspicions that she was involved with the Communist Party. Her radical activism led her to take an official position in the presidential campaign of former Vice President Henry Wallace, on the ultraliberal Progressive Party ticket. In the same year, she provided major leadership to the Cultural and Scientific Conference for World Peace, the famous "Waldorf Conference" held in New York that was denounced by the State Department and by most of the country's press as being pro-communist.

The 1950s were turbulent times for Lilly and Dash. Like Hammett, Hellman was forced to appear before Senator McCarthy and the House Un-American Activities Committee. Both of them were handed an unexpected and hefty bill for back taxes that many interpreted as a politically motivated punishment. Unlike Hammett, Hellman did not go to jail, but with no other resources at her disposal, she was forced to sell her beloved Hardscrabble Farm, a bitter blow.

Hellman's FBI file contains 307 censored pages, thirty-seven of which are withheld altogether. In addition, there are several Army, State Department, and CIA documents. She was branded a "key figure" in the FBI's New York Field Division, and files reveal that surveillance, mail watch, and records of what she read were maintained by the FBI for many years.

Hellman was a complex and controversial woman. She was funny, tough, and courageous on the one hand, and temperamental, obstinate, and dogmatic on the other. She abounded in contradictions: fierce loves and fiercer hatreds, dogged adherence to principles and questionable maneuvers, rock-hard strength and frightened vulnerability.

Reviewed as often as Hemingway and Tennessee Williams, to whom she was often compared, Hellman was a highly intellectual and prolific writer whose plays are well constituted and well observed, with very strong moral centers. Having broken the Broadway gender barrier, Hellman was described as the one, clear role model for any girl with crusading literary ambitions.[4]

Lillian died of a heart attack at the age of seventy-nine on June 30, 1984. She was feisty and combative to the end. "If you don't give me a cigarette this minute," she told a nurse, "I'm going to start screaming."[5]

## A CONTEMPORARY CHRISTIAN CONTEXT
## FOR THE IDEA OF SPIRIT

How do we speak of God in the current age? By way of response, a second inquiry is necessary, namely, what is happening in the world today? These two questions form the basis of a contemporary notion of the Spirit. Speaking about God from the history of the world is rather a recent development within Christian theology.[6] The history of Christian traditions demonstrates that the development of the third person of the Trinitarian model of God was late in coming. The stress especially in Western, Protestant systems of thought on divine transcendence contributed to the neglect of the notion of Spirit as a relational idea. By privatizing the range of the Spirit's activity, it focused on the justifying and sanctifying work of the Spirit in the life of the individual believer and emphasized the Spirit's gift of personal certitude.

Feminist theologians observe that another reason for the neglect of the idea of Spirit in Christian thought is that the ancient languages of the Bible speak of Spirit as indwelling and wisdom (Ruach, Shekinah, Hokmah, and Sophia) which relate Spirit with feminine reality.[7] It is not difficult to imagine that the neglect of the development of Spirit is linked to the marginalization of women within the history of the Christian tradition.

The real danger of an underdeveloped idea of Spirit in Christian thought is that the depth and breadth of the mystery of the God/world relation is left significantly unexplored. The fuller development of Spirit in contemporary theological thought opens the doors to expansive and richer meanings of the relationship between divine presence and human action. The dynamic of the presence of God is dialectically active and alive in every aspect of life. The life of the Spirit can be traced from the origins of the universe, within the primordial soup at the start of the evolutionary process, within the twists and turns of human history, to the final destiny of the planet. This expanded view of the Spirit can address and define the widest ranges of human experience and imagination.

In every historical epoch, it is the Spirit that vivifies the questions of meaning, purpose, and identity, stimulating the imagination and creativity to call forth life, freedom, compassion, and liberation. Through the dialectic of the Spirit's presence and absence in the world, we can begin to probe the mystery of divine immanence and transcendence in such a way that neither characteristic is lost, but rather artfully held in delicate tension.

Focusing on the model of God as Spirit corresponds with feminist wisdom and integrates the feminine within the idea of God. The dialectic of Spirit is known in experiences of new life, energy, and creative work. Fruits of the Spirit are peace, justice, resistance, and liberation. Spirit is the foundation of hope, wisdom, courage, and love. Women of Spirit especially have consistently found ways to resist constriction of their lives and at times to mount public challenge in the Spirit of prophecy.

Specifically, it is within this expanded notion of Spirit that all human work to resist injustice and oppression, to insist on freedom and compassion, to strive for peace and integrity is understood by Christians as God's presence and action within the world in the broadest and deepest reaches possible. The expansiveness of Spirit within the universe also permits Christians to stand in solidarity with people outside the community of faith who find the courage to resist oppression and to interpret their efforts as a manifestation of Spirit.

Once we grasp the relational capacity of Spirit, we can understand and appreciate the ways in which the voices of modern consciousness have contributed to the formation of the idea of Spirit. It is possible to say that secular challenges to the Christian life have assisted the idea of Spirit to come into its own. Further, the reciprocity between divine presence and the world that constitutes the notion of Spirit compels the community of faith to respond to the needs and challenges of the world.

This is no better noted than in the influences of two modern schemes of human thought that motivated resistance in the life and work of Lillian Hellman. Marxism and the countermovement to Western economic growth and progress were great secular movements of her day, and they weighed heavily in Hellman's brand of resistance. They also provided major impetus for the church to engage the world in the modern period, by challenging it to be a spiritual, transforming power for the good in human affairs and offering alternative interpretations of the nature of being human.

Certainly, Hellman saw her dialogue with these movements as having nothing to do with a Christian response to them. The way she used and developed them to fuel her own resistance to the injustices of the social, political, and economic orders of her day, however, are exemplary for the church's own prophetic voice.

## SPIRIT AND RESISTANCE

The notion of Spirit as a relational concept that imbues and vivifies the whole of creation also embraces human action in the world in the name of justice and compassion. The gifts of the Spirit which renew and empower human action in these areas are universal and not limited to whether or not humans attribute them to any particular religion or symbol system. It is religions, however, that make thematic the gifts of Spirit in narrative and ritual.

As we take up the life and times of Lillian Hellman and survey the devastated landscape of the twentieth century, the danger of not linking spiritual power to any specific definition in human experience is frighteningly clear. The Third Reich, for example, was able to galvanize immense energies that can only be called "spiritual" even as perverted as they were. In contrast, the measure of the Spirit's gifts in regard to human self-defintion and action in the world is for the Christian paradigm the life, teachings, and ministry of Jesus Christ. Lillian Hellman's formidable resistance of major forces to social and political oppression in the name of justice and freedom certainly finds an agenda in the spirituality, teaching, and compassionate politics of Jesus. As previously noted, the fact that Hellman did not claim this basis for her motivations and actions does not halt the empowering of Spirit and the liberating effects of Hellman's resistance.

To pose the dual inquiry of how we speak of God in the current age and what is happening in the world today is to speak of God from the experience of Spirit. The notion of Spirit has the advantage of corresponding with certain broad perspectives of existential, historical, and religious interpretations of reality. The definitions of wisdom are logical, theological, and feminist. Spirit as a theological category invites an inductive approach to the God/world relationship. With such a methodology, religious meanings become more intelligible to many contemporary minds as a way to engage a wide range of religious sensibilities.

The Christian narrative makes clear that the universal presence of the Spirit of God freely pervades the world before there is an incarnation of God in Christ. This insight is vital for Christians in their task of interpreting the lives and actions of those who stand outside the Christian paradigm and respond with integrity to the ethical dilemmas of their day with formidable resistance against oppression and injustice. Christian traditions teach that even where belief in the Incarnation does not exist, there is a universal presence of the Spirit of God fully embedded in the world. From both perspectives, the function of Spirit is to renew all creation.

To begin with Spirit is to acknowledge the existential experiences of acts of resistance in the context of historical patterns by which faith in God emerges. From this perspective, it is useful for Christians to assess the resistance of figures such as Lillian Hellman as edification for life in the Spirit.

## RESISTANCE AS VOCATION AND LIFESTYLE

Hellman's literary creativity and her personal life are deeply enmeshed with her passionate political convictions and actions. Her convictions and actions placed Hellman at the center of the socialist critique of capitalism, the anti-fascist movement of the 1930s and 1940s, and resistance to McCarthyism in the 1950s. These experiences constitute the three major social and political critiques in Hellman's work and activism. The three major critiques define her resistance and stimulate her to use her literary talent to articulate her protest.

### *The Critique of American Capitalism*

The Great Depression left many Americans confused and uncertain about the economic and political future of their country. It is not surprising that many intelligent and thoughtful people like Hellman turned initially in a socialist direction. Socialism and communism drew interest because of the wide-ranging programs they offered. These movements appeared to be useful in understanding the failure of capitalism. Concerned Americans appreciated socialist perspectives because they addressed the devastation of the Depression. Communism seemed to offer the strongest critical analysis of an economic system badly in need of reconstruction.

No doubt the socialist critique of capitalism prompted Hellman's ambivalence toward the wealth she herself enjoyed under a capitalistic economy. While her highly successful plays situated her well financially at different times in her life, she despised the greedy pursuit of wealth, which she saw as an ever-present danger under a capitalistic system. In an attempt to resolve this struggle in her own life and give voice to her political convictions concerning American capitalism, she picked up her pen and wrote her most powerful and memorable play. *The Little Foxes*, which opened February 2, 1939, on Broadway, reveals her own family's evolution from poverty to prominence.

The play takes place in the American South in 1900. The Hubbard family, which is wealthy but not wellborn, is eager to develop its modest mercantile success into a vast fortune. Hellman's family had actually amassed great wealth by riding the wave of the industrial explosion in the years following the Civil War. The central theme of the play is the Hubbards' desperate pursuit of power and wealth. Hellman develops the moral center of the play by demonstrating that the Hubbard family's increasing lust and greed lead to the demise of all family ties and human decency. The figures in her play are clearly drawn from strong characters in her childhood whom she despised for their ruthless drive for wealth.

The dominant character in her play is Regina, who is smart, good looking, and funny. She and her brothers, Oscar and Ben, are driven to possess great wealth from the textile industry. Hellman weaves into her play the injustice of a society that makes women socially and economically dependent on men. Regina, however, does not let such an obstacle get in the way of what she wants. She and her brothers agree to put up an equal share of money to close a financial deal that will secure their dreams. The dilemma is that Regina's share is controlled by her husband, Horace, who has a severe heart condition and is under medical care in a nearby institution.

Anxious to get Horace to agree to release the money she needs, Regina badgers him mercilessly at the expense of his fragile health. Horace, observing the greed of the Hubbard clan, refuses to give in. Growing impatient for Regina to come up with her share, the brothers go behind her back and force Leo, Ben's son, to steal valuable bonds from Horace's safe deposit box. Horace discovers the theft and tells Regina. Recognizing her leverage, she blackmails her brothers by threatening a jail sentence. Horace counters Regina's plan by telling her he lent the bonds to her brothers, eliminating the accusation of theft.

The final scene takes place in Regina's living room. Realizing that the last chance to secure the wealth she is determined to have has failed, she mounts her most ruthless attack on Horace. Under her verbal abuse, Horace suffers a heart attack and begs her to get his medication. When she refuses, he drags himself up the stairs in agony. Regina retreats behind a curtain in the living room, listening to the dying gasps of her husband. Aside from Horace's efforts to thwart the greed and lust of the Hubbard family, the only element of salvation in the play is depicted in Alexandra, the innocent and naive daughter of Regina and Horace. Assisted by an honest, decent, working-class friend who is in love with her, Alexandra finally acknowledges her mother's relentless greed and her complicity in her father's death. After denouncing her mother and her values, she moves out of the house. The play concludes with Regina watching her daughter escape with her friend. At first she is affected by her loss, but her pained expression quickly changes to steely determination to have what she wants the most, power and wealth.

Hellman creates her characters to make a point that, in a conflict of evil versus evil, evil triumphs. The decent characters look on helplessly as the Hubbards wreak havoc and destruction. The best reflection in the play comes from the maid, Addie: "Well, there are people who eat the earth and eat all the people on it . . . and other people who stand around and watch them do it. . . . Sometimes I think it ain't right to stand around and watch them do it."[8]

Hellman leaves it to the audience to decide whether or not she is making a broad statement on capitalism and the industrialization of the South. Certainly the characters throw light on the culture from which they spring. In this sense, the audience comes away with a deeper view of a type of individual that is molded by American society, and the picture is not flattering.

Hellman's timing of the play could not have been better. The Depression was ending. Americans were preoccupied with reexamining the values of their society. To say that Hellman's personal situation and political perspectives did not influence the point she was trying to make would be naive. Her ambivalence to her own wealth and her strong socialist leanings at the very least raise the question of whether adjusting oneself to a society that is enmeshed in oppressive practices could be counted as progressive. The corruption of the Hubbard family as a product of unchecked greed is more than a subtle theme in Hellman's play.

The social-critical analysis of the capitalist system, which identifies the greed that Hellman exposes in *The Little Foxes*, offers opportunity for the renewing work of Spirit in the world. For Christians, this is fertile ground as universal Spirit finds definition in the person and work of Jesus. The vivifying power of Spirit expresses itself in Jesus' teachings, ministry, and spirituality. Jesus understood the Spirit as central to his relationship with God. The encompassing presence of Spirit in his life led him to understand compassion as political. In first-century Palestine and in every historical epoch, societal institutions including the church are ordered in such a way that protest and reform are necessary components in avoiding corruption and distortion of the original intentions of the institutions themselves. Spirit provides the impetus for renewal in the form of compassion and justice. Compassion necessarily becomes political as it stands over against oppressive and unjust power.

## Anti-Fascism

Anti-Fascism played an enormous role during the mid-1930s in radicalizing many American writers and intellectuals. Hellman was no exception. She and other concerned Americans became alarmed that fascism was spreading without effective resistance. Mussolini in Italy and Hitler in Germany brought fear of growing anti-Semitism, especially for American writers and intellectuals who were of Jewish descent. The Nazi threat forced tough and risky decisions. Hellman and her colleagues were well-situated liberals who understood this threat and were not passive. She picked up her pen, which was her best weapon, and wrote the anti-Nazi play *Watch on the Rhine* during the period of the Russian-German alliance. It received the Drama Critics Award and opened eight months before the United States entered World War II. She used her considerable creativity for writing to demand action against Nazism.

In this lucid dramatization of a young couple's work in the anti-Nazi underground, Hellman presents the heavy-handed moral dilemma facing America at that time. *Watch on the Rhine* is a vehicle for Hellman to assert that fascism was the greatest evil of the day. Like her main character, Kurt, who risks all he values in life to keep his resistance work alive, Hellman compels her audience to commit to radical resistance to fascism.

Resistance motivated by the Spirit's presence in the world is a vehicle for the moral questions that arise in circumstances of injustice and oppression. It is the function of Spirit to promote ethical action and creativity. More specifically, resistance is human action that confronts the suffering caused by injustice. The Christian response to injustice is more complex than this, however. Christian teaching based on the life and ministry of Jesus also advocates nonviolence as a central value, and thus presents the dilemma of violence in the name of justice. The majority of Christians have adopted the justifiable war doctrine to resolve this dilemma. The doctrine states that if certain criteria of justice are met, a Christian may participate in violent acts in the context of war. Still, the crucial question of whether or not war or any violent action can be identified with the Christian paradigm remains.

The ethical dilemma of violence versus nonviolence also confronts all people of integrity. In *Watch on the Rhine*, Hellman raises to a universal level the moral issues involved in violent actions that thwart systems of destruction. Kurt, the main character, is by no means an unambiguous hero. Threatened by exposure as a Nazi resistor, he kills his well-paid betrayer in order to silence him and to preserve his community of resistance. The play closes with Kurt getting away with murder. The audience is left struggling with an ethical dilemma. Should Kurt be punished for the murder or should the resistance community be permitted to continue its fight against fascism? The audience must now weigh the price of resistance as a moral issue.

The dilemma in the play prompts the question: Can a violent response to injustice in such circumstances be the mysterious, ambiguous presence of Spirit or is it the conspicuous absence of Spirit? Spirit is the mystery of divine presence in the ambiguity of the world. We cannot give simplistic answers to complex life questions. Spirit is present in renewing and liberating power in the midst of historical struggle. Diverse experiences and actions, especially those that preserve hope in the midst of hopelessness, signify the presence of Spirit.

Hellman's Kurt is the leader of a community that resists its own destruction and the destruction of many others. Such communities work for renewal and freedom within the discontinuities and meaninglessness of history. Spirit's liberating and compassionate power is universal in scope and resists the limitations of human experience and categories of thought. The ambiguous conclusion to Hellman's play leaves Christians and non-Christians alike to wrestle with the moral quandary of violent/nonviolent action in the face of oppression.

## The McCarthy Hearings

On February 21, 1952, Hellman received a subpoena to appear before the House Committee on Un-American Activities. Hellman, who had always voiced her politics with great conviction, was clearly shaken by the command to appear before Joseph McCarthy and the committee. The real prospect of going to jail terrified her. Her lawyer drafted a letter for her to send to the committee. It stated that she had nothing to hide and that she would waive her constitutional right to claim the Fifth Amendment that gave her the right to decline to answer any questions about her political opinions, activities, and associations on the grounds of self-incrimination.

Hellman rewrote the letter herself in the hope of stretching the Fifth Amendment to fit her conscience. She would waive her right, except she would not name any names. At the hearing, in a quick strategic move, her lawyer handed out copies of the letter to all in attendance and to the press, an act that greatly angered the committee. As a result, the committee made it harder on Hellman than on others who testified. Her letter made headline news. Eloquently crafted, it carried subtle defiance of the political tyranny of the McCarthy witch-hunts. Hellman wrote:

> I am ready and willing to testify before representatives of our Government
> as to my own opinions and my own actions, regardless of any risks or con-

sequences to myself. . . . I am not willing now or in the future to bring bad trouble to people who in my past association with them were completely innocent of any talk or any action that was disloyal or subversive.[9]

At the time of her hearing, Hellman believed her money-making days as a playwright were over. Yet, with her usual flair, she purchased an expensive Balmain dress, a hat, and white kid gloves. If she were going to jail, she would do so in style. Her letter articulated the morality and necessity of resistance to the abuse of political power. Further excerpts from the letter, which she read aloud to the committee, are prophetic in nature.

> I do not like subversion or disloyalty in any form and if I had ever seen any, I would have considered it my duty to have reported it to the proper authorities. But to hurt innocent people whom I knew many years ago in order to save myself is to me, inhuman and indecent and dishonorable. I cannot and will not cut my conscience to fit this year's fashions.[10]

She continues with some surprising statements concerning the roots of her own morality by drawing on Judeo-Christian teachings and linking them to American patriotism. Her political intent clearly was to shame committee members in their violation of foundational principles of American society.

> I was raised in an old-fashioned American tradition . . . and it taught me to try to tell the truth, not to bear false witness, not to harm my neighbors, to be loyal to my country and so on. In general I respected these ideals of Christian honor and did as well with them as I know how. It is my belief that you will agree with these simple rules of human decency and will not expect me to violate the good American tradition from which I spring.[11]

During McCarthy's witch-hunts and previous to Hellman's famous letter, the Hollywood Ten mounted significant resistance to the congressional hearing. The Hollywood Ten were writers and actors in the film industry who openly defied the committee and were cited for contempt of Congress. Unlike others in the film industry, they received prison sentences for their refusal to answer questions. On March 30, 1977, Hellman was a presenter at the Academy Awards ceremony. It was clear to the audience that they were not only honoring a talented playwright but also asking for forgiveness for disassociating themselves from the purges of the 1950s. One author describes the event as Hellman moved center stage to address the audience.

> Onto the huge stage stepped a tiny old lady wearing a no-nonsense dark evening dress, bookish reading glasses covering a corrugated face that carried the scars of Siberian flights, HUAC terrors and Hammett's binges,

whose name meant for these people a number of plays they had grown up with, a number of films they had studied and a number of books they were embarrassed not to have read. Hollywood rose to its feet and gave Hellman a prolonged standing ovation, the only standing ovation of the evening. Hellman took the occasion to chastise Hollywood for its superficiality and its materialism. Accolades and a nationwide audience notwithstanding, she was not to be silenced or brought off so cheaply by that tainted crowd.[12]

Life that is imbued by Spirit exhibits justice-making activity and liberating power. Spirit empowers the capacity of humans to work for freedom. This potentiality in the human experience made possible by the Spirit's presence is actualized in bold resistance to oppressive powers. When abusive power devalues human community by robbing human transactions of basic common decency, it calls forth imaginative intellect and courageous effort to resist. Hellman used her considerable intellectual gifts, her passionate political commitments, and her creativity to confront what she thought had been laid to rest with fascism she had battled in the past.

Spirit shapes freedom and liberation in the world sometimes in unexpected ways through acts of resistance that often involve suffering. To speak the prophetic word has always been dangerous for people in and outside of the Christian paradigm. Hellman's decision to shake up the entrenched ideology of the McCarthy era through her creative and intelligent protest challenged the assured certainties of the hearings. The claim of conscience is the boldness of the Spirit to enable people to follow their deepest impulses for freedom and compassion and to do so at great risk. Hellman risked her freedom and livelihood for the sake of her conscience and for the loyalty and compassion she had for her friends and colleagues.

Spirit generates discomfort among the comfortable, and it was Hellman's righteous anger that fueled her ability to press critical questions that eventually contributed to discrediting the McCarthy hearings in the eyes of most Americans. A difficult aspect of Spirit for many people to recognize is the importance of righteous anger to motivate communities of resistance to stand over against injustice and oppression. Spirit involves both passion and intellect. On the one hand, it insists on unwavering commitment, and on the other resists uncritical acceptance of the goals and strategies of resistance. Within the complexities of human life, Spirit empowers human community by holding in creative dialectic, compassion and justice, sustaining and liberating power, love and truth, peace and righteous anger. Hellman found the courage to taste her righteous anger against injustice and oppression and to allow it to motivate her to resist those who violated the freedom and integrity of individuals and human community.

## CONCLUSION

Hellman did not rely on Christian sources for motivation for her social and political resistance. In so far as Christian ideas become integrated within secular ethical thought, her activism and the moral themes of her plays reflect similar proposals for Christian resistance to oppression and injustice in the world. The grace-filled movement of Spirit that gives rise to compassion and justice in Christian expression challenges Christians to learn and appreciate various proposals from a secular social order.

Expanding the experience of Spirit outside its conventional role in Christianity leaves room for the Spirit to inspire novel opportunities for renewal of human institutions based on justice and compassion. This reforming work of the Spirit enables Christian resistance to value and celebrate reciprocal interchange with secular forms of activism engaged in the work of justice. Reciprocity assumes the openness and ability to learn from and to integrate the contributions of others in dialogue. Spirit resists Christian expression that lacks the imagination to formulate a new relation to society.

Hellman's social and political dialogue with socialism was labeled as communist by Christians who were comfortable with "privatized" religion. The challenge of Spirit to Christian religion is for it to relate to the world. It is important for Christians to recognize that the passionate concern for relating the promises of Spirit to human existence is a way in which all moral beings from a variety of perspectives can discover the limitless possibilities of that promise. In this way, the universal work of Spirit can be evidenced in human acts and communities of resistance wherever they are found to uphold the values of compassion and justice.

## NOTES

1. As quoted in William Wright, *Lillian Hellman: The Image, the Woman* (New York: Simon and Schuster, 1986), p. 423.

2. As quoted in Wendy Wasserstein, "Foreword" to Lillian Hellman, *An Unfinished Woman* (New York; Little, Brown, 1999), p. viii.

3. To this day, there is controversy surrounding the authenticity of some aspects of her memoirs. While the accusations will never be resolved, Hellman's documented work and actions indisputably amount to a life of honesty, integrity, and courage. For biographical information, see Wright, *Lillian Hellman*; Davis Falk, *Lillian Hellman* (New York: Ungar Press, 1978); Richard Moody, *Lillian Hellman, Playwright* (New York: Pegasus, 1972); Carl Rallyson, *Lillian Hellman: Her Legend and Her Legacy* (New York: St. Martin's Press, 1978); Lillian Hellman, *An Unfinished Woman* (New

York: Little, Brown, 1969); Lillian Hellman, *Pentimento* (New York: A Signet Book, New American Library, 1973); Lillian Hellman, *Scoundrel Time* (New York: Little, Brown, 1976).

4. As quoted in Wasserstein, "Foreword," p. vii.

5. As quoted in Wright, *Lillian Hellman*, p. 161.

6. Elizabeth Johnson, *She Who Is: The Mystery of God in Feminist Theological Discourse* (New York: Crossroad Publishing, 1998), p. 128.

7. Johnson, *She Who Is*, p. 128.

8. As quoted in Wright, *Lillian Hellman*, p. 153.

9. As quoted in Wright, *Lillian Hellman*, p. 246.

10. As quoted in Wright, *Lillian Hellman*, p. 247.

11. As quoted in Wright, *Lillian Hellman*, p. 247.

12. As quoted in Wright, *Lillian Hellman*, p. 378.

# 19

# Theology of Resistance in Bonhoeffer and Tillich

## Matthew Lon Weaver

*N*ational political systems create policies that are more or less just. International political processes lead to circumstances more or less conducive to peace. It remains a responsibility of religious ethics in general—and Christian ethics in particular—to trace the twists and turns of the elusive path that may lead to more permanent conditions of peace and justice. In this chapter, two works by two German theologians writing near the beginning of Adolf Hitler's rule function as the tools for extracting elements of such a path: Dietrich Bonhoeffer's *The Cost of Discipleship*[1] and Paul Tillich's *The Socialist Decision*.[2] If we see Bonhoeffer's book as the product of a thinker prior to his political radicalization and Tillich's book as the fruit of one whose political thought had experienced radicalization a decade and a half before, they become fruitful instruments for sifting out some of the necessary elements of faithful political ethics.

### PAUL TILLICH AND *THE SOCIALIST DECISION*

Paul Tillich was born in 1886. The relatively new German Empire was at its zenith. When the call to battle was sounded for World War I, he entered the service of the imperial army with the patriotic ardor shared by many on both sides of the conflict. A product of the church, his politics were those consistent with the conservative German Lutheranism of the time. As a chaplain, he preached a sermon each year honoring the birthday of the Kaiser.[3] However, by 1918, in his thirty-second year, the annual sermons had ceased. By war's end, the politically submissive chaplain had become a theologian readily engaging in radical socialist criticism of the many levels

of Germany's cultural existence. The horrors of war and the sense of betrayal by leaders toward whom idolatrous loyalty was offered had transformed Tillich into one who saw theology as properly concerned with the
depth dimension of all existence: all of reality became the realm within
which to search out the ground of existence about which religious people
were to be ultimately concerned. No area was exempt from such scrutiny:
certainly not the political arena. This was not a matter of religion's intrusion
into the creative processes of culture. For Tillich, "The theologian . . . never
fail[ed] to respect the complete autonomy and independence of the various
disciplines, even while . . . bringing the normative criticism of religious import to bear on all realms of meaning."[4] For the decade-and-a-half-long in-
terwar period, Tillich carried out this critical task,[5] setting the basis for his
most extensive response to the Nazi phenomenon, *The Socialist Decision.*

As a theological interpreter of culture, Tillich attempted to formulate
political theory possessing a dimension of depth that would provide the theoretical bases and practical strategies that will result in a just society. In *The
Socialist Decision,* Tillich asserted that 1932 was a decisive moment for both
the socialist and the anti-socialistic forces of Germany. He had experienced
the vagaries of political existence under the Weimar Republic. He shared the
worries of others that the mixed results of Germany's democratic experiment
combined with popular discontent with the pressures of meeting Germany's
postwar obligations under the Treaty of Versailles would open the door to re-
actionaries of the Nazi ilk. He called socialists to decide for a new vision for
their cause. He called the enemies of socialism—particularly Nazism—to
cease propagating attitudes and policies that threatened the survival of Germany and Western civilization.[6] Three political principles form the focal
points of Tillich's discussion: the principle of political romanticism, the bourgeois principle, and the socialist principle.

Political romanticism is nurtured by primal myths of origin exalting soil,
blood, cyclicality, sacrality of space, and the holiness of being.[7] Here, "time is
always under the domination of space,"[8] leading inescapably to polytheism,
and allowing for a single ethic: "Might makes right."[9] Tillich affirmed the
substance-giving function of the powers of origin in the principle of political
romanticism while strongly opposing its destructive irrationality.[10] He described the latter in this way:

> [I]t is spirit with which spirit is opposed; the disappearance of the concept
> of progress is considered to be progress; myth is verified by documents; and
> the organic society is to be achieved by force, through parties. . . . [T]he
> body receives its new dignity through the spirit, which wants to retire in
> favor of the body. Thought is to be negated by thinking, and action by act-
> ing. This is romantic theory and practice.[11]

The bourgeois principle is rooted in the Enlightenment and its exaltation of the powers of reason. Reality is no longer seen in relationship to its primal sources but by means of the tools of rationality and empirical analysis. The myths of origin are utterly sapped of their power: "Just as there is nothing that cannot be solved by thinking, so there is nothing that cannot be shaped by action": revolutionary human autonomy is the consequence.[12] According to this principle, whether through the "free play of productive resources" (as in classic economic liberalism) or in the subjection of nature by the decisive action of individuals (as in democracy), a progressive harmony would result.[13] When economic disruption occurs, the bourgeoisie is forced into an alliance with the forces of prebourgeois feudalism, that is, the bearers of the myths of origin from which the bourgeois principle had allegedly detached the bourgeoisie. As a consequence, the belief in a harmony arising out of the rational mastery of resources is proven false, and the democratic, prophetic demand for justice—which is necessary for keeping the expansive forces of the myths of origin in check—is lost.[14]

Tillich rooted socialism—and the socialist principle—in the experience of ancient Israel. There, in the destruction of its national power, the sacredness of space (central to political romanticism) was broken, a breaking (or, at least, an important tempering) of a particularizing myth of origin:

> On the basis of a powerful social myth of origin, Jewish prophetism radicalized the social imperative to the point of freeing itself from the bond of the origin. God is free from the soil, the sacred land, not because he has conquered foreign lands, but precisely because he has led foreign conquerors into his own land in order to punish the "people of his inheritance" and to subject them to an unconditional demand.[15]

The shattering of a space-limited myth or origin is what Tillich called "the world-historical mission of Jewish prophetism."[16] Here, time rules over space, what will be challenges what is, and expectation takes on central significance: "time, the unconditional demand, and the 'Whither' [is enabled] to be victorious over space, mere being, and the 'Whence.'"[17] To be taken seriously as a force in opposition to the dehumanizing effects of the romantic and bourgeois principles, Tillich believed socialism had to be understood in both its particularity and its universality: "Insofar as socialism is the expression of this opposition, it is bound to the existence of the proletariat; insofar as it seeks to eliminate proletarian existence, and thus the opposition of the classes, it transcends the proletarian situation and includes all of society."[18] As it arose in Germany, Tillich saw it in relation to the groups who radicalized the bourgeois principle and refused alliance with prebourgeois forces: socialism arises out of this radical element among the bourgeoisie, demanding—among other things—market control on behalf of justice in place of free market economics.[19] However, to offer effective leadership for German society, Tillich believed, socialism had to confront an inner conflict manifesting itself in several areas of its thought. The present discussion will summarize Tillich's interpretation of the conflicts within three of those areas—human nature, society, and community—and then Tillich's prescriptions for resolving those conflicts.[20]

By arguing for the necessity of human transformation by means of reason, Tillich believed socialism echoed the bourgeois principle in ignoring each person's "spiritual, vital center, quite apart from his rational formation or standing," misunderstanding charismatic personalities, symbolism, and the yearning for mythic origins.[21] As much as Tillich valued Marx, this was a significant flaw:

> The innate weakness of Marxist socialism is that it has rejected *a priori* this depth dimension of reality, by reason of its protest against established, bourgeois religion. Marxist socialism had not distinguished between authentic and inauthentic religion, and had thereby lost a dimension of reality, the ultimate one in terms of meaning.[22]

To resolve the inner conflict regarding human nature, Tillich believed socialism had to abandon its mechanistic and superficial understanding of both human nature and human needs wrought by bourgeois rationalism. The reality of that human center "that is more primordial than the abstractions of subjective reason on the one hand or than an objective drive mechanism on the other"[23] is acknowledged in all its creative and destructive force. The fact that life "is made up of a vital complex of vital, erotic, aesthetic, and religious impulses that in many instances lead to an ascendancy of so-called 'spiritual' impulses over the life-preserving tendencies" is regained.[24] Further, the legitimacy and power of symbolism and mythic origins can be affirmed when they are put to their "original and authentic use."[25]

In its understanding of society, socialism's position that proletarian interests are consistent with both those of society and those of the international community conflicts with several facts: the proletariat must gain and maintain its power through power struggles; its interests are disharmonious with other political interests; within its own movement power struggles exist. This conflict between its principle and its historical embodiment made socialism uncomfortable and tentative in bearing the instruments of governmental power in Germany of the 1920s and early 1930s.[26] For socialism to correctly apprehend society, Tillich argued that it had to understand power in a positive way that renounced the belief in harmony.[27] It had to see power as the means for fulfilling the primal claim of the true origin for jus-tice, justice in the concrete situation: "Justice is not an abstract ideal stand-ing over existence; it is the fulfillment of primal being, the fulfillment of that which was intended by the origin. . . . [Socialism] must understand the power that it wins and defends as a realization of *this* justice for *this* time and in *this* social situation."[28] In considering the power structure most con-ducive to justice, Tillich pointed to democracy, but in an ambiguous way: democracy should be corrective rather than constitutive. Democratic gov-ernmental processes can potentially be used by power holders as tools for domination.[29] "[T]he powers of origin . . . support the structure of society and the democratic corrective . . . subjects it to the demand of justice."[30] Thus, socialism "must restrict democracy, on the one hand, while radicaliz-ing it on the other."[31]

On the issue of community, socialism confronts two matters: the in-ability of bourgeois principle to create harmony by severing the individual from tradition and offering reason in its place, and, thus, the necessity of returning to the powers bearing the myths of origin to establish commu-nity. The nation is the level at which community must be found, yet it is the actor in the international class struggle: "Socialism thus falls into the conflict of having to be internationalistic over against national imperialism, and on the other hand, nationalistic over against the ideology of interna-tional citizenship."[32]

Here, Tillich called socialism to affirm national community while resist-ing the exultation of any particular nation. In doing this, it measures all na-tions against the standard of justice. In arguing for socialism's superiority to nationalism, Tillich wrote, "Nationalism can provide the nation with an em-pire, but it cannot so relate it to the course of history as to free it from the cy-cle of birth and death. Socialism . . . frees the nations from the law of death by subjecting them to the prophetic demand."[33]

Tillich called Germans to a decision for socialism in a Europe on the brink of disaster:

> The salvation of European society from a return to barbarism lies in the hands of socialism. Only socialism can make certain that the unlimited possibilities for technical domination of the world that have been created in the bourgeois period will remain under human control and will be em-ployed for the service of humanity.[34]

The criticism of Nazism within the book led to its suppression within weeks of its publication. The views Tillich expressed here and elsewhere led to his removal from his chair at the University of Frankfurt on April 13, 1933.

## BONHOEFFER'S *THE COST OF DISCIPLESHIP*

For Dietrich Bonhoeffer, the Hitler years were ones of a growing level of resistance, carried out in ever greater secrecy, by means of a freedom of expression that was increasingly restricted. Thus, unlike Tillich—who was a political radical at the moment Hitler came to power—Bonhoeffer grew into a
radical political viewpoint during the course of Hitler's rule. On February 1,
1933—two days following Hitler's ascent to power—Bonhoeffer had the occasion to speak to the meaning of the *Führer* principle on a radio broadcast.
Written out of a still-conservative political philosophy that acknowledged the
potential need for strong political authority, Bonhoeffer's speech argued that
if such a principle could be defended, it had to be safeguarded from the temptation of the masses to idolize such a leader. The broadcast was cut off before
he finished. That same year found Bonhoeffer participating in the Pastors'
Emergency League—which led to the establishment of the Confessing
Church, in opposition to the official (and much larger) German Christian
movement—as well as speaking out against the exclusion of Jews from the
church. In 1935 he began his work as head of the Confessing Church's seminary at Zingst and, later, Finkenwalde. Bonhoeffer was prohibited from
teaching at German universities in 1936. When police closed the Finkenwalde seminary in 1937, he facilitated the continued training of pastoral candidates through collective pastorates at Köslin and Schlawe (later moved to
Sigurdshof). In 1938 Bonhoeffer had initial contacts with members of the
*Abwehr* (German counter-intelligence), which became a center of political resistance to Hitler. The year 1939 was decisive for Bonhoeffer's political resistance: he had important discussions with George Bell, Bishop of Chich-
ester, and Visser t'Hooft of the provisional World Council of Churches; and
he made his two-month-long trip to New York, where he determined that he
must return to Germany and engage in political resistance. Bonhoeffer began
his service in the *Abwehr* in 1940. He was forbidden to speak in public that
same year. By 1941 he was no longer allowed to publish his writings. In
1941–1942, he made visits to Switzerland, Norway, and Sweden related to resistance activities under the cover of his *Abwehr* position.[35]

Given these circumstances, to interpret the ethics of Dietrich Bonhoeffer—
especially his political ethics in response to Nazism—exclusively through *The
Cost of Discipleship* would be misrepresentation of a significant order. However,
this book is a necessary starting point for establishing the case for the growing
radicalizing of his thought. According to his biographer, colleague, and friend
Eberhard Bethge, *The Cost of Discipleship* (while published in 1937) was firmly
rooted in Bonhoeffer's experience of 1933 in the church struggles at the beginning of the Nazi era: "The book clearly owes its conclusive style and momentum

to a preoccupation with the Sermon on the Mount that had begun long before 1935. . . . Both the theme and underlying thesis of *Discipleship* were already fully evolved before 1933, but the book owes its single-minded, exclusive claims to that year."[36]

The book begins with an argument for understanding Christianity as a matter of particular, costly grace over against the distortion of a general, cheap grace: Luther epitomized the former, his followers the latter.[37] Bonhoeffer wrote, "In the depth of his misery, Luther had grasped by faith the free and unconditional forgiveness of all his sins. That experience had cost him his very life, and must continue to cost him the same price day by day."[38] But for his followers, "The justification of the sinner in the world degenerated into the justification of sin and the world. Costly grace was turned into cheap grace without discipleship."[39] The consequence was that "[d]eceived and weakened, men felt that they were strong now that they were in possession of this cheap grace—whereas they had in fact lost the power to live the life of discipleship and obedience."[40]

Bonhoeffer saw "discipleship" as primarily practical action rather than abstract dogma.[41] Faith and obedience go hand in hand. In fact, disobedience is a barrier to faith.[42] The subtleties and paradoxes of faithfulness at points lacking clarity are worked out in light of obedience, rather than in a way that undermines it.[43] Bonhoeffer described obedience in terms of self-denial, abandoning worldliness, forgiveness of others, and acceptance of that which is beyond comprehension, the depth dimension, in faithfulness. Christian discipleship means the end of all other immediate relationships apart from that with Christ. All other relationships are mediated by Christ.[44]

In the second part of the book, Bonhoeffer turned to the Sermon on the Mount. His interpretation of Matthew 5 begins by setting the self-renunciation, suffering, pity for others, and nonviolence of the beatitudes over against the power and violence of the world, making Christianity a contradiction to the world.[45] Bonhoeffer was calling for the embodiment of these values in the world by Christians as the salt of the earth.[46] Christ was the only one who could and did fulfill the law.[47] Yet, Christ's followers also work to carry it into effect through reconciliation with adversaries: anger is out of bounds, and healed relationships are the goal.[48] Within the community of discipleship, this emphasis on Christ-like relationships roots marriage in selfless and self-giving love. In all relationships, it means a commitment to truthfulness and the refusal to seek revenge.[49] Based upon the latter, Bonhoeffer argued that the church should not involve itself in politics:

> The right way to requite evil, according to Jesus, is not to resist it. This saying of Christ removes the Church from the sphere of politics and law. . . . [The Church] has abandoned political and national status, and therefore it

> must patiently endure aggression. Otherwise evil will be heaped upon evil.
> . . . The only way to overcome evil is to let it run itself to a standstill be-
> cause it does not find the resistance it is looking for. Resistance merely cre-
> ates further evil and adds fuel to the flames. But when evil meets no op-
> position and encounters no obstacle but only patient endurance, its sting is
> drawn, and at last it meets an opponent which is more than its match.[50]

All of this is consistent with the "extraordinary" Christian attitude toward the
enemy, one exclusively based on love, especially toward those utterly hostile
toward our love, ultimately expressed in praying for our enemies.[51]

Moving to Matthew 6, Bonhoeffer focused on both the "hiddenness" of
Christian life and simplicity. Christian piety must be practiced in unselfcon-
scious, single-minded obedience to Jesus: "We must be unaware even of our
love for our enemies."[52] The practice of simplicity—being stewards rather
than consumers of God's creation—is rooted in the wisdom that "God and
the world, God and its goods are incompatible, because the world and its
goods make a bid for our hearts, and only when they have won them do they
become what they really are."[53]

Based on Jesus' comments on the narrow gate in Matthew 7, Bonhoeffer argued that Christ's mediation of all relationships means that Christ is the
criterion upon which Christians relate to people, *Christ* rather than their own
estimation of the righteousness or unrighteousness of others. This path divides the church from the world, the nominal Christian from the real Christian, and those who profess faith from the doers of faithfulness.[54]

The commission of Jesus to the disciples in Matthew 9–10 is the anchor
of the third part of the book. Bonhoeffer was convinced that all aspects of the
commission had to be perceived in light of obedience to the Word of God:
the identity of those to be "harvested," the laborers and the power to bring
about the harvest, and the shape and scope of the labor to be done all are defined by Christ.[55] Those to whom the followers direct their message are to be
treated like Christ himself, and the bearers of the message are destined to experience community with Christ as the fruit of their obedience.[56]

In the fourth and final set of chapters, Bonhoeffer expounded upon the
relationship of discipleship to the meaning of baptism, the body of Christ, the
visible community, sainthood, and the idea of the image of Christ. In baptism,
the old person—that which belongs to the world—dies, that the new person
may be wholly Christ's.[57] Christians could have fellowship with Christ exclusively through the church which, as Christ's body, has a unique quality of personhood, the "person" within which peace is accomplished between God and
humanity.[58] Bonhoeffer echoed Paul's call for the church to be subject to political authority: "The antithesis between the world and the Church must be
borne out in the world. That was the purpose of the incarnation. That is why
Christ died among his enemies. That is the reason and the only reason why

the slave must remain a slave and the Christian remain subject to the powers that be."[59] Sainthood is related to political activity in this way:

> Like a sealed train traveling through foreign territory, the Church goes on its way through the world. . . . The sanctification of the Church means its separation from all that is unholy, from sin; and the method by which it is accomplished is by God's sealing the Church and thus making it his own possession, his habitation on earth, the place from which judgment and reconciliation go forth into all the world. . . . The world is the world and the Church the Church, and yet the Word of God must go forth from the Church into all the world, proclaiming that the earth is the Lord's and all that therein is. Herein lies the "political" character of the Church. . . . The sanctification of the Church is really a defensive war for the place which has been given to the Body of Christ on earth. The separation of the Church and the world from one another is the crusade which the Church fights for the sanctuary of God on earth.[60]

Finally, while the Fall meant humanity's loss of being in the image of God, Christ breaks through the subsequent and futile human attempts to regain that image by means of righteous acts. Christ re-creates that image within humanity by becoming human and by offering the body of Christ (the church) as the continuing means by which humanity can experience, and be re-created into, the image of Christ.[61]

## BONHOEFFER AND RADICAL POLITICS

The dynamics within German and world history as well as his discontent with circumstances within the church moved Bonhoeffer away from the political positions reflected by *The Cost of Discipleship*. Larry Rasmussen has done significant work in the relationship of the ethics and theology of Bonhoeffer. Rasmussen has argued that "being-there-for-others" is the unifying theme in Bonhoeffer's thought, a theme anchored in his Christology. Bonhoeffer ultimately developed a "christocratic understanding of all reality," resulting in a definition of ethics as living "in accordance with reality," which is the same as conforming to the way of Christ.[62] Bonhoeffer's ethics is relational ethics, developed in the context of one's relationship to Christ and Christ's mediation of all human relationships.[63]

The radicalizing of Bonhoeffer's thought between the time of *The Cost of Discipleship* and his later writings (the *Ethics* and *Letters and Papers from Prison*)[64] is rooted in a broadening of the implications of his Christology: "ethics as formation in *The Cost of Discipleship* is strictly a churchly ethic. It is what disciples do regardless of the world's response. In *Ethics* it is clearly an ethic of the

Christian in the world."[65] While the world is "'prematurely written off' as *the* place where formation to Christ takes place" in *Discipleship*,[66] the later writings "make clear that it is only by standing in the midst of the world" that one negotiates the "dialectics of 'resistance and submission'" to governmental authority.[67] In *The Cost of Discipleship*, responsibility corresponds to obedience, while in *Ethics* it is tied to freedom. This is because "Jesus Christ [of *Discipleship*] is the Author, Giver, and Fulfiller of divine law," while the *Ethics* interprets Christ as "the Responsible Man par excellence, the Bestower of Freedom, and the Redeemer of the man who incurs guilt in venturing the deeds of free responsibility."[68] Rasmussen helpfully emphasizes the very precise place resistance has in Bonhoeffer's Christologically rooted construction: resistance is an exceptional act rather than a normative one. Within the ethical framework, neither passive conformity nor radical revolutionary behavior are normative. However, the latter is considered ethical in rare, exceptional cases. This is conformation worked out within the three-fold pattern of Christ's mission, "that is, determining whether the conforming action is one of 'incarnation' (affirmation and cooperation), 'crucifixion' (judgment and rejection) or 'resurrection' (bold creativity and newness)."[69]

In the *Ethics* Bonhoeffer stated the practical implications for such a Christology in this way:

> In the course of historical life there comes a point where the exact observance of a formal law of a state . . . suddenly finds itself in violent conflict with the ineluctable necessities of the lives of man . . . [in which] responsible and pertinent action leaves behind it the domain of principle and convention, the domain of the normal and regular, and is confronted by the extraordinary situation of ultimate necessities, a situation which no law can control.[70]

Following this way is to follow the path of Jesus, who "refused to shun the fellowship of guilt and took upon himself the guilt of others" and "stood in solidarity with those enmeshed in inescapable responsibilities that could not but incur guilt in an evil order."[71] With this, Bonhoeffer has established the theological basis for his political resistance. As a consequence of that activity, he was arrested on April 5, 1943, nearly ten years after Tillich's dismissal. Two years later, the Nazis executed him.

## A FRAMEWORK FOR RADICAL POLITICS IN TILLICH AND BONHOEFFER

The contours of the thought of Tillich and Bonhoeffer as reflected in these pages provide a framework for radical political thought. Here, "radical" does not refer to drastic, extreme political behavior, although it does not exclude this. Rather, it refers to the behavior possessing at least these three characteristics: it is deeply rooted; it seeks out the dimension of the infinite; it bravely copes with the dimension of the finite.

### Radical Politics as Rooted Politics

This first characteristic of radical political behavior is true to the primary etymological meaning of "radical," that is, having to do with roots and origins. Tillich took seriously the fact of—and search for—a nation's mythic origins. This was not a matter of pandering to distorted nationalistic tendencies but one of savoring the richness of the primal creative forces behind existence in general and nations in particular. This was vitally important labor to him because otherwise the interpretation of these mythic origins was left vulnerable to dangerous manipulation. Tillich saw the business of cultural interpretation as crucial because the creative depth of these primal origins manifested itself in all of life's realms. Yet he knew that the temptation was ever present to unduly exalt the cultural creations—including political ones—that confused the creation with the creative force behind it, at its root. This is why prophetic, democratic, justice-bearing criticism that bore the space-transcending and time-driven expectation was so central to his political analysis. Tillich directed this critique at the positions of others as well as his own positions. Again, it was always the issue of getting at the depth, the root of the matter.

Bonhoeffer took faithfulness with utter seriousness. Perhaps the most popular theme of *The Cost of Discipleship* is his call away from cheap grace and toward costly grace. In one of the most frequently quoted lines from the book, Bonhoeffer declared: "When Christ calls a man, he bids him come and die."[72] His ever-developing Christological roots were the basis for the increasing intensity and scope of his ethics. Radical politics is rooted politics.

### Radical Politics Unendingly Seeks Out the Infinite

In the autobiographical work he wrote to introduce himself to the English-speaking world, Tillich defined himself as a person "on the boundary."[73] Using twelve existential and dialectical pairings, he described those tensions within which he lived that were formative for his thought. The most impressive part of Tillich's self-revelation is the dignity with which he treated each half of the pairings. He did not renounce one in favor of the other but held each pair together as poles of the dialectical search for truth. Tillich did not restrict his search for the truth to traditional, orthodox patterns of Christian theologizing. His search for the infinite led him to explore a variety of intellectual and spiritual disciplines. That same search led him to take seriously the complexity of human vitalities, that is, the varied life-giving dimensions of intellectual-spiritual-artistic life, captured by the nearly untranslatable German term *Geist*. Thus, *The Socialist Decision* was not an exceptional work. It was an altogether natural extension and fruit of Tillich's trust that the infinite manifested itself in manifold ways within the entirety of existence.

The growth from the almost anti-worldliness of *The Cost of Discipleship* to the strong world-affirmation of the later writings reflects a similar pattern in Bonhoeffer's journey. To say one conformed to Christ or that one lived in a way that was consistent with reality was to say the same thing. That the church and other cultural institutions failed their duty under Nazism was tragic. That nonchurch people behaved like Christians testified to the infinite's capacity to transcend the boundaries of orthodoxy. Radical politics seeks the infinite in all places.

### Radical Politics Copes with the Finite

Tillich's discussion of the discomfort of socialism in wielding the mechanisms of governmental power was an admonishment to face and cope with the ambiguities of power. We are to see power for what it is. We are to understand it for all its potential for tyranny as well as justice. We are to exercise it with a courage informed by a mature expectation of the results when finite creatures are involved.

For Bonhoeffer, political resistance finally became a tenable alternative when it could be correlated with Christ's enmeshment within sinful existence. Then the unavoidable, non-normative boundary cases of radical, extreme behavior became an acceptable part of the picture, even if tragically so. Then he could see the ambiguities of faithfulness as part of a complete picture of ethical Christian behavior.

Radical politics copes with the finite with courage.

## NOTES

1. Dietrich Bonhoeffer, *The Cost of Discipleship* (London: SCM Press, 1959).
2. Paul Tillich, *The Socialist Decision*, trans. Franklin Sherman (Potsdam: Alfred Protte, 1933; Washington, D.C.: University Press of America, 1977).
3. On January 27, 1915, he preached on Matthew 22:21, "'Render unto Caesar what is Caesar's; and to God what is God's.'" On that date in 1916 he preached on I Peter 2:17, "fear God, honor the King." On the same date in 1917 his text (Psalm 29:10f.) led him to encourage the soldiers to fight for a peace rooted in love and strength, rather than selfishness and weakness. Paul Tillich, *Frühe Predigten*

*(1909–1918): Ergänzungs und Nachlassbände zu den Gesammelten Werken von Paul Tillich, Band 7* (Berlin: Walter de Gruyter, 1994), pp. 383, 433, 537.

4. Raymond F. Bulman, *A Blueprint for Humanity: Paul Tillich's Theology of Culture* (East Brunswick, N.J.: Associated University Presses, 1981), p. 77.

5. Tillich's *The Protestant Era* has eight articles from this period. The posthumously published *Political Expectation* has five.

6. Paul Tillich, *The Socialist Decision*, trans. Franklin Sherman (Potsdam: Alfred Protte, 1933; Washington, D.C.: University Press of America, 1977), pp. xxxi–xxxii.

7. Ibid., pp. 13–19.

8. Ibid., p. 17.

9. Ibid., p. 19.

10. Ibid., pp. 38–39.

11. Ibid., p. 40.

12. Ibid., p. 24.

13. Ibid., pp. 50–51.

14. Ibid., pp. 54–56.

15. Ibid., p. 20.

16. Ibid.

17. Ibid., pp. 21–22.

18. Ibid., p. 61.

19. Ibid., pp. 57–58.

20. Tillich analyzed six areas of socialist thought in the book: the potential for social harmony, human nature, society, culture, community, and economics.

21. Ibid., p. 74.

22. Bulman, pp. 68–69.

23. Tillich, *The Socialist Decision*, p. 71.

24. Ibid., p. 136.

25. Ibid., p. 137.

26. Ibid., pp. 75–78.

27. Ibid., pp. 137–141.

28. Ibid., pp. 140, 141.

29. Ibid., p. 142.

30. Ibid.

31. Ibid., p. 144.

32. Ibid., p. 88.

33. Ibid., p. 152.

34. Ibid., p. 161.

35. Eberhard Bethge, *Dietrich Bonhoeffer—A Biography: Theologian, Christian, Man for His Times*, trans. Eric Mosbacher et al., revised and edited by Victoria J. Barnett (Minneapolis: Fortress Press, 2000), pp. 187ff, 238ff, 259–260, 272–276, 309ff, 425, 516, 583–584, 588ff, 622–632, 637ff, 648ff, 698, 723ff, 730.

36. Bethge, pp. 451, 457.

37. Ibid., pp. 45–48.

38. Ibid., p. 53.

39. Ibid.

40. Ibid., p. 59.

41. Ibid., pp. 61, 63, 73–74.

42. Ibid., pp. 72–73. "Our sinner has drugged himself with cheap and easy grace by accepting the proposition that only those who believe can obey. He persists in disobedience, and seeks consolation by absolving himself. This only serves to deaden his ears to the Word of God. We cannot breach the fortress so long as we merely repeat the proposition which affords him his self-defence. So we must make for the turning point without further ado, and exhort him to obedience" (p. 77).

43. Ibid., pp. 87–94.

44. Ibid., pp. 95–104, 110.

45. Ibid., pp. 117–128.

46. Ibid., p. 129.

47. Ibid., pp. 135–141.

48. Ibid., pp. 142–146.

49. Ibid., pp. 151–161.

50. Ibid., pp. 157–158.

51. Ibid., pp. 162–170.

52. Ibid., p. 177.

53. Ibid., p. 196.

54. Ibid., pp. 210–217.

55. Ibid., pp. 223–235.

56. Ibid., pp. 236–246.

57. Ibid., pp. 259–261.

58. Ibid., pp. 266–267, 269, 276.

59. Ibid., p. 297.

60. Ibid., pp. 313, 314, 315.

61. Ibid., pp. 337–344.

62. Larry L. Rasmussen, *Dietrich Bonhoeffer: Reality and Resistance* (Nashville: Abingdon, 1972), pp. 21, 22, 23.

63. Ibid., p. 31.

64. Dietrich Bonhoeffer, *Ethics*, ed. Eberhard Bethge, trans. Neville Horton Smith (New York: Macmillan, 1965) and *Letters and Papers from Prison: The Enlarged Edition*, ed. Eberhard Bethge, trans. Reginald Fuller et al. (New York: Macmillan, 1971).

65. Ibid., p. 28.

66. Ibid., p. 77n20.

67. Ibid., p. 43.

68. Ibid., pp. 50, 51.

69. Ibid., p. 43.

70. Ibid., pp. 45–46.

71. Ibid., pp. 62, 63.

72. Bonhoeffer, *The Cost of Discipleship*, 99.

73. Paul Tillich, *On the Boundary: An Autobiographical Sketch* (New York: Charles Scribner's Sons, 1936).

# 20

# Resisting Malpraxis in Religion

*Edward LeRoy Long Jr.*

$\mathcal{M}$ost of the chapters in this volume explore ways in which religious faith provides a standing ground for resisting social evils. Thinking, for instance, about resistance that communities of faith have offered to public threats from time to time—such as the heroic stance of the German Confessing Church against the evils of Nazi totalitarianism, or the opposition to apartheid on the part of some religious groups in South Africa—these essays direct our attention to social evils that we are called to resist with the aid and reinforcement of our faith. They rightly celebrate the capacity to stand up against public wrongs, and they affirm the value of religious conviction as a resource for overcoming forces of hate and destruction.

But another important matter must be examined: the way or ways in which religion can become a threat to human well-being—creating behavior that needs to be resisted. Although religion is often a resource for resisting evil, it is not immune from becoming destructive of the very peace and wholeness it purports to foster. The resistance of the Huguenots in the sixteenth century, commemorated in museums in southern France, was a struggle for freedom of conscience against the oppressive religious power of the time. Misguided religious zeal made the persecution particularly severe. Today, as in former times, some of the most troublesome forms of the behavior that we are called to resist are exacerbated by religion and may even be engendered by religion. While the call to resist malevolent social behavior is a deeply important aspect of Christian discipleship, it is sometimes necessary to resist religiously instigated wrong with the same faithful tenacity with which we resist demonic forces in the society at large.

Although religious persecution such as that visited on the Huguenots can be readily recognized as oppressive, many other forms of religious behavior are more difficult to discern because they are less obvious and more complex. Identifying and describing the nature of religious behavior that calls for resistance can be a difficult undertaking. There will often be disagreement as to what constitutes an improper use of religion. It can be especially difficult to see one's own practices or the practices of one's own religious group as the source of social malfeasance. Idealistic secularists and even cultured despisers of religion may help us to be aware of the moral blindness to which religion can be prone, but the proposal to do away with religion to cure ills it may create is not the only possible way to counteract problems caused by misguided religious zeal. To repudiate religion altogether often destroys valuable resources for dealing with problems that frequently are faced only with the courage and conviction religion offers.

The key to mature resistance to the misuse of religion lies within religious devotion exercised with the safeguards offered by the prophetic model. This model provides for the correction of the misuse to which religion can be put without jettisoning religion in order to overcome the consequences of its misuse. Prophets see the dangerous consequences that the misuse of religion can foster, yet they cling to the conviction that this evil must be addressed and resisted from within the covenant of faith and not from outside it.

Alas, religious groups do not have an enviable record of respecting this prophetic role. Religious authority is not immune from protecting its turf or refusing to acknowledge its own shortcomings. It can be stubbornly hostile to being criticized. The Bible helps us understand that prophetic awareness of unfaithfulness and of moral wrongdoing within the covenant group is likely to create severe opposition—not least from members of the very community of faith whose misdeeds are being challenged. Of all the resistances to which we are called, resistance to wrongdoing within the religious group with which we are associated is possibly the least likely to be discerned and most costly to resist. In political jurisdictions where freedom of religious practice is a reality, as in the United States, the most flagrant forms of religious persecution are less likely to acquire horrendous dimensions. But even in these jurisdictions, many practices sponsored by religion must be resisted as socially corrosive. Some of the most subtle and invidious of these take place when the freedom to practice religion prompts people to protect rather bizarre and destructive practices when carried out under religious auspices. Behavior that otherwise would be subject to a commonsense repudiation by the public may be tolerated because it is done in the name of religion.

## SEEKING A TERM FOR THE MISUSE OF RELIGION

While it is relatively easy to recognize the general proposition that religious behavior must sometimes be resisted, the difficulties involved in agreeing about when this is the case can be enormous. Blatant examples that rear up and beg to be resisted are relatively few, but many forms of religious behavior that play havoc with humane sensibilities have numerous adherents and defenders. We do not have a good vocabulary for describing the various forms that faith-based malfeasance can take. Many of the terms that come to mind are so intertwined with the divisions of our contemporary culture wars that their use is problematic.

The term "religious fundamentalism" is frequently employed to designate groups whose behavior is feared or resented. Among conservatives the terms "liberal" or "secular humanist" are used to designate persons or movements that are considered dangerous. While there may be certain attitudes and practices associated with fundamentalism that call for resistance, and occasions when fundamentalism poses threats to the well-being of a religious community as well as to the public sector, the term itself is not adequate for delineating the kind of religious practices that call for resistance. The term "fundamentalism" should be reserved for describing the faith stances of particular groups rather than used as a blanket designation for threatening behavior. Similarly, while there are forms of secular humanism that need to be challenged because they deny the possibility of legitimate belief in God, the term itself is not adequate for delineating outlooks that are always and everywhere so dangerous as to require vehement resistance. Some secularism is essentially nihilistic and fraught with socially irresponsible practices, but much of it is highly idealistic and has many aims and commitments that are quite compatible with those of religion.

Another set of terms used in discussions of these matters are the designations "religious right" and "religious left." To be sure, there are persons with conservative social and political convictions whose attitudes and whose behavior constitute serious breaches of Christian charity and threats to the peace and harmony of the church or the surrounding society. The same can sometimes be said of persons whose convictions stand at the opposite end of the political spectrum. There is no inevitable connection between holding conservative political and social views and behaving in ways that endanger the viability of the body of Christ. There is no guarantee that holding socially liberal views assures behavior that always makes for peace and harmony. The terms "religious right" and "religious left" are too broad and their meanings too equivocal to serve as adequate ways of designating a misuse of religion.

Used by themselves these terms have relatively little capacity to delineate with sufficient care potentially dangerous religious practice.

Still another term that is often used as a polemic against certain views is "extremism." While the term is most often applied to the political right and to those whose moral stances are narrow or prudish, it can equally well be used for polar opposite positions that are held with insensitive tenacity. The term "extremism" is pejorative rather than descriptive and is not very helpful as a general designation for socially destructive behavior. It may be a bit more helpful than the previous terms because it does indicate that certain beliefs can be held in unthoughtful ways, but it is insufficiently specific to help identify just what constitutes a misuse of religion.

Another term is called for. The term "malpractice" might be used, albeit employed with caution and broadened in meaning, to designate religious behavior that is counterproductive to humane social values and inimical to a healing and compassionate practice of religion. Just as malpractice in the case of the professions can consist of doing wrongful acts that inflict harm, or not doing needed acts, so malpractice in religion can involve both performing harmful acts and omitting necessary obligations.

There has been much of late written, particularly in liberation theology, about the importance of orthopraxis—that is, of right or good religious practice. This has been a helpful contribution to theological reflection because it emphasizes the profound truth that correct belief by itself is an insufficient measure of being wholesomely faithful—that what people do as a result of their beliefs is even more important than whether or not those beliefs are correct and proper. It would also be possible, and perhaps even helpful, to use the term "benepraxis" to denote behavior and policies that are helpful or healing rather than merely correct. But if there is right practice or helpful practice, it is also the case that there can be wrong practice, and it is wrong practice that the term "malpraxis" can be used to designate. Malpraxis can designate a contrast to orthopraxis or to benepraxis without causing confusion with malpractice.

Malpraxis in religion needs to be resisted because it damages human community and undercuts compassionate fidelity. There may be no greater task confronting persons of religious faith today than to discern and resist various forms of religious behavior of the type that crucified Jesus, made martyrs of prophetically faithful people throughout history, and sowed seeds of distrust and division wherever it has been operative. What follows may not exhaust the catalog of such behavior but will furnish some examples of how it works and will indicate why such behavior must be resisted. It will also indicate how difficult it can be at times to identify the difference between practices that stem from extraordinarily deep and profound commitments that

may have unfortunate auxiliary features but which are not necessarily dangerous and those which are counterfunctional to the very ideals of the traditions
from which they spring.

## RELIGIOUSLY DRIVEN VIOLENCE AS MALPRAXIS

When religion gets involved in conflicts, it can escalate disagreements between
parties with differing political purposes or moral objectives into struggles between antagonists who oppose each other with furious self-righteousness and
an unrestrained hostility. Although such behavior may occur without the sanction of religion, those who assert that God is on their side in conflicts very frequently behave with a uniquely driven zeal. Religion can become an engine of
emotive excess, an instigator of hate, and a polarizing force that greatly inten-
sifies conflicts.

Few religious traditions entirely escape this form of malpraxis on the
part of some of their adherents. Currently it is likely to be most popularly recognized in the behavior and attitudes of terrorists associated with the Muslim tradition. Their fanatical devotion, spurred by the belief that they are doing the will of Allah, is a source of great concern to those against which it is
directed and even a source of great concern to the majority of the members of
its own tradition. The stark excesses to which violence can mount when embraced as an expression of devotion frightens a good deal of the world and
demonstrates the possible dangers in religious zeal. Most devout Muslims understand such behavior to be an aberration of their own tradition, not one of
its distinguishing features. Hence, it is a form of malpraxis within that tradition even as it is a source of concern to others.

But to focus on this particular instance of religious zeal gone awry is to
overlook the extent to which this same infatuation with violence has been
found in other traditions as well, not least within certain periods and certain groups in Christian history. Christianity's role in creating and sustaining the Crusades was a form of malpraxis. Likewise, the extent to which a
great majority of American pulpits rallied support for the First World
War—a zealotry that has been subsequently regretted in most mainline religious thinking—is one of the sorry episodes in American religious history.
Nor is the religiously motivated embrace of violence confined to the wag-
ing of war. Those individuals who mistakenly believe that they are called to
destroy abortion clinics, or threaten the lives of those who work within
them, are guilty of this same malpraxis. They appeal to the need to protect
unborn life as a justification for taking the viable life of adults and are not

infrequently supported by a small group of clerics and believers who have made stopping abortions into a holy crusade the pursuit of which sets aside all normal restraints.

Religiously driven violence is a form of malpraxis because it tends to make violence furious by demonizing the enemy and to undercut the extent to which those who practice it are willing to acknowledge their own short-comings and to realize their own contributions to the conditions which give rise to conflicts. It separates "we" from "them" in a polarizing contrast that is blind to common humanity and incapable of understanding that human struggles are always tinged with ambiguity. Instead of concentrating on an evil to be deplored, it directs hostility to evildoers who must be destroyed. It is not necessary to do this in order to restrain and eliminate socially destructive be-havior. It is possible to be resolute without being fanatical, to resist evildoing without annihilating evildoers, to fight wars without making them crusades. When the task of opposing evil is understood as a necessary obligation, yet accepted with the moral agony of those who understand their own role in the creation of conflict and the tragic nature of what is required to combat evil, then conflict can be followed by a reconciliation that accepts former enemies as friends when their attitudes and behaviors undergo a change. The purpose of a legitimate or just use of coercion should not be to destroy opponents as much as to bring them to a point where interchange and reconciliation are possible. The way the Allied nations, and particularly America, treated Ger-many and Japan following the Second World War illustrates the importance of this perspective. Evil goes away when it is transformed; its mere defeat merely invites its resurgence.

Moreover, when violence is exacerbated by religiously sanctioned self-righteousness, moral restraints are often cast aside. The result is that the en-emy's behavior often shapes responses and tends to replace the restraints commended by our own scruples. If the enemy uses surprise and stealth, we respond with covert action; if the enemy attacks civilians, we tend to accept the use of bombing that is insufficiently discriminate or to become some-what callous to the horror of collateral damage. One of the gravest dangers in terrorism is that it is so provocative and so threatening that it may prompt responses we would never otherwise make. It could propel us back into a stance that is more akin to the crusade than to the just war, undoing many of the restraints which otherwise have begun to mark the use of military power in ways short of total warfare. If opposing terrorism can only be suc-cessful with methods that approach those of the terrorists, what is the profit? We must resist the impulse to let their religious zeal become an occasion for our religious malpraxis.

## LITMUS TEST EXCLUSION AS MALPRAXIS

An essential aspect of religion is the sharing of beliefs and agreeing to commitments. Ideally this process of holding convictions in common is an expression of shared purposes and responses that bring people together to celebrate things that bind them to one another on the basis of freely and devoutly held convictions. When beliefs stem from positive experiences, when they are expressions of gratitude for liberating and redeeming encounters that are profoundly felt by all who have had them, then convictions are expressions of joy and matters of celebration. Religion cannot live without them.

But religion often turns beliefs into instruments of exclusion rather than sources of community. Instead of celebrating that which binds people together in gratitude, it begins to judge who must be excluded from the community of faith. This tendency often arises after the initial response that creates a religious group has eroded, or when persons within the group develop different judgments about certain matters of faith and seek to impose their views on everyone else in the group. Creeds can be written to capture the central features of the beliefs that define the group, but they are often written to exclude views considered unacceptable by those in power or seeking power. While creeds often indicate the legitimate parameters of belief, in the very process of doing so they make possible practices that catapult believers into bitter controversies. These controversies, in turn, can escalate into practices such as heresy hunts and condemnations that transform the religious community from one that joyfully celebrates its common faith into one that becomes preoccupied with condemning and excluding those it judges to be apostate. Throughout history this form of malpraxis has bedeviled many communities of faith. It continues to do so today.

In Protestant circles, this process often occurs with respect to arguments about the role which the Bible is to be accorded in shaping the life and thought of the church. The Bible legitimately holds a high and crucial place as a source of truth and insight. But the message and content of the Bible can be utilized for the shaping of Christian faith only through human appropriation and interpretation. Christians must struggle to make that interpretation as faithfully as they can, but the necessity and the potential dangers of interpretation cannot be avoided by creating theories of biblical authority that seemingly override the inherent human elements in this process. To move from deep and appreciative affirmations about the reliability and authority of scripture to certain doctrinal assertions about how scripture must be embraced is to open the possibility for moving from a condition in which beliefs cohere the group to a situation in which beliefs divide it.

The life of a religious group is greatly altered when, instead of standing in humility and wonder before the Bible as a marvelously rich and complex source of spiritual guidance that is taken as the ultimate rule of faith and practice, people begin to use assent to certain narrow or specific propositions about the Bible as litmus tests of the fidelity of others. The Holy Bible is a rich compendium of insights and perspectives bequeathed to us over many years by writers inspired to record the significance and the meaning of their encounter with the divine. To accept it in its totality as the ultimate rule of faith and practice is to be challenged to self-examination, to scrutiny of one's own and one's group behavior, and to weighing a rich complexity that is far more profound than any single person's premature closure. Interpreting the Bible does not offer absolute certainty or total adequacy for our faith (although claims that it does abound), but rather it invites a continual search and inquiry that should be more like a pilgrimage than a manifesto. There is no checklist by which the correct appropriation of biblical faith can be guaranteed. Even when the Bible is read in communities of faith (and some traditions insist it can be read validly only in such communities), variations still arise and persist that indicate reading the Bible is a human venture and the correctness of any particular view can never be asserted with categorical certainty.

Efforts to overcome this inherent aspect of being faithful are numerous and, alas, often the very ingredients of bitter and destructive divisions. When a religious group, or faction within a group, becomes preoccupied with requiring a particular way of looking at the Bible to be affirmed, it usually makes a certain belief about the Bible into a litmus test of orthodoxy. This dynamic is at once so widespread and so seemingly persuasive that its potentially divisive consequences are often overlooked. The idea of literal inerrancy, for instance, is often asserted vehemently in an effort to give the Bible a special authority, one that gets beyond faithful responsiveness to unambiguous certainty. It has enormous appeal. It is almost always associated with a view that takes each and every passage in the Bible to be equally authoritative. The Bible then becomes a collection of texts that can be chosen at will to support a position espoused by those doing the selection. Instead of standing in awe, wonder, and humility under the rich totality of the Bible, this technique subordinates the Bible to the predilections of the reader. If every single text is viewed as equally valid as every other text, it is easy to use one part of the Bible as a guidepost with which to exclude all those with differing understandings of a particular issue or problem. Although usually trumpeted as the highest form of fidelity, it is frequently something much closer to idolatry.

Far from bolstering the functional authority of scripture, this approach undercuts it. If readers can insist that any texts they select are totally and completely authoritative, then they can control the biblical message rather than letting the biblical message control them. Such a process is often employed to prove others unfaithful. Thus, the assertion of biblical inerrancy becomes an instrument of power rather than of submission. It is no small wonder that the doctrine of inerrancy has been the key point at issue in many controversies that threaten the peace, harmony, and unity of Christian groups and has been a device that has divided, and continues to divide, many denominations—sometimes with disastrous consequences.

To be sure, sometimes it is necessary to make judgments as to whether certain beliefs are incompatible with the convictions of a religious community. But we would do well to avoid focusing on single issues, devising test issues that become the instruments for condemning others. No person's faith is so completely correct in every detail as to represent the only legitimate and proper way of being faithful. To hold otherwise is to embrace belief-correctness as a form of works-righteousness. Having an unusual view about a specific matter should not necessarily label a person as unfaithful. If a person's outlook in its totality becomes incompatible with a religious group's total understanding of faith, charitable separation may be needed, but a religious group which exercises a viable capacity for diversity is far less prone to malpraxis than one that is marked by a demand for complete and narrow doctrinal conformity.

My own personal experience helps me to realize that a great variety of faith stances can be full and legitimate without falling into this form of malpraxis. When I was in college and considering entering the ministry, the pastor of the Presbyterian church that I attended had a very conservative theology, a theology not much different in many respects from those of fundamentalists. But the manner in which he embraced those beliefs was entirely different from that of fundamentalists. He knew my understanding of Christian faith was quite different from his, yet he accepted and supported me in the process of seeking ordination (possibly hoping I would eventually come to perspectives more like his own). My liberal friends could not understand how we could resonate with one another, and possibly his conservative friends wondered about his openness to a young upstart. This relationship would not have been possible had either of us made particular beliefs about specific theological matters into a litmus test for approval, thus overriding the sense both of us had that the devotion to Jesus Christ held by the other was genuine and adequate.

## MORAL WEAPONRY AS MALPRAXIS

A third example of religious malpraxis stems from the misuse of the concern for moral behavior that is crucial to living faithfully. Religion rightly furnishes moral guidance and holds up standards of behavior to which people of faith should adhere. When these standards are used as ideals to inspire morally responsible living, they furnish much-desired guidance and inspiration for wholesome newness of life.

But religions are also prone to moralism—especially to making one particular moral requirement (often minor in importance or the focus of an immediate cultural controversy) the key measure of what it means to be righteous. They are also prone to making adherence to that particular moral expectation a requirement for acceptance—thus setting up a narrow test of orthopraxis. Those who do not, or will not, live accordingly are held up to contempt and often subjected to hostile criticism and disapproval. Moral haughtiness makes many religious people arrogant in their own goodness and prone to censor others. Religious zealots who have assumed that their achievements of righteousness warrant holding others in disdain or contempt have done much havoc in human history. This is a particularly divisive form of religious behavior.

The dynamic involved is seen with great clarity in the New Testament story about the woman caught in adultery who was brought to Jesus by a group of devoutly moral persons seeking to see her condemned for her misdeeds. Jesus refuses to be a party to the use of morality as a weapon and undercuts the religious self-righteousness that it feeds upon. His example should instruct us.

But this has not stopped such behavior. The dynamics of moral weaponry continue to appear in devout circles. One of these, reported years ago by Langdon Gilkey, occurred in the southern Bible Belt. A graduate student at the Vanderbilt Divinity School was pastoring a church. He was invited to the home of a church officer and, having been accustomed to somewhat more liberal attitudes in the North, agreed to accept an alcoholic beverage when it was offered to him. Almost immediately, when the word got out, he was called before a congregational meeting and his pastorate terminated. He might have been set up for this, and the vote against him might have stemmed from other causes of discontent. Nevertheless, this story illustrates how morality can become a weapon.

In another instance, involving quite contrasting moral stances, an Air Force officer with considerable military experience attended a church-related seminar that prompted him to come to new appreciation about the importance of peacemaking. He literally decided to devote the remainder of his life to a new calling. When he applied for the directorship of the peacemaking program of a major denomination, his appointment was challenged (albeit unsuccessfully) by a contingent of pacifists within the church on the ground that a person with military background could not validly lead a peacemaking program. This effort to block an appointment was probably less potentially vindictive than the move to sever a pastoral relationship, but it does indicate how people can employ a moral standard as a weapon against persons with whom they disagree.

I experienced something akin to moral weaponry during the Vietnam War. Twice, while being interviewed for possible teaching positions, I was asked about my judgment of that conflict. As a pacifist I did not support it, but I was unwilling to say that Christians who did were apostate. I could not make being opposed to that particular conflict a matter of absolute importance. I have subsequently learned I was turned down for both positions because of this.

The two decades from 1980 to 2000 were marked by a widespread use of moral weaponry in American political life. Political controversy was not infrequently carried on by using moral condemnation as a psychic club with which to defeat opponents, either by shaming them for indiscretions or by catching and castigating them for misdeeds. Morality used as a partisan club has a very different impact upon public life than morality that envisions the importance of responsibility and encourages people to seek the good life for themselves and others. Moral condemnation instigates suspicion and cynicism rather than inspiring exemplary conduct.

Much that happened in the political situation in this country in the period between the Vietnam War and the terrorist attacks on September 11, 2001, illustrates how this way of using morality can poison the political process. For a long and dreary period we witnessed a simultaneous erosion of moral behavior coupled with efforts to demonstrate the misbehavior of political opponents so as to discredit or to unseat them. These two developments fed on each other destructively. Whereas in the idealism of the social gospel the focus was on what moral ideals can contribute to public life, the tendency in this kind of politics is to concentrate on what can be morally condemned. Unfortunately, religion has often been a party to this process.

Indeed, the mindset of which such behavior is an expression is associated with other attitudes and policies that have dysfunctional consequences. It helps us to understand why we condemn abortion but overlook the far more important moral challenge of improving conditions of life for those who are born. We fight "wars" against drugs but do little to support programs that challenge persons to more satisfactory ways of living. We build prisons more readily than we build schools. Unlike the situation which faced theologians fifty years ago (when there was some moral idealism that was naive in viewing social realities), we are no longer about to be swamped by an excess of moral idealism that does not take the use of power seriously. Rather, we are likely to be anesthetized by a moral anomie that erodes the dependability of social interaction but which is curiously intermixed with the use of morality to wage partisan battles.

The repudiation of moral weaponry does not mean we cannot uphold moral standards. It simply means that we treat those standards as something to which all should aspire, not as something with which to condemn others. Although theologians have often recognized moral law as a basis for convicting us of our transgressions, the condemnation of others for political purposes is distressingly different from the traditional perspective. Rather than using the law to convict all persons of their shortcomings so as to prompt them to repentance and amendment of life, it becomes an instrument for the condemnation and even the destruction of those with whom we disagree or wish to discredit in the political or ecclesiastical process. Moral judgment exercised apart from efforts to seek forgiveness and redemption has little place in compassionate religion.

The unique and remarkable thing about the gospel is that it enables people to admit faults without suffering defeat. Moral weaponry works in the opposite direction—thwarting this possibility by citing faults in order to create defeats. It prompts one group to overlook its own faults so it can scrutinize and criticize the misdeeds of others in order to exclude them from community. Because it functions to counter the very process that is at the heart of the gospel, it is an invidious form of religious malpraxis.

The possibility of religious malpraxis appearing in any of the three forms which have been discussed seems to be rising. Terrorism seems to heighten the impulse to subdue wrongdoing by the use of violence; arguments over beliefs grow in number and intensity as religious pluralism casts doubt upon the finality of particular doctrinal assertions; the lowering of the moral tone of a culture prompts the condemnation of behavior that does not fit traditional mores. That makes the period in which we live and believe especially problematic—one in which divisiveness and rancor seem more evident than acceptance and mutual forbearance.

Religious malpraxis must be resisted because it threatens to discredit religion by endorsing behavior that is divisive, often self-serving, and deeply at odds with the most fundamental insights of a biblically grounded response to God. All of its forms are driven by a human impulse to exclude others rather than to transform them by inclusion and acceptance. Religious malpraxis can make us morally and spiritually misguided, less humane than we would be without the embrace of religious faith, and even a danger to others. To resist such practices and all similar misuses of the great power of the spirit to affect our attitudes and our behavior is the most important challenge we can face. Unless a righteousness infused by grace overcomes ungracious righteousness, religion will only contribute to, rather than help ameliorate, the agonies of our times.

# Index

# About the Contributors

**Frances S. Adeney** is the William A. Benfield Jr. Associate Professor of Evangelism and Global Mission at Louisville Presbyterian Theological Seminary.

**Brian K. Blount** is Associate Professor of New Testament at Princeton Theological Seminary.

**F. E. Bonkovsky** is Professor and Program Director at the Center for Advanced Studies at the University of Leipzig in Germany, and the Austrian University of Vienna and Webster in Vienna.

**Robert A. Chesnut** is Pastor Emeritus of East Liberty Presbyterian Church, Pittsburgh, Pennsylvania.

**Mark Douglas** is Assistant Professor of Christian Ethics at Columbia Theological Seminary.

**Gordon K. Douglass** is Professor Emeritus of Economics at Pomona College.

**Lora M. Gross** is Visiting Assistant Professor of Religion at Pacific Lutheran University.

**Heidi Hadsell** is President of Hartford Theological Seminary.

**Paul Hertig** is Professor of Global Studies/Sociology at Azusa Pacific University.

**Young Lee Hertig** is Lecturer at Azusa Pacific University, Department of Global Studies/Sociology.

**Edward LeRoy Long Jr.** is the Pearsall Professor Emeritus of Christian Ethics and Theology of Culture at Drew University.

**Ronald E. Peters** is the Henry L. Hillman Associate Professor of Urban Ministry at Pittsburgh Theological Seminary.

**John C. Raines** is Professor of Religion at Temple University.

**Laura Stivers** is Assistant Professor of Religion at Pfeiffer University.

**Robert L. Stivers** is Professor of Religion at Pacific Lutheran University.

**Ronald H. Stone** is the John Witherspoon Professor of Christian Ethics (retired) at Pittsburgh Theological Seminary.

**Matthew Lon Weaver** is Co-Pastor with his wife, Robyn, of Glen Avon Presbyterian Church in Duluth, Minnesota.

**Dana W. Wilbanks** is Professor of Christian Ethics at the Iliff School of Theology.

**Scott C. Williamson** is the Robert H. Walkup Associate Professor of Christian Ethics at Louisville Presbyterian Theological Seminary.